GLOBAL MEDIA STUDIES

Global Media Studies explores the theoretical and methodological challenges that are defining global media studies as a discipline. Emphasizing the connection of globalization to local culture, this collection considers the diversity of modes of reception, reception contexts, uses of media content, and the creative relationships that audiences develop with and through the media. Through ethnographic case studies from Brazil, Denmark, the UK, Japan, Lebanon, Mexico, South Africa, Turkey and the United States, the contributors address such issues as what links media consumption to a lived global culture; what role cultural tradition plays globally in confronting transnational power; and how global elements of mediated messages acquire class, regional and local characteristics.

Patrick D. Murphy is Associate Professor and Chair in the Department of Mass Communications at Southern Illinois University.

Marwan M. Kraidy is Assistant Professor of International Communication in the School of International Service at American University.

GLOBAL MEDIA STUDIES

Ethnographic perspectives

*Edited by Patrick D. Murphy
and Marwan M. Kraidy*

Routledge
Taylor & Francis Group

NEW YORK AND LONDON

First published 2003
by Routledge
29 West 35th Street, New York, NY 10001

Simultaneously published in the UK
by Routledge
11 New Fetter Lane, London EC4P 4EE

Routledge is an imprint of the Taylor & Francis Group

© 2003 Edited by Patrick D. Murphy and Marwan W. Kraidy

Typeset in Garamond by
Keystroke, Jacaranda Lodge, Wolverhampton
Printed and bound in Great Britain by
MPG Books Ltd, Bodmin

Library of Congress Cataloging in Publication Data
Global media studies : ethnographic perspectives /
edited by Patrick Murphy and Marwan Kraidy.
p. cm.
Includes bibliographical references.
1. Communication, International. 2. Ethnology. 3. Globalization.
I. Murphy, Patrick, 1964– II. Kraidy, Marwan, 1972–
P96 .I5 G564 2003
302 .2—dc21
2002156107

British Library Cataloguing in Publication Data
A catalogue record for this book is available from the British Library

ISBN 0–415–31440–2 (hbk)
ISBN 0–415–31441–0 (pbk)

A NUESTRAS MEXICANAS

CONTENTS

CONTENTS

CONTRIBUTORS

Fay Yokomizo Akindes is Assistant Professor of Communication at the University of Wisconsin-Parkside. Her work problematizes culture and identity in Hawai'i and the United States, and has appeared in *Diegesis, Discourse, Qualitative Inquiry*, and a few book anthologies. Her doctoral dissertation, "Hawaiian-music radio as diasporic habitus: A rhizomatic study of power, identity, and resistance," was selected the most outstanding dissertation completed in 1999 in the areas of international and intercultural communication by the National Communication Association. Prior to entering academe, she worked for eleven years in public radio (San Diego) and public and commercial television (Honolulu). She was born and raised on Molokai.

Ece Algan is Assistant Professor in the Communication Studies Department at the University of Iowa. Her research interests include the globalization of media and culture, the impact of new media technologies in the Middle East, and the role of global and local media in Turkish women's negotiation and reinterpretation of patriarchy, traditions and gender identities. She has conducted fieldwork in southeast Turkey on the role and meaning of the emergence of commercial radio and internet cafés in the lives of young Turkish audiences. Her recent work appears in *Political Communication*, and she has chapters forthcoming in the books *Globalization and Corporate Media Hegemony* (SUNY Press) and *Waking the Titans of New Communications: The Emerging Battleground of Media and Technology in a New World Order* (Hampton Press).

Heloisa Buarque de Almeida holds a Ph.D. in Anthropology at the State University of Campinas (Unicamp), Brazil. She has worked as a researcher at CEBRAP (Centro Brasileiro de Análise e Planejamento) and coordinates a regular panel on gender at Brazilian Anthropological Association (ABA) biannual meetings and the Gender Study Group at Unicamp. She has published articles on media reception and leisure practices in the city of São Paulo, and has a chapter in the forthcoming book *Television, Families and the Dynamics of Change: Brazilian Audiences and the Fertility Transition, 1965–1985*. Her Ph.D. research focused on gender and the promotion of consumption in Brazilian telenovela production and reception.

Anna Clua is Assistant Professor at the Department of Journalism and Communication Sciences, Universitat Autònoma de Barcelona. She teaches journalism and communication theory. Her research interests are the politics of identity formations, media reception, and cultural geographies as in-roads to the study of social change and political agency. Her doctoral dissertation was on the spatiality of media reception processes, taking cultural studies and critical geography as main theoretical references. Her work has been published in *Voces y culturas*, and *Anàlisi. Quaderns de Comunicació i Cultura*.

Nick Couldry is Lecturer in Media and Communications at the London School of Economics and Political Science and Director of its Masters Programme in Media and Communications Regulation. He is the author of *The Place of Media Power: Pilgrims and Witnesses of the Media Age* (Routledge, 2000) and *Inside Culture: Reimagining the Method of Media Studies* (Sage, 2000). His main research interests are media power and its anthropological basis, the media's relationship to questions of citizenship and ethics, and individual reflexivity in an age of cultural complexity.

Fabienne Darling-Wolf is Assistant Professor in the School of Communication and Theatre at Temple University. Her theoretical and research interests range from the global impact of new media technologies to popular constructions of femininity and masculinity in Japan. Her work has been published in the *Journal of Communication Inquiry*, in the *Reader's guide to women's studies*, and as chapters in several books. Originally from France, Fabienne has lived in Japan for extensive periods at several points in time. She is still in frequent contact with the women who opened their lives to her and allowed her to conduct her research.

Vamsee Juluri is Assistant Professor of Media Studies at the University of San Francisco. He completed his undergraduate education in Hyderabad and New Delhi and his graduate study at Bowling Green State University and the University of Massachusetts. His book *Becoming a Global Audience: Longing and Belonging in Indian Music Television* is forthcoming from Peter Lang publishers. His work on globalization, media, and audiences has been published in *Critical Studies in Mass Communication* and *European Journal of Cultural Studies* and further publications are forthcoming in *Television and New Media* and the anthology *Asian Media Studies*.

Marwan M. Kraidy is Assistant Professor, Division of International Communication, School of International Service, American University. His publications include articles on globalization, cultural hybridity, audience ethnography, and Middle Eastern media in *Critical Studies in Mass Communication*, *Communication Theory*, *Journalism and Mass Communication Quarterly*, *Journal of Broadcasting and Electronic Media*, *Journal of Transnational Broadcasting Studies*, and *Media Culture and Society*. He has won several awards from, among others, the National Communication Association, the Association of Educators in Journalism and Mass Communication, and the

Broadcast Education Association. He previously was Director of Graduate Studies, School of Communication, University of North Dakota.

Antonio C. La Pastina is Assistant Professor at the Speech Communication Department at Texas A&M University in College Station. He holds a Ph.D. from the Radio-TV-Film Department at University of Texas at Austin. His research interests are on media reception, the representation of otherness in mainstream media and its role on diasporic cultures as well as the implications of the digital divide to peripheral communities. He teaches courses in intercultural communication, globalization, media, gender and race, and US and Latin American popular culture. His work has appeared in *Journal of Broadcasting and Electronic Media, International Journal of Cultural Studies, Children's Association Quarterly Journal, Communication Research*, as well as *Intercom and Communicação e Sociedade* in Brazil. Before moving to the United States in the late 1980s he work as a journalist in São Paulo, Brazil, his native country.

Bent Steeg Larsen, Ph.D. in Media Science from the University of Copenhagen, has conducted qualitative research concerning the integration of media technologies in everyday life, and is currently working as a researcher at *Politiken*, a leading Danish newspaper.

Sweety Law is Assistant Professor of Communication at Texas A&M International University, a member of the Texas A&M system. Her research interests focus on mass media processes and effects, innovation diffusion, communication for social change, community development, and intercultural communication. She has published work on audience letter-writing and audience letter-writers to mass media programs in journals including *Gazette* and *Journal of Communication*. Her paper "Organizing for social change in a postmodern world: Rethinking participation" was adjudged Top Student Paper (International and Development Communication) at the International Communication Association Conference (1999) in San Francisco.

Patrick D. Murphy is Associate Professor and Chair in the Department of Mass Communications at Southern Illinois University, Edwardsville, where he teaches transnational media, media critical theory, and documentary media. He is a former Fulbright-García Robles fellow, and has published on the topics of media reception and cultural change, ethnographic method, the political economy of transnational media, and Latin American communication theory. His work has appeared in *Cultural Studies, Howard Journal of Communication, Journal of Communication Inquiry, Journal of International Communication*, and *Qualitative Inquiry*, as well as chapters in several books.

Jacob J. Podber is Assistant Professor at the College of Mass Communication and Media Arts at Southern Illinois University. His research interests are in electronic media usage in rural Appalachia and other "outsider" communities. His article "Early radio in rural Appalachia: An oral history" appeared in the *Journal of Radio Studies*. He has won several awards, including the Outstanding Dissertation of the Year Award from the Broadcast Education Association, the Carl A. Ross Paper of the Year Award from the Appalachian Studies Association, the Top Paper Award from the Broadcast Education Association, and the Top Paper Award on an American Theme from the Ohio University-American Studies Steering Committee. In addition, he was Graduate Production Supervisor for the videotape accompaniment to the book *Entertainment-Education: A Communication Strategy for Social Change* by Everett Rogers and Arvind Singhal.

Larry Strelitz is Associate Professor at the Department of Journalism and Media Studies at Rhodes University, South Africa. His current research interests include an ongoing study of how South African youth experience global media, and the effectivity of South African television edutainment programmes in communicating to local youth about HIV/AIDS. His recent work appears in *Media, Culture and Society* and *Communication*, and he has a chapter forthcoming in the book *Race/Gender/Media: Considering Diversity Across Audiences, Content, Producers* (AB-Longman).

Thomas Tufte is Associate Professor at the Department of Film and Media Studies at the University of Copenhagen, Denmark, and also teaches Communication for Development at the University of Malmö in Sweden. Audience ethnography has been a central approach throughout most of his research, with fieldwork conducted in Brazil, Denmark and South Africa. Recent books include *Living with the Rubbish Queen: Telenovelas, Culture and Modernity in Brazil* (2000), co-editor of *Global Encounters: Media and Cultural Transformation* (2001) and editor of *Media, Ethnic Minorities and the Multicultural Society: Scandinavian Perspectives* (forthcoming). Tufte is co-editor of the Danish Journal of Communication (*MedieKultur*), and member of editorial boards and advisory boards of several Latin American journals of communication and culture.

Part I

INTRODUCTION

1

TOWARDS AN ETHNOGRAPHIC APPROACH TO GLOBAL MEDIA STUDIES[1]

Patrick D. Murphy and Marwan M. Kraidy

For much of the early history of the study of media reception, qualitative researchers in communication and media studies produced ethnographies of audiences that were often theoretically sophisticated but empirically thin. Inspired by cultural studies, most markedly by Stuart Hall's model of encoding and decoding, qualitative media research adapted concepts from semiotics, reader-response theory, and even psychoanalysis, to construct increasingly polished conceptual arguments. In spite of ethnography's place in this cultural turn and its subsequent influence on the field, theoretical growth occurred at the expense of methodological development. Rather than demonstrating a commitment to immersion, building of trust, long-term observation, or participation in the daily lives of research participants, the corpus of reception work was marked by its reliance on discussion groups, solicited and unsolicited letters and in-depth interviews. This gap fostered a tradition of "ethnographic" inquiry where rigorous participant observation and description were largely absent (Abu-Lughod, 1997; Nightingale, 1993), and often replaced by an increasingly textual and rhetorical usage of ethnography.

But what are the reasons for this drift towards "quasi-ethnographic" studies? And why have so many studies that clearly lack ethnographic credentials been formulated under the ethnographic rubric? Three factors shaping the politics and practice of media ethnography account for the division between the declared application of ethnographic techniques and the concomitant underdevelopment of field experience. The first factor shaping the relationship between ethnographic theory and practice is the "political economy" of ethnographic scholarship. Extended fieldwork is costly, requiring significant institutional and time resources that tend to be concentrated in a select group of elite universities. Ironically, the study of media audiences, itself a democratic recognition of the importance of mass entertainment in the daily lives of working-class and middle-class audiences, is constantly under threat of becoming the epistemological privilege of well-funded scholars at elite institutions.

Second, many media scholars encountered the theoretical concerns of the "posts" (poststructuralism, postmodernism and postcolonialism) before the messiness of fieldwork was initiated and worked through. As a result, a growing body of media ethnography has been shaped more by the critique of ethnography's association with colonialism and Western discourse than by the surprise and productivity of the field encounter (Murphy, 1999a). In other words, political concerns over ethnography have in large part trumped epistemological issues – a point of tension that has somewhat hobbled ethnography's induction into the broader tradition of qualitative inquiry in communication, at least as an empirically rigorous enterprise. As is made clear in the development of this chapter, we are not dismissing the inclusion of issues of power and inequality in ethnographic scholarship. In fact, ethnography has a central place in critical-cultural scholarship and shoulders a special burden when it comes to questions of power and inequality because its gaze is fixed on the practices of everyday life. What we are arguing against, rather, is letting these issues define ethnographic practice in such a way that the researcher's task becomes little more than tapping oppressed voices or moments of tactical resistance and articulating them to theory. Instead, if questions of power and inequality are to be taken seriously, they need to be relocated at the heart of ethnographic practice and given the kind of close study that allows us to think concretely and creatively about how they work through and are shaped by cultural practice.

The third, and perhaps the most fundamental reason for the gap between the application of ethnographic techniques and the field experience is the very challenging nature of fieldwork on media reception. For example, how does one "participate" in the somewhat "closed" contexts (bedroom, automobile, living room, headphones, etc.) of much media consumption? Unlike the less closed-in and more performative-ritualized spaces that have been the customary sites for ethnographic inquiry throughout anthropology's history, media technologies are creating increasingly intimate, microcosmic and virtual reception environments and practices. This makes the notion of participant observation of media audiences extremely arduous in many cases, and suggests a rethinking of what constitutes "doing fieldwork." Here we suggest that media ethnography be understood as a research process of forming communities and making conversations that underscore a systematic and long-term investment in form, purpose and practice.

Examining the forces that have shaped ethnographic inquiry in the discipline of communication also means reconsidering its potential to nourish and challenge theory. This chapter takes up that task specifically in the realm of global media studies. By exploring the history and regional trajectories of media ethnography, as well as the epistemological and political issues of representation that have confronted anthropology and which are relevant to media studies, we attempt to map a path for media ethnography as a means through which to engage and engender a vision of global media studies theory grounded in the practices of everyday life.

Ethnography and the complexity of media reception

When considering how the three factors outlined above converged over the years and fostered a history of quasi-ethnographic media ethnographies, one must ask: what makes a "good" media ethnography? More recent studies such as those by Gillespie (1995), Mankekar (1999), Tufte (2000) and some of the research presented in Ginsburg, Abu-Lughod and Larkin (2002) have shown signs of bridging the gap between description and fieldwork, concretely demonstrating that cultural immersion and long-term participant observation have a central place in media ethnography. However, even in light of these fine examples of media ethnography, the unique research dilemmas of the study of media reception lead one to ask: *must* media ethnography be based on something akin to participant observation to be "ethnographic"? Is a commitment to immersion, the building of trust, long-term observation, and the participation in the daily lives of research participants the only (or even best) road for researchers interested in studying the relation between media reception and cultural practice? The very diversity of modes of reception, reception contexts, uses of media content, and the performative and creative relationships that audiences develop suggest that media ethnography is a highly complex, multifaceted endeavor. Indeed, even the notion of research site has become much more fluid in recent years, as the *mise en scène* of "the field" is increasingly loaded with local adaptations of global cultural capital mediated via new "spaces," practices and imagined communities of media reception. Here the social and the symbolic display the sort of deterritorialized formations and borderlessness that postmodernists have been talking about for years.

Engaging this complexity is pivotal for the elaboration of a broader ethnographic project committed to understanding how the phenomenon of globalization is played out locally in relation to particular traditions, systems of belief, and texts which have altered them. The point of analysis, therefore, should be the resulting hybrid cultures: that is, the stylistic features of local cultural life that emerge materially and discursively as "tonalities" (Geertz, 1983) of global culture. To seek out and understand such features of mass mediated intercultural encounters (e.g. how cultural hybridity is constituted and what its ingredients are), researchers in the field of international communication must commit themselves to methods of inquiry that reposition the importance of context and everyday life in theory. Such an ambitious research agenda evokes the following questions. What patterns and practices link media consumption to a lived global culture? How do audiences negotiate global messages locally? How do the global/ideological elements of mediated messages fix to and acquire class, regional, and/or community characteristics? What role does popular memory play globally in confronting and/or altering transnational power? How does the introduction of Western ideals about consumption shape local notions of resource control and management? A second set of questions about globality are in fact inherent in the practice of ethnographic knowledge. What/where is the research site? What investment does the ethnographer have with the research community? How do the subjects/participants of the research speak through the ethnographic text and what voice do they have?

Articulating ethnography and international communication

With its largely localized focus, media ethnography offers much to the internationally oriented and increasingly intercultural field of global media studies. Just as ethnography faced a representational crisis in anthropology, which we explicate later in this chapter in relation to media ethnography, theories of international communication have been mired in debate around issues of power and influence. For much of its development, ideological power (involvement, control, participation, resistance, and negotiation) has been a central problematic and common thread in international communication theory. The cultural imperialism thesis is grounded in theories of dependency that emerged as a reaction to the paradigm of modernization that dominated the field since the early works of Lerner (1958), Schramm (1964) and Rogers (1969). In stark opposition to modernization theory's functionalist grounding, the notion of cultural imperialism was firmly rooted in critical political economy (Schiller, 1976, 1996). It questioned modernization theory and propelled issues of power and culture to the forefront of international communication research. However, the cultural imperialism thesis's almost singular focus on structural issues of ownership and distribution, in addition to the rise of political conservatism in the United States and Great Britain in the 1980s, caused its demise. While Schiller (1991) insisted that we were "not yet [in] the post-imperialist era," other writers (Boyd-Barrett, 1998; García Canclini, 1990; Mattelart, 1994 and 1998) called for the recognition and exploration of mediated cross-cultural hybridities, and Mowlana (1994) advocated epistemological reorientation. These calls were accompanied by scholarship that shifted attention to the rising importance of "the local" as a space for media and cultural theory and research (Appadurai, 1996; Braman, 1996; Kraidy, 1999). However, the stance that locality and its cultural manifestations (e.g. hybridity, reconversion) embody qualities of resistance rather than accommodation has received much more theoretical treatment than empirical engagement; and in postcolonial studies, the concept of hybridity itself is at the center of a heated debate concerning the cooptation of concepts of ethnic and cultural difference for the marketing needs of global capitalism (Kraidy, 2002).

The elaboration of audience ethnography for global media studies offers a heuristic opportunity to examine the local implications of globalization, which concern how the majority of the world population experiences globalization in its everyday life. After all, ethnography's main preoccupation has been the construction of what Geertz (1983) called "local knowledge," even if that focus on the local was not always explicitly stated. And even much earlier it was Geertz (1973) who reminded us that it is through

> almost obsessively fine combed field study in confined contexts that the mega-concepts with which contemporary social science is afflicted (modernization, post-modernity, conflict, oppression, structure, meaning, etc.) can be given the kind of sensible actuality that makes it possible to think not only realistically and concretely about them, but, what is more important, creatively and imaginatively with them.
>
> (p. 23)

Geertz's assertion resonates with a renewed sense of urgency in today's heated debates on globalization, because of the theoretical dilemmas of globalization as a phenomenon, process, and predicament given form and sustenance locally. That is, if global media studies is to establish a more grounded theoretical orientation toward globalization, as in our opinion it should, then that theorizing needs to be informed by the material produced through fieldwork. This means that global media studies must establish a more salient commitment to ethnographic inquiry – one both nourishing to and driven by theory.

Such a commitment is not a simple task, as it requires a certain investigative flexibility in the study of media audiences: one sensitive to a range of political and economic forces and distinct reception communities, in addition to subject positions tied to gender, ethnicity, class, religion, and sexual orientation, while also paying homage to the epistemological critiques levied against the ethnographic enterprise in the 1980s and 1990s. As a result, media ethnography faces a complex challenge as a central method of inquiry in international communication theory: how to develop more contextually grounded ethnographies while at the same time expanding the notion of the field to address the unique dilemmas of localized research in relation to the global issues raised by transnational media processes. It is this very challenge that requires the ethnographer to address, ultimately, the interplay between ideology and experience (or, in more ethnographic terms, between history and biography) by seeking out what Colombian communication scholar Jesús Martín-Barbero (1993) has described as the echo of the hegemonic within popular culture.

This is an important objective in global media studies because while globalization may be discursively situated in terms of broad economic, political and cultural trends, media consumption is one of the defining activities of the global–local nexus as it is perhaps the most immediate, consistent and pervasive way in which "globality" is experienced. Most of the previous treatments of these dynamics have restricted themselves to the realm of theory (e.g. Ang, 1990; Ferguson, 1995; Sreberny-Mohammadi, 1985), or when the contributions ιphic inquiry are engaged, they often appear like attachments to the ς of theorizing globality (Skovmand and Schrøder, 1992; Sreberny-ιdi et al., 1997). In contrast, *Global Media Studies: An Ethnographic .ιe*'s contributors present a more complete landscape on the crucial role ∪. εthnography in unraveling the global–local articulations that various authors have argued are at the heart of transnational media and cultural dynamics (e.g. Kraidy, 1999; Sreberny-Mohammadi, 1985; Thussu, 1998). While some expand the theoretical debate by establishing fresh conceptual combinations or rethinking established research domains (Algan; Couldry; Clua; Juluri; Kraidy; Larsen and Tufte; Law; Strelitz), other contributors offer "tales from the field" which speak to the dialogical dynamic of long-term fieldwork and sustained participant observation (Akindes; Buarque de Almeida; Darling-Wolf; La Pastina; Murphy; Podber).

Through these chapters a unique dialogue unfolds between theory and practice and between ethnographic inquiry and international communication: an interparadigmatic borrowing that unveils central connections and the broader implications of elaborating global media studies grounded in locality. The significance of such a collection lies in its articulation of three areas of communication and media studies that have experienced their own difficulties: namely (1) the crisis of representation in ethnographic inquiry; (2) the locational complexity which characterizes all social and cultural phenomena; and (3) the post-cultural imperialism theoretical malaise in international communication. To frame the potential and limits of an ethnographically informed approach to global media studies, the next section of this chapter draws attention to some trajectories, debates and points of tension that have shaped media ethnography produced in the last twenty years and colored the work put forward in this book.

Traditions of media ethnography

Drotner (1994 and 1996) argues that we should recognize that interest in ethnographic approaches appeared roughly at the same time in a variety of geographical and disciplinary research environments. She notes that this diversity is not always salient, however, as English-language publications tend to privilege an Anglo-American perspective that restricts our understanding of broader socio-political contexts. For example, the work of writers such as Ien Ang, Thomas Lindlof, James Lull, David Morley, and Janice Radway has often dominated discussion about what constitutes the qualitative study of audiences and what ethnography means within the confines of mass communication research and cultural studies. But even within this broader Anglo-American trajectory it is important to take note of different points of departure, different political and epistemological motivations for moving toward qualitative and ultimately ethnographic forms of inquiry. For example, the British qualitative tradition emerged from cultural studies' interrogation – via Marxist, struc-turalist, semiotics, and feminist theory – of the power of social texts. The adoption of ethnographic techniques was also driven by a desire to find alternatives to traditional social science research on media effects associated with the United States, e.g. surveys, experimental research. In the seminal *The Nationwide Audience*, Morley (1980) was concerned with moving beyond inadequate models of audience reception (e.g. "media effects" and "uses and gratifications") and toward an understanding of audiences that "differentially read and make sense of messages which have been transmitted, and act on those meanings within the context of the rest of their situation and experience" (p. 11). As Morley (1996) notes, the 1980s "boom" in ethnographic audience research that followed was "the result of the critique of overly 'structuralist' approaches, which had taken patterns of media consumption to be always-ready-determined effects of some more fundamental structure – whether the economic structure of the culture industries, the political structure of the capitalist state or the psychic structure of the human subject" (p. 15).

Opposition to the positivist paradigm, behavioral science, and quantitative methodology dominating the social sciences shaped early ethnographic work in the United States (Drotner, 1996; Moores, 1993). The notion of the active audience emerged as the centerpiece of much of this research, and various studies detailed the ritual and performative ways in which people integrated and interacted with media technologies (e.g. Lindlof, 1987). Most of these studies focused on the notion of the audience, while some others such as Lull (1990) pursued a research agenda on the family as a micro-environment within the larger audience. While this approach shared the British school's rejection of audience passivity and acknowledged how individuals used media as resources, a sustained attempt to analyze ideology was absent. Subsequent theorizing about the relationship between texts and audiences, particularly by minority and feminist writers, began to lead US media ethnography towards a more critical and cultural orientation. This writing wrestled with the politics of representation by directing theory toward issues related to social injustices based on race, class and gender discrimination. The shift in emphasis was influenced heavily by literary criticism's preoccupation with the "text" as well as anthropology's own crisis over representation, but was charged politically through perspectives of writers who felt part of disempowered and/or marginalized segments of society (e.g. hooks, 1990; Trinh, 1989). The result has been an increased sensitivity around questions of textualization, often revolving around concerns such as who is constructing ethnographies, and in whose interest?

These epistemological and political trajectories are clearly reflective of a certain socio-cultural ethos, as well as, more generally, the relationship between (Western) academia and knowledge production. While they have provided very important pathways into the enterprise of media ethnography, and ethnography itself seems to has achieved a "special appeal" in British and American cultural studies (Marcus, 1998a), even recent Anglo-American scholarship remains emphatic about the limitations and partialities of audience ethnographies, and thus implicitly disparages ethnographic practice (Juluri, 1998; Murphy, 1999a). For example, in the final chapter of *The Audience and its Landscape*, Hay (1996) asks: "[w]hich social practices and knowledge practices, through the apparatus and normative institutions that sustain and drive any kind of 'research,' become privileged (foregrounded) and accepted in representing a social structure – a sense of the way things are?" (p. 361). Such provocations are meant, of course, to stir the thick soup of qualitative audience research, rethink established protocols of inquiry and analysis (observation, artifacts, thick description and imaging through film, video or written text), and challenge the disciplinarity of media reception theory. But as the placement of Hay's provocations as an "Afterword" seems to suggest, these points are offered as conclusions about the slippery and problematic nature of reception studies, not as points of departure that reception researchers have been able to address methodologically. In our opinion, the cultural complexities of media reception (e.g. recognition of everyday life practices and patterns, reception context, mobility, tactics and strategies of audiences) evoked by Hay and others as significant yet "phantom-like" concerns in audience research are precisely the empirical fruit that media ethnography brings to the table – points which this book takes up in detail in the following chapters.

Other regional "schools" of media reception have had their own development, emerging largely outside of the British and US trajectories but now appearing to be in a dialogue of sorts. For instance Latin American scholars have a long and complex history of theoretical developments and qualitative research on communication and culture – an outgrowth of the region's own traditions of anthropology and sociology, as well as the critical pedagogy of Paolo Freire (Rodríguez and Murphy, 1997). Moreover, the Indian, the Spanish and especially the Scandinavian communication schools have created rich bodies of reception work in their own rights. Products of these "lesser known" trajectories are now more frequently available in English, and their influence is visible in the bibliographies of English-language scholars. For instance, the work of Latin American media theorists Jesús Martín-Barbero, Néstor García Canclini, Ondina Fachel Leal, Valerio Fuenzalida, Jorge González, Jesús Galindo, Sonia Muñoz, Leoncio Barrios, and Guillermo Orozco is now familiar to many European and US researchers; and Scandinavian writers Ulf Hannerz, Kristen Drotner, Kim Schrøder, Klaus Jensen, and Thomas Tufte are quoted and/or occasionally publish in Spanish and Portuguese language communication publications.[2]

When considering the implications of this global theoretical and method-ological cross-fertilization, it is difficult not to ask: is there a "global" media ethnography? This is precisely what Indian media ethnographer Vamsee Juluri (1998) ponders, but not without a sense of irony. He notes that in the past few years the work of seminal Western media ethnographers has come dressed in a sort of nostalgia, as if to suggest that the opportunity to do "real" audience work has somehow passed:

As someone entering the field in the mid 1990s, I wonder what it means that the high moment of audience studies seems to have passed, perhaps to travel, like old American sitcoms, to the rest of the world. This is not so much a statement about the intentions and fallacies of the many scholars who have worked in the field as a comment on the situatedness of the field itself in the geopolitics of history.

(p. 86)

Paradoxically, Juluri's work, like that of many other non-Western media scholars (e.g. Kraidy, 1999; Leal, 1990; Mankekar, 1999; Parameswaran, 2001), represents a new sort of pluralism grounded in both its own situatedness and, to borrow from his own use of Stuart Hall, its "detour through the West."[3] Because of this growing global trend, it is becoming as important to locate from where and with whom authors are exchanging ideas as it is to ask how writers are constructing ethnographic texts because both of these factors suggest much about the epistemological roots and geopolitical climates through which media ethnography and global media studies are taking shape. This means it is important to examine what ontological and epistemological ghosts of ethnography's past reside in this "detour," because they certainly haunt recent ethnographic inquiry in media studies.

The politics of ethnography

From its birth in early anthropology, the ethnographic approach has been utilized in the enterprise of taking events "from the field" and describing them in an effort to match the hard data requirements of positivist science (Asad, 1994). But the scientific notions of objectivism and interpretive processes of cultural translation ("the native's point of view") that colored these ethnographic accounts came under fire as a minor industry of "crisis" scholarship called into question the epistemological moorings and political connections of anthropology (Clifford, 1983; Clifford and Marcus, 1988; Marcus and Fisher, 1986; Rosaldo, 1989). Specifically, critiques were levied against traditional ethnography's preoccupation with context and realism, and against the notion that the field experience was little more than the collection of yet-to-be-processed data. These critiques challenged the assumption that the reality of any given cultural community is readily available for interpretation as long as the ethnographer has the proper tools (e.g. good field notes, genealogies, maps, demographic data gathering, etc.) to engage in and dislodge its essence for the ethnographer's specific descriptive and analytical purposes.

Critics also accused traditional ethnography of embodying elitist and ethnocentric perspectives, implicitly associated with colonial discourses. This charge focused mainly on how the "write-up" of the field experience simultaneously objectified (participants become objects for study as if museum pieces)

11

and subjectified (subjugated via power relations) the "Other." Critics questioned the way in which ethnography acted to re-inscribe and maintain oppressive power relations through surveillance techniques of distance and control of description while the ethnographer remained invisible within his or her own text. Along these lines media ethnography has experienced its own criticisms. Lotz (2000), for one, argues that what reception researchers typically do is a sort of hit-and-run version of participant observation, not ethnography, noting that:

> Much participant observation is the equivalent of Geertz stopping in to visit with the Balinese once a week – or even every day for a few hours – but returning home to sleep at the end of the day. Do these participant observation studies provide deeper understanding of media use than survey data or textual analysis? Unquestionably. However, identifying this work as ethnographic diminishes the distinction deserved by research engaging in truly extended field study and obscures the potential of immersing oneself deeper into media use by groups and individuals.
>
> (p. 450)

Her point is that the body of research under question does not suffer from data problems of a quantitative sort, but rather lacks consistency and the inter-subjective knowledge and relationships between the observer and the observed. Various authors have sought ways to move away from the surveillance techniques and colonizing tendencies of traditional ethnographic practice, calling for the elaborations of ethnographies that foreground the role of the ethnographer (e.g. Fox, 1991). Such calls have done much to alter the established protocols regarding the textualization of ethnographic research, and many ethnographies are now increasingly marked by accounts of personal experience: that is, who "we are" and "where we are coming from" (Behar, 1996). This epistemological turn is meant, in large part, to monitor the marginalizing effect of ethnographic practice by inscribing oneself in lieu of inscribing the Other. As such, these renderings can often be quite intimate as they provide personalized accounts of interpersonal tensions, the limits of ethnographic authority, field dilemmas and epiphanies – textual domains that have become the foundational ingredients of autoethnography, as well as providing shape and substance to other self-reflexive approaches (e.g. native ethnography, the observation of participation, dialogical process, feminist ethnography, sensuous ethnography) (see, for example, Behar, 1993; Kraidy, 1999; Lotz, 2000; Murphy, 1999b and 2002; Narayan, 1993; Parameswaran, 2001; Stoller, 1997).

Informants, participants, co-researchers, or cultural interlocutors?

Another site of ethnographic struggle, and one that is in many ways more important and challenging to the form and practice of ethnographic description, is that of the place of the voices of research participants. To address this concern, authors have borrowed Russian Formalist notions such as polyvocality and dialogical knowledge from Mikhail Bakhtin to argue for the construction of multivocal ethnographies (Conquergood, 1991; Quantz and O'Connor, 1988) and examine the limits of ethnographic collaboration (Hüwelmeier, 2000; Shokeid, 1997). In this context writers attempt to draw on a variety of individual opinions to recognize the multiple dimensions of cultural life. At their best, multivocal texts draw on disparate voices to restore the importance of unique individuals and resistance to social order, while at the same time maintaining an understanding of how utterances are historically and ideologically located. But multivocal texts can run the risk of appearing forced and sterile, positioning the Other as more comfortable and proactive in the ethnographic text than they might have actually been during the ethnographic encounter (Marcus, 1986). Rhetorical devices such as "co-researchers" and "cultural interlocutors" have been applied to soften disparities between voice, text, ethnographer and power, but these labels may not necessarily function to make ethnographic descriptions any "thicker." Rather they may only serve to help fashion descriptions that appear more communal, open and empowering than, say, "informant" or "subject." Moreover, they can be abused, as the incorporation of the Other as an active speaker in an ethnographic text often erases rather than challenges relations of power (Grossberg, 1989), making one wonder if the elaboration of polyvocal texts actually democratizes ethnographies or if multivocality merely camouflages the authoritative voice of the writer.

Consequently, ethnographers must consider the important dynamic between themselves and their informants. These relationships often mark the most intimate dimension of ethnography and can be a combination of the most fruitful and frustrating aspects of long-term fieldwork, as with the passing of time sincere friendships can develop, expectations can change, and the identity of the ethnographer as well as informants can transform and alter who and what they represent to one another. The evolving relationship between ethnographer and informant is a process framed by the boundaries of race, class, ethnicity and gender, which shape meaning and define culture. But also important are the ways that relationships are formed in reference to hierarchical hegemonic structures such as nationhood, regionality, or in the case of native ethnographers, access to cultural capital ("foreign" education, travel, material goods, etc.) (Gillespie, 1995; Kraidy, 1999; Mankekar, 1999; Murphy, 1999b; Parameswaran, 2001). That is, relationships unfold not only in relation to the researcher's perception of informant, but also in relation to the participant's perception of the ethnographer.

Acknowledging such dynamics, asserts Weiss (1993), "implies that Orientalism is not simply a product of the Logos of the West. There is objectification on both sides, which is part of the process of understanding begun by defining ourselves first through the opposition of 'the other'" (p. 187). This negotiation and definition of Self-through-Other is one of the main reasons why

13

a sustained and intimate commitment to the audience under study is important for media ethnography. It is through this process of self-destabilization that a sort of productive discomfort emerges – a "place" within the ethnographic encounter where dialectically produced configurations of subjectivity give shape to and reveal ethnographic knowledge. In this volume, Ece Algan (Chapter 2), Fabienne Darling-Wolf (Chapter 7) Antonio La Pastina (Chapter 8), Fay Yokomizo Akindes (Chapter 9), Heloisa Buarque de Almeida (Chapter 10), Jacob Podber (Chapter 11) and Patrick Murphy (Chapter 14) provide contingent, historically and culturally reflexive accounts of how this dynamic defined their research and the data it produced. What each of the studies show is that "field research is *impossible without the active cooperation* of the people and communities understudy" (Sandstrom, 1995, p. 172, emphasis ours). They also show, as Nightingale (1996) pointedly argued in her critique of active audience research, that the ethnographer's commitment to "cultural translation," that is the heart of interpretation in any intercultural process, remains essential. In this sense, it is clear that participants not only can, but also do provide direction for the research and negotiate a constitutive voice in the production of ethnographic knowledge, but it remains the delicate and inescapable task of the ethnographer to translate that voice.

Site, place, space, ritual

The positionality of voices, relationships, friendships and experiences might give the impression that media ethnography, in the name of locating globalization in the local, must fix itself to a coherent internal understanding of local culture. But as Geertz (1973) asserted many years ago, we do not study research sites, we study *in* them. In other words, the situatedness of the local is not a site, place or space merely to pin down and capture, but rather a point of reference through which to engage the emergent dimensions of globalization. For the purposes of audience ethnography this is key as it suggests something about how fieldwork needs to be in constant dialogue with how biography relates to history, and how the performative, ritualized, distinct and plural manifestations of local life nevertheless echo hegemonic culture. This global interrogation through the lens of the local requires that we do not, as Marcus (1998b) cautions, "succumb to relying on 'canned' visions of what the world historical system is like (e.g. relying too heavily on Marxist views of capitalism), rather than taking the appropriately ethnographic view that macro system terms of analysis should be radically rethought from the ground up" (pp. 39–40).

Taking the micro-knowledge about places, spaces, rituals and performance derived form ethnographic inquiry and articulating it in a way that nurtures, sustains and at the same time challenges macro-level theoretical frameworks of media, globalization and culture demands that we "risk" making some broader claims about the relationship between ideology and experience. Livingstone (1998, pp. 202–203) notes that this chore has been consistently refused by cultural/audience studies via the claim that the construction of generalizations about audiences imposes artificial categories on diverse, contingent and elusive practices. However, the point remains that while media theorists working through ethnography as a means to "make things out" (to echo Geertz) may hesitate in taking the (hazardous) initiative of making such generalizations, others – particularly those working in the global commercial sector – will express no such trepidation. Moreover, if media ethnographers have a political commitment to a *critical* ethnography – one that is concerned with how power is taking shape and transforming people's lives on a global scale – then they must overcome their queasiness with the possibility of making generalizations and of objectifying/commodifying/inscribing the Other. Indeed, it is necessary, as Fine (1998) has argued, to "barter privilege for justice" in an effort to "represent stories told by subjugated Others, stories that would otherwise be discarded" (p. 150).

Confluences

It is with some irony, perhaps, that within the current theoretical wrestling match over "Self" and "Other" and micro- or macro-cultural processes that ethnography finds its purpose for global media studies. Anthropologist Paul Willis (2000) argues that there is a need to move away from the "dominant individualistic view" of cultural negotiation, and instead re-engage the notion that cultural creativity is usually collective and socially originated, and meaning-making intrinsically framed, enabled, and constrained by powerful external structural determinants. For international communication researchers such a return to structural concerns of meaning-making needs to involve a combined commitment to macro and micro questions of power and culture. Ethnographic inquiry, with its base in local practices and the performative features of culture, offers the material to bridge the gap between meaning and structure without losing sight of the complexity, context and inherent power imbalances of cultural consumption. This contribution to global media studies should not be underestimated, especially at a time when some media scholars, intentionally or unwittingly, celebrate difference via micro-assessments of postcolonial locales and the plurality of cultures without attempting to consider global structural concerns.

In fact, rendering the multiple mediations of cultural interactions is what ethnography does best via the questions it asks, the procedures it uses to answer them, and the stories it ultimately tells. It is precisely through this multiplicity, this negotiated sense of how media audiences in various contexts engage or bear the transformative power of globalization through local cultural practice, that media ethnography is positioned to address the hegemonic echoes of global power. Ethnography's focus on the local, therefore, should not be grounded in ontological opposition to processes of globalization. Rather, the commitment to the local that is at the heart of ethnographic work should be directed at fleshing out, giving concrete manifestations to the large-scale forces of globalization. In closing, an ethnographic approach to global media studies is a heuristic trail towards a better understanding of the dynamics between global forces and local specificities.

Notes

1 This introduction draws substantially from, and includes revised segments of, P. D. Murphy and M. M. Kraidy (2003), International communication, ethnography, and the challenge of globalization, *Communication Theory* 13(3).

2 For selected readings in English, see Barrios, 1988; García Canclini 1992; Gonzalez, 1992 and 1997; Leal, 1990; Martín-Barbero, 2000; Orozco, 1995.

3 The "detour" that scholars from the developing world are often required to take has been recognized by many scholars. See Keyan G. Tomaselli's (2001) account of his interactions with Western academia for a more recent and very telling version of the center–periphery imbalance. Chapter 2: The problem of textuality in ethnographic audience research Global Media Studies.

References

Abu-Lughod, L. (1997). The interpretation of culture(s) after television. *Representations* 59, 109–134.

Ang, I. (1990). Culture and communication: Towards an ethnographic critique of media consumption in the transnational media system. *European Journal of Communication* 5(2–3), 239–260.

Appadurai, A. (1996). *Modernity at large: Cultural dimensions of globalization.* Minneapolis: University of Minnesota Press.

Asad, T. (1994). Ethnographic representation, statistics and modern power. *Social Research* 61(1), 55–88.

Barrios, L. (1988). Television, telenovelas and family life in Venezuela. In L. Lull (ed.), *World Families Watch Television* (pp. 49–79). Newbury Park, CA: Sage.

Behar, R. (1993). *Translated woman: Crossing the border with Esperanza's story.* Boston: Beacon Press.

Behar, R. (1996). *The vulnerable observer: Anthropology that breaks your heart.* Boston: Beacon Press.

Boyd-Barrett, O. (1998). Media imperialism reformulated. In D. K. Thussu (ed.), *Electronic empires: Global media and local resistance* (pp. 157–176). London: Arnold.

Braman, S. (1996). Interpenetrated globalization, In S. Braman and A. Sreberny-Mohammadi (eds), *Globalization, communication, and transnational civil society* (pp. 21–36). Cresskill, NJ: Hampton Press.

Clifford, J. (1983). On ethnographic authority, *Representations* 1, 118–146.

Clifford, J. and Marcus, G. (eds) (1988). *Writing culture: The poetics and politics of Ethnography.* Berkeley: University of California Press.

Conquergood, D. (1991). Rethinking ethnography: Towards a critical cultural politics. *Communication Monographs* 58, 141–156.

Drotner, K. (1994). Ethnographic enigmas: "The everyday" in recent media studies. *Cultural Studies* 8(2), 208–225.

Drotner, K. (1996). Less is more: Media ethnography and its limits. In P. I. Crawford and S. B. Hafsteinsson (eds), *The construction of the viewer* (pp. 28–46). Hojbjerg, Denmark: Intervention Press.

Ferguson, M. (1995). Media, markets, and identities: Reflections on the global–local dialectic. *Canadian Journal of Communication* 20(4), 28–46.

Fine, M. (1998). Working the hyphens: Reinventing self and other in qualitative research. In N. K. Denzin and Y. S. Lincoln (eds), *The landscape of qualitative research* (pp. 130–155). Thousand Oaks, CA: Sage.

Fox, R. (ed.) (1991). *Recapturing anthropology: Working in the present.* Santa Fe, NM: School for American Research Press.

García Canclini, N. (1990). *Culturas hibridas.* Mexico, D.F.: Grijalbo.

García Canclini, N. (1992). Cultural reconversion. In G. Yudice, J. Franco and J. Flores (eds), *On edge: The crisis of contemporary Latin American culture* (pp. 29–43). Minneapolis: University of Minnesota Press.

Geertz, C. (1973). *The interpretation of culture.* New York: Basic Books.

Geertz, C. (1983). *Local knowledge.* New York: Basic Books.

Gillespie, M. (1995). *Television, ethnicity and cultural change.* London: Routledge.

Ginsburg, F., Abu-Lughod, L. and Larkin, B. (eds) (2002) *Media worlds.* Berkeley: University of California Press.

Gonzalez, J. (1992). The confraternity of (un)finishable emotions: Constructing Mexican telenovelas. *Studies in Latin American Popular Culture* 11, 59–92.

Gonzalez, J. (1997). The willingness to weave: Cultural analysis, cultural fronts and networks of the future. *Media Development* 44, 59–92.

Grossberg, L. (1989). On the road with three ethnographers. *Journal of Communication Inquiry* 13(2), 23–26.

Hay, J. (1996). Afterword. In J. Hay, L. Grossberg and E. Wartella (eds), *The audience and its landscape* (pp. 359–378). Boulder, CO: Westview Press.

hooks, b. (1990). Culture to culture: Ethnography and cultural studies as critical intervention. In *Yearning: Race, gender and cultural politics* (pp. 123–143). Boston: South End Press.

Hüwelmeier, G. (2000). When people are broadcast their ethnographies: Text, mass media and voices from the field. *Social Anthropology* 8(1), 45–49.

Juluri, V. (1998). Globalizing audience studies. *Critical Studies in Mass Communication* 15(1), 85–90.

Kraidy, M. M. (1999). The global, the local, and the hybrid: A native ethnography of glocalization. *Critical Studies in Mass Communication* 16(4), 456–476.

Kraidy, M. M. (2002). Hybridity in cultural globalization. *Communication Theory* 12(3), 316–339.

Leal, O. F. (1990). Popular taste and erudite repertoire: The place and space of television in Brazil. *Cultural Studies* 4(1), 19–29.

Lerner, D. (1958). *The passing of traditional society.* New York: Free Press.

Lindlof, T. (1987). *Natural audiences: Qualitative research of media uses and effects.* Norwood, NJ: Ablex Publishing.

Livingstone, S. (1998). Audience research at the crossroads: The "implied audience" in media and cultural theory. *European Journal of Cultural Studies* 1(2), 193–217.

Lotz, A. (2000). Assessing qualitative television audience research: Incorporating feminist and anthropological theoretical innovation. *Communication Theory* 10(4), 447–467.

Lull, J. (ed.) (1990). *Inside family viewing: Ethnographic research on television's audiences.* New York: Routledge.

Mankekar, P. (1999). *Screening culture, viewing politics: An ethnography of television, womanhood and nation in postcolonial India.* Durham, NC: Duke University Press.

Marcus, G. E. (1986). Contemporary problems of ethnography in the world system. In G. E. Marcus and M. J. Fisher, *Anthropology as cultural critique* (pp. 165–193). Chicago: University of Chicago Press.

Marcus, G. E. (1998a). What comes (just) after "post?": The case of ethnography. In N. K. Denzin and Y. S. Lincoln (eds), *The landscape of qualitative research* (pp. 383–406). Thousand Oaks, CA: Sage.

Marcus, G. E. (1998b). *Ethnography through thick and thin.* Princeton, NJ: Princeton University Press.

Marcus, G. E. and Fisher, M. J. (1986). *Anthropology as cultural critique.* Chicago: University of Chicago Press.

Martín-Barbero, J. (1993). Latin American cultures in communication media (trans. E. Fox). *Journal of Communication* 43(2), 18–30.

Martín-Barbero, J. (2000). The cultural mediations of television consumption. In I. Hagen and J. Wasko (eds), *Consuming audiences? Production and reception in media research* (pp. 145–161). Cresskill, NJ: Hampton Press.

Mattelart, A. (1994). *Mapping world communication: War, progress, culture.* Minneapolis: University of Minnesota Press.

Mattelart, A. (1998). Généalogie de nouveaux scénarios de la communication. In J. Berdot, F. Calvez and I. Ramonet (eds), *L'Après-Télévision: Multimédia, virtuel, Internet.* Valence, France: CRAC.

Moores, S. (1993). *Interpreting audiences: The ethnography of media consumption.* London: Sage.

Morley, D. (1980). *The Nationwide audience.* London: British Film Institute.

Morley, D. (1996). The audience, the ethnographer, the postmodernist and their problems. In P. I. Crawford and S. B. Hafsteinsson (eds), *The construction of the viewer* (pp. 11–27). Aarhus: Intervention Press.

Mowlana, H. (1994). Shapes of the future: International communication in the twenty-first century. *Journal of International Communication* 1(1), 14–32.

Murphy, P. D. (1999a). Media cultural studies' uncomfortable embrace of ethnography. *Journal of Communication Inquiry* 23(3), 205–221.

Murphy, P. D. (1999b). Doing audience ethnography: A narrative account of establishing ethnographic identity and locating interpretive communities in fieldwork. *Qualitative Inquiry* 5(4), 479–504.

Murphy, P. D. (2002). The anthropologist's son (living and learning the field). *Qualitative Inquiry* 8(3), 246–260.

Narayan, K. (1993). How native is a "native" ethnographer. *American Anthropologist* 95(3), 671–686.

Nightingale, V. (1993). What's "ethnographic" about ethnographic audience research? In J. Frow and M. Morris (eds), *Australian Cultural Studies* (pp. 149–161). Urbana: University of Illinois Press.

Nightingale, V. (1996). *Studying audiences: The shock of the real.* London: Routledge.

Orozco, G. (1995) The dialectic of television reception. *Mexican Journal of Communication* 2, 93–106.

Parameswaran, R. (2001). Feminist media ethnography in India: Exploring power, gender, and culture in the field. *Qualitative Inquiry* 7(1), 69–103.

Quantz, R. A. and O'Connor, T.W. (1988). Writing critical ethnography: Dialogue, multivoicedness, and carnival texts. *Educational Theory* 38(1), 95–109.

Rodríguez, C. and Murphy, P. D. (1997). The study of communication and culture in Latin America: Form laggards and the oppressed to resistance and hybrid cultures. *Journal of International Communication* 4(2), 24–45.

Rogers, E. (1969). *Modernization among peasants*. New York: Holt, Reinhart and Winston.

Rosaldo, R. (1989). *Culture and truth: The remaking of social analysis*. Boston: Beacon Press.

Sandstrom, A. (1995). The wave: Fieldwork and friendship in northern Veracruz, Mexico. In B. Grindal and F. Salamone (eds), *Bridges to humanity: Narratives on anthropology and friendship* (pp. 172–192). Prospect Heights, IL: Waveland Press.

Schiller, H. (1976). *Communication and cultural domination*. White Plains, NY: International Arts and Sciences Press.

Schiller, H. (1991). Not yet the post-imperialist era. *Critical Studies in Mass Communication* 8(1), 13–28.

Schiller, H. (1996). *Information inequality*. London and New York: Routledge.

Schramm, W. L. (1964). *Mass media and national development: the role of information in the developing countries*. Stanford, CA: Stanford University Press.

Shokeid, M. (1997). Negotiating multiple viewpoints: The cook, the native, the publisher and the ethnographic text. *Current Anthropology* 38(4), 631–646.

Skovmand, M. and Schrøder, K. C. (1992). *Media cultures: Reappraising transnational media*. London: Routledge.

Sreberny-Mohammadi, A. (1985). The local and the global in international communications. In J. Curran and M. Gurevitch (eds), *Mass media and society* (pp. 136–152). London: Arnold.

Sreberny-Mohammadi, A., Winseck, D., McKenna, J. and Boyd-Barrett, O. (eds) (1997). *Media in global context*. London: Arnold.

Stoller, P. (1997). *Sensuous scholarship*. Philadelphia: University of Pennsylvania Press.

Thussu, D. K. (1998). Localising the global. In D. K. Thussu (ed.), *Electronic empires: Global media and local resistance* (pp. 273–294). London: Arnold.

Tomaselli, K. G. (2001). Blue is hot, red is cold: Doing reverse cultural studies in Africa. *Cultural Studies-Critical Methodologies* 1(3), 283–318.

Trinh, M.-H. T. (1989). *Woman, native, other: Writing postcoloniality and feminism*. Bloomington: Indiana University Press.

Tufte, T. (2000). *Living with the rubbish queen: Telenovelas, culture and modernity in Brazil*. London: University of Luton Press.

Weiss, W. A. (1993). Gringo . . . Gringa. *Anthropological Quarterly* 66(4), 187–196.

Willis, P. (2000). *The ethnographic imagination*. Chicago: University of Chicago Press.

Part II

SITUATING ETHNOGRAPHY IN GLOBAL MEDIA STUDIES

2

THE PROBLEM OF TEXTUALITY IN ETHNOGRAPHIC AUDIENCE RESEARCH

Lessons learned in southeast Turkey

Ece Algan

Istanbul has always determined the cultural agenda in Turkey. The country's print media, music and film industries have always been centered in Istanbul, a city which not only is located in the northwest or European side of Turkey, but also mimics, appropriates and borrows from the West. After the 1990s when the state monopoly in broadcasting was broken, Istanbul also commanded the broadcasting industry, with many new commercial broadcast networks airing throughout Anatolia, the Asian part of Turkey. Being from Istanbul and having witnessed this enthusiastically embraced change in the media environment, I was eager to see how these new stations and programs were experienced outside of Istanbul. Which national stations were Anatolian Turks listening to? What kind of programs did their local radio and television stations run? Were audiences also interacting with local radio personalities? What kind of music was preferred? What did people like best about the stations in their provinces? How were they experiencing and interpreting local media and Istanbul-based national networks in their daily lives? With these questions in mind and the belief that an ethnographic approach can best capture and respect the practices which people in different parts of the world invent in their everyday dealings with the changing media and cultural environment (Ang, 1990, p. 257), I decided to conduct media ethnography in Sanliurfa – a province in the underdeveloped southeast of Turkey along the Syrian border – to examine the role and meaning of these newly emerged commercial channels in the lives of Turkish audiences. I wanted to investigate how their media use intersects, contradicts or contests existing cultural practices and to map how local meanings and alternative responses are made within and against prevailing social structures – such as traditions – and messages provided by the national and global networks.

Although I was clear about my research questions and goals, recent criticisms and debates over the "state of audience research and the place of ethnography in it" confused my efforts to design my research because all the suggestions and recipes about how to establish a comprehensive theory of audience research frequently criticized, negated or contradicted one another. Yet, despite the research re-assessing audience and reception studies and the warnings about the pitfalls of ethnographic audience research – especially the charge that it analyzes micro-narratives – there has been widespread agreement that the study of everyday life is central to the study of media (Ang, 1990, 1993; Drotner, 1994; Grossberg, 1989; Moores, 1993; Morley, 1992, 1993; Radway, 1988, 1996; Silverstone, 1989, 1994). While the study of everyday life ultimately points us toward a more ethnographic approach to the study of media consumption, our concerns lead us to question how far personal narratives on media use and interpretation can go beyond the celebratory display of the polysemy of audiences. Conducting ethnographic inquiry into the everyday practices of media users instead of conducting bounded, regionalized investigations of singular text–audience circuits is one of the approaches proposed to overcome the shortcomings of studying media audiences (Radway, 1988).

The question then becomes how to study audiences' experience of media in their everyday lives so as to illuminate the social responses to media embedded in macro-structures of society rather than detail personal narratives on media (Ang, 1990; Morley, 1993, 1997; Gibson, 2000). The usual approach to this goal is often articulated as the need for a more contextual framework to expand our understanding of the social, political and ideological structures within which media consumption takes place, although there is a lot of debate over the issues surrounding context. On the one hand, Ang (1996) proposes to take into consideration not only the contexts of media consumption but also the contexts of ethnographic knowledge production itself. On the other hand, Morley (1997) agrees with Corner (1991) that "more context" regarding the ethnographic research process does not solve any problems. He argues that the self-reflexive character adopted by postmodern ethnography to cope with the power relations between researcher and researched, as well as questions of representation, have focused attention on how ethnographies are (and/or should be) written rather than what they tell us. Similar dilemmas arise in the debate over polysemic power and the resistance of the active audience versus the power of media institutions and texts, as well as in the criticisms regarding the lack of analysis of the political, social, economic and ideological determinants in ethnographic studies on media consumption.

It is certainly naïve to expect a clear-cut scholarly consensus to guide me in my research, but I also agree with Gray (1999) that the lack of agreement on methodology and the politics of producing ethnographic audience research have inhibited many young ethnographers from conducting such research and instead have created an abundance of studies discussing the state of ethnographic audience research. Drawing on these debates, and in light of my fieldwork experience, this chapter is an account of my struggle to conduct ethnographic research on media consumption that is not genre- or text-based, and it also examines the challenges that recent criticisms on the state of the scholarship pose for media ethnographers. An exploration of these challenges will contribute to the arguments about why cultural studies fail to draw on ethnography (Murphy, 1999a), and it will suggest new ways of conducting media ethnographies, such as the multisited approach.

I believe that one of the most important reasons for the lack of studies on everyday life and media consumption – despite the overall agreement on the need for such studies – is that reception studies have always focused on how a particular text is received. By providing a detailed discussion of the problem of textuality in reception studies, I aim to illustrate the need for an ethnographic approach that prioritizes the *audience* in its unique geographical, cultural and social environment rather than the media *text* or *genre*. Therefore, this chapter also deals with the issues of context in ethnography with reference to the interconnectedness of the context of ethnographic knowledge production and the socio-cultural context of media consumption. In addition, my fieldwork experience illustrates that conducting ethnographies on multiple sites of media consumption instead of a single media text constitutes a crucial starting point for conducting media ethnographies that aid not only the study of everyday life but also the social, political and ideological contexts of media use.

What is wrong with genre-based ethnographic audience research?

Five years ago, in my first year of graduate school in the United States, I was taught that the best examples of reception studies are those which combine audience research with a textual analysis of the media genre or text under investigation. First, the researcher had to provide an audience interpretation of a text or genre. Second, the researcher had to deconstruct the text by applying structuralist, semiotic, feminist, literary or (most important) ideological analysis. Third, the researcher had to illustrate how the content of the text was constructed by media corporations to *reinforce* the state ideology, patriarchy, consumerism, or some other oppressive system by supporting his/her analysis with statements from the informants. I recall wondering about the need to conduct audience research if the audience analysis was only used to support the researcher's arguments and if the conclusion was always to be based on the scholar's identification of the constraints and determinants dictated by the content of the text.

What I wish to emphasize here is that reception studies or audience research has often been seen as secondary to or supportive of other types of cultural studies work, and what it is and why it should be done is still subject to

25

speculation. Ang (1996) argues, for instance, that audience research informed by cultural studies has produced "considerable epistemological confusion over the concept of 'audience' as an analytical object," a confusion that has "also reanimated the persistent critical preoccupation with the political standing of scholarship: What does it mean to do 'audience research,' and why do it in the first place" (p. 247)? As Ang's observations suggest, the crisis in the study of media audiences is thus neither purely theoretical nor merely methodological but both epistemological and political. Reception studies have been thought of as a way to examine how a particular *text* or *genre* – such as *Dallas*, *The Cosby Show*, *Star Trek*, romance novels, soap operas and so on – is received and interpreted rather than as a way to study how *audiences* consume and interpret media or what the meaning and place of media are in their daily lives. Therefore, in these studies, audiences under investigation usually are grouped by their allegiance to a particular show or media text. A perspective that views the media as a collection of texts treats the audience as readers. "Active readers" is a term that has still been used to recognize the power of audiences over texts. However, Jensen and Pauly (1997) argue that conceptualizing people who watch television, listen to music, read the newspaper, and generally attend to media events as readers (rather than as social, interpretive actors) invokes a much longer heritage of assumptions about texts and their power (p. 157). In order to address these assumptions, many scholars have called audiences "interpretive communities," but as Jensen and Pauly (1997) put it:

> To consider the audience an interpretive community is still to locate people through texts rather than through the social processes by which texts influence and engage people in actual circumstances. Because they construct people as readers, text-based approaches will understand family, friendship, and community as secondary or nontextual forces that "construct" the reader subject, not as the experienced rubric in and through which people read, think, love, and plan.
>
> (pp. 157–158)

Many scholars still strongly believe that there is a definite need for a textual object of study when conducting ethnographic audience research. The following passage is from a very insightful article on how to construct a critical ethnography of media audiences that is neither populist nor determinist but examines media consumption in everyday life. A close look at how the methodology and methods that are necessary for such a project are articulated in this article gives us some more hints regarding the common assumptions about what "ethnographic media research" is and how it should be conducted.

> In the first stage, the collection of interpretations, most successful ethnographic audience studies organize their investigations around

the specific relationships that arise between media genres and audience subgroups. . . . Once an important genre or program is specified, a variety of creative methodological tactics are typically employed to extract audience interpretations of cultural texts under question.

(Gibson, 2000, p. 266)

These assumptions regarding what audience research is and how it should be conducted explain the failure of the scholarship to draw on ethnography. When we all acknowledge that reception studies' emphasis on how a mass-produced text is received by media audiences centralizes the use of a particular text and thus hinders understanding of the relationship between media use and the cultural practices of the audience, then we can start looking for ways that are not text- or genre-based to investigate those relationships. As Radway (1996) writes:

Despite my continued commitment to ethnography, I also believe we risk languishing at an impasse in audience research if we reproduce exactly the same sort of studies we have generated in the past. I am thinking here of studies like my own, studies that are genre-based despite their interest in audiences. Such studies are also predicated upon certain assumptions about the coherence of the reader, viewer, or consumer and, therefore, concomitantly upon certain assumptions about the identifiability and stability of audiences as aggregates of individuals. . . .

What I am getting at here is the fact that a significant portion of audience-based research begins with specific literary, cinematic, televisual, and musical forms, that is, with romances, horror movies, soap operas, television news, heavy metal, or punk. . . . Thus we are trained to deal with *either* printed texts, with filmic and televisual forms, *or* with music. However, to import our confidence about the distinctiveness of media and genre to the study of their fans and consumers may well be to construct an unwarranted formalism of the audience, a formalism that renders invisible the complex ways in which media consumption is multiple, overlapping, contradictory, and stitched together at every turn with many other daily practices.

(p. 244)

Since many of us worry about justifying our choices of who we study and what we find, we have a tendency to form homogenous, measurable, comprehensible audiences. Choosing an audience gathered around a text gives us such a manageable audience. Focusing on a particular text or genre and its fans not only creates an assumption that the audience is a coherent, stable and identifiable entity but also reduces the definition of the audience almost to a group of people

27

who consume a certain media text religiously. This narrow perspective of audience leads many scholars to draw easy conclusions about the polysemic power of the active audience. However, as Radway (1996) suggests, perceptions of media activity that see audiences as either passive or creative/active readers tend to simplify media use as a linear process of reception and response (p. 244). Understanding how media consumption is embedded in people's daily practices will also change our view of the relationship between audience and text.

It is important to note here that I do not negate the polysemic power of audiences, nor do I suggest we should completely abandon text- and/or genre-based approaches for the study of audiences and focus solely on everyday media use. Nevertheless, beginning with Stuart Hall's encoding/decoding model and gaining momentum with Morley's (1980) *Nationwide* study, the focus on text and acknowledgement of its multiple meanings was instrumental in creating a paradigm shift in media studies from the positivistic uses of the gratifications tradition of audience research toward an interdisciplinary cultural studies approach. In that sense, my interest in audience research that does not focus on a particular media text and/or genre does not imply a rejection of studying audience experiences of media through the meanings they make from a single text in favor of mapping everyday media use. On the contrary, I am interested in audience research that captures the social, cultural, historical, political and ideological contexts that shape the meanings audiences make in their everyday lives, as well the meanings they draw from media. I also believe that studying audience responses to the content of media texts alone is not always sufficient for a broader understanding of media's changing role, meaning and function in a global world. Given the number of texts on such questions, I will briefly summarize two main arguments that emerge in the critique of ethnographic audience research and review a couple of responses to these criticisms, since those remarks reveal the confusion regarding the issues of "context" in the debates about reception studies.

The problem of textuality and context

One criticism of ethnographic reception studies, which is also referred to as the "new audience studies," is that it presumes and celebrates the power of the audience over media texts while ignoring the power of the producers of media. While disagreeing with this criticism, Morley (1997) points out that some work in cultural studies reflects an "unhelpful romanticization of consumer freedoms" and forgets that the original objective of reception studies was to illustrate the question of cultural power by moving cultural studies from a simple-minded dominant ideology model to a complex model of hegemony (p. 137). A second criticism is that reception studies analyze the micro-narratives of media consumption and fail to discuss the macro-narratives of political, economical and/or social aspects surrounding media reception (Corner, 1991; Curran, 1990). According to Gray (1999), accusing the "new audience studies" of lacking a political and critical edge indicates a problem with what constitutes the political, since many studies inspired by feminist scholarship – which investigates women's personal or micro experiences and interpretations of media – challenge existing models and approaches in communication and audience research (p. 25). As Gray (1999) puts it:

> Although many of the critics take the new audience research to task for attending only to the "micro" dimension, I would argue that what underpins the questions and problematics of the studies are those of agency and structure. Studies show how public and private are absorbed into the everyday, the mundane, the ordinary. Such studies recognize the false distinctions between micro and macro, and demonstrate how discourses flow in and out of constructions of identity, self, private and public, national, local and global. Boundaries, thus, are permeable, unstable and uneasy, demanding a new way of thinking and looking at the "audience," the user, the text, and the complexity of relations and discourses which surround and are part of it.
>
> (p. 31)

Morley (1997) also thinks that these criticisms are based on an assumption that the macro equates with the "real" and the micro equates with the realm of the epiphenomenal (p. 126), and he adds that "the developing backlash against micro-ethnography is in danger of encouraging a return to macro political issues which is, in fact, premised on a mal-posed conception of the relation between the micro and the macro" (p. 126). Indicating that macro-structures can only be reproduced through micro-processes, Morley (1997) responds to these criticisms by reminding us that one of the important motivations behind the shift toward a "new" audience research was to attempt to find better ways to articulate the micro and macro levels of analysis, not to abandon either pole in favor of the other (p. 126). He believes that our objective must be to attempt to integrate the analysis of the broader questions of ideology, power and politics with the analysis of the consumption, uses and functions of television in everyday life. That is, the question is not simply how to understand media's domestic, socially organizing and/or ideological-representational roles, but rather an integrated one which strives to "understand the articulation of micro and macro issues and processes" (Morley, 1997, p. 128).

However, as Ang (1996) observes, these critiques and their responses pose a challenge for ethnographers who fear to be critiqued by cultural studies skeptics for failing to achieve a "comprehensive theory of the audience." The challenge is to identify how micro-narratives are formed, contested and reproduced within macro-structures of society while trying to accomplish the impossible task of contextualizing each and every emerging micro-narrative. Ang (1996) proposes that we should mark out the search for a "comprehensive theory of the audience" and acknowledge the partial and incomplete nature of our theorizing and research for a better realization of the complex dynamics of media consumption practices (p. 248). According to her, this requires conceptualizing the media more radically and without conceptualizing television, radio, the press, and so on in isolation (p. 248). She observes that many reception studies still conceptualize television as a given phenomenon with fixed features and intrinsic potential to be used or interpreted in different ways by different audience groups: "From a radical contextualist perspective, however, television's meanings for audiences – textual, technological, psychological, social – cannot be decided upon outside of the multidimensional intersubjective networks in which the object is inserted and made to mean in concrete contextual settings" (p. 250). She states that this epistemological move toward radical contextualism in audience studies resulted in a growing interest in ethnography as a means of empirical inquiry. As she puts it:

> Ethnographically oriented research is considered the most suitable to unravel the minutiae of difference and variation as they manifest themselves in concrete, everyday instances of media consumption. What ethnographic work entails is a form of "methodological situationalism," underscoring the thoroughly situated, always context-bound ways in which people encounter, use, interpret, enjoy, think and talk about television and other media in everyday life. The understanding emerging from this kind of inquiry favors interpretive particularization over explanatory generalization, historical and local concreteness rather than formal abstraction, "thick" description of details rather than extensive but "thin" survey. But this ethno-graphic interest is neither uncontroversial nor unproblematic.
>
> (p. 251)

Even though Ang favors radical contextualism, she realizes the unfeasibility of such an analysis since "radical contextualism in principle involves the impos-sibility of determining any social or textual meaning outside of the complex situation in which it is produced" (p. 253). Therefore, she suggests that instead of "wanting to be epistemologically perfect," we should draw our attention to the "uncertain trajectories of the politics of narrative and narration, of story and discourse" (p. 254). Thus by revealing that the ethnographer must "always speak and write from 'somewhere,'" Ang (1996) argues:

> we can leave remnants of logico-scientific thinking (as embodied in the epistemology of radical contextualism) for what it is in favor of narrative modes of reasoning and representation, in which not only the contexts of media consumption, but also the contexts of ethnographic knowledge production itself are taken into account.
>
> (p. 254)

Morley (1997) cautions us against just these "contexts of ethnographic knowledge." Drawing from Hall, Morley points to the tendency toward the textualization of cultural studies, which treats power and politics merely as matters of language and/or discourse and ignores the social and material foundations of the cultural phenomena under analysis. As Morley writes:

> one of the crucial features of the American (and predominantly literary) appropriation of British cultural studies has been the loss of any sense of culture and communications as having material roots, in broader social and political processes and structures, so that the discursive process of the constitution of meanings often becomes the exclusive focus of analysis, without any reference to its institutional or economic setting.
>
> (p. 123)

Furthermore, Morley agrees with Probyn (1993) that ethnography, which has been a popular method for media consumption and reception studies, is becoming textual. In fact, he charges that ethnography's textualization has in part made it fashionable within cultural studies, along with the discovery of "the virtues of its postmodern inflection" which are "now widely assumed to be self-evident, as are those of a constructivist epistemology, and a heavily textualist form of discourse theory, which has little regard for questions of socio-economic determination" (1997, p. 122). He observes that since Clifford and Marcus's collection *Writing Culture* (1986) has drawn attention to the fact that ethnographies are written accounts, and thus they must be analyzed as forms of writing and representation, there is a tendency to believe that the awareness of the politics of writing is always, in itself, the solution to methodological problems. However, Morley (1997) states that neither the provision of more context "nor an address to its textual characteristics will solve all its problems" (p. 129). While I share Morley's concern that an emphasis on textuality and the politics of knowledge may have a disabling effect that makes it "pretty hard for anyone to say anything about anyone (or anything) else, for fear of accusation of ontological imperialism" (p. 122) and may result in ethnographies which are mere mimicry of the informants' statements, I also think it is not possible to create an ethnography which is capable of informing about the processes of the micro and macro without a detailed account of the context. Also, without providing a detailed description of the ethnographic processes and accounts and problematizing the ethnographer's relation with his or her informants, ethnographers might not feel comfortable enough to move on to the next step of making cultural judgements – especially after reviewing the scholarship about how ethnography and/or anthropology should be conducted in order to distance itself from its colonial past. More context on ethnographic knowledge production may not solve the methodological and ideological problems of the field of ethnography, but it can solve the problem of mimicry by creating rooted groundwork for the ethnographer to work with in forming meta-narratives about the phenomenon under inquiry.

Press's (1997) approach to audience research might be one way to ease the concerns over how textuality hinders the contexts of media consumption. She argues that audience, despite being an arbitrary construction in qualitative research, is a concrete, living subject in ethnography and that audience researchers should treat audience as such. Thus, Press suggests the application of sociological analysis to audience research in order to define and analyze the context in which subjects make meanings of media. Another approach is conducting media ethnographies that utilize traditional ethnographic methods in order to analyze "how various forms of media intertwine, creating new codes of understanding and experience on public agendas and in our private lives" (p. 174). Emphasizing how media ethnography departs from reception studies and ethnographic audience research, Drotner proposes that media ethnography should be seen as "an epistemological alternative to other forms and not as their extension" (p. 172). In that sense, she points out that media ethnographies "take as their analytical point of departure a particular group of people, not a particular type of medium" and define the group as media users (Drotner, 2000, p. 172). In doing so, she argues that "one studies the informants as recipients as well as producers of mediated communication," and thus the ethnographer should visit different locations of media use (p. 172). Revisiting early studies on media use and new trends in anthropological theory, I will give an account of my fieldwork experience in order to discuss how one can locate media ethnographies outside the text.

Locating media ethnographies outside the text

Some of the earliest studies that aim to identify everyday media use are on women's daily experiences of radio and television (Hobson, 1980), social uses of television among American families (Lull, 1990), social roles of video recorders at home (Gray, 1987), power relations in a domestic viewing context (Morley, 1986) and the family use of domestic technology (Silverstone and Morley, 1990). These studies were instrumental in shifting the focus, in Morley's words, "from the analysis of the pattern of differential audience 'readings' of particular programme materials, to the analysis of the domestic viewing context itself – as the framework within which the 'readings' of programmes are (ordinarily) made" (Morley, 1986, p. 14). Even though the focus shifted from text or genre to the domestic context of reception, this time it limited itself to the domestic sphere in an attempt to understand the macro-structures of viewing, and thus participant observation became a method of watching people watch television in many studies. Neither watching television with the informant families nor talking about certain television programs or genres reveals much about the relation between media use and their everyday realities and practices outside the domestic context. Moreover, a research project such as mine, which does not aim to investigate family viewing but seeks to explore local responses to global and national media products and how those responses correspond to everyday life both inside and outside of the domestic context, requires a different research direction than that taken by the studies mentioned above. Otherwise, limiting oneself to the study of the domestic sphere could exclude media use in the public sphere, such as internet cafes and radio use in workplaces, and the sphere of media production.

While the constraints that reception studies pose in their emphasis on text discouraged me from following an ethnographic approach, new trends and debates in anthropology and media ethnography made them more viable for my research agenda. Criticisms about the practice of these disciplines resulted in questioning not only conventional methods and assumptions of writing and representing cultures, but also how much these methods are able to capture and study cultures in a global and interconnected world system. Anthropology's assumption that cultures occupy naturally disconnected spaces is being challenged because we no longer live in the era of small isolated villages but in an era where global media and cultural artifacts blur both cultural and geographic boundaries and where most of the world's population lives in urban areas (Gupta and Ferguson, 1992). Marcus (1998) observes the emergence of a new mode of ethnographic research which arose from anthropology's engagement with a number of interdisciplinary fields that have evolved since the 1980s, such as media studies, feminist studies, science and technology studies, and cultural studies. This mode of ethnography, which Marcus refers to as multisited research,

> moves out from the single sites and local situations of conventional ethnographic research designs to examine the circulation of cultural meanings, objects, and identities in diffuse time-space. This mode defines for itself an object of study that cannot be accounted for ethnographically by remaining focused on a single site of intensive investigation. It develops instead a strategy or design of research that acknowledges macrotheoretical concepts and narratives of the world system but does not rely on them for the contextual architecture framing a set of subjects.
>
> (pp. 79–80)

Before beginning my fieldwork, I was not sure if multisited research would help me understand the role of local media in people's lives and capture global and national impact on their interpretation of media because I wanted to focus on Sanliurfa, which is mostly an agrarian province composed mainly of Kurds and Arabs and located in the underdeveloped southeast region of Turkey. However, as I learned more about the area from both officials and inhabitants and saw the drastic changes caused by the Southeast Anatolia Project (as well as the breakup of the state media monopoly), I embraced a multisited approach because it encouraged me to move "between public and private spheres of activity, from official to subaltern contexts" (Marcus, 1998, p. 97).

One of the reasons why I wanted to conduct my research in Sanliurfa was the Southeast Anatolian Project (GAP). By producing electricity and dramatically expanding irrigation agriculture through the construction of twenty-two dams built on the Euphrates and Tigris Rivers, this project aims to develop the region while supplying energy for the whole country. When I talked to the officials and scientists behind the GAP project, I found that the socio-economic structure in southeast Turkey drastically changed upon the introduction of irrigated farming and GAP's other development initiatives. Besides the increase in agricultural production due to irrigation, industry also developed significantly with the help of financial incentives given by the government. This project displaced many people throughout the province and increased the population of and immigration to the city center of Sanliurfa and other urban areas. In 1993 Harran University was built in Sanliurfa city, which brought many students and faculty from other provinces. Both the university's diverse population and the large number of GAP project staff – in addition to the draw from rural areas – contributed to the changes in the traditional nature of what Appadurai (1990) called the "ethnoscape" of the region. Money accumulated as a result of investments and incentives, increasing the overall income and adding many upscale neighborhoods to the city's landscape. The city had to adapt to these drastic changes and outside influences.

In learning about the province and the city, talking to officials helped me understand the social changes faced by Sanliurfans. Next I talked to Sanliurfans about their media use and reception to see how they were interpreting and responding to these changes through media and how media aided them in their understanding. When I talked to students, farmers, shopkeepers and merchants, I saw that the new lively commercial mediascape of Turkey was welcomed by Sanliurfans and overlapped with both the other changes in their lives and their traditions. For instance, Sanliurfans are proud of their music and the province has produced many nationally acclaimed musicians. "Sira gecesi" is the very old Sanliurfa tradition of sharing the music and folk songs of the region in which men get together to create and recite songs. Since 1993, local radio and television channels often broadcast this music and ritual. However, arabesque and political pop music are the most consumed music genres among the youth of Sanliurfa. Discussions with DJs about what songs they choose to play made me more aware of how the young identify with the sad mood and lyrics depicting impossible love stories, economic difficulties, and the problems of belonging to the fringes of society.

The personal narratives of the individuals who built the first local radio and television stations in 1993 provided me with not only an oral history of local media in Sanliurfa but also the legal, technical and financial challenges that current media stations face, including the media owners' battles with the authorities which constantly monitor their broadcasts. These stations' competition with national networks, their aims and missions as local media channels, and their views of their audiences gave me various clues to understand the media environment better.

One challenge I faced regarding how to conduct my research without isolating a certain media form was how to capture and study radio audiences in an ethnographic audience research tradition that almost became equivalent to television studies. Except for Hobson's (1980) research on housewives' use of radio and television and Tacchi's (1998) exploration of the ways in which radio sound is used in the home, radio audiences are completely ignored. In the nostalgic oral histories of early media use, radio is often treated as an ancient medium and as being historically significant because of its role in nation-building in Europe after World War I. Other cultural studies research on radio emphasizes its didactic use in the Third World for development purposes.

Even though radio is often seen as a local and/or national medium as opposed to other electronic media, such as television and the internet which are assumed to cross local and national boundaries easily, my research on radio audiences illustrates the ways in which the youth of Sanliurfa encounter, negotiate and respond to global messages and culture via their local radio. Moreover, in a region where traditions, the feudal social structure, and the strict interpretation of Islam result in many rigorous constraints on the lives of youngsters, radio plays a crucial role in overcoming these constraints. Although marriages are arranged, dating is not tolerated, and young women are not allowed to walk the streets alone in Sanliurfa, the young people not only make their voices heard via these interactive channels but also manage to experience love and dating via the messages they send through arabesque songs and their conversations with DJs. Many stories are told in Sanliurfa about radio functioning as a matchmaker. For many youth, these message exchanges encourage hope and keep them informed about their acquaintances' struggles with love. For some, these exchanges are "fun to follow, just like a soap opera."

Any research that attempts to capture a media environment in Sanliurfa cannot ignore the multiple roles that the internet and internet cafés play in the lives of Sanliurfa's youth. Over 100 internet cafés exist in the city of Sanliurfa alone. While teenage boys use computers to play video games, older ones and young men often chat with others, hoping to meet in the ether with a woman. Some of them have girlfriends in other provinces of Turkey whom they have only met on the internet. They occasionally call each other and send text messages via cellular phones, which are very popular among young men despite their economic difficulties. In Sanliurfa, internet cafés also function as spaces to meet people, socialize and learn about the new sites and games. According to one of my informants, they had already caused the closure of many traditional café houses in Sanliurfa, where most men regularly visit to chat and play backgammon.

My research required me to talk to people at different sites, such as DJs in radio stations, young men in the internet cafés, young women in cafés, homes and the multi-purpose community centers (CATOM), the GAP administration, radio and television station owners, Harran University students, children of farmers, as well as to investigate different media such as radio, television, cellular telephones, and the internet. These experiences resonated with Marcus's (1998) notion of multisited ethnography, where the research is "designed around chains, paths, threads, conjunctions, or juxtapositions of locations in which the ethnographer establishes some form of literal, physical presence, with an explicit, posited logic of association or connection among sites that in fact defines the argument of the ethnography" (p. 90). Not isolating one particular medium but attempting to capture a city's media environment illustrated the complex ways that young people experience love, dating, etc., in a traditional society that arranges marriages and does not tolerate dating.

Space and place in media ethnographies

Even though some ethnographic methods are widely utilized in audience studies, ethnography's and/or anthropology's emphasis on place is rarely an issue for the study of media audiences, except for some recent media ethnographies, such as Mankekar's (1999) book on national identity and television in India, Kraidy's (1999) work on local/global identities and media in Lebanon, Gillespie's (1995) work on British Asian teen culture and television in London, and Murphy's (1999b) study of television and everyday life in Mexico. Place is often emphasized only if the fieldwork involves original sites of research (instead of an office or conference room arranged by the researcher for focus groups). When the emphasis is on the text, then it automatically places the text as a site of inquiry. Another important reason for the dearth of discussion of place in current media ethnographies is that most ethnographers think of themselves as insiders, the bearers of "local knowledge." Alasuutari (1999), for instance, believes that if ethnographers study their own cultures then they have the advantage of "a very long personal field experience" (p. 8). Alasuutari asserts that in light of "our abundant" experience, "it is ridiculous to think of a media ethnography in terms of so-and-so many months of participant observation: 'fieldwork' has actually started years before we knew anything about a particular site we are going to study" (p. 8).

What Alasuutari omits from the discussion is what happens when a middle-class, middle-aged, educated ethnographer from a certain city chooses to study a young, lower-class, blue-collar, poorly educated audience from the "other side" of the same city. Even though the ethnographer studies his/her own culture, can he/she still claim that he/she shares the same culture with the informants if their cultural practices and everyday life realities differ dramatically? For instance, I am an urban, well-educated, middle-class Turkish woman from a modern, industrial city (Istanbul) researching ethnically diverse lower/middle-class, poorly educated/uneducated Turks, Turkish Kurds and Turkish Arabs in the underdeveloped, agrarian southeast of Turkey, and I do not really know if I can call myself a native ethnographer, even though I share with them the same nationality, history, religion and language (although many of them have Kurdish or Arab ethnic backgrounds, they are at the same time bilingual). Then the significant differences in cultural practices and everyday realities, not only between the ethnographer and the informants but also among the informants themselves, require us to place a special emphasis on where ethnographies take place – both the overall geography, such as a city, town or country, and smaller locations, such as shops, a radio station, home, etc. Situating our informants geographically, socially and culturally might help us better understand the relationships between their media consumption and everyday practices.

In this chapter my goal was to illustrate the need for a more ethnographic approach to the study of media audiences by problematizing the issues of textuality and context. Such an approach requires not only a radical contextualism of the ethnographic account and the physical location where the ethnography takes place, but also the spatial context of media consumption. Instead of focusing on a specific radio channel or show and its audience, I attempted to map the media use in a specific geographic location in the periphery of Turkey in order to understand the hegemonic interplay between the center and periphery, the global and local, and the West and the East. At the end of my fieldwork, I realized that multisited ethnographic method not only made it possible for me to avoid the constraints of a text or genre but also helped me to locate my research, situate myself, and contextualize the social, cultural, political, geographic and ideological elements that shape people's engagement with media in Sanliurfa.

References

Alasuutari, P. (1999). Introduction: Three phases of reception studies. In P. Alasuutari (ed.), *Rethinking the media audience: The new agenda* (pp. 1–21). Thousand Oaks, CA: Sage.

Ang, I. (1990). Culture and communication: Towards an ethnographic critique of media consumption in the transnational system. *European Journal of Communication* 5, 239–260.

Ang, I. (1993). *Desperately seeking the audience*. London and New York: Routledge.

Ang, I. (1996). Ethnography and radical contextualism in audience studies. In J. Hay, L. Grossberg and E. Wartella (eds), *The audience and its landscape* (pp. 247–262). Boulder, CO: Westview Press.

Appadurai, A. (1990). Disjuncture and difference in the global cultural economy. *Public Culture* 2(2), 1–24.

Clifford, J. and Marcus, G. E. (eds) (1986). *Writing culture: The poetics and politics of ethnography*. Berkeley, CA: University of California Press.

Corner, J. (1991). Meaning, genre and context: The problematics of "public knowledge" in the new audience studies. In J. Curran and M. Gurevitch (eds), *Mass media and society* (pp. 267–284). New York: Edward Arnold.

n, J. (1990). The new revisionism in mass communication research: A reap-
isal. *European Journal of Communication* 5(2/3), 135–164.

er, K. (1994). Ethnographic enigmas: "The everyday" in recent media studies.
Cultural Studies 8(2), 341–357.

Drotner, K. (2000). Less is more: Media ethnography and its limits. In I. Hagen and
J. Wasko (eds), *Consuming audiences? Production and reception in media research*
(pp. 165–188). Cresskill, NJ: Hampton Press.

Gibson, T. A. (2000). Beyond cultural populism: Notes toward the critical
ethnography of media audiences. *Journal of Communication Inquiry* 24(3), 253–273.

Gillespie, M. (1995). *Television, ethnicity and cultural change*. London: Routledge.

Gray, A. (1987). Behind closed doors: Video recorders in the home. In H. Baehr and
G. Dyer (eds), *Boxed-in: Women and television*. London: Pandora Press.

Gray, A. (1999). Audience and reception research in retrospect: The trouble with
audiences. In P. Alasuutari (ed.), *Rethinking the media audience: The new agenda*
(pp. 195–205). Thousand Oaks, CA: Sage.

Grossberg, L. (1989). The circulation of cultural studies. *Critical Studies of Mass
Communication* 6, 413–20.

Gupta, A. and Ferguson, J. (1992). Beyond "culture": Space, identity, and the politics
of difference. *Cultural Anthropology* 7(1), 6–23.

Hobson, D. (1980). Housewives and the mass media. In S. Hall, D. Hobson, A. Lowe
and P. Willis (eds), *Culture, media, language* (pp. 105–114). London: Hutchinson.

Jensen, J. and Pauly, J. J. (1997). Imagining the audience: Losses and gains in
cultural studies. In M. Ferguson and P. Golding (eds), *Cultural studies in question*
(2nd edn) (pp. 155–169). Thousand Oaks, CA: Sage.

Kraidy, M. M. (1999). The global, the local, and the hybrid: A native ethnography of
globalization. *Critical Studies in Mass Communication* 16, 456–476.

Lull, J. (1990). *Inside family viewing: Ethnographic research on television's audiences*.
London: Routledge.

Mankekar, P. (1999). *Screening culture, viewing politics: An ethnography of television,
womanhood, and nation in post-colonial India*. Durham, NC: Duke University Press.

Marcus, G. E. (1998). Ethnography in/of the world system: The emergence of multisited ethnography. In G. E. Marcus, *Ethnography through thick and thin*. Princeton,
NJ: Princeton University Press. (Reprinted from *Annual Review of Anthropology*, 24
(1995), 95–117.)

Moores, S. (1988). The box on the dresser: Memories of early radio and everyday life.
Media, Culture and Society 1, 25–40.

Moores, S. (1993). *Interpreting audiences: The ethnography of media consumption*. Thousand
Oaks, CA: Sage.

Morley, D. (1980). *The Nationwide audience*. London: British Film Institute.

Morley, D. (1986). *Family television: Cultural power and domestic leisure*. London and
New York: Routledge.

Morley, D. (1992) *Television, audiences and cultural studies*. London and New York:
Routledge.

Morley, D. (1993). Active audience theory: Pendulums and pitfalls. *Journal of
Communication* 43(4), 13–19.

Morley, D. (1997). Theoretical orthodoxies: Textualism, constructivism and the "new
ethnography" in cultural studies. In M. Ferguson and P. Golding (eds), *Cultural
studies in question* (pp. 121–137). Thousand Oaks, CA: Sage.

Morley, D. (1999). 'To boldly go . . .'. The third generation of reception studies. In P. Alasuutari (ed.), *Rethinking the media audience: The new agenda* (pp. 195–205). Thousand Oaks, CA: Sage.

Murphy, P. D. (1999a). Media cultural studies' uncomfortable embrace of ethnography. *Journal of Communication Inquiry* 23(3), 205–221.

Murphy, P. D. (1999b). Doing audience ethnography: A narrative account of establishing ethnographic identity and locating interpretive communities in fieldwork. *Qualitative Inquiry* 5(4), 479–504.

Press, A. L. (1997). Toward a qualitative methodology of audience study: Using ethnography to study the popular culture audience. In J. Hay, L. Grossberg and E. Wartella (eds), *The audience and its landscape* (pp. 113–130). Boulder, CO: Westview Press.

Probyn, E. (1993). *Sexing the self: Gendered positions in cultural studies*. London: Routledge.

Radway, J. (1988). Reception study: ethnography and the problems of dispersed audiences and nomadic subjects. *Cultural Studies* 2(3), 359–76.

Radway, J. (1996). The hegemony of "specificity" and the impasse in audience research: Cultural studies and the problem of ethnography. In J. Hay, L. Grossberg and E. Wartella (eds), *The audience and its landscape* (pp. 235–245). Boulder, CO: Westview Press.

Silverstone, R. (1989). Let us then return to the murmuring of everyday practices: A note on Michel de Certeau, Television and Everyday Life. *Theory, Culture and Society* 6(1), 77–94.

Silverstone, R. (1994). *Television and everyday life*. London: Routledge.

Silverstone, R. and Morley, D. (1990). Families and their technologies: Two ethnographic portraits. In T. Putnam and C. Newton (eds), *Household choices* (pp. 74–83). London: Futures.

Tacchi, J. (1998). Radio texture: Between self and others. In D. Miller (ed.), *Material cultures: Why some things matter* (pp. 25–45). Chicago: University of Chicago Press.

3

PASSING ETHNOGRAPHIES

Rethinking the sites of agency and reflexivity in a mediated word

Nick Couldry

The problem of ethnography has cast a long shadow over the practice of media and cultural studies. The disputes concerning the ethics and epistemological coherence of fieldwork that split anthropology in the 1980s seem to have transferred some of their force to recent debates about how we can study media audiences across the world. It would, however, be a mistake to discuss the epistemology of the media audience as if the audience researcher carried a pale version of the colonialist's historical burden – although the rhetoric of some attacks on audience research suggests this (Hartley, 1987 and 1996; Nightingale, 1996) – for that would obscure a more interesting question, whose significance stretches well beyond media analysis: what kind of "location-work" (Gupta and Ferguson, 1997b, p. 5) will enable us to address the locational *complexity* which characterizes all social and cultural phenomena today, not least those marked by the multidirectional flows of media images?

Even when stripped of its colonial connotations, ethnography's fiction of "being there" – "there" where the systematic order of a wider culture is "revealed" to a sensitive observer – remains problematic. But its problem can now be seen as a problem for conducting any research in today's dispersed, mediated societies. Put simply: how *do* we conceive of the order, or system, at work in today's world, and where do we need to be to grasp it better? We can formulate this in more specific ways, for example as the question of how, and from exactly where, can we track the movements which all our lives as self-reflexive agents in such societies entail, and the movements across our lives of media flows from countless sources?[1] Or, recalling Donna Haraway's (1991) provocative term from an earlier, rather different epistemological crisis: how can we produce "situated knowledge" of mediation's place in the lives of others and ourselves?

The study of media, then, is entangled with the problem of ethnography, but in interesting ways that transcend old debates on the colonial encounter. The issue of complexity, and how to study it, affects all branches of the social sciences and humanities that are attempting to give accounts of what goes on "inside" today's "cultures" (both sets of scare quotes being necessary). It is a matter of grasping, first, as I have said, the complexity of "order" and "space," but also the complexity of agency and reflexivity, so we can produce more satisfactory accounts of what "subject" and "object" of ethnography share. Both, after all, are self-conscious agents (Cohen, 1994), who are highly mobile, living and reflecting across many different sites. I want to argue that the situated analysis of *mediation's* place in our lives has resonance for today's reconceptualization of ethnography in general (Gupta and Ferguson, 1997a; Marcus, 1998), and in particular the shift towards an ethnography that is *"places* – rather than *place-focused"* (Marcus, 1998, p. 50).

This chapter will approach these difficult issues in three stages. The first section will review the critique of "culture" within anthropology and the ways beyond this critique that have recently suggested a different mode of cultural analysis. The second section will explore how that general debate about "culture" plays out when we think specifically about mediated culture and media uses: what contribution can media analysis make to an ethnography of "places" within a wider analysis of cultural complexity (here, I suggest, anthropology and media and cultural studies are partners, not rivals)? The third section will review the method of my own empirical research in which was at least a partial attempt to address these issues. The chapter will, in these various ways, flesh out its title's metaphor of "passing ethnographies."

Disappearance of the ethnographic agent?

The implication of the apparently innocent object of research – "cultures" – in the practices which comprised, and in some respects still continue to comprise, colonialism is well-known. As Lila Abu-Lughod (1991) has put it, "culture is the essential tool for *making other* . . . anthropological discourse gives cultural difference (and the separation between groups of people it implies) the air of the self-evident" (p. 143, added emphasis). And not just that: applied to "ourselves," a belief in a distinctive, shared culture is the touchstone of nationalism in all its often disturbing forms, even if the evidence for what it is we share with our compatriots is often problematic or absent (Schudson, 1994). For some writers, a shared national "culture" is always the projection of a mythical unity (Bhabha, 1994; Zizek, 1990), desired but never possible.

To say this, however, is only to pose a problem, not to resolve anything. What happens when we attempt to study cultural processes *without* relying on the notion of "cultures" – that is, stable, coherent, localized "units" of cultural analysis? What are the implications for the practice and theory of ethnography, when both its object (a distant "culture") and its subject (the agent who moves with privileged status outside his/her own "culture" to study another) disappear, at least in their familiar forms?

There are no straightforward answers, but to move forward we need to draw, for example, on the new model of cultural processes and flows developed by Ulf Hannerz (see Couldry, 2000b, chapter 5 for more detail). The reasons for this can be seen best if we briefly recall the old model of culture that must be superseded. The older model pictures the space of culture primarily in terms of a series of separate "cultures," with the interactions between them being of secondary importance. Each "culture" is understood as a natural unit: coherent (so that hybrid cultures are an exceptional case), and associated with a particular shared place and time.

Paradoxically, that older model on which classical anthropology depended was formulated most clearly by its anthropologist critics. As Ulf Hannerz (1992) puts it, it is "the idea of culture as something *shared*, in the sense of homogeneously distributed in society" (p. 11, added emphasis). This holistic model, with its "fiction of the whole" (Marcus, 1998, p. 33), is supported by various metaphors which James Clifford (1988) did much to excavate. There is the organic metaphor of culture as *growth*, "a coherent body that lives and dies," or alternatively survives, provided it remains uncontaminated by outside influences (pp. 235 and 338). Closely linked with growth is the metaphor of *place*, an issue which will be particularly important in the rest of this chapter. Just as everybody occupies one, discrete place, so too from the point of view of the old notion of culture the "place" of culture is the site where its reality is lived, the focus where all the possible lines of diversity in a culture intersect in a unity (Auge, 1995, p. 58). They intersect there, so that they can be "read," a third metaphor: "culture as *text*" (pp. 49–50), a text with finite boundaries.

These metaphors are problematic not least because they exclude others: metaphors emphasizing the connections between multiple cultural sites, the uncertainty of cultural boundaries, in a sense therefore the opaqueness, not the transparency, of culture. The old metaphors encourage us to look for *less* complexity in cultural phenomena, when we should be prepared to look for more.

The old holistic model of culture has, however, been extremely influential not only in anthropology, but also in sociology (it was at the root of functionalist models of social integration, such as that of Talcott Parsons) and cultural studies, where its influence on Raymond Williams's (1958) early account of culture as a way of life is obvious. Yet it is clearly inadequate to deal with a world of complex flows of people, images, information and goods, in which local culture everywhere incorporates "transculturality" (Welsch, 1999), and we live in "imagined worlds" that are complex amalgams of elements from all over the world (Appadurai, 1990). In this context, the idea of culture as necessarily tied to a place can be seen for what it always was: an *assumption*. We must look for cultural processes in different places, or (better) through imagining a different relation of cultural production from place and space. If we do, then new spaces and new mobilities come into view: Paul Gilroy (1992) has famously argued for the study of the Black Atlantic (a space of passage between nations); Marc

Auge (1995) has argued for the study of "nonplaces," the "cultures" of ordinary places of transit, such as airports, tourist zones; and there are many other examples which could be given.

Here, though, a further difficulty with the old metaphors must be addressed, which results from debates in spatial theory, rather than anthropology. If "culture" has been deconstructed as a simple object, so too has "place." No place, argues Doreen Massey (1997), is reducible to a simple narrative, a coherent set of meanings. Places are points where many influences, operating on many different scales (up to and including the global), intersect. Instead of a traditional notion of "place" as bounded locality, we need "a global sense of the local" (1997, p. 240). In every place, multiple scales of connection are overlaid.

Once we complicate our idea of how culture is embedded in place, then we must question our assumption that cultures have a simple relation to time. We must, for example, as Homi Bhabha (1994) has argued, raise "the essential question of the representation of the nation as [itself] a temporal process" (p. 142): national "culture" cannot be reduced to a simple object describable as it exists at one point in time. Material processes for constructing past, present and future are wrapped up in our sense of the national "present". We have to challenge what Charlotte Brunsdon and David Morley (1978) called "the myth of 'the nation, now'" (p. 27). And the problem of time applies to other descriptive terms as well, including those that try to capture the open-ended process of the self, at which point the dimensions of space and time become entangled. Quasi-spatial language for describing the self (such as "subject-positions") is problematic, precisely because it closes off the self's reflexive processes in time (Battaglia, 1999, p. 117; Couldry, 1996, p. 327).

The result of all these moves is not to divorce our notion of cultural production and cultural experience entirely from space, place or time. Rather we need a more complex notion of that relation. The question is too complex to resolve in a few pages, but one initial consequence is clear: the dissolution of that apparently innocent methodological presumption, the ethnographic "present," present "there" in "the field" where the ethnographic agent is based.[2]

To take these thoughts a stage further, I want to draw specifically on Ulf Hannerz's (1992) work on cultural space in his important book *Cultural Complexity*. "Complex societies," according to Hannerz, are distinctive in a number of ways. Most relevant here is the fact that their meanings have to be *distributed* to that society's members, who are dispersed across space. There is no reason to assume that distribution is even. On the contrary, "in a society where the cultural flow is varied and uneven, it is an open question which meanings have reached where and when" (p. 81). But people are not monads taking inputs from the wider culture in isolation from everyone else; they are also engaged in making sense of *other people's* meanings and interpretations (p. 14). This adds a second layer of complexity to the distribution of meanings, which cannot be simply extrapolated from the first: a dimension of reflexivity which itself is a material process that takes place here, and not there.

The idea of cultural "holism" – that cultures comprise principally the meanings that people share – is thus untenable. As Hannerz (1992) puts it:

> we must recognize the real intricacy of the flow of meaning in social life. As each individual engages in his [sic] own continuous inter-preting of the forms surrounding him, how can we take for granted that he comes to the same result as the next fellow [sic]? There is nothing automatic about cultural sharing. Its accomplishment must rather be seen as problematic.
>
> (p. 44)

In other words, our idea of cultures as large-scale structures has to take account of the "local" complexity of agents' reflexivity about culture, not just academics' reflexivity of course, but the reflexivity of every agent they study. Everywhere processes of agency and reflexivity intersect. Given the resulting complexity, ethnography's situated knowledge can no longer be based on the ethnographer's movement (or lack of it) perfectly tracking culture's movement (or lack of it). The intersection between "ethnography" and "culture" is necessarily more partial than that: it takes the form of *passing ethnographies*, which yield, we hope, knowledge under particular conditions.

Accepting partiality in this sense (at the level of guiding metaphor) does not mean renouncing claims to generalizable knowledge, as I explain below. But it does mean thinking about generality from a starting-point that takes complexity seriously. There is no reason any more to suppress or reduce the complexity all around us. Lives are stretched across many sites and many roles, without necessarily cohering into a unity; communities are not tied to a single nation-state, but are informed by the experience of moving between many. We must take seriously "identities that resist classification" (Kearney, 1995, p. 558), which of course may mean working at odds with the definitional strategies of states or markets. We don't know, and certainly can't assume, that people accept the market-led identities that are prepared for them, which means that we must take seriously people's journey's across cultural space, whether they are voluntary or involuntary. Culture, in short, emerges "on a differently configured spatial canvas" (Marcus, 1995, p. 98) where the connections between sites matter as much as and sometimes more than, the sites of imagined closure (the village, the city, the nation-state, or even the globe).

The nature of this methodological shift has been brought out well by Anna Lowenhaupt Tsing (1993) in her book on her time spent with the Meratus Dayak people from the mountainous forest regions of southeast Kalimantan in Indonesia. They are in various ways managed and marginalized by the central Indonesian government, but at the same time engage in a complex set of negotiations of their identity with many "centers," not just Jakarta, but more locally, and globally. Tsing found there were no "villages" to study, but rather a shifting network of cultural dialogues across scattered populations. Her own practice – as reflexive ethnographic agent – involved ceaseless movement as well. In a powerful passage, Tsing (1993) describes how her own movements across cultural space made irrelevant the attempt to reduce that space to a closed cultural order:

> As I involved myself with a network that stretched across the mountains, I moved increasingly further from structural models of local stability and came to recognize the open-ended dialogues that formed and reformed Meratus culture and history. My own shifting positioning made me especially alert to continual negotiations of local "community", to the importance of far-flung as well as local ties . . . a culture that cannot be tied to a place cannot be analytically stopped in time.
>
> (p. 66)

I want now to explore what this means specifically for the analysis of mediated cultures.

Analyzing our mediated lives

Anna Lowenhaupt Tsing expresses very clearly that existing notions of how cultural analysis fits with reality are inadequate. Tsing was, however, in one respect writing still in a classic ethnographic situation, one that was not intensely mediated. Mediation, as communication which crosses contexts and borders in pervasive and regular ways, changes the boundaries of the ethnographic situation, just as it changes the boundaries of the political situation, the family situation, and the educational situation (Meyrowitz, 1985). The consequences of this for ethnographic practice have only recently been explored.

Lila Abu-Lughod (1999), whose subtle work on television audiences in Egypt has been important here, has recently argued that television is in fact central to ethnographic practice today. Television often provides a ready-made link between ethnographers and their subjects (p. 111), of a sort that earlier ethnographers in "strange" countries could never call upon. More than that, television – as its genres, styles and knowledges and often, of course, specific programs too cross the world – has reconfigured the cultural space which ethnographers need to cross. As a result, Clifford Geertz's famous methodological tool of "thick description" (which Abu-Lughod endorses) "needs some creative stretching to fit mass-mediated lives" (p. 111). This raises a question: where exactly is the entry-point for ethnography in studying "the significance of television's existence as a ubiquitous presence in [people's] lives and imaginaries?" (p. 111). Or, more bluntly: thick descriptions of *what*?

On the face of it, there is common ground between anthropology and the significant tradition of situated qualitative research in media sociology since the mid-1980s. It is unfortunate therefore that Abu-Lughod undermines this ground through a very partial account of media sociology. She takes no account of the methodological debates in audience research about the difficulties of fully contextualizing research into audience practices in the home (Morley and Silverstone,1991; Silverstone, Hirsch and Morley, 1991); this makes unfair her criticism of certain texts (such as Silverstone, 1994) which never purport to be fresh ethnographic work themselves. Her analysis seems designed to create the space for anthropology "proper" to do fully contextualized research into media consumption, as if for the first time. There are two problems with this position, in addition to its very partial account of the work already done in audience research: first, it operates within a rather polarized view of the boundaries between anthropological work and media and cultural studies, which is no longer helpful (cf. Thomas, 1999); second, it implicitly makes a claim for methodological advances in Abu-Lughod's own work which seem rather exaggerated. Her analysis in the same chapter of audiences and producers of the Egyptian television drama *Mothers in the House of Love* is certainly suggestive in detail and it is a "mobile ethnography" (Abu-Lughod, 1999, p. 122) in the limited sense that the ethnographer moves between locations, asking questions. But it provides no account, for example, of the mobility of the people it studies, of how people's interpretations of the serial might change as they interpret it in different contexts, or of how media themselves might affect the circulation of interpretations in significant ways. While Abu-Lughod's recognition of mediation's centrality to ethnographic method is welcome, we need, I suggest, to turn elsewhere to clarify exactly how that relationship should work.

An important advance is represented by George Marcus's (1999) essay "The use of complicity in the changing mise-en-scene of anthropological fieldwork." This is a thoroughgoing rethinking of what "thick description" can mean in today's complex cultural spaces. Marcus abandons the idea that what is feasible or desirable in fieldwork is "rapport," that is, a close *fit* between the ethnographer's and her/his interlocutor's understandings of the world, achieved within the confines of the ethnographic situation. Instead of "rapport" as the "foundational commonplace of fieldwork" (1999, p. 87), Marcus develops the notion of "complicity," which emphasizes not the knowledge so much as the questioning and curiosity that ethnographer and interlocutor share.[3]

Marcus's first characterization of this "complicity" is as "an awareness of existential doubleness on the part of *both* anthropologist and subject; this derives from having a sense of being *here* where major transformations are under way that are tied to things happening simultaneously *elsewhere*, but not having a certainty or authoritative representation of what those connections are" (p. 97, original emphasis). The result of this uncertainty may be anxiety (p. 98), as well as a shared sense of questioning that extends far beyond the dilemmas of the (post-) colonial encounter. Indeed, the uncertainty which the interlocutor feels is not the product of being approached by the ethnographer at all; it is a pre-existing condition of *any* self-reflexive life in a world of complex cultural flows and influences. It is this self-reflexiveness and uncertainty within everyday life that the ethnographer has to reflect in her or his accounts.

The result, Marcus (1999) argues, is to change the focus of fieldwork itself: only when an outsider begins to relate to a subject also concerned with outsideness in everyday life can these expressions (of anxiety) be given focal importance in a localized fieldwork that, in turn, inevitably pushes the entire research program of the single ethnographic project into the challenges and promises of a multisited space and trajectory – a trajectory that encourages the ethnographer literally to move to other sites that are powerfully registered in the local knowledge of an originating locus of fieldwork (p. 99).

What the two figures in the ethnographic "situation" share, then, is "an affinity," based on their "mutual curiosity and anxiety about their relationship to a 'third'" – that is, to the sites *elsewhere* that affect, or even determine, their experiences and knowledges *here* (p. 101). When the anthropologist travels, she is not therefore doing something exclusive to the (still generally privileged) position of the anthropologist, but instead she is materializing a concern with external determinations that is shared with her interlocutor. This, at least, is the intriguing alternative metaphor for fieldwork that Marcus offers.

It is a powerful analysis because it takes seriously the mobile reflexivity and agency of both ethnographer and interlocutor; and because it emphasizes that the ethnographer's discourse must be adequate to the doubts and uncertainties already lived by the interlocutor (cf. Battaglia, 1999, p. 115). Complexity and uncertainty, in other words, are not just an academic projection onto the world, but already woven into the fabric of everyday life, part of what situated knowledge must capture. Crucially, however, Marcus's analysis emphasizes not only doubt, but knowledge. Ethnographer and interlocutor are perplexed precisely because they both want *to know* something that holds true beyond their own partial situation. A romanticization of the purely local is not Marcus's point, nor could that satisfactorily reflect our attempts to make sense of a complex, largely opaque world (hence the failure of visions of anthropology based on avoiding "representation" entirely, such as Tyler (1986)). We try, even if we often fail, to make sense of our location in "places [that are] simultaneously and complexly connected, by intended and unintended consequences" (Marcus, 1998, p. 551). Ethnography must aim to do no less.

While this new conception of ethnography has roots going back for example to Hannerz's (1980) early work on our dispersed lives in the modern city, which long predates recent concerns with mediation in anthropology, it is peculiarly apposite to today's concern with the media's role in our lives. The media operate as a "third" space within our lives, both close and distant, and whether we are ethnographers or not – a paradox which Raymond Williams (1973) expressed better than anyone when he described modern communications as:

> a form of unevenly shared consciousness of persistently external events. It is what appears to happen, in these powerfully transmitted

and mediated ways, in a world within which we have no other perceptible connections but we feel is *at once central and marginal to our lives*.

(pp. 295–296, added emphasis)

Media provide common contexts, language and reference-points for use in local situations, even though media production takes place outside most localities and its narratives cut across them from the outside. The frameworks within which we reflect on ourselves and others are shared with others, because they have a common source in media flows, and yet those frameworks are never entirely "ours"; we can grasp them alternately as "inside" or "outside." Indeed "complicity" (in Marcus's sense – of a shared awareness of the importance to us as agents of the *external* forces that act upon and across us) may be a useful metaphor precisely for the ways in which city life itself has been changed by mediation. As Nestor García Canclini (1995) has asserted:

> Since . . . even the accidents that happened the previous day in our own city reach us through the media, these [the media] become the dominant constituents of the "public" meaning of the city . . . More than an absolute substitution of urban life by the audiovisual media, I perceive a *game of echoes*. The commercial advertising and political slogans that we see on television are those that we reencounter in the streets, and vice versa: the ones are echoed in the others. To this circularity of the communicational and the urban are subordinated the testimonies of history and the public meaning constructed in longtime [*sic*] experiences.
>
> (pp. 210–212, original emphasis)

The media, in other words, by providing so many shared resources through which we can (and in a sense must) frame the social world, change the terms on which we can offer individual testimony as well. Our sense of public history has already been displaced before we can articulate our personal place within it. If so, media's implications for ethnography go well beyond the problems of studying the immediate viewing situation in the living room.

We need an ethnography that adequately reflects the complexity of how media flows together produce *the mediation* of our social life (cf. Martín-Barbero, 1993). At the very least, this requires a methodology that recognizes the stretched-out nature of that process of mediation: encompassing not only the stereotypical site of media consumption (the home), but also the countless other sites where media circulate (the street, the shop, the office, the bar, and so on), the sites of media production (the studio, the live event), and those hybrid sites where audience members travel to see the process of production close up.

Before I explore some of these possibilities in more detail, let me make one broader point which explains why studying such complexity in the mediated landscape is more than academic self-indulgence. "Ethnography'" – seen in Marcus's terms, as a commitment to grasp the situated reflexivity of actual agents – is part of what elsewhere I have called the "principle of accountability" in cultural research (Couldry, 2000b, chapter 6). Quite simply: the language and theoretical framework with which we analyze others should always be consistent with, or accountable to, the language and theoretical framework with which we would hope to analyze ourselves. And, equally, in reverse: the language and theoretical framework with which we analyze ourselves should always be accountable to the language and theoretical framework with which we analyze others.

The reversibility of the principle is crucial: it is this that prevents us from falling into a spiral of endless self-interrogation, never to resurface! There must be a dialectic between the way we think about others and the way we think about ourselves; what we say about one must reflect what we know about the complexities of the other. Put another way: every attempt to speak in one's own name is tied to an obligation to listen to the voices of others; and every attempt to describe others must allow them the complexity of voice that one requires to be acknowledged in oneself. Deliberately here I am combining ethical issues with methodological ones. The methodological challenge to grasp the real complexity of "cultures" only has force because we in turn recognize the ethical obligation to listen to (multiple) others. In our commitment to account for how we think about self and others, methodology and ethics converge. We cannot, as analysts, safely turn our backs on the complexity which mediated cultures display.

Passing ethnography, or notes on an emergent method

I want now to reflect in some detail on my own attempt to research aspects of mediated culture in *The Place of Media Power* (Couldry, 2000a). The strategies I adopted and their limitations are, I would suggest, relevant to the wider questions – of the role of ethnography in media sociology, and the development of ethnography generally – which this chapter has tried to address.

My starting-points, long before I formulated my exact research strategy, were, first, a commitment to the underlying principle of audience research as practiced by David Morley and others – that is, a commitment to the empirical study of how actual people put media texts to use in their lives – but also, second, a concern about whether detailed study of how particular texts are interpreted in particular contexts can answer the question that, in Britain at least, audience research was designed to address: what is the role of media in the legitimation of wider power structures and inequalities?[4] There is a gap between the ambitions of audience research and its actual achievements, given the limitations which it initially imposed upon itself. None of which means that media are *without* social impacts, only that there is a question about the best entry-point for analyzing them (I agree with Lila Abu-Lughod to this extent).

I tried to answer that question in my research through two moves (this, perhaps, is to give more order retrospectively to my strategy than it had at the time). First, I had the hunch (later developed as a theory: Couldry, 2000a, chapter 3) that one way to research the media's social impacts was to look at how media institutions and media people are thought about: what, in other words, are our beliefs about media power and how do they contribute to the usual legitimation of that power? My research therefore aimed to find moments where the vast, society-wide process of legitimating media power was explicitly articulated or at least could be traced in behavior and language. Second, I had the hunch (see Couldry, 2000a, chapter 2) that while mediation has very broad impacts on a territory such as Britain, those impacts are never simple or even, and therefore that there must be moments – or rather sites – where the legitimation of media power is open to challenge, or is negotiated in some way: fissures, if you like, where, as in Victor Turner's (1974) model of liminal behavior, wider structural patterns are revealed.

The result of these two hunches was to encourage me to research not conventional sites of media reception or production, important though these are, but instead more exceptional sites where the status of media institutions and media authority was in some way negotiated, whether playfully or seriously. Hence my choice of two very different situations for field research: first, leisure sites where people get close up to the process of media production, such as Granada Studios Tour in Manchester, which contains the set of Britain's longest-running prime-time soap opera, *Coronation Street* (the American parallels, while not exact, would include Universal Studios in Florida and NBC Studios Tour in New York: Couldry, 2000a, pp. 65–66); and, second, protest sites where people without media experience became involved in a mediated event and therefore saw the media process close up. In the latter case, my fieldwork was inevitably limited by what protests were under way at the time of the research, and my main research was on people's reflections about a protest that was completed the year before my fieldwork, the protests against the export of live animals through the small British east coast port of Brightlingsea in 1995. Since the detailed political context of these protests was not my main concern, but rather their status as an access-point to the media process, I will not detail it further here (but see Couldry, 2000a, pp. 123–124).

My approach to such sites was on the face of it based on conflicting principles: on the one hand, I wanted to do as detailed a contextual analysis as possible of why people visited Granada Studios Tour and how people understood their experience of participating in the mediated protests at Brightlingsea, since it was through their detailed accounts of those localized encounters that I hoped to obtain insights into people's orientations towards media institutions in general. On the other hand, both types of site were temporary, in the sense that my interviewees had merely passed through them, either in the space of a day (as at Granada Studios Tour) or over the space of a few months (as at Brightlingsea). They were not the type of permanent living or working space in which ethnography has normally been conducted. Their interest was precisely as *exceptional* sites, which meant that they could not be fully contextualized in the lives of their participants, or indeed fully contextualized at all. (Which is not to say that they were exceptional in exactly the same way: the Brightlingsea protest site was a space closely linked to a real, inhabited place, whereas Granada Studios Tour was much closer to a "nonplace" in Auge's (1995) sense.[5]) I was drawn, in other words, to do a maximally contextual study of sites which lacked a full context, a quasi-ethnography that I decided was better not called an ethnography at all (2000a, p. 198).[6] Only much later did I realize that it had parallels with the shift in 1990s anthropology to a pluralistic notion of ethnography that might include the study of "accidental communities of memory" (Malkki, 1997, p. 91) such as those formed at Granada Studios Tour and Brightlingsea.

In any case, the apparent theoretical contradiction was less intractable in practice. First of all, I was quite clear that these sites were worth studying – they were public sites where significant events or practices occurred, the like of which had rarely been researched. Second, I was convinced that ethnography in the sense of total *immersion* in what happened at such sites was in principle impossible. Granada Studios Tour was a commercial site visited by up to 6,000 people a day, well beyond the grasp of even the largest army of ethnographers; and the protests at Brightlingsea were already firmly in the past, even if the recent past. Ethnography on the traditional model could not then be the answer to the methodological problems posed by researching those sites, and yet those problems were surely typical of many other non-trivial sites of "sociality" where people come together on a temporary basis, often without knowledge of each other's full context for being there (cf. Maffesoli, 1996). If such sites were significant, yet not susceptible even in principle to ethnographic work in the traditional sense, then a different possibility, and necessity, was opening up for qualitative research.

This alternative model – which I can now see as a version of Marcus's ethnography as "complicity," not "rapport" – involved renouncing the aim for an impossible immersion in context and instead seeking as much context as could reasonably be obtained. I pursued this in various ways. For the sites themselves, I relied on participant observation (at Granada Studios Tour) or (at Brightlingsea) on a mixture of observations and close study of local and national press materials on the protest. From interviewees, I obtained, where possible, long open-ended interviews, usually in their own homes. At Brightlingsea this was my main source, but at Granada Studios Tour the home interviews were a supplement to a large number of interviews conducted on site. Unfortunately in the latter case, there was only one person interviewed on site who was willing to meet me again at home – not surprisingly, since Granada Studios Tour represents precisely a day-off from commitments! This revealed, however, in another guise, the limits to "ethnographic" context built into the very structure of this particular public site. My third source of context was provided by the interviewees themselves, as they reflected on their engagement with the site in question. They chose the relevant context within which to talk about their time at the studios or on the protest. They could have related it to any event in their lives whatsoever, but it was the context *they* chose, usually in retrospect, in which I was most interested.

A full ethnographic context for their visit to Granada Studios Tour or the protest experience at Brightlingsea was in principle impossible, but this did not mean that the context obtained was trivial. On the contrary, it was useful evidence of what the site had meant to those I interviewed. In effect, by pursuing this strategy, I made a choice. I could have chosen a radical contextualist approach (cf. Ang, 1996), which might have led me to abandon research altogether – since the context available was never going to be complete enough! Instead, I took a more pragmatic approach, working in each case with what context I could obtain, and building up from there a larger picture of the way people talked about those sites, and the patterns in such talk.

That choice was grounded in a growing sense that there was a striking pattern, even or especially at the level of the banal language people used about those sites and their significance (cf. Couldry, 2000a, pp. 104–105, 143–144, 197 for further explanation). It was this patterning, and its pervasiveness, that was the most important aspect of the various interviews and observations I had conducted: a wider pattern that did not contradict or undermine the self-reflexivity of those I interviewed, but which instead worked itself out through their reflections. Indeed such patterns of thinking – their characteristic categories, such as the underlying hierarchy between "media world" and "ordinary world" (Couldry, 2000a, chapter 3) – emerged most strongly in the passages where they were put under greatest pressure by the interviewees themselves, by being argued with or renegotiated. Rarely, however, were those patterns entirely deconstructed, or absent; and this, I realized, was the wider point towards which my scattered quasi-ethnography was leading.

In effect, I had conducted a contextualized, multisited study of people's talk about visits to two sites (not themselves connected), which revealed patterns of thinking that were more than just multisited: they were the type of pervasive and banal categories (Billig, 1995) through which wider ideological structures get produced, in this case the ideology of media power. To grasp such patterns, and their influence, we need paradoxically to study them in action, as they are put to work in particular cases. This means doing research in multiple contexts which have to be grasped as *rhetorical* contexts – as contexts of argument and negotiation – which is not the same as knowing the total life-context in which those arguments took place. Listening closely and effectively to people's talk need *not* require a full ethnographic contextualization for that talk.

Only through work *across* a number of such contexts (without necessarily immersing myself in any of them) could I grasp the patterning of language, thought, and action through which media power is reproduced and legitimated. The "place of media power," I had discovered, is latent everywhere, even if our naturalized beliefs about the media emerge most clearly at those places (for example, sites of media production) where they are called into question.

Final reflections

These reflections on my own research might seem a long way from the traditional notion of ethnographic method: the ambition for what Marcus calls "rapport" within the ethnographic situation. My approach has tried rather to engage with as much context as is available for some of the passing acts and reflections we make as we pass through a mediated world. The result is a passing "ethnography," but one no less serious for that. It represents a serious commitment to engage with the texture of our dispersed but mediated lives. And it is a real ethnography, if we accept George Marcus's wider rethinking of what ethnography entails: an engagement with the situations of others based in a shared attention to the complex webs of determination within which we think and act. This involves qualitative work that crosses a number of places, and travels to some which we would not necessarily first think of as sites where we engage with media.

Even so, it might seem that this new dispersed notion of ethnography and in particular media ethnography has sidestepped some important questions of politics. Even if "the circumstantial commitments that arise in the mobility of multi-sited fieldwork provide a kind of psychological substitute for the reassuring sense of 'being there' of participation in traditional single-site fieldwork" (Marcus, 1998, p. 99), too mobile an ethnography of mediated space risks running free of the ethical questions which the ethnographic encounter so powerfully brought into focus. It is important to emphasize, therefore, that what I am *not* arguing for is a footloose analysis that follows media images wherever it chooses. Our sense of complexity, and why studying complexity matters, must be more grounded than that. It should be grounded in an awareness that it matters to study power and its disguises.

Media have the vast power that they do because we all, systematically even if usually unobtrusively, work to produce their authority as natural (Couldry, 2000a, chapter 1). Our presence as analysts at *one* place (whether it is the home or the studio) will not be sufficient to unlock the workings of media power. To believe otherwise would ironically be to reproduce the type of mystification upon which media power itself relies:[7] that there is one place, the place in the media, where society's important things happen, the myth that it matters to "be there." If we are fully to understand the dispersed symbolic order that underlies the media's myth-making powers, we must avoid the ethnographic myth that we can only do so by "being there" ourselves.

Acknowledgements

Many thanks to Patrick Murphy and Marwan Kraidy for their helpful criticisms of an earlier draft, which allowed me to sharpen its argument. Thanks also to

Roger Silverstone, whose comments on my earlier research sparked, much later, these reflections.

Notes

1 I am using the term "societies" here guardedly, as there is a growing debate about its usefulness (Urry, 2000).
2 For an important exploration of the problems with the classic ethnographic notion of "the field," see the essays in Gupta and Ferguson (1997a).
3 Cf. also Paul Rabinow (1996, p. 17) on the "tacit sharing of curiosity" between researcher and researched.
4 For a valuable restatement of the values of the "critical" audience research tradition, which is clear about the methodological challenges it has faced, see Ang (1996).
5 Thanks to Roger Silverstone for drawing my attention to this point.
6 I was aware of the valid criticisms of some inflated claims for ethnographic research in media studies. See for example Gillespie (1995, p. 23) and Nightingale (1996, pp. 110–112).
7 Like Marcus, I am interested in a "grounded study of the mystifications" of culture. In my case it is "media culture" and in Marcus's case it is "capitalist culture": see Marcus (1998, p. 159 n. 2).

References

Abu-Lughod, L. (1991). Writing against culture. In R. Fox (ed.), *Recapturing anthropology: Writing in the present*. Santa Fe, NM: School of American Research Press.

Abu-Lughod, L. (1999). The interpretation of culture(s) after television. In S. Ortner (ed.), *The fate of "culture": Geertz and beyond*. Berkeley: University of California Press.

Ang, I. (1996). *Living room wars: Rethinking media audiences for a postmodern world*. London: Routledge.

Appadurai, A. (1990). Disjuncture and difference in the global cultural economy. In M. Featherstone (ed.), *Global culture*. London: Sage.

Auge, M. (1995). *Non-places: An introduction to an anthropology of supermodernity*. London: Verso.

Battaglia, D. (1999). Towards an ethics of the open subject: Writing culture in good conscience. In H. Moore (ed.), *Anthropological theory today*. Cambridge: Polity.

Bhabha, H. (1994). *The location of culture*. London: Routledge.

Billig, M. (1995). *Banal nationalism*. London: Routledge.

Brunsdon, C. and Morley, D. (1978). *Everyday television: Nationwide*. London: BFI.

Clifford, J (1988). *The predicament of culture: Twentieth century ethnography, literature and art*. Berkeley: University of California Press.

Cohen, A. (1994). *Self-consciousness: An alternative anthropology of identity*. London: Routledge.

Couldry, N. (1996). Speaking of others and speaking personally: Reflections after Elspeth Probyn's *Sexing the self*. *Cultural Studies* 10(2), 315–333.

Couldry, N. (2000a). *The place of media power: Pilgrims and witnesses of the media age*. London: Routledge.

Couldry, N. (2000b). *Inside culture: Reimagining the method of cultural studies*. London: Sage.

Couldry, N. (2001). The hidden injuries of media power. *Journal of Consumer Culture* 1(2), 155–177.

García Canclini, N. (1995). *Hybrid cultures*. Minneapolis: University of Minnesota Press.

Gillespie, M. (1995). *Television ethnicity and cultural change*. London: Routledge.

Gilroy, P. (1992). *The black Atlantic*. London: Verso.

Gupta, A. and Ferguson, J. (eds) (1997a). *Anthropological locations: Boundaries and grounds of a field science*. Berkeley: University of California Press.

Gupta, A. and Ferguson, J. (1997b) Discipline and practice: "The field" as site, method and location in anthropology. In A. Gupta and J. Ferguson (eds), *Anthropological locations: Boundaries and grounds of a field science*. Berkeley: University of California Press.

Hannerz, U. (1980). *Exploring the city*. New York: Columbia University Press.

Hannerz, U. (1992). *Cultural Complexity: Studies in the Social Organisation of Meaning*. New York: Columbia University Press.

Haraway, D. (1991). Situated knowledges: The science question in feminism and the principle of partial perspective. In *Simians cyborgs and women*. London: Free Press.

Hartley, J. (1987). Invisible fictions. *Textual Practice* 2, 121–138.

Hartley, J. (1996). *Popular reality*. London: Arnold.

Kearney, M. (1995). The local and the global: The anthropology of globalisation and transnationalism. *Annual Review of Anthropology* 24, 547–565.

Maffesoli, M. (1996). *The time of the tribes*. London: Sage.

Malkki, Lisa (1997). News and culture: Transitory phenomena and the fieldwork tradition. In A. Gupta and J. Ferguson (eds), *Anthropological locations: Boundaries and grounds of a field science*. Berkeley: University of California Press.

Marcus, G. (1995). Ethnography in/of the world system: The emergence of multi-sited ethnography. *Annual Review of Anthropology* 24, 95–117.

Marcus, G. (1998). *Ethnography through thick and thin*. Princeton, NJ: Princeton University Press.

Marcus, G. (1999). The use of complicity in the changing mise-en-scene of anthropological fieldwork. In S. Ortner (ed.), *The fate of "culture": Geertz and beyond*. Berkeley: University of California Press.

Martín-Barbero, J. (1993). *Communication culture and hegemony*. London: Sage.

Massey, D. (1997) A global sense of place. In A. Gray and J. McGuigan (eds), *Studying culture: An introductory reader*. London: Arnold.

Meyrowitz, J. (1985). *No sense of place*. New York: Oxford University Press.

Morley, D. and Silverstone, R. (1991) Communication and context: Ethnographic perspectives on the media audience. In K. B. Jensen and N. Jankowski (eds), *A handbook of qualitative methodologies for mass communication research*. London: Routledge.

Nightingale, V. (1996). *Studying audiences: The shock of the real*. London: Routledge.

Rabinow, P. (1996) *Essays on the anthropology of reason*. Princeton, NJ: Princeton University Press.

Schudson, M. (1994). Culture and the integration of national societies. In D. Crane (ed.), *The sociology of culture*. Oxford: Blackwell.

Silverstone, R. (1994). *Television and everyday life*. London: Routledge.

Silverstone, R., Hirsch, E. and Morley, D. (1991). Listening to a long conversation: An ethnographic approach to the study of information and communications technologies in the home. *Cultural Studies* 5, 204–227.

Thomas, N. (1999) Becoming undisciplined: Anthropology and cultural studies. In H. Moore (ed.), *Anthropological theory today*. Cambridge: Polity.

Tsing, A. (1993). *In the realm of the diamond queen*. Princeton, NJ: Princeton University Press.

Turner, V. (1974). *Dramas fields and metaphors*. Cornell: Cornell University Press.

Tyler, S. (1986). Post-modern ethnography: From document of the occult to occult document. In J. Clifford and G. Marcus (eds), *Writing culture*. Berkeley: University of California Press.

Urry, J. (2000). *Sociology beyond societies*. London: Routledge.

Welsch, W. (1999). Transculturality: The puzzling form of cultures today. In M. Featherstone and S. Lash (eds), *Spaces of culture: City – Nation – World*. London: Sage.

Williams, R. (1958). *Culture and society*. Harmondsworth: Penguin.

Williams, R. (1973). *The country and the city*. London: Hogarth Press.

Zizek, S. (1990). Eastern Europe's empires of Gilead. *New Left Review* 183, 50–62.

4

WHERE IS AUDIENCE ETHNOGRAPHY'S FIELDWORK?

Anna Clua

What is a place? What gives a place its identity, its aura? These questions occurred to the physicists Niels Bohr and Werner Heisenberg when they visited Kronberg Castle in Denmark. Bohr said to Heisenberg:

> Isn't it strange how this castle changes as soon as one imagines that Hamlet lived here? As scientists we believe that a castle consists only of stones, and admire the way the architect put them together. The stones, the green roof with its patina, the woodcarvings in the church, constitute the whole castle. None of this should be changed by the fact that Hamlet lived here, and yet it is changed completely. Suddenly the walls and the ramparts speak in a quite different language. The courtyard becomes an entire world, a dark corner reminds us of the darkness in the human soul, we hear Hamlet's "To be or not to be." Yet all we know about Hamlet is that his name appears in a thirteenth-century chronicle. No one can prove that he really lived, let alone that he lived here. But everyone knows the questions Shakespeare had him ask, the human depth he was made to reveal, and so he, too, had to be found a place on earth, here in Kronberg. And once we know that, Kronberg becomes quite a different castle for us.
>
> (Heisenberg, 1972, p. 51, quoted in Tuan, 1977, p. 4)

In 1999 I spent five months in Denmark. One day I decided to visit Kronberg. What I could see, after a first gaze at the map, was that Kronberg was labeled there as Kronborg. When placing myself at the middle of the castle's courtyard I could not hear any human soul's deep whisper, but instead the reverberating sound of a repertory of military marches played by a band of Danish girls dressed in red and white miniskirts. I felt just like a tourist. And then I realized that Hamlet's castle could only become possible as an imagined castle, whatever its name.

Contested spaces

During the 1970s, the conversation that Heisenberg and Bohr maintained about Kronberg was a very useful illustration of the relations of space and place in geographical terms (Tuan, 1977). For "space" was an abstract concept that became concrete when turned into "place." "Place," thus, was the lived, perceived, experienced space invested with human values. The 1970s were precisely the period when the so-called "humanistic geographers" like Tuan came into terms with phenomenology. They were engaged with trying to challenge positivistic physical geography by introducing the issue of human perception of space (or, more concretely, the issues of spatially constricted human perceptions and of humanly constricted space perceptions).

By the same period, another kind of critical geography (expressed, like humanistic geography, on the margins of the hegemonic academic expression of "Geography") was developed through radicalism and Marxism. Borders between (abstract) space and (particular, perceived, individualized) place began to blur, and new topics attracted the researchers' attention. One important issue was that of social transformation. "Radical geographers" claimed for themselves political commitment and activism, within and beyond academic borders (Peet, 1978). Changing social structure, they said, means changing space, as well as changing space means changing social structure. Richard Peet (1998) explains how radical geography transformed into Marxist geography as follows:

> Radical geography was a quest for social relevance at a time of contradiction and crisis in capitalist society. But social relevance produced a contradiction inside radical geography, between political objectives which were virtually unlimited (i.e. aimed at the transformation of society) and analytical capacities which were claustrophobically constrained by the techniques, methodologies and paradigmatic boundaries of conventional scientific concepts. Thus, radical geography was radical in topic and politics, but not in theory or method of analysis.
>
> (p. 75)

Marxist geographers defined space as the material product of the labor forces as well as the social struggle scenario. Social structure (both as product and as mode of production), Marxist geographers said, forms part of the dialectics of historical materialism.[1] Power, knowledge and space became very important features for the understanding of historical social inequalities, which were also seen as spatial inequalities (via center–periphery increasing dichotomization, in many senses), under capitalism.[2]

From the 1980s, the development of critical geography has been influenced by a great diversity of perspectives (e.g. poststructuralism, realism, social theory, postmodernism, cultural studies) that have produced new forms of conceptualizing space. The 1990s generated a prolific development of "new geographies" (Philo, 1991, 1999) coinciding with an extraordinary expansion of Anglo-Saxon publishers beyond disciplines and national markets (Barnett, 1998). I am going to focus attention here on recent debates about the controversial definition of "critical geography." Nowadays, there is a rich internal debate between different kinds of "radicalism" (mainly Marxist and postmodernist) within critical geography. Often the discussion is arbitrated by mutual misunderstanding, for Marxism is considered by some postmodern geographers as a deterministic-economicist grand theory, and postmodernism is considered by Marxist geographers as a market product and as a politically correct academic option. We can find the same tension in recent debates about the constitution of so-called "cultural geography." Andrew Sayer (1994), for instance, has interestingly presented this tension in terms of the political economy/cultural studies split within critical geography.[3] Nevertheless, there are many authors who go beyond all these confronted positions, as we may see through the interesting work of Edward W. Soja. Below I examine his important contribution and its relevance for media ethnography.

Spaces for going beyond

Edward W. Soja focuses his attention on the way postmodernism makes explicit the usual lack of interest that social theory has in spatial issues. In Soja's opinion, postmodernism helps us to break away from the binary kind of modern thought, offering an alternative, a third way that is also an expression of the cultural politics of difference.[4] He argues that social theory has traditionally been elaborated around conceptions of history and human relations' temporality, but has failed to consider spatiality. Soja extends this argument by showing the limited way in which space has been observed through institutional academic disciplines such as Geography, Architecture, Urban and Regional Studies, and Urban Planning (expressed with capitals). In his critique of the limits of the academic/institutionalized knowledge of space, Soja makes an exception when talking about those academics in spatial disciplines "who have been engaging seriously with the recent literature in the broad new field of critical cultural studies" (Soja, 1996, p. 12, emphasis added).

Despite this critique, Soja's task has been in large part to bridge borders between fields of knowledge. First, he vindicates the inclusion of space in sociological and humanistic explanations. His effort to extend the academic constrictions of geography (as discipline) is concretely expressed by approaching Lefebvre's and Bourdieu's spatial thought (in a manner that helps to question the traditional confrontation of Marxist and postmodern thought), and also drawing from cultural studies (concretely through bell hooks's effort to take space into account from a radical postmodern position). Second, he appeals to our existing understanding of space by expanding those dichotomies (time/space, space/place, material-real space/symbolic-imagined space) that have traditionally grounded social science epistemology. And third, and most importantly, he emphasizes the importance of going beyond abstract conceptions of space by constantly developing empirical research. Soja's contribution is not an easy one. He wants us to think, live and perceive space differently. This means to think space not only from our academic position (as a merely "*conceived* space"), but also from our position on (and transition through) the world as a "*lived*" and "*perceived* space," both "real-and-imagined," historic and dynamic, socially produced and reproduced under conditions of uneven development.

Soja (1996), thus, does not limit his claims to recover space as a "real space" (the Firstspace, as he calls it) as well as an "imagined place" (the so called Secondspace), but he also vindicates the *other* way of conceiving space: that is, "simultaneously real and imagined and more (both and also . . .)." This Thirdspace "can be described and inscribed in journeys to 'real and imagined' (or perhaps 'real-and-imagined'?) places" (p. 11). The term Thirdspace, although used here in another context, is borrowed from Homi Bhabba (1990, 1994), whose works Soja takes into account (just like other works about "difference" developed within cultural studies by Cornel West, Paul Gilroy, Stuart Hall or the above-mentioned bell hooks). The author posits the need for "the creation of another mode of thinking about space that draws upon the material and mental spaces of the traditional dualism but extends well beyond them in scope, substance, and meaning" (Soja, 1996, p. 11). Soja also attempts to develop, from a Marxist perspective, the definition of a cultural politics where space, knowledge and power are historically intertwined in order to shape the "spaces of representation" and the "representation of spaces." Soja takes these ideas from the work of Foucault and Lefebvre – two authors who have long reflected on "other spaces" where social differences are expressed.

Foucault (1980, 1986), for instance, talks about the other spaces as "heterotopias," which he defines as "the space in which we live, which draws us out of ourselves, in which the erosion of our lives, our time and our history occurs" (quoted in Soja, 1996, p. 15). Soja is also interested in the way Foucault criticizes social theory historicism, with all the consequences that this criticism may have when reconsidering the spatiality of human relations:

> Foucault asked why is it that time has tended to be treated as "richness, fecundity, life, dialectic" while in contrast space has been typically seen as "the dead, the fixed, the undialectic, the immobile"? He answers his question by referring to a persistent overprivileging of the powers of the historical imagination and the traditions of critical historiography, and the degree to which this privileging of historicality has silenced or subsumed the potentially equivalent powers of critical spatial thought.
>
> (Soja, 1996, p. 15; citing Foucault, 1980, p. 70)

Lefebvre's (1991) claim for a "radically open" kind of knowledge is, according to Soja, an essential contribution. Lefebvre's Marxism is not only a theoretical approach, but also a way of demonstrating, all through his trajectory, that it is possible to be an idealist without having to renounce being a materialist – a position that Soja draws from to argue that it is possible to be a postmodern researcher *and* maintain a political commitment.

Significantly, Lefebvre's ideas opened up the possibility of thinking of space beyond the wall that modern Western thought has built between physical space and mental space (as well as between objects and subjects or between academic spatial disciplines). Lefebvre also made possible thinking beyond Marxist dialectics based on historical materialism. It was necessary to add spatiality to the historicity and to the social character of human relations (described by Marx as relations of production in a capitalist world). Lefebvre called this "triple dialectics," by insisting that the social, the historic and the spatial were real as well as symbolic (Soja decides to call it "trialectics"). To the question "Is it the consciousness that produces the material world or the material world that produces the consciousness?" Lefebvre answered yes to both, and posits in addition that there will always be an alternative answer that goes beyond constrictive formulations (of the scientific expression, the social expression, the political expression).

Another important contribution of Lefebvre's work is, in Soja's opinion, defining space as a terrain for social struggle and for vindicating the right to be different against the worldly homogenization imposed by capitalism. The struggle for the right to difference may be represented at many levels, from "body and sexuality" to "global responses to geographically uneven development and underdevelopment":

> [Lefebvre] embedded these multi-sited struggles for the right to difference in the contextualized dialectics of centers and peripheries, the conceived and the lived, the material and the metaphorical; and from these concatenated dialectics of uneven development and differentiation he opened up a new domain, a space of collective resistance, a *Thirdspace of political choice* that is also a meeting place for all peripheralized or marginalized "subjects" wherever they may be located.
>
> (Soja, 1996, p. 35)

How space is represented differently and how difference is represented spatially are very important questions that should not be neglected by critical researchers. By expressing this idea (via Foucault and Lefebvre), Soja is calling for a political commitment that goes beyond the "objectivity" logic, the reason/ideology dichotomy, as well as the conservative immobility that still defines the academy and the academic definition of social reality.

Audience geography

At this stage in the evolution in audience studies, to assert that mass media reception is a contextualized process might seem an obvious remark. But how audience studies produce the field where work is located, or how different "real and imagined" places produce different audience studies, are very important questions. Trying to answer them implies not only looking at the prevalent notion of "audience geography," but also looking at the prevalent notion of "geography."

Media reception studies often summarize audiences' activity as their ability to negotiate resistance in relation to hegemonic messages. As a result, by focusing attention on texts (both media and audiences' texts), researchers have been defining contexts as mere containers. Canadian communication researcher Jody Berland (1992) asserts that audience studies have been limiting the practices of the active audience within a "social-environment-as-given" (p. 47). To bridge this gap, the study of the social uses of communication technologies must not neglect the question of how media technologies produce space; that is, how landscapes are both constructed around the uses of mass media, as well as described by mass media contents. Berland (1992) points to an interesting issue when asking why the changes in social production of space are related to changes in communication technologies.[5] As she states, those changes need to be located "in the technological proliferation, cumulative privatization, and spatial expansion of global capitalization" (p. 47).

To facilitate talking about audience geography in a different way, there is first a need to conceive of places as having changing conditions, as the cultural geographer David Harvey (1989) suggests. Understanding places as transformative also leads us to the very important question of what is the researcher's place, because this "place" is also dialectically produced (as well as the ontological positioning, or the political commitments and social paths, or even the different ways of perceiving distances between the object and the subject, the real and the imagined, the possible and the impossible, the known and the unknown . . .). Fieldwork landscapes may be represented very differently by researchers' accounts, depending on being (and/or feeling) a woman or a man, black or white, young or old, foreigner or native, as well as on being (and/or feeling) a well-established researcher or not being (and/or feeling) it at all. These are questions, in fact, that do not have to be considered apart from ontological positioning, political commitments and different ways of perceiving distances. Neither do they have to be considered apart from placing ourselves on the move. As Doreen Massey (1993) argues, the problem of talking about location arises when considering space as *being* instead of *becoming*: that is, when assuming a conservative or even a reactionary intellectual position.

Assumed forms of thinking about audience location have often produced a poorly dimensioned, and even static understanding of geography. The problem is not merely this way of assuming what is space (often reproducing the terms of pure physical geography), but its definition as a context *per se*, and at the same time as one more context just like "others" (as race, gender, social class, etc.). Space is thus considered in a flat and superficial way. Although past audience research has attempted to consider contexts in relation to their dynamism and complexity, the vast majority have treated space apart from time and from the "other" contexts mentioned above. In fact, these other numerous contexts are scarcely observed in relation to time/space and, then, in relation to each other.

By thinking about space we may look at the way audiences are located not only geographically but also historically. This means trying to look at local media reception practices within the Western communication system of late capitalist society that is becoming more and more "global." Hegemonic political economy talks about the new information's spatial order that shapes the world. In this "global village" consumerism landscapes are called the "natural environments" for social action. And this is, in fact, the idea of "natural environment" that many researchers reproduce when locating audiences' activity. On the other hand, critical political economy recognizes the influence of capitalism in producing and organizing social spaces, through processes of privatization of media ownership and regulation, as well as through "mobile privatization" (Williams, 1974) of media reception.[6] In my opinion, there is an extended confusion when defining audience contexts as "natural environments" and pretending at the same time to be defending a critical point of view. What becomes problematic is not the context of media reception (as a place for consumerism), but precisely its taken-for-granted definition within researchers' discourse. Thomas Tufte (1997), for instance, has interestingly analyzed the generalizations about television and everyday life (as well as about the location of their encounter) made from a naturalized British point of view in Roger Silverstone's work (1994).

David Morley has recently developed a very comprehensive definition of "home" in relation to other concepts like "media," "identity" and "space" (Morley, 2000). Nevertheless, trying to see how this theoretical concept of "home" works in practice is, as Morley recognizes, not easy. On the other hand, his way of thinking about ethnographic fieldwork (Morley, 1992) does not help to answer this question either. Morley's methodological assumptions have already been discussed elsewhere (Flores, 2001). My concern here is the argument that Morley has been using all through his works (see also Morley and Silverstone, 1990) to defend the idea that fieldwork must be placed in the sitting room. As an example, consider the author's last words in a 1996 text entitled "The geography of television":

> If we are to understand how any (post) modern sense of identity, community, or nation (at any level) is produced, then we shall need to confront, among other things, the domestic setting of its production, via the consumption and use of broadcasting and other ICTs. To this extent, a "retreat" into the domestic sphere may

precisely be the detour we need to make, if we are effectively to
understand these "larger", more obviously "political" questions.

(Morley, 1996, p. 338)

Precisely because of presenting the postmodern approach as the starting point
for including space in a more open kind of audience research (as in fact Morley
does in his text), it makes no sense to conclude that what "we *need* to make"
is a "retreat" into a "sphere" (the domestic one). Positioning ourselves far from
the "global village" kind of discourse does not necessarily mean that we have to
locate fieldwork in what may be considered the opposite extreme (the household).
On the other hand, by equating the political "obviousness" with "larger"
questions, are we as ethnographers not retreating in many more senses? In any
case, where does the "detour" on the way back home take place (as the scenario
for identity production via broadcasting and electronic media consumption)?

There is not a simple answer to this last question. The construction of cultural
identity (around the sense of community, even the sense of nation, to which
Morley refers) is not *necessarily* better placed "into" the domestic sphere than *in
relation to* those "other things" among which television "consumption" may be
considered. I think, for instance, about the bars on the street where I live.
During a football game between the traditionally rival teams of Barcelona and
Madrid, these places become specially overpopulated. Streets and bars are
important locations for people encounters, to the extent that they constitute
places where identities (for example, Catalan and Spanish national identities)
are represented or even confronted. At least that is what happens in the
neighborhood where I live in Barcelona, as well as in the little village where I
come from, although the sense of "we" and of "others" may differ from one place
to another. For instance, being a woman in a bar of a little village where
everybody knows each other (that is, the village where I come from) makes me
almost an invader specifically when a football match is on the television.

Rather than saying that we need to retreat into the micro-scale, what we
need is to get out of the generalizations that this academic prescription may
involve. We should ask, for instance, who is the *we* that we mention, whose
detours are we talking about, or which ones may be seen not only in a theoretical
way, but as the common detours through which we *use* to go home everyday
(whatever it might be understood and lived as *home* – just like bars or streets –
in the different places where fieldwork is located)?

Where is audience ethnography's "somewhere"?

James Hay (1996) has analyzed Janice Radway's call for an interdisciplinary
kind of research through which to approach "dispersed audiences and nomadic
subjects" (Radway 1988), as well as Lawrence Grossberg's response to Radway's
proposal (Grossberg 1988). In both cases, ethnography's way of looking at space
is shown as a problematic issue.

In many respects, Radway's proposal for a multidisciplinary project offered a useful way of beginning to rethink assumptions underpinning communication and media studies that had set the parameters of audience analysis for decades. And her valorization of ethnographic methods has also been central to debates reshaping audience study since the 1980s. But ethnography, as Lawrence Grossberg (1988) noted in his response to her essays and as others have argued since, has not been particularly sensitive to the *mobility* of subjects through everyday life. What remains implicit in Radway's proposal (and even in Grossberg's response to it) is the spatial problematic – a more full-fledged consideration of the issue of everyday life as a spatially constituted field of practice (Hay, 1996, p. 363).

One interesting point of Hay's analysis is the consideration of the important role that critical geography has to play in order to rethink ethnographic audience research. In fact, some Latin American authors were also calling, by the same period, for a more dimensioned way of defining space (Gonzalez, 1995; Jacks, 1994). Hay's approach to critical geography, thus, is part of a broader (although unconnected) current. This current also includes critical geographers' interest in approaching cultural studies. Hay (1996) asserts that, by that time, "critical, Marxist geographers" had not "discussed media or the issue of the audience" (p. 370). But if we look at "critical geographers" without relegating them to the category of "Marxists," we can find quite a few exceptions to Hay's assertion (see, for example, Burgess and Gold, 1985; or Jackson, 1989, 1993; or Morley and Robins, 1995).

Moreover, according to Hay, critical reception studies' tendency has been to map audiences in a "Euclidean geometry" way, while critical geography has already gone far beyond this. Hay offers Doreen Massey's (1993) work on "power geometry" as an effective way to "describe how the relative mobility of different social groups and different individuals is part of a terrain of other kinds of flows and interconnections." Or, as Hay notes, Massey's elaborations of power geometry conceptualize mobility as "part of non-Euclidean *geometries of social relations and power*" (Hay, 1996, pp. 369–370).

There are some other interesting works in critical geography through which we may approach "change" and "mobility" questions. Doreen Massey's previous works on regional geography and the study of "localities" (Massey 1984, 1985) are excellent examples of how critical geography has approached social structuration theory (concretely through Anthony Giddens's proposal). Torsten Hägerstrand's (1982) *time-geography* has had an important role to play in Giddens's works (1984, 1985), as well as in cultural geographers' works dealing with social paths and rhythms in everyday lives, in biographies, and in collective histories.

Ien Ang (1996) analyzes what adopting a "radical contextualism" perspective means for audience research. Stating from this perspective that media reception takes place in a dynamic and complex process means adding the problematic of placing researchers' activity in the fieldwork. "The ethnographer cannot be 'everywhere' but must always speak and write from 'somewhere'" (p. 254). As she points out, it makes no sense to try to find a solution for this. What Ang rather vindicates is the ethnographer's consciousness of where he or she is placed in every specific studied case. The very important thing, in any case, is to maintain coherence with political positioning. For "our curiosity about the audience is never innocent" (using Ang's starting point).

Drawing on Clifford Geertz (1988), Ang states that ethnography may "help us to locate and understand the *gradual spectrum of mixed-up differences . . . .* that comes with the progressive transnationalization of media audiencehood" (Ang, 1996, p. 260). Ang's suggestion of observing contexts ethnographically also requires avoiding "succumbing to sweeping generalizations" of cultural imperial- ism and globalization issues. Nevertheless, to avoid talking about globalization issues does not mean talking about decontextualized particularities. In my opinion, one of the most difficult and interesting questions recently posed by media ethnographers is how to deal with the global/local hybridization (Kraidy, 1999; Jacks, 1999; Tufte, 1999, 2000; Jacks and Tufte, 1998).

Conclusions

Media ethnography should not consider space as a fact, but as a challenge: that is, as the object/subject of critically inquiry. This requires the introduction of new questions and thus opening the "field" to new horizons. For instance, how are social change and social difference represented on space? How does space change and differ (genealogically as well as geographically) in people's minds and everyday life? How do media – and their social use – change and differentiate space? To what extent does space – as conceived, perceived and/or lived space – create changing and different media uses? Can these changes and differences help us to define different cultural identities within the so-called "information society"? How can it contribute a deeper understanding of "the global era"?

Media ethnographers have just begun to locate fieldwork in spatial terms. However, there has not been a sufficient effort to look at audiences beyond naturalized places (for instance, the household). Looking at space differently (as the geographer Edward Soja suggests) means asking new questions and thus opening the scope of media ethnography. It means also opening research to a more interdisciplinary understanding and practice. When doing fieldwork, media ethnographers need also to explicate place "on the move": that is, as transformative yet situated in terms of power, economics, history, etc. As such, we have to be able to recognize and talk about the difference (and also the inequalities) that space makes in media reception. The question is not so much whether space is global or local, the public sphere or the private sphere, the rural or the urban, the "in" or the "out," the "here" or the "there," etc., but rather what is the constant friction that is revealed and given shape by space, and how does that friction serves as a creative force?

Why is space important for media ethnographers to take into account when defining "fieldwork"? Above all, there is the question of not conceiving space from a totalizing and/or a constrictive point of view. I also have tried to show that theoretical statements can only become operative in practice starting from constantly putting into question our condition as researchers within the academy and as political actors within society. Thinking of space in that way gives us the possibility of reflecting on this paradox, and on the insufficiency of just talking theoretically or just doing empirical research.

In fact, nothing keeps us from going beyond. Jody Berland and James Hay (from very different theoretical statements) call for a "non-taken-for-granted" definition of space in audience research. As Hay (1996) asserts:

> "Defining" audiences is a spatial project. It underscores that listening, reading, and viewing occur in and around particular sites and through a social world organized geographically. But it acknowledges that these activities simultaneously produce "paths" – from one site to another – through everyday life, and that these paths elude modes of inquiry that privilege certain sites in everyday life.
>
> (p. 364)

Some audience researchers have already focused their attention on the global/local encounter (often better defined as "friction"). In any case, what this text has been trying to convey is thinking of space as *problematic*. This is the very reason why space matters. Soja's "postmodern geographies" could provide media ethnographers with suggestions for critically redefining the "field" in which empirical work has been traditionally placed. Fieldwork should not be described as something placed on a specific, fixed, determined, or even taken-for-granted space. On the one hand, fieldwork has to be placed in the struggle scenario of difference's representation (as far as space has a political meaning that media ethnographers use to neglect). On the other hand, media ethnographers need to locate their footsteps on a space that is both part and container of people's (and our own) vital paths, of our transient histories and biographies, of our hybrid identities, of our transpiring feelings and transgressor imaginations.

The main purpose of this chapter has not been to talk about field experience, nor do I pretended to offer an exhaustive account of the different perspectives from which space has been treated in audience research. Rather, it represents an attempt to bridge borders between complementary but yet for the most part disjointed theoretical trajectories. During the last ten years audience cultural studies and critical geography have been trying to approach each other within a theoretical frame. Up until now they have been reflecting on common methodological issues using exactly the same terms, and sharing the same critical and non-positivistic epistemological positions (Evans, 1988; Herbert, 2000). But, at least in my own academic context, audience ethnography has not been developed, for instance, by going beyond the kind of boundaries (that separate departments or faculties, that separate theory and fieldwork) marked on the academic map. Nevertheless, as Clifford (1992) has stated, placing ethnographic work in the *field* also has its constrictions, and I think it may specially be true in the case of interdisciplinary and *international* research teams, where cultural boundaries may also exist. In order to approach it in a different way, in this chapter I have tried to pinpoint the idea that researchers, as well as any other members of a studied community, can be "travelers" in some sense, crossing moving borders. And this creates another kind of gaze into real-and-imagined "common" places.

By trying to focus attention on the claim for "bridging borders," I have found challenges everywhere. The most important one has been that of approaching critical geography as a media ethnographer. In any case, it wasn't my intention to remain within these pages like a frozen Mediterranean in the courtyard of Hamlet's castle. I am aware that I have been talking about ideas (or about questions that may arise from these ideas) more than about facts and practical or relieving answers. But I really hope to have just made a little step towards taking space into account when doing fieldwork, and to have found a place for it here, among the pages of this book.

Notes

1 Concretely, Edward Soja uses the term "socio-spatial dialectic" (Soja, 1980), while David Harvey talks about the "historical-geographical materialism" dialectics (Harvey, 1989). Richard Peet has expressed it as the "spatial dialectics" (Peet, 1981).

2 We can find a good example of what "radical geography transforming into Marxist geography" was about by looking at the journal *Antipode: A Radical Journal of Geography*, founded in 1969 at Clark University in Worcester, Massachusetts. David Harvey's (1989) trajectory is a good example too.

3 For going deeply into the roots and further meanings of geography's controversial "cultural turn," see Cosgrove (1989), Jackson (1989), Philo (1991), the provocative Mitchell (1995), or Sayer (2000).

4 This idea has been developed through Soja's trilogy (1989, 1996, 2000), although I only quote here the second book.

5 Jay G. Blumler poses another interesting question that may be considered complementary to Berland's one: "Do prevalent notions of 'the audience' change in response to changes of media structure, and if so, how?" (Blumler, 1996, p. 97).

6 William's (1974) concept of "mobile privatization" has been used by media researchers during the last decade (see for instance Berland, 1992; Morley, 2000; Silverstone, 1994; Tufte, 1999).

References

Ang, I. (1996). Ethnography and radical contextualism in audience studies. In J. Hay, L. Grossberg and E. Wartella (eds), *The audience and its landscape* (pp. 247–262). Boulder, CO: Westview Press, Harper Collins Publishers.

Barnett, C. (1998). The cultural turn: Fashion of progress in human geography, *Antipode* 30(4), 379–394.

Berland, J. (1992). Angels dancing: Cultural technologies and the production of space. In L. Grossberg, C. Nelson and P. Treichler (eds), *Cultural studies* (pp. 38–55). New York: Routledge.

Bhabba, H. K. (1990). The third space. In J. Rutherford (ed.), *Identity, community, culture, difference* (pp. 207–221). London: Routledge.

Bhabba, H. K. (1994). *The location of culture*. New York and London: Routledge.

Blumler, J. G. (1996). Recasting the audience in the new television marketplace?. In J. Hay, L. Grossberg and E. Wartella (eds), *The audience and its landscape* (pp. 97–111). Boulder, CO: Westview Press, Harper Collins Publishers.

Burgess, J. and Gold, J. R. (eds) (1985). *Geography, the media and popular pulture*. London: Croom Helm.

Clifford, J. (1992). Traveling cultures. In L. Grossberg, C. Nelson and P. Treichler (eds), *Cultural studies* (pp. 96–116). New York and London: Routledge.

Cosgrove, D. (1989). Geography is everywhere: Culture and symbolism in human landscapes. In D. Gregory and R. Walford (eds), *Horizons in human geography* (pp. 118–135). London: Macmillan.

Evans, M. (1988). Participant observation: The researcher as research tool. In J. Eyles and D. M. Smith (eds), *Qualitative methods in human geography* (pp. 197–218). Cambridge: Polity Press.

Flores, C. (2001). La metodología cualitativa en la investigación de la recepción televisiva. Análisis comparativo de las técnicas y los supuestos. Research work presented at the Department of Journalism and Communication Sciences, Universitat Autònoma de Barcelona (October).

Foucault, M. (1980). *Power/knowledge: Selected interviews and other writings, 1972–1977*, ed. C. Gordon. New York: Pantheon.

Foucault, M. (1986). On other spaces. *Diacritics* 16, 22–27.

Geertz, C. (1988). *Works and lives: The anthropologist as author*. Chicago: University of Chicago Press.

Giddens, A. (1984). *The constitution of society: Outline of a theory of structuration*. Cambridge: Polity Press.

Giddens, A. (1985). Time, space and regionalisation. In D. Gregory and J. Urry (eds), *Social relations and spatial structures* (pp. 265–295). London: Macmillan.

Gonzalez, J. A. (1995). Coordenadas del imaginario: Protocolo para el uso de las cartografías culturales, *Estudios sobre las culturas contemporáneas* 1(2), 135–161.

Grossberg, L. (1988). Wandering audiences, nomadic critics. *Cultural Studies* 2(3), 377–391.

Hägerstrand, T. (1982). Diorama, path and project. *Tidscrift voor economische en sociale geografie* 73(6), 323–339. Also in J. Agnew, D. N. Livingstone and A. Rogers (eds), *Human geography. An essential anthology* (pp. 650–674). Oxford: Blackwell.

Harvey, D. (1989). *The condition of postmodernity*. Oxford: Blackwell.

Hay, J. (1996). The place of the audience: Beyond audience studies. In J. Hay, L. Grossberg and E. Wartella (eds), *The audience and its landscape* (pp. 359–378). Boulder, CO: Westview Press, Harper Collins Publishers.

Heisenberg, W. (1972). *Physics and beyond: Encounters and conversations*. New York: Harper Torchhook.

Herbert, S. (2000). For ethnography. *Progress in human geography* 24(4), 550–568.

Jacks, N. (1994). Televisión e identidad en los estudios de recepción. In G. Orozco (ed.), *Televidencia: Perspectivas para el análisis de los procesos de recepción televisiva.* (pp. 55–68). Mexico DF: Universidad Iberoamericana, Programa Institucional de Investigación en Comunicación y Prácticas Sociales.

Jacks, N. (1999). *Querência. Cultura regional como mediação simbolica. Um estudo de recepção.* Rio Grande do Sul: Editora da Universidade, Universidade Federal do Rio Grande do Sul.

Jacks, N. and Tufte, T. (1998). Televisão, familia e identidade (parte de um projecto integrado). In A. A. Canelas Rubim, I. M. Ghislene Bentz and M. J. Pinto (eds), *Produção e recepção dos sentidos midiaticos.* Petrópolis RJ: Vozes.

Jackson, P. (1989). *Maps of meaning: An introduction to cultural geography.* London: Unwin Hyman.

Jackson, P. (1993). Towards a cultural politics of consumption. In J. Bird, B. Curtis, T. Putnam, G. Robertson and L. Tickner (eds), *Mapping the futures: Local cultures, global change* (pp. 207–228). London: Routledge.

Kraidy, M. (1999) The global, the local, and the hybrid: A native ethnography of glocalization. *Critical Studies in Mass Communication* 16, 456–476.

Lefebvre, H. (1991). *The production of space.* Oxford: Blackwell. (French original text: *La production de l'espace.* Paris: Anthropos, 1974.)

Massey, D. (1984). *Spacial divisions of labor: Social structures and the geography of production.* New York: Methuen.

Massey, D. (1985). New directions in space. In D. Gregory and J. Urry (eds), *Social relations and spatial structures* (pp. 9–19). London: Macmillan.

Massey, D. (1993). Power-geometry and a progressive sense of place. In J. Bird, B. Curtis, T. Putnam, G. Robertson and L. Tickner, *Mapping the futures: Local cultures, global change* (pp. 59–69). London: Routledge.

Mitchell, D. (1995). There's no such thing as culture: Towards a reconceptualization of the idea of culture in geography. *Transactions of the Institute of British Geographers* 20, 102–116.

Morley, D. (1992). *Television, audiences and cultural studies.* London: Routledge.

Morley, D. (1996). The geography of television: Ethnography, communications, and community. In J. Hay, L. Grossberg and E. Wartella (eds), *The audience and its landscape* (pp. 317–342). Boulder, CO: Westview Press, Harper Collins Publishers.

Morley, D. (2000). *Home territories: Media, mobility and identity.* London: Routledge.

Morley, D. and Robins, K. (1995). *Spaces of identity: Global media, electronic landscape and cultural boundaries.* London and New York: Routledge.

Morley, D. and Silverstone, R. (1990). Domestic communications. *Media, Culture and Society* 12(1), 31–55.

Peet, R. (ed.) (1978). *Radical geography: Alternative viewpoints on contemporary social issues.* London: Methuen.

Peet, R. (1981). Spatial dialectics and Marxist geography. *Progress in Human Geography* 5, 105–110.

Peet, R. (1998.) *Modern geographical thought.* Oxford and Malden: Blackwell.

Philo, C. (ed.) (1991). *New words, new worlds: Reconceptualising social and cultural geography.* Lampeter: St David's University College (Social and Cultural Study Group).

Philo, C. (1999). Más palabras, más mundos: Reflexiones en torno al "giro cultural" y a la geografía social. *Documents d'Anàlisi Geogràfica* 34, 81–99.

Radway, J. (1988). Reception study: Ethnography and the problems of dispersed audiences and nomadic subjects. *Cultural Studies* 2(3), 359–376.

Sayer, A. (1994). Cultural studies and "the economy, stupid." *Environment and Planning D: Society and Space* 12, 635–637.

Sayer, A. (2000). Critical and uncritical turns. In I. Cook, D. Crouch, S. Naylor and J. Ryan (eds), *Cultural turns/geographical turns* (pp. 166–181). Harlow: Pearson Education.

Silverstone, R. (1994). *Television and everyday life*. London and New York: Routledge.

Soja, E. W. (1980). The socio-spatial dialectic. *Annals of the Association of American Geographers* 70, 207–225.

Soja, E. W. (1989). *Postmodern geographies: The reassertion of space in social theory*. London: Verso.

Soja, E. W. (1996). *Thirdspace: Journeys to Los Angeles and other real-and-imagined places*. Oxford: Blackwell.

Soja, E. W. (2000). *Postmetropolis*. Oxford: Blackwell.

Tuan, Yi-Fu. (1977). *Space and place: The perspective of experience*. London: Arnold.

Tufte, T. (1997). Televisión, modernidad y vida cotidiana: Un análisis sobre la obra de Roger Silverstone desde contextos culturales diferentes. *Comunicación y sociedad* 31, 65–96.

Tufte, T. (1999). Gauchos going global: Mobile privatization and ritualized media use. Paper presented at the 14th Nordic Conference for Media Researchers, Kungalv, Sweden.

Tufte, T. (2000). *Living with the rubbish queen: Telenovelas, culture and modernity in Brazil*. Luton: University of Luton Press.

Williams, R. (1974). *Television: Technology and cultural forms*. London: Fontana.

5

AUDIENCE LETTERS
AND LETTER-WRITERS

Constituting the audience for radio in
transnational contexts

Sweety Law

The search for "the audience" has intensified worldwide among broadcasting media and development planners who use mass media intensively. This is a fact even in developing countries where, during the 1980s and 1990s, mass media had ensured large captive audience groups. Development planners and non-governmental organizations (NGOs) continue to rely on broadcasting media in addition to other communication media. Ethnographic techniques in general, and their potential use of audience letters and letter-writers in particular, might offer an important approach to the search for the audience. For media ethnographers, audience letter-writers could help produce richer texts and extend the notion of the field. For development planners, the socio-cultural and political dimensions of ethnography, especially postmodern ethnography, could provide an enhanced knowledge of and dialog with the audience they seek to change. Letter-writing is but one road into the hearts and minds of audiences, and a significantly useful one in the case of radio programming in developing countries.

Unlike in industrialized countries, audience members in developing countries write letters in the hundreds and thousands. However, most audience letters are lost due to lack of facilities, resources, or plans to put them to use. For instance, according to Papa and associates (2000), an estimated 150,000 letters were received by All India Radio in response to its serial *Tinka Tinka Sukh* (Happiness in Small Things) during its one year of broadcast 1995–96. Within six months of its broadcast beginning in March 1995, the Kenyan radio program *Youth Variety Show* received 348 letters from all parts of the country; about 58 percent of the letters came from adolescent men and 40 percent came from adolescent women (Kenya Youth Initiative Project, 1996). Could any research tradition on audience ignore these individuals? Until recently, this segment of the audience has been mostly ignored if not suppressed because it constitutes a socio-demographic group with "high involvement" of the media. In concrete terms of any public identity, this imposes a closure on the interpretive processes in which the voice of the non-expert, the uninitiated, the Other, is marginalized. This view also ignores other possibilities of viewing audiences, such as treating this group simultaneously as a legitimate group alongside those who use media but do not write letters.

In developing countries, illiteracy is still a prevalent problem and other socio-economic and infrastructural challenges still exist. However, media institutions manage such situational constraints by setting up listeners' clubs, arranging for "local scribes" to assist with letter-writing, and instituting other motivational mechanisms for audience letter-writing. Still, there are many individuals who write in independently. Also, there have been a number of instances of group letter-writing where an individual initiates a letter on behalf of a small group of associates and acquaintances (Law and Singhal, 1999). Clearly, in some developing country contexts, audience letter-writing is a socio-cultural production that could also provide the ethnographic site for audience studies. Viewed in totality, audience letter-writing might be seen as pointing to a popular cultural practice extending media reception and articulating perhaps mostly the subjective but also including the objective as well as both micro and macro processes.

Mapping ethnography for audience letter-writing

Audience letters and letter-writers could be invaluable ethnographic resources for audience research and development planners in presenting important links for both research methodology and ontological and epistemological platforms. To distill the epistemological and methodological terms of naturalistic inquiry, media ethnography and the narrower reception studies have mostly focused on participant observation and in-depth interviews, in the field. Outlining a discursive history of media ethnography, Drotner (1993) observes that "ethnographic media studies differ from other interpretive traditions in their temporal and spatial organization of the empirical investigation" (p. 8). This view, generally labeled the cultural approach, seeking historical and fine particulars, often contends that "the central object of analysis of mass communication research lies outside the media, in the cultures and communities of which media and audiences are constituents" (Jensen, 1990, p. 143). From this vantage point, some leading researchers have gone to the extent of dismissing any notion of audiences.

Inherent in the temporal and spatial organizing view of media ethnography is what Philipsen (1977) calls a weak commitment to a linear ethnographic process because each stage moved through is also a potential point of return. According to Carbaugh and Hastings (1992), the linear process involves three general phases – pre-fieldwork, fieldwork, and post-fieldwork – sometimes, during post-fieldwork, leading back to the field, both geographically and intellectually, in order to generate better perspectives. Following Philipsen (1977), Carbaugh and Hastings (1992) advocate an ethnographic approach to interpersonal communication that is a cyclical research process involving theorizing that moves through phases from a basic orientation to evolution of theory based upon evaluating the relationship between the situated theory and the basic orientation. What is proposed is that the ethnographer should have strong theoretical grounding before venturing into the field, in order for communication theorizing to occur. What is assumed also is a situated socio-cultural site, a field visit or visits during which the ethnographer cycles through theorizing phases.

Another level at which the cyclical theorizing process might occur, or begin, is before the field visit. For media ethnographic inquiry, audience letter-writers and their letters have the potential both to instantiate and to collaborate on the ontological and epistemological terms of the inquiry. The letter-writing between the ethnographer and the audience letter-writers inscribes a cyclical research process for both sides wherein all individuals have a fair chance of speaking and being heard. Entering the field from such a relationship base makes it easier for more active participation by all sections of the audience, in contrast to the assumption that somehow upon entering the field the kind scientist can engage the cooperation of the audience.

That audience letters form part of the variety of classical anthropological and ethnological methods of investigation including material documents such as diaries and government documents is perhaps their obvious known value. This chapter argues for the importance of viewing the research and theorizing processes that might be generated by those letters. Briefly, study of audiences could commence before the field visits. This starting point would help in centering the audience as the proper subject of ethnography even during pre-fieldwork, rather than after entering the field. Such an outlook extends the temporal dimension of media ethnography and compels the researcher to take an enhanced view of the spatial organizing of the research, the proper subject, and the evoked relationship between researcher and researched. It might therefore be argued that during pre-fieldwork, when the researcher would be setting up the general theorizing foundations of the research, audience letters and their letter-writers could also be engaged in drawing out the contours of the field study and setting up some of its main arguments. The relationship-building context could situate both researcher and audience in a metaphorical space that previews and extends field visits.

The engagement with audience letter-writers might be paralleled in importance with the search for appropriate entrées, key informants and other logistical details. By furthering communication through exchange of letters, the ethnographer enables the audience to become active participants, rather than passive objects, in the research. By their responsiveness, obliging attitude, cooperative support, and managing of the continuation of the dialog, if you will, audience letter-writers can become as articulate as desirable articulate interviewees. As Kauffman (1992) said:

> Knowledge is contingent. This is not to say that knowledge is merely relative, for in a world in which certain knowledge and ways of knowing have been and continue to be privileged by virtue of class-race-gender positioning, the knowledge and ways of knowing of historically oppressed groups are sorely needed, the continued absence of them perpetuates incompleteness in our understandings of societies and cultures.
>
> (p. 188)

Kauffman's standpoint was feminist; audience letter-writers might be described as similar muted groups rendered invisible, if not voiceless, by much of the same class-gender-race positioning of privileged systems that anchor, unconsciously or consciously, most pre-fieldwork and post-fieldwork.

Perhaps the strongest ontological and epistemological reason for viewing audience letters and letter-writers as valuable ethnographic tools for audience research and development planners is provided by Kim Schrøder. Schrøder's (1994) conceptualization of "interpretive communities" demonstrates how a Peircean perspective could still enable "real" media ethnography and where "people come first." Thus media signifying processes are not conceptualized within general abstract linguistic systems where meanings are fixed and might be assumed to be transferable unmodified to the audience's minds. Rather, meanings are only potential until actualized in a communicative context, in this case in the audience letters. On this level, media ethnography distinguishes interactive social communities (constituted independent of any media use) and "interpretive communities" which are defined by their media use alone. The socio-demographic dimensions disappear as fundamental social influences and the audience members become defined by their "interpretive repertoires . . . a product *of* the language community as a whole, *of* the cultural positionings that become established in the course of the individual's life history, *of* the communicative interactions in the interpretive and social communities of everyday life, and finally, *of* the unique assemblage of these influences constructed by the individual from moment to moment" (Schrøder, 1994, p. 345). Methodologically, Schrøder proposed the individual interview in the informant's home as the best research setting. In both the theory and methodology of "interpretive communities," audience letters and letter-writers seem fitting material for media ethnography.

In terms of specific methodology, micro-scale ethnographic audience research has not been entirely without difficulties either. Radway (1988) and others have pointed to how the practice of conducting bounded, regionalized investigations of a singular text-audience – which is common – may be limiting for most kinds of media. Issues of entrée into the community, gaining rapport for the case being studied, and accessing sensitive or inaccessible information are important methodological factors in qualitative research (Creswell, 1998; Douglas, 1976; Janesick, 1994; Lindolf and Grodin, 1990). Denzin (1991) observes that qualitative researchers have spent most of the time on resolving "the myth of an observer with a method who could somehow prevail upon this subject to reveal her inner world of experience to the kindly knowing scientist" (p. 68). Ang (1991) makes a powerful case for an ethnographic principle by way of "methodological situationalism" of audiences that would foreground their situational practices and experiences; but she does not quite address how such goals might be achieved in the research setting. Rather, she suggests that we should not attempt to contain the social world of actual audiences because the very fluid nature of that world resists full representation (p. 164). Schrøder (1994), while agreeing with Ang that the world of actual audiences is too polysemic and polymorphic, is reluctant to write the audience out of reality, into the pure realm of situational discourses – and empirical paralysis (p. 341; Bird, 1992, p. 257). She urges: "let's get on with it and produce incompletely articulated accounts of audience readings and practices which may, in spite of their (no doubt) multiple shortcomings, provide illuminating insights into the polysemic and polymorphic relationships between media and people in the world we live in" (p. 341).

The communication phenomenon of audience letter-writing might serve to an extent in mitigating some pragmatic questions in audience research such as bounded regionalized study and access issues. Importantly, audience letters might provide insights into the inner world that Denzin (1991) finds even the most empathetic scientists struggle with. In both industrialized and developing countries, letter-writing is a known activity of audience reception; and media institutions, particularly print, institute it as a strategic business mechanism. Thus, while the quest to define and understand the audience remains a goal, an important link connecting the audience has been mostly overlooked. Planned efficiently, it is a link that can be significantly incorporated and explored, particularly by ethnographic techniques.

An important fact about audience letter-writers in developing countries is simply that they self-define themselves into reality by their writing. They would certainly be characterized as highly involved, and possessing a loose yet defined membership (perhaps like political party affiliations of most ordinary citizens) by virtue of a belief in their letter-writing agency. The general view is that audience letters are "[l]imited and disorganized" and consequently "these audience self-representations are easily accommodated, belittled or ignored" (Ang, 1991, p. 6). Ang observes that more organized forms of audience self-presentation than letter-writing, such as pressure groups for "better" television or less violence, have a better chance to be heard. This approach is still the better-known and more effective strategy. It would be interesting to investigate the role of audience letter-writing in pressure groups and their agenda. Whereas signature and email campaigns are beyond the scope of this essay, their existence and common use do generate the view of audience letter-writing as having both organizational pressure and impact value. Under existing social and organizational structures, their consequence depends on media institution goals and media program stimuli more than on the culture and motivation of the audience letter-writers. Audience letter-writers may be fewer than the actual audience size but they are a distinctive group nonetheless and part of the notion of audience. In the search for the audience, these groups of individuals who come forward, mostly voluntarily, are important to acknowledge.

In some contexts, particularly where government and management exert unilateral asymmetrical control over media institutions, audience letters would still be ignored or easily accommodated. More recently, informal investigations in the United States have revealed that a number of media programs (e.g. *Touched by an Angel*) and media outlets (e.g. faith-based; print) receive audience letters and use them in significant ways. Enhancement of communication media, especially email and fax, might explain the spurt in audience letter-writing and their determined acknowledgement by some media producers. Also, if some media issues involve the community and stimulate pressure groups, audience letter-writing could extend beyond writing only to the media program in question. Letter-writing is still a recognized technology of self-presentation, only its salience is more subtle than its functionality and in most cases it is made subsidiary to the face-to-face interpersonal. Could ethnographic researchers, who are seeking the particular and not the general, afford audience letter-writers a chance to be heard? In some transnational contexts, lacking in communication technology resources, audience letters might still represent the best available form of audience self-presentation and possibly the primary context for their chance to be heard.

First of all, I will outline some of the basic issues with audience letters, letter-writers and development programs in developing countries. Next, the importance of audience letter-writing will be argued. A role for audience letters and letter-writers will be discussed. Finally, I propose how audience letters, letter-writers and ethnography might be mutually enriching in both the epistemology and methodology of media ethnography. In particular, the role of the ethnographer is explored. This essay grew out of my work on communication for social change programs and audience letters (e.g. Law and Singhal, 1999; Papa et al., 2000). I have researched media audiences and their letters in a number of transnational contexts such as India, Kenya, and other countries. Using content analysis of the primary texts (letters), I have mostly applied the qualitative approach and also experimented with a quantitative method. An overall triangulation framework guided the analysis of each of the letters. Thus, several data sets (letters, personal communication with audience letter-writers and program producers, content analysis of media programs, surveys) were compared and contrasted. The letters and letter-writers were organized by media program and studied separately. In each case, an important outcome was the realization of the rich ethnographic potential of audience letters and letter-writers.

Audience letter-writers and development programs

All development campaigns and their communication programs identify an aggregation of individuals who are intended to be the object or audience for the program. The receiver-related communication plan to produce the aggregate of individuals includes requiring written feedback, exclusivity of audience club memberships, and other interaction by audiences. In many developing countries, radio is the more viable media for mass reach; and for many radio programs focused on social change, a common practice is to establish radio listener clubs. Both general listenership and listeners' clubs are often sustained by audience letter-writers. Thus, conceptually, in the case of development campaigns, audience letter-writers would form an audience, identifiable and united by the common activity and interest in listeners' club membership and letter-writing to the media program.

My argument to promote recognition of audience letters, and consequently letter-writers, as constituting an audience arises from a need addressed by critical cultural politics. It is ironic that audience letter-writers are not viewed as audience by the same media programs that seek to produce them. The popular view is that the letter-writers are atypical, diffused and too few in number to make any difference. Such an unexamined view becomes self-defeating especially where audience letter-writers are numerous and need to be heard. The prevalence of the popular view might be a basic problem for the extensive invisibility of audience letters and letter-writers to media programs for social change, particularly in many developing countries. There might be some truth that audience letters and their letter-writers are quantitatively limited but that should hardly negate their status as audience. Also, it is true only in some contexts and there has been little questioning of the assumptions for this assertion. It would be informative to investigate to what degree audience feedback is promoted relative to promoting the program or the sponsors, producers and advertisers. Another important question centers on the conceptualization of feedback by the institution: is it "feedback mechanisms" (e.g. Earley, 1986) or "response to a message" (e.g. Jacoby et al., 1984; Martin and Jacobs, 1980)? In either case, the object of interest is solely the media institution and its entities. Gonzalez (1989) argued for a social view of audience interactivity, as opposed to a linear information processing view, compelling recognition of feedback as a process rather than as an object. Such a perspective might likely restore some ground for considering all categories of audiences, especially audience letter-writers, as a legitimate entity, as well as enabling the actualization of feedback processes rather than simply viewing them as a program symbol.

Where the number of audience letters has been substantial and there has been a good response from audience letter-writers, the problem of organization is evident. While the popularity or success of a media program is an indeterminate factor, the economic market model of the audience plans for success whether it is realized or not. Media programs for social change that adopted the market model need similar plans that factor in situational variables such as the cultural importance of audience letter-writing in certain audience contexts. In the absence of any planned role for audience letters and their letter-writers, the letters are used for producing formal information for program content as well as what Ang (1991) terms "informal knowledge" of the audiences that comes into circulation only through discursive practices such as board meetings and story conferences.

Although not addressed as a distinctive audience grouping, audience letter-writers are projected as one for summary reporting purposes. All evaluation reports of media programs for social change cite and detail the number of audience letters they received to indicate their audience. In the absence of other dependable indicators of media function, which is a field reality in most developing countries, audience letters are appropriated to represent real and potential audiences. This approach may not be entirely faulty in light of the importance of letter-writing within certain socio-cultural contexts of audiences. However, the convenience and value of audience letters as an indicator of audience presence is overshadowed by the absence of any particular methodology to incorporate their knowledge, and consequently audience letters and their letter-writers are denied legitimate status as constituting an audience.

Audience letter-writers and developing countries

Where telecommunications are still a luxury, letter-writing is the preferred communication mode for both rural and urban audiences. For example, in India there are only 13 telephones per 1,000 people (Sarma, 1998). Under the circumstances, when audiences write, the communication act is significant. The audience letter-writers display agency for participation in the public forum created by the media program. Whereas a preponderance of fan mail might be expected, there is as much representation of active engagement with social issues examined in the media program. Lacking access to or knowledge of other public fora for discussion about public affairs, the audience letter-writers discuss issues within the space permissible by a letter format. There is an attitude and awareness similar to the more educated readers/letter-writers of urban national print media. From a cultural perspective, audience letter-writers might be defined as "active audiences" of their communities, the informal observatory of its everyday character and challenges. By demonstrating agency for participation in public life, they also perform their citizenship as any other active group.

Ironically, letter-writers are not acknowledged for their initiatives in public discourse. The methods mostly utilized in media effects research (such as surveys, focus groups, interviews, and quasi-experiments) elicit linear information processing or perceptions that are activated at a given contemplation of a mass media. Babrow (1988) believes there may be many more associated outcomes present in an interpretive structure than are activated in any given contemplation of a media object. Ang (1991) believes that a more thorough cultural approach would go beyond the pseudo-intimate moment of media/audience encounter to address differentiated meanings in articulating more general social relations of power. Generally, the issue of access to sensitive information persists. The issues of access to the audience group (or community) and access to sensitive information have not been problematized as much as merited for the goals of ethnographic or critical cultural studies. Letter-writing to participate in public discourse, traditionally led by the dominant classes, as generated by media programs with social change goals could de-center the roles of "knower and known" and shift information flow from source to audience, from dependence to reciprocity. In developing countries, letter-writers might be viewed as "historians," informal chroniclers of micro/macro processes in contexts that might not enable access to such information or more democratic participation.

For critical cultural ethnographers, the initiation of communication by active audiences through letter-writing enables *interaction* as a focus of interest, thereby resolving some of the challenges of gaining trust and support. In presenting sensitive and inaccessible information in their letters, letter-writers risk vulnerability and self-disclosure to participate in public discourse. Recognition of the audience's initiative in letter-writing could establish the communication basis of ethnographic tasks in audience research. As Conquergood (1991) observed, "the rethinking in ethnography is primarily about speaking and listening . . . [to] voices, utterances, intonations, and multivocality" (p. 183). The audience letters might be viewed as the first opportunity for ethnographers to listen to other voices and utterances, not simply what they are looking to hear.

Most criticisms against audience letters and letter-writers are from the positivist frame of reference. The personal accounts, whether in the form of opinion or personal stories, inscribe the role of reasoning in the process of letter-writing. According to Fisher (1984), the material and stuff of stories is "good reasons" or "elements that provide warrants for accepting or adhering to the advice fostered by any form of human communication that can be considered rhetorical" (p. 206). Fisher argues that values may serve as reasons, and what we usually call reasons are value-laden. The concept of good reasons coincides with the assumption that human beings are as much valuing as they are reasoning beings. Thus, even one isolated personal story in an audience letter, without other analytical features, represents value for an enhanced understanding of the audience. The stories and personalization narrate interests and values important to the audience letter-writers, and are consequently often different in the reasoning and reasoning style from the discourse stained by scholarly orientations.

The motivations for writing letters are varied. Some individuals write because they are "registered listeners" of the radio program, although they need not write. Some simply wish to hear their names broadcast, although there is no guarantee or set policy for that across most institutions. Certain people are interested in gaining access to the performers and producers for themselves. A number of individuals write to identify with the program's issues or to celebrate with certain actors. Thus, letter-writing, whether voluntary or prompted by institutional organization, is an important activity by listeners and can be a key to an enhanced understanding of the extension of issues central to the letter-writers' lives that the mass-media program seeks to mediate and change.

Media programs in developing countries cannot afford to overlook the cost-effective, realistic, and practical dimensions of identifying their audiences via the collection of audience letters, particularly for popular programs. Consider the example of *Hum Log*. Approximately 200,000 audience letters were received in response to this television program in India.[1] In addition, approximately 200,000 letters were received by *Hum Log* actors and actresses, making an overall total of 400,000 audience letters that were received during the seventeen months[2] in which the highly popular series (ratings of up to 90 percent) was broadcast (Singhal, 1990). In terms of sheer magnitude of implementation of mass communication programs in developing countries, for logistical reasons foremost, it is not feasible to identify all audiences or to collect feedback from all audience members. Therefore, letters from involved audience members comprise an important source of feedback and knowledge about the program's audiences.

Audience letters, particularly those unsolicited, lessen a variety of research problems such as giving socially desirable answers and selection bias. Like other personal documents, the criticism of self-selection can also be applied to audience letters as an information source. The problem of self-selection may also be generally levied against focus group and certain survey techniques. But its influence may be much less than face-to-face evaluative situations because letters afford anonymity for freer communication by the audience member.

The letters also represent a potentially rich source of "information exposure," i.e. the measure of an individual's access to information environments, intra-organizationally as well as inter-organizationally. Studies by Law and Singhal (1999) and Papa et al. (2000) of letter-writers to a popular radio soap opera in India, *Tinka Tinka Suk* (Happiness in Small Things), indicated a number of instances of collaborative writing, reporting of group discussions, and initiation of collective social change action. In terms of information exposure at the individual level, audience letters can thus present more in-depth knowledge of audiences than surveys and interpersonal influence studies. And should audience letter-writers be enlisted as points of entrée into a community, it might be proposed that an insider, and not someone who has gained insider status for purposes of the research, anchors the ethnographic study.

The systemic view of information exposure outlined above has another implication for social change media programs. Historically, opinion leadership in developing countries was viewed as vested in the village chief or local elites. Most literature on interpersonal influence is situated in interpersonal face-to-face communication and defines key players as communication nodes of influence. By extension in many developing transnational contexts, this communication model again foregrounded local elites. For purposes of knowing audiences better, the definition of opinion leadership and interpersonal influence may need elaboration to include written testimonials and their authors who are generally not local elites.

Thus far, I have attempted to outline the significant role of audience letters and letter-writers for media programs in developing countries. Methodologically also much work needs to be done. The research on audiences of media programs for social change has been mainly positivist and theoretical in approach. Hassan and Zakariah (1993) attempted to analyze audience participation in developing programs on radio in Malaysia. Audience letter-writers were a variable in the investigation. However, in the absence of identifying what systems were set up for audience participation, audience letter-writers were treated as objects, objectified in letters that were only a feedback mechanism for assessing program reach. An earlier study by Shtarkshall and Basker (1985) outlined that audience letter-writers to a radio program on family planning in Israel could be categorized as various kinds of help-seekers. More recently, Law and Singhal (1999) explored manifestations of efficacy in audience letters. Identifying audiences via their letter-writing and viewing them as active participants in the public discourse of their communities would require some rethinking in the philosophy and practice of audience research.

Audience letters and letter-writers: enriching the ethnographic approach

Ethnographic techniques could easily be applied to study audience letters. Mostly provided by audience members on a voluntary basis, as a collection of texts, audience letters represent a plethora of what Conquergood (1991) would call "voices, utterances, and intonations." In practical terms, ethnography works primarily with "unstructured data, that is, data that have not been coded at the point of data collection in terms of a closed set of analytic categories" (Atkinson and Hammersley, 1994, p. 248). According to Atkinson and Hammersley (1994), the ethnographic analysis of data involves explicit interpretation of meanings and functions of human actions, with quantification and statistical analysis playing a subordinate role at most (p. 248). These are some features of ethnographic methods that might enable stand-alone research of audience letters.

For media ethnographers, audience letter-writing could help produce richer texts and extend the notion of the field – by enriching both the ethnographic process and the research outcome. In terms of mediating the process, the letters might present a significant opportunity to develop interpersonal communication and access into the community. Letter-writing is an involved process requiring time and constant self-reflexivity on the part of researchers as they must remind themselves of being "interlocutor" if not coeval partner of other participants in the study. Like the development of any interpersonal relationship, perhaps starting from uncertainty and anxieties, working with audience letter-writers could also be a long process that might transform the relationship, change the researcher and perhaps the audience letter-writers. Ultimately, the outcome of the process would depend on the position or positions adopted by the researcher.

Audience letters could situate the researcher as listener foremost, in the audience research process. This differs from ethnography's distinctive starting point of participant observation. However, the definition of participant observation is subtler than "immersion in the day-to-day lives of the people" (Creswell, 1998, p. 58) or an intensely sensuous way of knowing (Conquergood, 1991). There are important subtleties in the typology within and between complete observer, observer as participant, participant as observer, and complete participant (Atkinson and Hammersley, 1994). A more dynamic observation locates the ethnographer on a continuum because "participant observation offers possibilities from being a complete outsider to being a complete insider" (Jorgensen, quoted in Creswell, 1998). This can be the case but it need not be. The researcher–participant continuum process is complex and the researcher may adopt varied roles at different times. Furthermore, the researcher's goals may change as the history of the relationship with participants change. Of interest to this essay are the researcher's beginning status of complete outsider and the transition processes and goals thereafter building towards entrée and relationship history. The processes and goals hinge around many relational and communication factors, and a starting position as listener is a valid and reliable ethnographic position afforded by the audience letters.

For the ethnographer on audiences, reading audience letters may be viewed as a form of participant observation. It might be considered a first step in the communication processes of a participant observation continuum in which the audience letter-writers themselves have invited the researcher for the first interaction. Although mostly written in a highly personal style, the letters are meant for reading by an anonymous other or "romanticized imagined" other. By committing time, interest, and labor to acquire insights into the letters and the audience letter-writers, the researcher would transit into a mode of "being-in-the-world" of the audiences. The appropriate labor invested in order to be immersed in the textual representations of the audience letter-writers' language and meanings can be as rigorous as studying other documentation and actual fieldwork. From the audience letters, the researcher could initiate the next stage in ethnography's interactive processes by an in-depth field study of the letter-writers in their everyday contexts.

Audience letter-writers might also be viewed as alternative gatekeepers to a group, a view that approximates more closely ethnography's ideal of providing a voice for the marginalized. Creswell (1998) writes: "[i]n an ethnography, access typically begins with a *gatekeeper*, an individual who is a member of or has insider status with a cultural group." This gatekeeper is the initial contact for the researcher and leads the researcher to other informants (Hammersley and Atkinson, 1983). Typically, in developing countries, local elites (especially men) have been established as gatekeepers in most rural communities. However, most instances of audience letter-writing from such contexts reveal that the letter-writers are not local elites but mostly high school or college students (including many women), and local village/town-level entrepreneurs. Furthermore, the reality of audience reception and media function is quite different in developing countries from that generally assumed in Western audience research. For example, in more rural neighborhoods, it is quite common to hear radios blare popular music or entertainment broadcasts from local stores – much like piped music in the glitzy malls of America or Europe – to attract and amuse clientele. A number of such local entrepreneurs are regular audience letter-writers as much as other groups of individuals. It might be claimed that in transnational contexts, businesses as well as the family or household are important audiences for regular radio listening. When only the head of household or family is surveyed, many features of the actual audiences are left out. When audience letter-writers are viewed as important gatekeepers to a social group as much as the local elites, the concepts of gatekeeping and participation in public life acquire more democratic features.

In view of the implied democratic goals of ethnography, the researcher must be sensitive as to which individuals are selected as gatekeepers (who provide entrance to a group or site) and key informants (who provide useful insights into the group). Access and entry are sensitive components in qualitative research and the researcher must establish trust and rapport (Janesick, 1994, p. 211). Initial interactions in the field are critical and could significantly mark the transition process of the researcher's status from outsider to somewhat participant or insider. Attention to the audience letters that preface the initial face-to-face field interactions helps to establish trust and rapport. Such recognition of the audience letter-writers privileges the processes of relationship-building that center on communication. My personal experience is that initial communication with audience letter-writers as a follow-up to their letters can provide a tremendous boost to the field interaction that primarily constitutes the practice of ethnography.

Audience letters and letter-writers: practicing ethnography

For audience research, audience letters could enable a discernable shift in ethnography's traditional "Other-as-theme" to "Other-as-interlocutor" (Theunissen, quoted in Conquergood, 1991) by privileging the letter-writers' point of view and opinions on some of the issues most relevant to them. When hundreds and thousands of audience letter-writers initiate communication through their letters, the ethnographer could have privileged access to a more encompassing understanding of audiences and the contemporary cultural condition, "in their own words." However, in attempting to de-inscribe audience letters and audience letter-writers who are inscribed into structural and historical relations of power, the ethnographer enacts a struggle towards rhetorical self-reflexivity. The gap between engaging others where they are and representing them where they aren't, always immense but not much noticed, has become extremely visible (Conquergood, 1991). For the ethnographer of audiences, to transform to "Other-as interlocutor' is both simplified and complicated by the textual nature of the letters.

Among the problems of using personal documents such as letters is their "fascination with style" (Gruhle, quoted in Allport, 1951) and their non-objectivity. Therefore, any analysis of audience letters must guard against the letter-writer's tendency to develop an aesthetic fascination with her/his task and consequently to allow art to take over sincerity and fact. To the latter criticism, Allport (1951) observed how extreme objectivism had disclosed its own weakness. Strictly speaking, by themselves, audience letters could be assessed for their quality independently by testing for "internal consistency or *self-confrontation*" (p. 128). This test is widely applied in literature and biography. Documents need not stand alone; supporting evidence can and should be obtained – which is where ethnographic fieldwork would be a useful follow-up strategy.

Recognizing the active culture of letter-writing is a step towards ethnography's empowerment goals. The varied criticisms of audience letters and their letter-writers as being opinionated and personal unveil political stakes that anchor practices of research, scholarship, and no less everyday audiences. Whereas the cultural politics of research and scholarship have been documented in various ways, there is scant work on audience letter-writing and cultural politics. Audience letter-writers, particularly from rural areas, are not generally from the local elite class. They might be more literate than other media audiences but it is overestimating to equate "active" with "powerful." By presenting a different perspective of "active audiences" other than recalcitrance or romanticizing, two widely held generalizations by the cultural leadership of dominant classes, audience letter-writers seek in their writing an opportunity to participate in the public discourse of the evoked community of audiences, if not the larger "public" arena.

Audience letter-writers have also been criticized for their combination of self-selection and untruthfulness. But should their letters be dismissed or discarded simply on that basis? Papa et al. (2000) concluded how contradictions imbue the processes of parasocial interaction and social learning for social change. Allport (1951) notes: "Writers know well enough what their *intentions* are, and what their *proximate* motives are, but seem lost when reporting 'ultimate' motives. But before regarding this as a fatal criticism, let us raise the question whether any psychological scientist knows the nature of anyone's *ultimate motives*" (p. 133). By the same token, it is hard to tap in survey responses and focus group interviews the audience's *objective* and *true* motives. Audience letters are as prone to errors of reporting, such as deception, or "perverse self-exhibitionism," or errors of mood, or blindness to motives, as any other approach. However, by recognizing the contradictory and continuous social process of all cultural production and admitting the politicized orientation of both research and writing, ethnographic research would enable a better understanding of audiences, letter-writers, and media function.

Clearly, audience letters and letter-writers have much potential to enrich both practice and principles of media ethnography.

Discussion

For media programs with specific goals of social change, there are imperatives to identify audiences and solicit their input and feedback. An ethnographic investigation of audience letter-writing could significantly shape the direction of any inquiry, especially a critical inquiry of mass media audiences in some transnational contexts. Particularly in contexts where letter-writing is the only means of participation in public life, and media and its institutions are in desperate search of audiences, encouragement of audience letters could be an easy solution for media. And if letter-writers are affirmed as an audience group, their letters could evoke an active site of more democratic and critical cultural politics. Foremost, the audience letter-writers need to be recognized as audiences.

Conquergood (1991) asserts that "[n]o group of scholars is struggling more acutely and productively with political tensions of research than ethnographers" (p. 179). Such a charge has certain implications depending on context. For example, in Europe and the US, the cultural politics focus of reception studies argues for the independence of audiences to negotiate meanings of text and even to resist preferred readings. But arguably these "negotiations" are geometrically intensified and weighted in developing countries. For instance, letter-writing by audiences is prompted by different motivations and framed by different cultural structures, and serves as a means for participation in public discourses otherwise denied or hierarchically inaccessible. By privileging those voices in the public discourse of scholarship and other knowledge-creating activity, the ethnographer would acknowledge her existence and shift her own role from representation (with all its challenges) to performance, from observer/researcher to coeval partner in the communication on social change.

Audiences write to a particular program amidst many competing discourses including history and other media programs. More than only discovering "the diversity and differences," or seeking "the diverse as well as the homogenous," the ethnographic approach can focus on epiphanies which radically alter and shape the meanings persons give to themselves and their life projects (Denzin, 1991, p. 60). The stories narrated in the letters are highly personal events whose epiphanic value is borne out in the letter-writing initiative and shared insights. Thus the ethnographer may approach certain audience letter-writers to study how human beings make history under conditions that are not of their own choice.

For audience research in some transnational contexts, rethinking ethnographic inquiry in terms of "speaking, listening, acting together, instead of observing" (Conquergood, 1991) and attaining "vividly felt insight into the life of other people" (Trinh, 1989) shifts the researcher's primary search. That is, rather than seeking the gatekeepers and key informants of pre-selected audiences, the ethnographer "relocates" the listener via the intonations and multivocality that accompany "the shift from space to time, from sight and vision to sounds and voice" (Conquergood, 1991). Reading and paying appropriate attention to audience letters is an important step in the listening role, and perhaps a key event for an "interiorizing experience" that is marked by that social-psychological moment of direct contact with the audience letters and stretching possibly to the communicative praxis of fieldwork.

Notes

1   According to Doordarshan, the Indian national television network, which broadcast *Hum Log*.
2   During 1984–85.

References

Allport, G. W. (1951). *The use of personal documents in psychological science*. New York: Social Science Research Council.

Ang, I. (1990). Culture and communication: Towards an ethnographic critique of media consumption in the transnational system. *European Journal of Communication* 5, 239–260.

Ang, I. (1991). *Desperately seeking the audience*. London: Routledge.

Atkinson, P. and Hammersley, M. (1994). Ethnography and participant observation. In N. K. Denzin and Y. Lincoln (eds), *Handbook of qualitative research* (pp. 248–261). Thousand Oaks, CA: Sage.

Babrow, A. S. (1988). Theory and method in research on audience motives. *Journal of Broadcasting and Electronic Media* 32(4), 471–487.

Bird, E. (1992). Travels in nowhere land: Ethnography and the impossible audience. *Critical Studies in Mass Communication* 9, 250–260.

Carbaugh, D. and Hastings, S. O. (1992). A role for communication theory in ethnography and cultural analysis. *Communication Theory* 2(2), 156–165.

Conquergood, D. (1991). Rethinking ethnography: Towards a critical cultural politics. *Communication Monograph* 58(2), 179–194.

Creswell, J. (1998). *Qualitative inquiry and research design: Choosing among five traditions*. Thousand Oaks, CA: Sage.

Denzin, N. K. (1991). Representing lived experiences in ethnographic texts. *Studies in Symbolic Interaction* 12, 59–70.

Douglas, J. D. (1976). *Investigative social research*. Beverley Hills, CA: Sage.

Drotner, K. (1992). What is "the everyday" in media ethnography? Paper presented to the Mass Media and Ethnography of Everyday Life seminar, Holbaek, Denmark, November.

Drotner, K. (1993). Media ethnography: An "Other" story? *Nordicom Review* 2, 1–13.

Earley, P. C. (1986). An examination of the mechanisms underlying the relation of feedback to performance. *Academy of Management Proceedings*, 214–218.

Fisher, W. R. (1984). Narration as a human communication paradigm: The case of public moral argument. *Communication Monographs* 51, 1–22.

Gonzalez, H. (1989). Interactivity and feedback in Third World development campaigns. *Critical Studies in Mass Communication* 6(3), 295–314.

Hammersley, M. and Atkinson, P. (1983). *Ethnography: Principles and practice*. London: Tavistock.

Hassan, M. S. and Zakariah, A. T. (1993). Audience participation in radio development programmes: A study of Radio Seremban, a Malaysian local radio station. *Asian Journal of Communication* 3(2), 128–140.

Jacoby, J., Troutman, T., Mazursky, D. and Kuss, A. (1984). When feedback is ignored: Disutility of outcome feedback. *Journal of Applied Psychology* 69, 531–545.

Janesick, V. J. (1994). The dance of qualitative research design. In N. K. Denzin and Y. S. Lincoln (eds), *Handbook of qualitative research* (pp. 209–219). Thousand Oaks, CA: Sage.

Jensen, K. B. (1990). Television futures: A social action methodology for studying interpretive communities. *Critical Studies in Mass Communication* 2, 1–18.

Kauffman, B. J. (1992). Feminist facts: Interview strategies and political subjects in ethnography. *Communication Theory* 2(3), 187–206.

Kenya Youth Initiative Project. (1996). *A dialog with young people through radio: Interim evaluation report*. Nairobi: Johns Hopkins Population Communication Services.

Law, S. and Singhal, A. (1999). Efficacy in letter-writing to an entertainment-education radio serial. *Gazette* 61(5), 355–373.

Lindolf, T. R. and Grodin, D. (1990). When media use can't be observed: Some problems and tactics of collaborative audience research. *Journal of Communication* 40(4), 8–28.

Martin, L. and Jacobs, M. (1980). Structured feedback delivered in small groups. *Small Group Behavior* 11(1), 88–107.

Papa, M., Singhal, A., Law, S., Pant, S., Sood, S., Rogers, E. M. and Shefner, C. (2000). Entertainment-education and social change: An analysis of para-social interaction, social learning, and paradoxical communication. *Journal of Communication* 50(4), 31–55.

Philipsen, G. (1977). Linearity of research design in ethnographic studies of speaking. *Communication Quarterly* 25(3), 42–50.

Radway, J. (1988). Reception study: Ethnography and the problems of dispersed and nomadic subjects. *Cultural Studies* 2(3), 359–376.

Sarma, N. (1998). The changing face of Indian Media: Implications for development organisations. http://www.comminit.com/review_indianmedia.html.

Schrøder, K. C. (1994). Audience semiotics, interpretive communities and the ethnographic turn in media research. *Media, Culture and Society* 16, 337–347.

Singhal, A. (1990). Entertainment-education communication strategies for development. Unpublished doctoral dissertation, University of Southern California.

Shtarkshall, R. and Basker, E. (1985). Radio and family planning in Israel: Letters to the broadcasters. *Journal of Communication* 35(1), 89–97.

Trinh, T. M. (1989). *Woman, native, other: Writing postcoloniality and feminism.* Bloomington, IN: Indiana University Press.

6

RITUALS IN THE MODERN WORLD

Applying the concept of ritual in media ethnography

Bent Steeg Larsen and Thomas Tufte

In recent years, the field of audience ethnography has grown significantly, with increased attention given to rapid technological development and cultural globalization. A growing number of empirical studies have sought to understand the relationship between local culture and global cultural discourses. The relations between identity formation, media uses and cultural change are thus increasingly the focus of attention in many audience ethnographies. This chapter draws on our own recent empirical studies conducted in the context of this wave. One study explores media uses in Denmark, the other studies media uses amongst families in southern Brazil (Larsen, 2000; Tufte, 2001).

Both our cases analyze the cultural organization of the more or less unheeded functions of media use in everyday life. One should expect quite a few dissimilarities between media habits in European and South American contexts – and there certainly are – but what struck us were the similarities: not similarities in terms of content preferences, media technologies, etc., but similarities in the way ritual aspects of everyday life rewardingly can be taken into account in order to explain media use that is carried out for no apparent reason by media users in everyday context. Through our line of argument, we wish to show how rituals – as we define them – configure a key element of principally any social use of the media and thus, ideally, of any audience ethnography. In our definition of the concept, rituals transform ordinary, mundane actions like eating, talking, watching television, and so forth, into actions that transcend the particularities of the situation and link the participants to a general social and cultural order that exceed the present time and space.

Our aim here is, by manner of empirical illustration, to introduce the classical anthropological concept of ritual into audience ethnography in a way that corresponds with the strong emphasis audience ethnography has on studying

90

everyday practices and the social interaction between people. Many concepts from anthropology have been "imported" into audience ethnography, and many media scholars refer substantially to the anthropological literature, especially on issues of methodological inquiry, reflexivity, and the need for coherent contextualization of media reception. However, we believe that substantial theoretical development remains to be done for audience ethnography to mature as a field of inquiry. Through an empirical analysis of the morning use of radio in a Danish family and the evening use of television in Brazil, we wish to show how media use can be reinterpreted as a ritual and hopefully thereby contribute to the further development of the field of audience ethnography.

With this chapter we hope to show that what appear as mundane practices can be highly charged, socially and culturally. When ritualized, mundane practices express, maintain and negotiate the existing social and cultural order, and by applying the concept of ritual the researcher gains access to this order. What people do and say is not always coherent. With the concept of ritual we introduce an analytical tool that can gather more knowledge about how local and global cultures are embedded in action, as opposed to knowledge gathered through members' discourses about what is significant for their culture.

First, we briefly introduce the concept of ritual, its origin in anthropology and how the concept is used in media research. We then present our empirical examples and argue how media use might be involved in ritual action. Finally we discuss the further relevance of the concept of ritual in media research.

What is ritual?

Audience ethnography, being a field developed within media studies over the past fifteen years, remains a dispersed academic enterprise, and has in large part been developed by media scholars with backgrounds in the humanities and cultural studies, and only few anthropologists. Ritual is a concept originating in anthropology. In the following, we briefly identify some of the original scholars and their contributions to the particular understanding of ritual that we seek to explore *vis-à-vis* media use.

Durkheim's sacred objects and mental states

By making a distinction between the *sacred* and the *profane*, the French sociologist Emile Durkheim (1995) analyzed religion as a set of ideas and practices by which people sacralize the social structure and bonds of the community. Ritual serves, Durkheim argued, to arouse a "passionate intensity," feelings of "effervescence," in which individuals experience something larger than themselves. For Durkheim, *rituals serve to promote feelings of collectivity, senses of belonging and of being brought together as a collective group*. Religion is the medium through which shared social life was experienced, expressed and legitimated. Religion and religious behavior were thus the object of Durkheim's sociology,

91

but in his approach to this object his focus was on its social nature and not the divine (Bell, 1997).

The main characteristics of Durkheim's concept of ritual lie in the ritual establishing a *shared focus* (the sacred object) within a group, and articulating *a particular mood* (a mental state). The ritual shows *respect* for the sacred object, and participants who do not show this respect will be (physically or symbolically) punished by the other participants. While Durkheim's work represents one of the very first theoretical treatments of religion and ritual, his theories were developed further, establishing a series of different understandings of ritual, following the major directions of social science: functionalism and structuralism.

Among the structuralists it is especially Arnold Van Gennep's (1960) invention of *rites de passage* which is of particular relevance. Van Gennep's sequential method studies a ritual in relation to what precedes and what follows it, thereby emphasizing aspects of past, present and future, a perspective on social practices and situations which Victor Turner (1995) later advanced.

Following Van Gennep, the English anthropologist Max Gluckman explored why some social relationships required rites of passage (Bell, 1997, p. 38). While Durkheim argued that the ritual is a projected expression of social cohesion and unity, Gluckman suggested that rituals are the expression of quite the opposite: of complex social tensions being negotiated and mediated. In other words, Durkheim emphasized the role of the ritual to maintain unity of a social group, whereas Gluckman defined rituals as a mechanism whereby social equilibrium and unity were constantly re-created.

The perhaps most influential theorist on ritual in contemporary social theory may be the British anthropologist Victor Turner. Combining Van Gennep's work on the structure of the ritual with Gluckman's work on the ritualization of social conflict, Turner (1995) developed his theory of structure and anti-structure. Turner argued that many rituals serve as *social dramas* whereby feelings of community (*communitas*) break through the established structures, in liminality. The term "limen" is Latin for "threshold" and with the liminal realm Turner describes an in-between space and time where the past is momentarily suspended and the future has not yet begun. In this process, he argues, social structures are transcended, accompanied by experiences that renew and redefine the social structures (Turner, 1983, p. 130). After the ritual, nothing is as before. The point is that social structure is not a static organization but a dynamic process, where rituals – performed as social dramas – serve not to restore a social equilibrium but to renew and redefine the social structure.

Ritual in modern social life

Turner (1983) makes an important distinction between rituals in traditional and modern societies. Whereas rituals in traditional agrarian cultures primarily work as a more or less institutionalized emotional confirmation of an existing social order, rituals in modern industrialized societies take place much more sporadically and are characterized by playful experimentation and often involve an element of social critique. Turner introduces the term "liminoid" to describe the ritual experience in modern societies, compared to the liminal experiences which are predominant in traditional societies. Liminal experiences tend to be collective, centrally integrated into the total social process, structured by collective symbols, and ultimately eufunctional. Liminoid experiences, on the other hand, are often individual, develop apart from central political process, are more idiosyncratic, and often contain social critique, exposing the injustices, immoralities etc. of the mainstream economic and political structures and organizations (pp. 157–158).

Turner emphasizes that both types of ritual experiences, liminal and liminoid, exist in modern societies. The point Turner wants to make is that the modern liminoid experience contains a transforming quality apart from the social and cultural confirming nature of the liminal experience.

The work of Erving Goffman contains an alternative view on what rituals are. In an attempt to "update" a Durkheimian definition of ritual to modern social life, Goffman (1967) suggested that in modern societies rituals do not mark a clear distinction between what is sacred and what is profane. But religious rituals, Goffman asserted, still exist, and it is the individual, the self, which is the sacred object: "in one sense this secular world is not so irreligious as we might think. Many gods have been done away with, but the individual himself stubbornly remains as a deity of considerable importance" (p. 95).

In what ways do Goffman's and Turner's concepts of ritual differ? The main difference, as we see it, is that Turner describes the liminoid experience in rituals as a suspension from an existing and constraining social order. Goffman, on the other hand, states that rituals in fact *are* the social order. Participating in rituals is not, Goffman would say, a withdrawal from the social world, but, on the contrary, an integration into it. Without competence in rituals, a both implicit and explicit knowledge of "how to do" rituals, access to the social world would be impossible. Rituals, then, are about positioning the self in the social world, regarded as a network of social relations.

So whereas Turner stresses the liminoid experience as an occasional suspension of social reality, rituals in Goffman's definition constitute social reality. We might illustrate the distinction between Turner's and Goffman's view on rituals in the following way:

Ritual as suspension	*Ritual as integration*
Individual	Social
Alternative reality	Social reality
Break from social position	Social positioning
Extra-ordinary	Ordinary
Occasional	Frequent

The problem with Goffman's concept of ritual is that it is almost all-embracing, and forces one to pose the question: what is *not* ritual? We return to this question later. In the following we will present some examples of how the concept of rituals has been applied by media researchers. Our point is that the concept is applied very much in the way Turner defines the concept. Our aim is to ask whether a Durkheimian and Goffmanian concept of ritual may be fruitful in understanding certain aspects of media use in daily life.

Ritual in media research

The concept of ritual is not a new phenomenon in communication studies. The distinction between communication as *transmission* and *ritual*, as suggested by Carey (1989), is perhaps the most well-known example. The role of communication in the ritual view is not transmission of information but confirmation (Carey, 1989, p. 19). Rather than changing people's beliefs, communication represents shared beliefs in society and plays an important role in a continuous confirmation of an underlying social and cultural order. According to Carey, rituals are not actions that are totally set apart from reality, but are constantly involved in defining and changing reality. Carey's concept of communication is not specifically directed toward analysis and he does not include a formal definition of what a ritual is.

For Roger Silverstone (1994) television viewing as ritual plays an important role in his theoretical attempt to understand the role of television in everyday life. Like Carey, Silverstone does not explicitly define what a ritual is, but he does apply the concept in a more narrow sense that makes it more operative in empirical analysis. Resembling Turner, Silverstone states that rituals take place as momentary suspensions of the ordinariness of everyday life. Opposed to the ordinariness of everyday life, a ritual marks a special space and time.

Silverstone, like Carey, stresses that even though rituals suspend the ordinariness of everyday life, rituals are *about* this ordinariness. The ordinariness, the culture of everyday life, is momentarily made into an object of reflection. Rituals, then, are not completely detached from everyday life, but are, on the contrary, a continuing reflection of one's place and position in it (Silverstone, 1994, p. 168).

The media have a role in these rituals because of their mythical quality. Previously, rituals took place in settings far removed for everyday life (e.g. churches, carnivals), but these highly charged ritual spaces have gradually been replaced by television because television is constantly representing reality in symbolic forms and thereby producing the raw material for reflection on the taken-for-grantedness of everyday culture (pp. 166–167).

It is the same line of thought that lies behind Klaus Bruhn Jensen's (1995) very clarifying distinction between "time-in" and "time-out" in everyday life (pp. 57–58). Time-in culture is the practical, action-oriented everyday life where structure and agency, in Giddens's (1984) terms, are incorporated in social action (Jensen, 1995, p. 57). Jensen defines time-out as "a separate social practice . . . which can be identified by social agents as such. It places reality on an explicit agenda as an object of reflexivity, and provides an occasion for contemplating oneself in a social, existential, or religious perspective" (p. 57).

Central to both Silverstone's and Jensen's assertions about the ritual role of mass media is that rituals and time-outs depend on establishing an attentive relationship between a "text" and a "reader." The media user literally steps out of everyday life into a realm where reality is represented in symbolic form, and that momentary suspension, of course, relies on a full attention to the content of the media, even though it may only be for a small period of time.

At this point, though, we would like to suggest other ritual uses of mass communication where the content of the medium (e.g. a television program) is not the main focus of attention. The US researcher Eric W. Rothenbuhler has thoroughly analyzed the ways in which anthropology has conceived of ritual, trying deliberately to draw the explanatory potential of ritual *vis-à-vis* everyday life over into the analysis of media uses. Our aim is, through Rothenbuhler, to advance the argument of ritual as social integration.

Ritualized media use

Eric Rothenbuhler's book *Ritual Communication: From Everyday Conversation to Mediated Ceremony* (1998) offers a very thorough analysis of the theories of ritual. Defining ritual, Rothenbuhler states: *"Ritual is the voluntary performance of appropriately patterned behavior to symbolically effect or participate in the serious life"* (p. 27). First of all, rituals are defined by their *formal qualities*, as either a way of doing things (ritual as adjective) or a type of thing done (ritual as noun). A multitude of markers together represent a systematic syntax that constitutes a ritual order of interaction. Among these markers may be different forms of media use. Ritual as noun refers to distinct events, for example the media events referred to by Dayan and Katz (1992). However, our interest lies mainly in ritual as adjective, focusing on the ritual aspects of everyday media use.

Rothenbuhler distinguishes very clearly between ritual and routine, emphasizing the participation in the serious life as the distinctive element which routines and habits do not contain: "Habits lack what energizes rituals: the purpose of symbolically effecting the serious life" (p. 28). Much media use is structured by habit, being far from ritual or even ritual-like. Thus, he opposes the notion of ritual as an empty convention, something that has lost its importance. However, he remains unclear as to how to distinguish the degree of seriousness of a particular social activity.

One indicator of seriousness lies in the "charging" of the situation. What is ritual in everyday life is a situation and an act which is charged by a larger order, or articulating a larger "feel." The situation is transformed into a Durkheimian *sacred object*, which each participant engages purposefully, thus transcending the particular situation. Recalling Van Gennep's *rites de passage*, and Turner's concept of *liminality*, "ritual action is action oriented toward transcendence of the particularities of the situation in which it is performed. A ritual situation is one constructed so as to offer transcendence of the particularities of the social circumstances surrounding it" (Rothenbuhler, 1998, p. 61).

This brings up two other characteristics: the voluntary aspect, and ritual as a customary behavior, governed by "oughts." The ritual participant agrees to enter and participate in a social order, accepting the rules of the game, despite the possible negative aspects of the ritual action. It may be necessary to pass through and participate in some particular ritual in order perhaps to obtain a different social role, a joint feeling of unity, or another state of mind. The ritual action is intentional action, performed, created, recreated and charged with a particular social meaning for a particular social group:

> The point is that people – both as individuals and institutions – are inventing rituals all the time, or at least they are ritualizing, that is, accentuating the ritual aspects of things. Indeed, if ritual is an element of all social action, then it is always there waiting to be accentuated, waiting for someone to invest their attention and make something more meaningful of the whole. At the level of institutions, this is just as reasonable and has yet further grounds.
> (Rothenbuhler, 1998, p. 51)

Recalling Van Gennep's sequential emphasis on past, present and future aspects of ritual, Rothenbuhler argues that ritual always refers both back (its symbolic meaning) and forth, toward the present situation and the social meaning the ritual is about to attribute to some performance. Thus, rituals are not suspensions but have communicative meaning in a continuous sequence of actions: "Ritual, then, is about both position in a cosmic order and alignment in a practical world" (p. 64).

In other words, and as a summary of Rothenbuhler's understanding of ritual, the ideal and the material unite in ritual action: "ritual is a communication device for uniting the ideal and the material, the general and the particular, the cosmic and the ordinary, the past and the future, the structures of history and the happenings of individual lives" (p. 64). This communicative device is characterized by many elements which can be summarized as: (1) ritual has external form; (2) ritual is socially integrative; (3) ritual is organized around a sacred object; (4) ritual provides a moral regulation of social activity; and (5) ritual transcends the particular social situation and links the ordinariness of everyday life with the larger cosmic aspects and meanings of life.

The immediate challenge that now arises is to try this concept out in practice. How do we operationalize the concept? Here, Rothenbuhler has less to offer. In his book, he offers some general suggestions, but leaves it to further empirical research to explore the validity of this approach.

In the following section we present two empirical examples of what we suggest is ritual action. The question is, of course, in what way can we regard them as rituals or ritualized behavior?

Media use as ritual: some empirical examples

The first empirical example is from a study on media use in everyday life in Denmark. It consists of focus group interviews, carried out with an "ethnographic" approach to media use, asking for the connections between media use and everyday life (Larsen, 1997).

In the following quote, an interviewee (Anna) employed the term "ritual" about her family's activities in the morning:

> We have exactly the same ritual every single morning. And mercy on the person who gets in the way for more than half a second. Because then, the time you have spared in the morning . . . I mean, morning activities are always carried out within a very tight schedule, especially if you have to leave the house at a certain time . . . and one of the first things that is done is that the radio is turned on.

Anna describes a typical morning situation where all the family members are very busy. Everybody has to be on time (school or work) so they all must keep a certain tempo in order to meet that demand. The use of radio in Anna's family has some very significant key characteristics. First, the radio is turned on *regularly* at the same time every morning, almost regardless of the content. Second the radio is an *integrated* part of a situation where listening to the radio is far from the only activity. Third, the radio is described as a *necessary* part of the situation, something that is hardly noticed when used, turned on almost automatically, but seriously missed if for some reason it is not there.

The next example stems from an audience ethnography conducted among four Brazilian families in the town of Porto Alegre. The fieldwork was conducted, periodically, over a two-year period (Tufte, 1998, 2001).

Marcia (29) and Yherar (26) are engaged and live together in a part-time manner, Yherar often spending time in Marcia's house. Marcia lives with her mother, Lorena Barcaro, in a flat in an upper-middle-class neighborhood in a big town in southern Brazil. Wanting to be together in their leisure time, Marcia and Yherar adapt to each other's interests and media preferences. This example illustrates how Yherar participates in Marcia's and her mother's media use.

Marcia is aware of Yherar's lack of interest in telenovelas, but nevertheless he does accompany her in exercising her media preferences. As Marcia states: "Novela, for example, he [Yherar] doesn't like much to watch, but he ends up watching." Yherar generally watches more television when in the Barcaro household than actually is his intent: "I see much more television there [with the Barcaros] than here [in his own family's flat]. It is because Marcia calls me in to watch. She likes novelas, she likes the 6 o'clock novelas, the 8 o'clock novelas, but I don't."

Yherar basically participates in this novela viewing for social reasons. He is in the living room during the novela screening "not because she [Marcia] calls, but because she and mostly her mother are there already. So I stay together with her. We are apart all week, so then we are together watching television and things. I have more time in the weekend" (Yherar).

Although the first example is about radio use and the second is about television use there are some characteristic similarities. First, the radio and the television are turned on *regularly* to the same programs at the same time every day. Second, both radio and television are used in *social settings*. Third, one can ask whether the specific *content* of the medium in these cases is the only reason for becoming engaged in media use. This is particularly the case for Yherar, who explicitly states that he doesn't like to watch telenovelas, but nevertheless does. In Anna's case it is hard to tell whether she is able to listen to the radio with undivided concentration for more than a few minutes, considering how busy she and her family are in the morning.

The point we want to make here is that the exact content of the medium and its connection to reasons for message consumption (e.g. for "pleasure" or "information") do not provide a satisfactory explanation of the media use. Media use is "more" than pure information chosen for rational reasons resulting in attentive relations between readers and texts. Few scholars would argue otherwise, but we make this statement here in order to stress the social implications of the media use: What, then, goes on in the examples we just quoted? What can explain Anna's and Yherar's behavior apart from the exact content of the medium? Rhetorically we ask: Is there a ritual going on? According to Anna there is. In Yherar's case, it is not stated explicitly, but we will try to show why we consider it a ritual.

Rituals are going on

If we look at Anna's mornings and Yherar's evenings, we might detect some elements that suggest that a ritual or at least ritualized behavior is actually taking place. First we could ask: Where is the ritual? Is getting up in the morning and getting ready for work not just sheer routine? And likewise, is throwing yourself onto the sofa in the living room next to your girlfriend every evening a ritual? In both cases we argue that it is not *only* routine, but also ritualized behavior. As noted earlier, rituals always, compared to routines, symbolically affect the serious life, and we believe that in these cases a ritual is going on that affects the social behavior of the co-present members of both Anna's and Yherar's families.

Serious life

A way to detect the ritual is to look for the sacred object. In Anna's case, the sacred object to be respected is best revealed in her expression of how violators of the morning ritual will be punished. She states: "mercy on the person that . . ." The important point to make is that radio is *not* the sacred object. The sacred object is, in the Goffmanian sense, the selves or the integrity of the co-present family members and the overall (social) situation. What is important, what has to be respected and protected, is a shared attention to a common goal: respect for the limited time that each family member has for preparing themselves for the day.

In Yherar's case his voluntary participation in the evening ritual in his girlfriend's family's home demonstrates his engagement in serious life. He dislikes telenovelas and generally does not watch a lot of television. Nevertheless, he enters into the living room and places himself on the sofa. The sacred object is definitely not the television and its content. His participation has to do with the "being together" – the family union in the living room. As with Anna's mornings, the sacred object in Yherar's evening is the integrity of (himself and) the co-present family members, and the overall situation. Yherar participates voluntarily, but his behavior also contains a degree of "I ought to" or "ought-ness." Sanctions will be imposed on him if he chooses not to participate.

The analysis of both cases can be pushed even further. If we ask *why* it is important to protect the integrity of the other family members, it becomes clear that it is Anna's family and Yherar's future family-in-law as concrete social units that are the sacred objects in these rituals. Because we can ask: What puts Anna in a position from where she is able to "punish" violators of the ritual? We believe that negative sanctions will (hypothetically speaking) refer to more or less implicit social obligations of family life and thereby to the violator's indifference to the maintenance of the family as a (in principle) lifelong project. Anna feels she is in a position where she would punish somebody who violates the ritual. Yherar clearly feels he would be punished if he avoided participation. Acting in accordance with the ritual works as a respectful integration into the larger project, the family project. In other words, what is going on in both rituals is a moral regulation of behavior, adjusted to the concrete situations that are implicitly recognized as rituals, rituals that in both cases integrate each member into the serious and socially obliged life of family membership. In the case of Yherar, the long-term perspective is very apparent: he seeks to integrate himself into the situation, on one hand probably pleasing his girlfriend and future mother-in-law, but also acting out a new social identity, investing himself and his self in the project of becoming a member of this family (as husband and son-in-law).

What would have happened if Yherar had chosen not to participate in the evening gathering in the living room, and instead had remained alone in the bedroom watching sport or doing something else? Non-participation in the family ritual could be interpreted as profane and provocative. Pushing it to the edge, it could lead to social disintegration *vis-à-vis* Yherar's relationship with Marcia and ultimately their breaking up. Or it would result in a very different evening situation, influencing the social relationships – these would thus be renegotiated, redefined.

It is very important to note that the family as a coherent unit is not a stable and pre-ordained construction. As Gluckman points out, rituals actually serve to create and re-create social units as coherent social groups and equalize tensions that are threatening the basis for social interaction within the group. The implication of this is that the members of Anna's family have ritualized their morning activities in order to balance tensions that might exist between family members, tensions which are momentarily put aside in order to meet the temporal demands in the mornings but also to symbolically maintain the family as a social unit. In this perspective it is clear that rituals integrate the particular with the general, serving both short-term and long-term purposes.

In the case of Yherar, his participation in the evening ritual definitely functions as socially integrative, by subduing his social practices to those of his girlfriend, Marcia, that again are linked to the presence of her mother, Lorena. Yherar integrates the social setting established by Marcia and her mother in the sofa corner of the living room, chatting and watching television. Giving up sports or homework in this particular moment in time and space is important for the larger project and for the maintenance of social equilibrium. As part of this social integration, he accepts Marcia's and Lorena's social and media practices, thus watching the 8 o'clock telenovela together with Marcia and Lorena. Obviously, his intention is to be especially with Marcia, so his social action is directed not necessarily towards watching television, but towards establishing a social relationship. It is thus his voluntary performance and intentional act to join Marcia and her mother in the living room.

In this light, participation in the ritual is a move towards establishing a social equilibrium, and the ritual becomes a moral regulator of social action – a regulatory process manifested as a negotiation or struggle between different interests, personalities and social identities. Possible tensions between the participants are reworked, smoothing out difficulties and establishing a mutually acceptable platform for social interaction.

Rites de passage

Both Anna's and Yherar's ritual might also be regarded as "rites de passage." Radio, seen in Anna's case, is widely used in the morning, both in private homes and in cars on the way to work places. It is evident that the radio plays an important role in the listeners' preparations for the public life they are about to enter when leaving the private household. Radio content (frequent traffic and weather updates, short news programs, sports, etc.) provides useful and instrumental information about the actual condition of the world "out there" on a particular day. But also the "feel" or the "pulse" of the radio (the music, the voice and tempo of the radio hosts, the pace of the programming, etc.) may constitute what Lull (1990, p. 35) has termed a "busy atmosphere" in the private home. The morning radio creates a space of action where the public (the radio programs) is interwoven into a private realm, (re-) introducing the pace and temporal pulse of everyday life. Radio thus plays a role in a necessary transformation from a private world of sleep into everyday consciousness. Turning on the radio is to "log on" to everyday life, an act of professionalization, adjusting one's behavior and mental state to the common social, temporal and spatial conditions of everyday life.

Similar characteristics can be drawn from Yherar's evening ritual, providing two perspectives affirming its role as a rite of passage. On one hand, it possesses elements similar to Anna's morning radio. The evening encounter of the family, talking, watching television and drinking coffee or eating by the sofa table constitutes a daily transition rite from public to private and from day to evening. Recalling Van Gennep's sequential understanding of rites of passage, this ritual occurs *after* work and other performance in public spheres and *before* withdrawing to the most private and intimate time and space of everyday life. Television, in particular the chosen content, the telenovela genre, is central in this transition process. The narrative – being repetitive in character, and with a very slow dramaturgical development – permits this. It sets a very relaxed pulse, establishes a collective audiovisual space, contributing to the formal setting of the ritual – a daily transition ritual, where rhythms and roles are transformed, revised, and particular social relationships and senses of belonging are reconfirmed.

On the other hand, this daily evening ritual is also a repeated ritual element in Yherar's long-term life project of moving from the status of an unmarried man to that of a married man. Yherar had at the moment of data collection been dating Marcia for three years, and after the completion of the data-collection they got engaged and planned a date for their wedding. Yherar's larger project is part of the basis upon which he acts also in the particular situation. His "voluntary performance of appropriately patterned behavior to symbolically effect or participate in the serious life" (Rothenbuhler, 1998, p. 27) has different levels or dimensions of seriousness. On one hand, the ritual helps regulate behavior and social relations in everyday life (as such constituting an immediate objective and aim of particular daily rituals). On the other hand, the rituals help regulate and develop social relations and social identities in a long-term perspective.

By participating in the evening ritual in the living room of his girlfriend's home, he is actively involved in identity work, preparing himself to become increasingly integrated into the family, and rehearsing and developing a social relationship to his future mother-in-law. This constitutes the longer-term perspective of the transition rite. It is practically impossible, in the ritual, to identify what social action relates to the immediate objective and what relates to the longer-term project inherent in everyday life. Both processes coexist. The agenda – what drives the action here – is not a suspension or non-suspension from everyday life, but a social project: wishing socially to relate (or not) with others.

Role of the media in the rituals

So far, we have argued that a ritual is taking place in both Anna's morning situation and Yherar's evening situation. However, do the radio or the television have any significance at all? Or could these media, in principle, be replaced by the washing machine? We argue that what makes the morning situation in Anna's family a ritual, and what makes the evening situation in Yherar's case a ritual too, is the fact that the co-present persons organize their behavior according to a sacred object. If we follow Durkheim's definition of ritual, we are able to identify the possible functions of the medium in each of these two rituals. As Durkheim states, the ritual has three characteristic elements: a *common focus*, a *common mood* and a *common space* (e.g. a church). We argue that in the micro-social setting of everyday life these elements are constituted in social interaction, and that the media use sometimes plays a part in the constitution of ritual settings – like the radio in Anna's mornings or the television in Yherar's evenings.

Anna states that one of the first things that is done in the morning is that the radio is turned on. The radio works as a kind of aural "boundary marker," a sound that demarcates that a certain activity has begun and gives the morning activities an overall episodic character with beginnings and ends (Larsen, 1998). The radio not only works as a temporal marker, but is simultaneously playing a part in establishing the setting for social integration. Turning on the radio is information "given off," a way of indirectly expressing a certain condition for the ongoing social interaction. In this perspective radio can be said to institute the ritual. It does so by demarcating a ritual space, transforming the physical surroundings in the private home into a specific symbolic space with certain (and in this case, implicit) behavioral rules that organize the action of the family members. The sheer sound from the radio informs the members that the daily ritual has begun. And, in the Durkheimian sense, it is the radio that, among other things, establishes and maintains each member's focus on their activities. The continual sound of the radio, then, both institutes and constantly reminds the co-present members of the family about the current conditions for social behavior. The radio, in other words, serves as a constant reminder of the fact that the activities are carried out within a larger framework of a ritual. In this respect we would say that radio plays an important role in ritualizing the morning situation.

In the case of Yherar, he enters into a living room where a pre-established mood, an aural boundary marker, already exists. The television contributes to the configuration of this symbolic space in various ways: (1) the sounds of the telenovela with their significant radiophonic sound track; (2) the large degree of visual images from domestic settings running across the screen; and (3) the repetitive narrative and slow dramaturgical rhythm (Tufte, 2000). All these aspects form part of establishing the boundaries, in time and space, of this symbolic sphere where a ritual is taking place.

The rules prevailing in this symbolic space have to do, among many other things, with the lifelong tradition and trajectory of telenovela watching in the family. The genre is very well known to Marcia and Lorena, less to Yherar. The common focus is the social relation and family unity, a focus emphasized by the large degree of domesticity and family life performed in the narrative. The family project is emphasized by the genre. Thus, we can say that the television, and especially the particular genre on the screen, contributes to the ritualization of this evening situation. Imagine what would happen if the television was turned off!

In summary, and referring to Durkheim, we would argue that the radio in Anna's case and the television in Yherar's case are not the sacred objects in the rituals we have analyzed. But we claim that these media play important parts in establishing the rituals as regular and regulating phenomena in Anna's and Yherar's social lives, although in slightly different ways. The sound of the radio and both the sound and images from the television organize the attention of the family members, and this attention is not necessarily directed towards the content of the programs, but towards the concrete social situation. The medium, we argue, creates a common mood that directs the family members' attention toward the sacred object: the family as a social unit that constantly has to be respected and protected, among other things through everyday life.

Conclusion and perspectives

In this chapter we have argued that the concept of ritual is a useful analytical route to understand some aspects of media use in everyday life.

We apply a concept of ritual that primarily stresses the social functions of rituals in daily life. This conceptualization differs from the notion that ritual is a momentary suspension of everyday life, turning everyday life into an object of reflection. By comparison, our definition of ritual stresses the "time-in" of everyday life, where the ritual is not a moment of suspension but rather a moment of social integration, affecting the serious life of the intersubjective world. This is not to say that one definition is necessarily wrong or that one form excludes the other. We believe that these two forms of ritual coexist in everyday life. Watching television with family members may be a ritualized act that symbolically integrates each member into the family as a social institution, (re-) establishing each member's place and position in it. But this ritual may coincide with occasional ritual "time-outs" from the situation, maybe triggered by the content of the television program.

The concept of ritual that we apply cannot account for the meaning-making processes related to media use. But we argue that from an ethnographic point of view some apparently irrational aspects of media use might be explained with the concept of ritual that we apply: for example the regularity of media use and the fact that people use media with content they do not attend to, or simply dislike. The point is that hours are spent with media in everyday life, and that far from all kinds of media uses can be explained with reference to the content by suggesting more or less instrumental use values. The regularity of media use might be explained with reference to ontological security, the constant reconstruction of reality as a stable and predictable "place to be." But we argue for a closer look at these apparently trivial aspects of media use in everyday life by suggesting that media use plays a part in establishing settings for everyday rituals. This is important because these rituals transcend the particularities of the situation and relate the participants to an overall social and cultural order *and* position each participant within the social group. This view on everyday behavior as saturated with rituals of social integration and positioning might explain some of the more (at first sight) ephemeral and unimportant media uses.

As media ethnographers, if we regard media use as a means of creating ritual spaces and times in everyday life, and if we ethnographically seek out those "sacred objects" that are not necessarily mediacentric, we might be able to detect how media use is deeply involved in the moral regulation of everyday behavior in social situations. The media are interwoven into daily practices and, as we argue, everyday rituals, creating moods and frames that define inter-actional conditions for co-present participants. These interactional conditions are not only practical but relate to and are ruled by "sacred objects" that exceed the current situation. The ritual creates a larger feel, a feeling of something that exceeds the individual and connects the individual to society, re-establishing and/or redefining its position in it. Following this line it is everyday rituals, with or without the media, that hold society and cultures together: the constant regulation of behavior that connects individuals to a social world where one's position is constantly being reconfirmed and negotiated.

Ritual, then, is certainly about identity, the feeling and sense of self in the social world, not only on a reflexive level, but on an everyday level where participation in rituals unnoticed places oneself within a cultural order – a position that might also be negotiated and resisted. One could argue that the feeling of self and integrity in the social world is a continuous project that is in part articulated in everyday rituals. Participation in rituals is entering the serious social world of moral obligations, or as Rothenbuhler (1998) puts it, the world of "oughts" (p. 5). The social world is not a "free world" in the sense that each individual can do whatever she or he wishes to do. On the contrary, it is almost impossible to go about in the social world without participating in rituals that constantly define one's place and position. The feeling of self, the feeling of "me," might stem from one's ability to resist or redefine these positions: the ability to express individuality in a world that is constantly reshaped through everyday ritual.

This is not to say that rituals are "bad," restraining people to a pre-given moral world. First, rituals are devices to manage the chaos of the social world. Rituals provide order, predictability, sense and obligation to social life. Second, if rituals are a way of constituting social order then the social order, consequently, can be changed through rituals, both confirming and commenting on social reality.

Reinterpreting media use from the perspective of rituals can help increase the attention towards cultural, national and historical similarities and differences. The perspective of rituals enables researchers to identify what initially may seem to be banal and peripheral as highly charged rituals that stem from non-verbalized and taken-for-granted cultural beliefs within a culture. What is taken for granted – as a sacred object – within one culture may not be taken for granted within another culture, and the concept of ritual can be a very useful tool to identify the culturally informed motives behind actions which may not be explained in interviews because the motives are not recognized by the interviewee. In other words, the researcher should look for sacred objects within a specific culture, sacred objects that might be universal or might be a characteristic and defining element within a specific culture.

In a globalized world, political and cultural discourses flow and change more rapidly than ever, and no doubt affect how we think and live our culture in the broad sense of the word. Ritual behaviour, we argue, is an important object of analysis because it enables us to identify to what extent local, regional or national cultures are influenced by global culture – not on the level of discourse, but on the level of action.

References

Bell, C. (1997). *Ritual: Perspectives and dimensions*. Oxford: Oxford University Press.

Carey, J. W. (1989). *Communication as culture. Essays on media and society* [1975]. New York: Routledge.

Dayan, D. and Katz, E. (1992). *Media events: The live broadcasting of history*. Cambridge: Harvard University Press.

Durkheim, E. (1995). *The elementary forms of religious life* [1912]. New York: Free Press.

Gluckman, M. (1962). *Essays on the ritual of social relations*. Manchester: Manchester University Press.

Gluckman, M. (1963). *Order and rebellion in tribal Africa*. New York: Free Press.

Goffman, E. (1967). *Interaction ritual: Essays on face-to-face behavior*. Cambridge: Pantheon.

Jensen, K. B. (1995). *The social semiotics of mass communication*. London: Sage.

Larsen, B. S. (1997). Media use and everyday life. In J. Koivisto and E. Lauk (eds), *Journalism at the crossroads: Perspectives on research*. Tartu: University of Tartu, University of Tampere.

Larsen, B. S. (1998). Media situations: A situational view on media use in everyday life. In *Sekvens 98, Dept of Film and Media Studies: Audiovisual media in transition*. Copenhagen: University of Copenhagen.

Larsen, B. S. (2000). Radio as ritual: An approach to everyday use of radio. *Nordicom Review* 21(2), 259–274.

Lull, J. (1990). The social uses of television. In J. Lull (ed.), *Inside family viewing: Ethnographic research on television's audiences*. London: Routledge.

Rothenbuhler, E. W. (1998). *Ritual communication: From everyday conversation to mediated ceremony*. Thousand Oaks, CA: Sage.

Silverstone, R. (1994). *Television and everyday life*. London: Routledge.

Tufte, T. (1998). Local lives, global media, multiple identities: Gaucho lives between Chimarrao and cable television. In *Sekvens 98, Dept of Film and Media Studies: Audiovisual media in transition*. Copenhagen: University of Copenhagen.

Tufte, T. (2000). *Living with the rubbish queen: Telenovelas, culture and modernity in Brazil*. Luton: University of Luton Press.

Tufte, T. (2001). Gauchos going global: A critical assessment of cultural globalization. In U. Kivikuru (ed.), *Contesting the frontiers: Media and dimensions of identity*. Göteborg: NORDICOM.

Turner, V. (1995). *The ritual process: Structure and antistructure* [1969]. New York: Aldine de Gruyter.

Turner, V. (1983). Liminal to liminoid, in play, flow and ritual: An essay in comparative symbology. In J. C. Harris and R. J. Park (eds), *Play, games and sports in cultural contexts*. Champaign, IL: Human Kinetics Publishers, Inc.

Van Gennep, A. (1960). *The rites de passage* [1929]. Chicago: University of Chicago Press.

Part III

RESEARCHING THE LOCAL

7

NEGOTIATION
AND POSITION

On the need and difficulty of developing
"thicker descriptions"

Fabienne Darling-Wolf

Multiple selves in theory

Scholars who have attempted to examine the complexity of individuals' lives have come to the conclusion that we all embody multiple selves (Caplan, 1988; Narayan, 1989; Skeggs, 1995). Not all of these selves, however, have equal value – or consequences – as far as our research is concerned. For instance, my position as a white European has generally proven a lot more politically compromising in conducting feminist research among Japanese women than my position as a woman. Indeed, Western scholars have been charged with constructing women from other cultural environments, Asian women in particular, as less feminist and more oppressed than their Western counterparts – asserting their own cultural superiority in the process. Aihwa Ong (1988) maintains that feminist academics tend to impose Western standards of evaluation on non-Western women and display little interest in exploring indigenous constructions of gender and sexuality. She argues that non-Western women's speech is consequently inscribed into the context of Western feminist scholarship, placing them in a position of subordination in feminist theoretical and textual productions. This tendency has certainly colored Western accounts of Japanese women's lives, as many have perpetuated the common stereotype of Japanese culture as particularly oppressive to women, and of Japanese women themselves as struggling to "catch up" with their more feminist Western "sisters" (see, for example, Condon, 1985).

Attempts by white Western feminist scholars to "give a voice" to women of a different cultural or racial background have similarly frequently resulted in reductionist and essentializing notions of identity developed in the process of searching for an "authentic" cultural Other (Callaghan, 1995; Sawhney, 1995). As Susan Stanford Friedman (1995) notes, "At its most extreme this embrace [of "other" women] tends toward a fetishization of women of color that once again reconstitutes them as other caught in the gaze of white feminist desire" (p. 11). But because the very structure of institutionalized academic production is itself implicated in systems of domination and subordination around the world, this potentially problematic position does not only apply to white Western scholars. It extends, at least to some degree, to all researchers located within the confines of the Western academic environment (Bauer, 1995; Ganguly, 1992). Rey Chow notes, for instance, that the activities of Chinese academics are sometimes less tied to oppressed women in China than to their own careers in the West. As she writes, "If it is true that 'our' speech takes its 'raw materials' from the suffering of the oppressed, it is also true that it takes its capital from the scholarly tradition, from the machineries of literacy and education, which are affordable only to a privileged few" (Chow, 1993, p. 114).

This critique has been particularly relevant to feminist anthropologists and ethnographers who have had to recognize the fact that the very structural features of their discursive practice necessarily create problematic power relationships between the privileged researcher, generally located in the West, and her subaltern subject. In the context of fieldwork, for instance, feminist ethnographers often find themselves directly confronted with the difficulty of negotiating their feminist sensibilities against the backdrop of a different cultural and/or socio-economic environment. Patricia Zavella speaks of her struggle with her academic feminist Chicana identity while conducting research among working-class women. She found herself confronted with her informants' rejection of the feminist label as white-identified, and their desire to construct their own identities in ways that appeared politically unpalatable to her (Zavella, 1996). Lila Abu-Lughod (1993) faced a similar dilemma in her interactions with Bedouin women, as she struggled to reconcile her feminist politics with some of the cultural practices she witnessed and in which her informants willingly engaged.

Because of this complex process of negotiation, the relationship between feminism and ethnography has frequently been described as inescapably caught in webs of betrayal and exploitation (Behar, 1993; Stacey, 1988), or at best – in Marilyn Strathern's much-cited article – awkward (Strathern, 1987). This awkwardness, however, has much less to do with feminism than with the process of conducting research. All research is necessarily situated and consequently runs the risk of betrayal. As Pat Caplan (1988) reminds us, what we find depends on the questions we ask and on the angle of vision from which we approach our material. It simply becomes most obvious in feminist ethnography because of feminism's stated political position and critique of objectivity (i.e. because feminism never pretended *not to be* situated) and ethnography's involvement with actual people in actual places (people who, unlike texts and statistics, can fight back). The awkwardness of the relationship between feminism and ethnography is, however, a useful awkwardness. It helps us understand how much our own experiences might influence the way we approach and conduct our research, requires us to recognize representation as both a political and an epistemological problem, and forces us to face the complexity of identity formation. It encourages us, in other words, to address on a practical as well as a theoretical level the aforementioned recognition that we all embody multiple and fragmented selves (Abu-Lughod, 1991).

Multiple selves in practice

It is with those theoretical issues in mind that I embarked on eight months of fieldwork in a small southern Japanese village. Like many researchers before me, I was quickly confronted with the complexity of my own position, as well as that of my informants' often seemingly contradictory identities. The circumstances through which I had come to do research in this particular place at this particular time, the specific history I shared with the women who became my informants, the new trajectories our relationships took through the course of my stay, all influenced the way my research developed and the final written product of my work.

Particularly significant was the fact that I had a chance to experience what became my field site as two different selves. My partner and I had lived in the village for about a year as English teachers three years before returning to conduct my study. At the time, I knew very little of the Japanese cultural environment and did not speak much of the language. Functioning in the village was at times a struggle. I had to learn to deal with the complete lack of privacy (the doors of our house had no locks and our neighbors enjoyed paying us visits at all hours of day and night), with the complex social rules of this small rural community, with the animosity of some and the overwhelming generosity of others. I even had to learn to plant potatoes the Japanese way! It was also the most rewarding experience of my life. The relationships I developed and the feeling of "belonging" I eventually reached left me wanting to come back.

When I started graduate school the year after returning from Japan, I decided to focus my research on this fascinating cultural environment that I felt I had only got a glimpse of during my months in the village. I chose the village as my field site because I felt that my partner and I had experienced a considerable amount of involvement in the daily lives of our friends and neighbors there. We had been frequently invited into people's homes, and allowed to participate in many of the significant events of the Japanese year, including the greatly awaited October festival that is the pride of the village. I believe this possibly unusual – at least for a foreign English teacher – amount of participation in the life of this community was facilitated by the rural environment and by the fact that our house, generously lent by a friend, was located in the middle of the densely laid-out village. This location made us a particularly visible target, as the only *gaijin* around, of our neighbors' curiosity and interest. Also helpful was the fact that our 100-year-old Japanese-style house was particularly decrepit and had no hot water, heating, or indoor plumbing, which brought us a considerable

111

amount of sympathy and respect for the fact that we should be able to handle this most extreme case of "*tatami* life."[1]

So I did return to our house in the village, but as a different person. I was now equipped with a theoretical knowledge of Japanese culture and history, with a working knowledge of the Japanese language, and with a specific agenda as a researcher. I developed new relationships with women I had interacted with before, and with some I had never met. I decided to let these relationships develop naturally and give my friends a chance to share their world with me before proactively attempting to explore their negotiation of media images – the topic I most wanted to address. Two three-generational families became particularly involved in my research, giving me a chance to share their daily lives. These women and their circle of friends and extended family provided me with the insights that would constitute the bulk of my research. They became my "key" informants in all matters related to the Japanese media, the conceptions of female attractiveness I wanted to explore, the Japanese culture, and a vast number of other topics unrelated to my research. Elizabeth Chiseri-Strater and Bonnie Sunstein (1997) define informants as people who guide researchers and help explain their culture. This is the role these women took upon themselves to play. But in the process of opening up their daily world to me, they did a lot more than describe a specific cultural environment. As we shared work and leisure, stressful and happy moments, my informants revealed a lot of themselves, and taught me about the complexity of the process of identity formation – a process complex no matter what cultural environment one evolves in.

Interacting with these individuals on a daily basis again also highlighted the complexity of my position in this community, by then familiar. While clearly an outsider in terms of race and cultural origin, I found my status within the village frequently blurred along other dimensions. My various selves worked for or against my inclusion within the group of women I conducted research with in various situations and at different points in time.

For instance, my status as a married woman – whose husband was also known in the community through his teaching – granted me a certain level of acceptance among women defining themselves as housewives.[2] When I interviewed these women's unmarried daughters, however, it became more of a detriment than an asset. My status as a graduate student generally facilitated my interactions with lower-class and younger women, but diminished my credibility among older upper-class informants. Because my husband and I were returning to a village where we had previously lived, we also acquired a paradoxical status as the village's outsiders. We were certainly *gaijin*,[3] but not any *gaijin*. We were THE *gaijin*, living in the "*gaijin*" house" – as the house where we lived had been known since our last stay. People welcomed us back into their homes with open arms and we did not have to go through the "warm up" period we had experienced during our first stay.

My status as a relative insider within certain groups of individuals in the village further evolved over time. For instance, when I became pregnant toward the end of my stay in the village, I suddenly reached a new level of "insiderness" among the women with whom I interacted on a daily basis. Women who were mothers shared stories of pregnancy and labor and provided childrearing advice. Younger women touched with excitement my growing belly and compared my physical evolution to their older friends' or siblings'. Female informants volunteered to take me to the hospital for check-ups and showered me with a variety of homemade morning sickness remedies. Thus, the common experience of this biological process was able to reduce to some extent the distance created by my different racial and cultural backgrounds.

My class position and education levels were other axes on which my insider/outsider status was determined as I spent considerable amounts of time with two families from very different socio-economic backgrounds. Whereas my level of consumption while in Japan on a meager graduate student fellowship was lower than most of my informants', I was "upper-class" in many other respects. Not only did I carry a laptop computer around, but I also knew how to use it to stay in contact with other individuals for whom owning a computer was also a normal part of life. I had traveled to and lived in numerous places that most of my lower-class informants could only dream of, and strongly felt the privilege of my position when asked to talk about them. In other words, despite my informants' awareness of my low income level – and despite the fact that I was raised in a rural working-class household – my current education level combined with my position as a researcher, even if only a graduate student, made me an outsider in terms of class among my informants of a lower socio-economic background.

On the other hand, I may not have had the right income level, but I had enough cultural capital to "pass" within the upper strata of the village's society. My level of education and the fact that I am familiar with several cultures allowed me to feel generally comfortable in the households of my upper-class informants, despite their clear awareness that my economic standing was not nearly as high as theirs, even when back in the United States. I could hold conversations with my friend Takako[4] about the best places to visit in Paris or New York, and knew what fork to eat with when she took me to fancy French restaurants. But when Takako's oldest daughter, Mako, came to visit from Tokyo, I suddenly became aware of my lower-class status in the presence of this very successful urban woman five years younger than I am, who regularly travels around the world staying in the best hotels and works in an office on Harajuku, one of Tokyo's busiest business streets. Even Takako suddenly looked more "rural" in the presence of her assertive urban daughter.

All this illustrates the fact that our position as researchers is much more complex than suggested by the insider/outsider dichotomy. As Kirin Narayan observes, "the loci along which we are aligned with or set apart from those we study are multiple and in flux. Factors such as education, gender, sexual orientation, class, race, or sheer duration of contacts may at different times outweigh the cultural identity we associate with insider or outsider status"

(Narayan, 1989, p. 23). In order to develop a more sophisticated understanding of the potential influence of our own position on our research, we must explore our "multiplex subjectivity" (Rosaldo, 1989, pp. 168–195) and, to borrow Zavella's words, "realize we are almost always simultaneously insiders and outsiders and discuss what this means for our particular research projects" (Zavella, 1996, p. 141).

Some individuals may, however, find this realization easier to negotiate because of the specific circumstances of their everyday lives "back home." As Narayan notes, these multiple planes of identification may, for instance, be most painfully highlighted among anthropologists who have identities spanning racial or cultural groups. I believe that my experience as a French woman originally from a working-class rural background living in the urban United States married to a Ukrainian Canadian has contributed to my coming to terms with the multiple selves constituting my identity. I never experienced my outsider status more strongly than when I came back to the United States after living in Japan for the first time. Having grown tired of the stares and extreme reactions that my different racial and cultural identity frequently occasioned in the village, I was eager to return home – only to find out that wherever I went people asked me where I was from and would not take the United States for an answer, even though it is the place where I have spent all of my adult life.[5]

The insights gained through such experiences should not, however, be overestimated. They should not blind us to the ways in which we – whoever we may be – are all implicated in multiple flows of power and systems of domination (Friedman, 1995). No matter how much of an "insider" we might feel we are at different points in our research, some aspects of our identity – if only the status of researcher – removes us from our informants' experiences. In other words, we must consider the factors blurring our understanding of our informants' lives as well as those contributing to it, the dimensions which make us potential oppressors as well as potentially oppressed.

My selves in a small Japanese village

In what ways, then, was my research among rural Japanese women influenced by my multiple identities as a female, French, living in the US, white, middle-class, heterosexual, feminist, young, married, graduate student – to name only a few of the selves that come readily to mind? To some extent, it is impossible for me to know, and I can only hope that a recognition – as honest as I can possibly produce it – of the position from which my work was conducted might inspire others to help me identify my most troublesome blind spots. I can also hope that taking this specific position into consideration, others will find my work useful, however situated it may be. There are nevertheless a few areas of my research on which I might suggest the filter of my multiple selves may have had a particularly powerful distorting effect.

Race is an obvious one. As, literally, one of the only two *gaijin* living in the village, I found myself particularly conscious of my whiteness throughout the course of my fieldwork. While my own relationship toward the color of my skin and my informants' reaction to it certainly evolved over the course of my stay, I was nevertheless reminded of my racial identity on a regular basis when participating in the daily life of the village.[6] This consciousness was exacerbated by the fact that issues of racial representation were at the core of my research on (Westernized) representations of female attractiveness in the Japanese media.

It was indeed when my informants and I talked about ideals of feminine beauty and their construction in Japanese popular cultural texts that I most strongly felt the significance of my skin pigmentation. I was faced, for instance, with the possibility that my racial identity might influence my informants' proclaimed opinions about the value of Westernized physical traits. Were the women I interviewed identifying such traits as particularly desirable simply because of my presence among them? In this case, the larger cultural environment and the everyday experience of living in the village provided clues to the sincerity of my informants' assertions. Women in the village not even remotely involved in my research frequently commented on how "beautiful" I was.[7] One such comment even occurred when I was bathing at one of the village's numerous hot springs, as a young woman approached me to express her belief that "all *gaijin* have really good bodies" – a statement clearly not empirically supported by my then four months pregnant (and starting to show) far-from-perfect naked body. The fact that the types of cosmetic surgery most popular in Japan are those designed to remove signs of Asian racial identity – such as eyelid or nose surgery – and my informants' otherwise negative attitude toward the presence of white Westerners in the pages of women's magazines provided additional clues that this may not be all about me.

More significant, and more potentially problematic, is the role my Caucasian racial identity might have played in influencing the way *I* interpreted my informants' relationship toward the imagery surrounding them. Throughout my stay in Japan, I struggled to embrace the complexity of this relationship and attempted to resist jumping to simplistic and essentializing conclusions potentially influenced by my position as a white feminist trained in a Western academic culture. The extent to which I succeeded in this task is yet to be determined and is open for debate with other scholars (and ordinary people) differently situated.

There are, however, a few instances in which I clearly remember using my personal experience as a guide to interpretation. I tended, for instance, to liken my informants' situation as women living in one of the most rural areas of Japan to my experience growing up in one of the most rural areas of France with a similar density of population. My Japanese friends' attitudes toward religion reminded me of attitudes I frequently observed in my culture of origin, where religious rituals have more cultural than spiritual meanings. I felt that I could relate to these women's experience of American movies or television programs having grown up in a cultural environment similarly invaded by such foreign texts. While these comparisons may have enhanced in some respects my understanding of the Japanese cultural environment, they are also admittedly limited and potentially misleading. One might argue for instance that it is unfair to compare the culture of a nation with a long violent history of colonialism to that of a culture which, despite its own colonialist bouts, actually exhibits many of the characteristics of a postcolonial nation. Furthermore, my own experience of American cultural influence while growing up in France was not complicated by racial difference, as my informants' was.

Our multiple selves, however, are all we have to help us understand and interpret a particular situation. Shying away from attempting to develop an understanding of other people in other places because of our fear of committing mistakes would be just as damaging as the mistakes we might commit (Alcoff, 1995; Elam, 1995). But we do need to recognize that we cannot represent reality totally, but can only produce partial, situated, truths (Abu-Lughod, 1991), and that our accounts of the world and ourselves are always necessarily incomplete descriptions rather than unmediated representations (Ganguly, 1992). Truths, however, are not rendered useless because admittedly partial and situated. As Lila Abu-Lughod (1991) reminds us, long-term processes are manifested locally and specifically, produced in the actions of individuals living their particular lives.

Developing thicker descriptions

Having recognized the complexity and significance of the researcher's position on the research process and production of academic texts, the next step is to do similar justice to our informants' position. In their attempts to address the epistemological difficulty of embracing difference, feminist scholars have come to the realization that we need to examine the various influences on people's experiences – or various sets of oppression – in relationship rather than addition to each other (Bow, 1995; Harding, 1995). This theoretical recognition has, however, proven difficult to put into practice, particularly by communication scholars. For instance, while Western feminist attempts to address the relationship between media and consumers in the form of "audience studies" have usefully challenged the notion that female readers are simply "cultural dopes" uncritically consuming media promoting an oppressive dominant ideology, these analyses nevertheless often fail to embrace fully the complex nature of identity formation. Audience studies are typically caught in a domination vs. resistance dichotomy, which prevents them from adequately addressing this complexity.

Some media scholars have certainly attempted to include several dimensions of women's experiences into their analyses – such as race and/or class – but have generally failed to truly examine these dimensions in relationship to each other. For instance, in her study of tabloid newspapers, Elizabeth Bird (1992) mentions the middle-class perception of tabloids and their readers as "trash" and includes a disturbing description of tabloid readers by middle-class informants as lower-class, female, and overweight. While she recognizes the obvious class stereotype in this description, she fails to relate it specifically to gender stereotyping and acknowledge how lower-class status intersects with gender to create oppressive representations of femininity specific to working-class females. Similarly, Andrea Press (1991) tends to rank forms of oppression in her argument that working-class women exhibit more class-specific readings of television while middle-class women exhibit more gender-specific ones. Her concept of "dual" oppression implies a problematic additive model. Press also fails to recognize that white working-class women might experience their class status differently from members of minority groups.

Even Janice Radway (1984) fails to address significant dimensions of women's lives. In the introduction to the second edition of her book *Reading the Romance*, she regrets having focused only on white middle-class women in her study, consequently missing important insights on how race or class might affect women's interpretation of romance novels. While greater racial diversity would have given her study more depth, Radway seems to forget in her comment that white middle-class women also have a race and a class (and a sexual orientation, and an age, and a degree of ability and a religious orientation and so on . . .) and that she could have paid attention to these even with her white informants rather than contribute to the stereotype that white middle-class women are "the norm" and consequently unaffected by such factors.[8]

In her article on the tension between issues of resistance and domination Sherry Ortner (1995) maintains that such studies suffer from "cultural thinning" (p. 180) and argues for a return to "thick ethnography" (p. 176) as a means to explore more fully the multiple and often contradictory selves that our informants embody. But how are we, as media scholars, to develop these thicker descriptions?

One thing we can do is move away from the texts we study to focus more deeply on our informants themselves, and the larger environment in which they evolve. By identifying a text to analyze, and then locating an audience for this text, analyses of media interpretation tend to keep the text as the focus of attention. While most studies do recognize the intertextual characteristics of media environments, few actually attempt to fully address how the fact that cultural texts often respond to each other might affect consumers' interpretation – or the possibility that it may be impossible to separate a text from its environment. I have argued elsewhere that the Japanese cultural environment beautifully illustrates the problematic nature of this separation (Darling-Wolf, 2000). Indeed, I quickly realized upon returning to the village that my informants' consumption of a specific cultural text could not in any way be separated from the rest of the extremely commercial media environment in which this consumption took place. My informants bought magazines because they had their favorite star on the cover, watched a specific television show because it featured their favorite singer, or bought a song because it was sung by a famous actor. The imagery I wanted to analyze was present everywhere in my informants' cultural environment – from subway stations to magazines read at the hairdresser – and it is within this much larger context that interpretation and negotiation took place.

Furthermore, placing the text at the center of analysis tends to *assume* the centrality of media representations in identity construction. In such a case, informants are perceived of as viewers or readers of a text – and their responses interpreted in relationship to this text – rather than as complex individuals with multiple identities. Hence the difficulty of addressing the complexity of sets of interlocking influences which informants may not necessarily relate to their media consumption. In order to add depth to our descriptions, we need to place *people* at the center of our research and let them connect their experiences to the text, if that is what they choose to do.

We also need to get involved in all aspects of our informants' lives to avoid too narrowly focusing on the topic at hand. I have often found that it is in the context of participant observation rather than in the course of interviewing that multiple selves and contradictions emerge. I had the opportunity to conduct in-depth interviews with twenty-nine women during my stay in Japan. But it is six individuals whose daily family lives I shared and who took it upon them-selves to educate me about their cultural environment who provided me with the most fruitful insights regarding the specific environment in which they evolved. While my conversations with other women were a useful means of contextualizing my key informants' words, sitting on the living room floor of the Yamaguchi house shelling beans in the middle of the night while talking about the latest television show, watching the New Year's Eve specials with the Suzuki family before getting up to ring the temple bell, or comparing body parts at the spa with my young friends Chieko and Yukiko greatly aided my efforts to locate my research in its proper context.

I am not arguing here for a simplistic return to the classic "native's point of view." Nor did I attempt in my research simply to give my informants a "voice." Neither of these concepts fully do justice to the *participant* in participant observation. The process of participant observation is a complex process of negotiation through which informant and researcher engage in a dialogue in order to attempt to understand more fully a particular situation at a particular point in time. In this process, the informant's understanding may be affected as well as the researcher's. For instance, Takako Suzuki and I frequently engaged in discussions over the meaning of culture. One day, as she talked about tea ceremony and flower arrangement, I picked up a small rubber Pikachu – the pocket monster – from a small basket of knick-knacks on the table in front of us. Holding it up, I shared my own understanding of culture – influenced by my involvement in cultural studies and other theoretical ventures – stating that "*this* is Japanese culture." She replied that she could not accept such an interpretation of her cultural environment. Weeks later, as I was hanging out with Takako's daughter, she commented that her mother had found the idea of Pikachu as the prime representative of Japanese culture particularly exciting. Today, the shelves of my office are stacked with the Pikachu figures Takako sends me on a regular basis.

Similarly, through the process of participant observation, one does more than simply give a voice to those being observed – unless "voice" is extremely loosely interpreted. What are we to do, for instance, when our informants' actions and behaviors contradict their statements? For example, while Takako often spoke about her lack of care about her appearance, she also spent hundreds of dollars every month on outfits and frequently commented on how many calories she had ingested after a good meal. In this case, voice can only fully embrace multiple selves and contradiction if it is rather fragmented and possibly incoherent. The concept of "giving a voice" suggests a somewhat dishonest lack of interpretation. It is impossible in the process of conducting and writing research to avoid being confronted with the need to provide interpretation. What we *can* do as researchers is acknowledge the moments when such interpretation takes place and highlight the contradictory factors having led us to a particular understanding of a situation:

> The result can be a textualization of the field experience that not only makes more explicit how researchers study and interpret popular culture but also the possibilities of rigorous, thick descriptions of fundamental ethnographic concerns (e.g. historical context, economic struggles, social reality, cultural practices) about the people who constitute the audience.
>
> (Murphy, 1999, p. 500)

Embracing complexity

Finally, once multiple selves and contradictions do arise, we need to attempt to embrace them, deal with complexity, and resist the temptation to make our informants' experiences neatly fit within our own pre-defined categories. This, again, is much easier said than done, and I certainly cannot claim to have always succeeded in doing so in my own research. Things in reality are often more complicated than in theory. The neat categories developed in academic research – gender, race, class, sexual orientation – are shifting and evolving.

For instance, because representations of female attractiveness are generally based on an upper-class model, one of the goals of my research was to explore how women's socio-economic background might influence their negotiation of this imagery. The concept of "class," however, quickly proved a relative one. The first difficulty in assessing my informants' "class status" came from the fact that women have traditionally tended to inherit this status first from their father, then from their husband. Thus, informants who exhibited all the signs of upper-class status at the time I conducted my research might actually have belonged to a different socio-economic stratum for most of their lives. For instance, I was surprised to find out that my key informant, Hanako-san, who had been married to the head of one of the most powerful Buddhist temples of the region for over twenty years, had actually spent most of her life raising her two children by herself after the death of her first husband. She had survived for thirty years or so by performing odd jobs, including office work for a construction company, selling insurance, sewing kimonos, and a thirteen-year stint as a cabaret dancer.

Class is also geographically relative. Because rural Japan is relatively economically depressed, even members of the upper class in the village where I lived might not ever enjoy the kind of income level reached by their urban counterparts. They might, however, enjoy a different quality of life, as many of the problems commonly associated with Japanese society – including overcrowding or pollution – are not as seriously felt in this farming region where land is frequently inherited, and generally less costly, than in areas with a higher density of population. Conversely, the majority of inhabitants of the region coming from a lower socio-economic background might fare relatively better than lower-income urban-dwellers.

On the other hand, an individual's income level might influence her experience of geographical location by allowing for – or preventing – frequent visits to major urban centers located on other islands. The concept of class was consequently very difficult to separate in my study from the concept of geographical location. While most of my informants in the village clearly stood on the lower echelons of the Japanese economic ladder, their experience of class was intimately tied to their rural status, and vice versa. In other words, it was difficult for me to assess how class and geographical location interlocked to influence my informants' negotiation of popular cultural texts.

This difficulty was exacerbated by the fact that my informants tended to define themselves in middle-class terms no matter where they stood on the socio-economic ladder, interpreting their own position to make it fit within middle-class standards. Most of the women I interviewed deemed themselves "housewives" even when their responsibilities extended far beyond those normally associated with marriage and motherhood. I interviewed "housewives" of factory workers or farmers who worked "part time" forty to fifty hours a week. Chizuko Ueno (1983) argues that the current concept of the typical Japanese family as composed of a housewife and working husband is actually a very class-specific ideal passed down from the upper strata of society throughout the industrialization process. By defining themselves as housewives rather than workers, my informants asserted their position within this ideal. I could not dislodge them from their chosen position. My decision to speak of class only in relative terms, as "lower" or "upper," rather than employ labels – including terms such as "working class" – that I knew my informants would probably not choose for themselves, only partially solved the problem. I was still imposing my own interpretation of where these people stood on the economic ladder and not fully dealing with the evolving nature of class status.

Other factors, of course, combined with class to cast added layers of complexity onto my informants' experiences. Age and race were other significant actors in my informants' negotiation of media representations of attractiveness working in often contradictory and shifting ways to occasion feelings of alienation, ambiguity, pleasure and/or rebellion toward popular cultural texts. For instance, women of different socio-economic backgrounds might experience aging differently within this process of negotiation. Particularly pressured to conform to upper-class standards of attractiveness, higher-class women did not always develop the kind of detachment toward the body and media representations afforded to some extent by age to women of a lower socio-economic status. Because Japanese cultural standards of feminine beauty are based on a young, upper-class, Westernized model, women from a higher socio-economic background were defining not only their gendered identity when attempting to match this ideal, but also their class status.

While I often reveled in the very complexity and contradictory nature of my informants' comments in the process of conducting fieldwork, I found complexity and contradiction much more difficult to deal with when attempting to write about it for academic purposes. The typical structure of academic texts is not particularly well suited to encourage embracing contradictions. We are supposed to write linearly organized pieces that "make sense," not narratives full of contradictory comments. It is thus in the process of writing that I found myself most clearly confronted with the problems associated with the institutionalization of feminism identified by Dale Bauer (1995). Even as I attempted to point out the complex, ambiguous and often contradictory nature of my informants' relationships toward popular cultural texts, I found myself having to twist the complexity to coerce it to fit within the format of a fairly logically organized written text. Even if relatively fragmented, repetitive, and contradictory in order to reflect – at least to some extent – the nature of my informants' comments, the written work that resulted from months of interactions with women in the village still strikes me as only a pale reflection of the experience of fieldwork.[9]

It is in this process of writing that I became most painfully aware of the power relationship between researcher and informants, of the ethical responsibilities vested in my attempts to communicate my informants' words to others. How was I, for instance, to report on the fact that all of my informants deemed Western women more liberated than Japanese women? Was I simply to report this fact and potentially contribute to the Western stereotype of Japanese women as particularly submissive and oppressed? Was I to report this fact and contradict it with my interpretation of the situation and take away my informants' power to define their own position? Should I have decided not to report on this fact for fear of misinterpretation and silence my informants in the process? While I opted to address this dilemma by attempting to locate my informants' comments within the specific context of our conversations, I cannot control readers' interpretations. Linda Martín Alcoff reminds us that authors partially lose control over the meaning of their utterances in the process of publication and distribution of academic texts. As she notes, "[t]he meaning of any discursive event will be shifting and plural, fragmented and even inconsistent. As it ranges over diverse spaces and transforms the minds of its recipients according to their different horizons of interpretation, the effective control of the speaker over the meanings that she puts in motion may seem negligible" (Alcoff, 1995, p. 105). But, as Alcoff continues, this partial loss of control does not entail the loss of responsibility. We can attempt to assess the possible trajectories our speech will take as well as locate it within the context from which it emanates.

I hope this essay has demonstrated that conducting ethnographic research, or even research based on an ethnographic methodology, confronts researchers with varied and numerous challenges. I agree with Judith Stacey's assertion that "elements of inequality, exploitation, and even betrayal are endemic to ethnography" (Stacey, 1988). Such elements are endemic to any kind of research, particularly if it is politically grounded. I consequently prefer to focus in conclusion on Stacey's more optimistic assertion that a critical ethnographic consciousness can also help us achieve a level of contextuality, depth, and nuance unattainable through other, less difficult research methods.

Notes

1 Traditional Japanese-style living, involving sleeping and sitting on floors covered with *tatami* mats made of plaited rice-stocks. In her ethnography of a Japanese factory, Kondo (1990) mentions that one of her informants confided to her that "only someone of Japanese descent was genetically capable of adjusting to life on *tatami* mats" (p. 13).
2 Most of my informants defined themselves as housewives even if they frequently worked outside their home for more than forty hours per week. Such work was generally defined as help to their husband's business in the case of farmers or small business owners, or as "part-time."
3 Literally, outside person, but generally used to refer to white Westerners.
4 All names have been changed to protect informants' anonymity.
5 I get similar reactions when going "home" to France, as my husband and I speak English to each other and my French has acquired English-sounding intonations over the years.
6 Carol Stack, a white researcher conducting research in an African American community, writes about how she was allowed to forget her skin color for long periods of time during her stay in the community. Ironically, this level of comfort with her different racial identity was reached after members of the community started calling her "white Caroline," a naming she identifies as both a sign of acceptance and an unfeigned marker (Stack, 1996). I experienced a similar process when referred to as "THE gaijin" in the village. While a marker of my racial identity and outsider status, the term also paradoxically carved a place for me in the community.
7 I do not typically get such comments when living in the United States.
8 These examples are not given here to undermine the work of these scholars who have greatly contributed to their field but rather to illustrate the extreme difficulty of putting theory into practice.

9   I have found more multimedia and interactive forms of expression to offer more potential for reflecting this complexity. However, in the typical academic context, these experimental forms do not get the kind of recognition afforded to more traditional texts, such as journal articles.

References

Abu-Lughod, L. (1991). Writing against culture. In R. G. Fox (ed.), *Recapturing anthropology: Working in the present* (Vol. 5, pp. 137–162). Santa Fe, NM: School of American Research Press.

Abu-Lughod, L. (1993). *Writing women's worlds: Bedouin stories.* Berkeley: University of California Press.

Alcoff, M. L. (1995). The problem of speaking for others. In J. Roof and R. Wiegman (eds), *Who can speak: Authority and critical identity* (pp. 97–119). Urbana: University of Illinois Press.

Bauer, D. M. (1995). Personal criticism and the academic personality. In J. Roof and R. Wiegman (eds), *Who can speak: Authority and critical identity* (pp. 56–69). Urbana: University of Illinois Press.

Behar, R. (1993). *Translated woman: Crossing the border with Esperanza's story.* Boston: Beacon Press.

Bird, E. (1992). *For enquiring minds: A cultural study of supermarket tabloids.* Knoxville: University of Tennessee Press.

Bow, L. (1995). "For every gesture of loyalty, there doesn't have to be a betrayal": Asian American criticism and the politics of loyalty. In J. Roof and R. Wiegman (eds), *Who can speak: Authority and critical identity* (pp. 30–55). Urbana: University of Illinois Press.

Callaghan, D. D. (1995). The vicar and the virago: Feminism and the problem of identity. In J. Roof and R. Wiegman (eds), *Who can speak: Authority and critical identity* (pp. 195–207). Urbana: University of Illinois Press.

Caplan, P. (1988). Engendering knowledge: The politics of ethnography. *Anthropology Today* 4(6), 14–17.

Chiseri-Strater, E. and Sunstein, B. S. (1997). *FieldWorking: Reading and writing research.* Upper Saddle River, NJ: Simon and Schuster.

Chow, R. (1993). *Writing diaspora: Tactics of intervention in contemporary cultural studies.* Bloomington and Indianapolis: Indiana University Press.

Condon, J. (1985). *A half step behind: Japanese women today.* Rutland and Tokyo: Turtle.

Darling-Wolf, F. (2000). Texts in context: Intertextuality, hybridity, and the negotiation of cultural identity in Japan. *Journal of Communication Inquiry* 24(4), 134–155.

Elam, D. (1995). Speak for yourself. In J. Roof and R. Wiegman (eds), *Who can speak: Authority and critical identity* (pp. 231–237). Urbana: University of Illinois Press.

Friedman, S. S. (1995). Beyond white and Other: Relationality and narratives of race in feminist discourse. *Signs* 21(1), 1–49.

Ganguly, K. (1992). Accounting for Others: Feminism and representation. In L. F. Rakow (ed.), *Women making meaning: New feminist directions in communication* (pp. 60–79). New York: Routledge.

Harding, S. (1995). Subjectivity, experience, and knowledge: An epistemology from/ for rainbow coalition. In J. Roof and R. Wiegman (eds), *Who can speak: Authority and critical identity* (pp. 120–136). Urbana: University of Illinois Press.

Kondo, D. (1990). *Crafting selves: Power, gender, and discourses of identity in a Japanese workplace.* Chicago: University of Chicago Press.

Murphy, P. (1999). Doing audience ethnography: A narrative account of establishing ethnographic identity and locating interpretive communities in fieldwork. *Qualitative Inquiry* 5(4), 479–504.

Narayan, U. (1989). The project of feminist epistemology: Perspectives from a nonwestern feminist. In A. Jaggar and S. Bordo (eds), *Gender/Body/Knowledge* (pp. 256–269). New Brunswick, NJ: Rutgers University Press.

Ong, A. (1988). Colonialism and modernity: Feminist re-presentations of women in non-Western societies. *Inscriptions* 3, 79–93.

Ortner, S. (1995). Resistance and the problem of ethnographic refusal. *Comparative Studies in Society and History* 37(1), 173–193.

Press, A. (1991). *Women watching television: Gender, class, and generation in the American television experience.* Philadelphia: University of Pennsylvania Press.

Radway, J. (1984). *Reading the romance: Women patriarchy and popular literature.* Chapel Hill: University of North Carolina Press.

Rosaldo, R. (1989). *Culture and truth: The remaking of social analysis.* Boston: Beacon Press.

Sawhney, S. (1995). The joke and the hoax: (Not) speaking as the other. In J. Roof and R. Wiegman (eds), *Who can speak: Authority and critical identity* (pp. 208–220). Urbana: University of Illinois Press.

Skeggs, B. (1995). Theorising, ethics and representation in feminist ethnography. In B. Skeggs (ed.), *Feminist cultural theory: Process and production* (pp. 190–206). New York: St Martin's Press.

Stacey, J. (1988). Can there be a feminist ethnography? *Women's Studies International Forum* 11(1), 21–27.

Stack, C. B. (1996). Writing ethnography: Feminist critical practice. In D. L. Wolf (ed.), *Feminist dilemmas in fieldwork* (pp. 96–106). Boulder, CO: Westview Press.

Strathern, M. (1987). An awkward relationship: The case of feminism and anthropology. *Signs* 12(21), 276–294.

Ueno, C. (1983). The position of Japanese women reconsidered. *Current Anthropology* 28(4), S75–S84.

Zavella, P. (1996). Feminist insider dilemmas: Constructing ethnic identity with "Chicana" informants. In D. L. Wolf (ed.), *Feminist dilemmas in fieldwork* (pp. 138–159). Boulder, CO: Westview Press.

8

"NOW THAT YOU'RE GOING HOME, ARE YOU GOING TO WRITE ABOUT THE NATIVES YOU STUDIED?"

Telenovela reception, adultery and the dilemmas
of ethnographic practice

Antonio C. La Pastina

Ethnographers immerse themselves in a culture, often different from their own, to retell the lives of a particular people, to narrate their rites and traditions, and to understand and explain their cultural practices. In doing so, ethnographers contain, even if unintentionally, the observed experiences, giving form and coherence to a multiplicity of simultaneous events, sensations, feelings, and emotions. The ethnographer tries to order the chaotic world in which theory and praxis are jumbled.

In the process of writing an ethnographic account, the ethnographer attempts to give voice to those whom he or she "consumed" during fieldwork. At the same time, the writer is containing and "rechanneling" the voices of his or her subjects/informants/collaborators. But can we represent the "reality" and desires of the members of the community studied? After almost a year in Macambira,[1] a small rural community in northeast Brazil, I felt as if I belonged, but the closer the time came for me to depart, the clearer it became that I did not. I was there as a transient observer, and few understood why I was there at all. On one of my last days in town I was talking with residents on the sidewalk in front of a friend's house when one said, "Now that you're going home, are you going to write about the natives you studied?" The man who uttered these words was playing with me, but the humor in his words also conveyed the bitterness that many in the community felt toward their powerlessness to shape their own image in the outside world.

That simple statement was fraught with meaning. First, there was an acknowledgment that their lives had been consumed by the ethnographer and soon would be exposed. Second, they saw me as placing them in the position of subjects, primitive and uncivilized, reducing them to "natives" when I turned my ethnographic gaze upon them. It is important to understand that the native connotation here refers to the Brazilian Indians, who, among members of the community, seemed to be perceived as primitive, savage, and uncivilized. Through informants' comments, their readings of Indian characters in the telenovela discussed here and other incidents in town, there was an attempt to distance themselves from native Brazilians who are invariably part of the genetic make-up of most of the population in the region. Third, the then-recent publication of a story in the national news magazine *Veja*, in which the community had been represented as extremely poor and with limited access to television (Sanches and de Lima, 1997), had increased their sense of powerlessness to control their representations and strengthened their uncertainty of my ability or intent to represent the community life in ways members of the community would deem appropriate.

No matter how much I engaged in the local daily routines, I was there to investigate the community and my presence was a reassurance that we were different. They were the "other." In a sense, my presence reinforced their views of the distancing between their lives and those of the "modern South" of Brazil they saw on television. They saw me as a part of the South, not only because I was a native of São Paulo living in the United States, but probably because of many subjectivities I embodied: white, wealthy (comparatively), educated, and traveled. This raises interesting questions in the debate on native ethnography. Who is a native? Are nations, communities, or particular subjectivities the site of one's native identity? This is not the place to delve into that discussion, but it suffices to say that I was certainly not a native, even though we shared a nation, a language, and a common national history.

No matter how aware I was of the importance of subjects retaining their voices, or how much I cared for the reality of the community, once I was removed from the field, my work was focused on recreating a world from memories, observations, notes, interviews, and archival and media sources. The objective scholar, defended by some (D'Andrade, 1995) and claimed to be a figment of an empiricist imagination by others (Scheper-Hughes, 1995), can try to present him/herself as a blank slate, the neutral observer. In reality, as the ethnographer, I experienced the fieldwork in its totality with all my senses (Stoller, 1992) and with the limitations imposed by my body and mind. My embodied experiences, the smells, the sights, and the sounds, all worked to create a greater understanding of local dynamics. My own sensations of pleasure and disgust, desire and anxiety, helped mark the cadenza of my research. These sensations and events became ways for me to understand the local existence in relation to my own.

In writing about telenovelas in community life, I am circumscribing a segment of the lives of those in Macambira, trying to use "them" to explain a social phenomenon for academic consumption.

I will try here to explain the process of converting a large body of data about many issues, collected through many methods, into an account of a particular process and topic. I focused here on viewers' engagement with *The Cattle King* (*O Rei do Gado*), a highly popular telenovela that aired in Brazil from June 1996 to February 1997, and their interpretations of the adultery theme to discuss the ethnography practice and its function in reception studies. What attracted me to Macambira on my first visit was what would become the center of my work: women's labor. Even in the heat of the afternoon, when many were resting, one could hear the embroidering machines at work. Nearly everyone I spoke with that first day told me that embroidery was the main source of income in a region where jobs were scarce. The number of economically independent women, along with the salient traditional patriarchal norms and gender roles, made Macambira a unique place to examine these tensions in a critical context. The fieldwork reported here was part of my dissertation research, but also part of a larger interdisciplinary investigation of the role of telenovelas in the demographic transition in Brazil.[2]

Ethnography and audience research

Although telenovelas share common roots with US soap operas, the two genres have evolved in different ways since the 1950s. Telenovelas in Brazil, and in most of Latin America, are broadcast daily in prime time, have definitive endings allowing for narrative closure (normally after 180 to 200 episodes depending on the program's popularity), and are designed to attract a wide viewing audience of men, women and children (Lopez, 1991). These narratives traditionally are dominated by a leading couple and rely on class conflict and the promotion of social mobility (Mazziotti, 1993).

In a review of Latin American studies on telenovela audiences, McAnany and La Pastina (1994) argued that, based on the available information, it seems that telenovela audiences "are active and derive a variety of meanings from those programs . . . make applications of these programs to their lives; . . . and are aware of the fictional nature of the genre and the function of its rules" (p. 883). They also found that "contextual variables such as family, class, gender, neighborhood, and others are often included to qualify the audiences' reaction" (p. 837) and that little is known about audience behavior since it is predominantly absent from most audience studies in the region.

In most studies of telenovela audiences in Brazil to date, researchers have adopted a single subject/interpretative position, whether it be class (Leal, 1986) or political engagement (Lins da Silva, 1985) or gender (Prado, 1987; Tufte, 1995). Most of these researchers used qualitative methods (in-depth interviews, life histories, participant observation), but few engaged in in-depth, long-term, community-based ethnography as defined by Marcus and Fisher (1986), and consequently limited the potential of the research to help our understanding of the complexity of viewers' readings and appropriations of media texts used in everyday life (McAnany and La Pastina 1994; Murphy, 1999). The problem of focusing on one subject position alone is that it might reduce the possibility of analysis. Viewers might present readings shaped by different subjectivities simultaneously. How can we separate them? How can we argue that one subject position might be shaping that reading instead of another? Arguably, the power of contextualization provided by the ethnographic method might help answer those questions.

For Morley and Silverstone (1991), ethnographic methods provide an "analysis of multiple structured contexts of action, aiming to produce a rich descriptive and interpretative account of lives and values of those subjected to the investigation" (pp. 149–150). The importance of ethnography for audience studies lies in the possibility of assessing the different elements involved in the reception process and how these elements interact within the context of the locality in which the observation is taking place, as well as with the culture and identity of the community members. Television audiences are fluid; they present different characteristics in different situations and toward different programs. "Watching television should be seen as a complex and dynamic cultural process, fully integrated in the messiness of everyday life, and always specific in its meanings and impacts" (Ang, 1991, p. 161).

One of the advantages of using ethnography to conduct audience studies rests on its potential to provide a domestic context of television and telenovela reception among the different groups in the community. It also facilitates an understanding of how the reception context can affect the interpretation of the message by viewers, individually and in groups. The ethnographic approach also allows the examination of the phenomena in their immediate social, political, and economic contexts. This resonates the idea of mediations proposed by Martín-Barbero (1993), among other Latin American scholars. With mediations, Martín-Barbero is attempting to articulate a broader understanding of the process of reception, taking into consideration the different structures that will mediate the process of interpretation, production and reception.

That said, the practice of audience ethnography remains a challenge. The need to focus on the complexities of the surrounding environment and on personal ideational values and attitudes makes this a process fraught with limitations. To observe and participate in the process of media consumption might limit a more general analysis of the societal process and the trends that can be described in a sociological study. Nevertheless, the understanding of individual and communal media consumption practices might help to apprehend the ways in which viewers engage with media texts in their totality. The goal of audience studies must be to build a solid understanding of the reception processes, establishing a basis for a better analysis of the long-term impacts that media texts might have on viewers.

The ethnographic process has the potential to provide an in-depth under-standing of what I term media engagement (La Pastina, 1999). The meaning intended for the word here is that of being engaged (with the media), from the verb to engage, which means to occupy the attention or efforts of a person (or persons). To engage with a telenovela represents more than just watching it. It means that the text becomes part of a routine. It will be used for gratification and leisure (Katz, Blumer and Gurevitch, 1974), as well as negotiated with other members of the family and the community in discussions in several venues, most of which are informal (Liebes and Katz, 1990). Viewers will reject some images and topics, embrace others, identify with certain situations and characters, and reject others. When referring to engagement, it also will be implied that this process is inserted in a context, such as home, community, and network relations, and is continuously evolving due to these social interactions. These structures, in Giddens's sense of the term (1979, 1984), enable and constrain media engagement. Giddens developed a theoretical framework that attempts to explain the role of human agency within the limits imposed by societal structures. Key to structuration theory is the duality between action and structure. Structures may enable and constrain human action, but they are also the result of human action. With engagement, I propose that to understand the process of media reception we need to acknowledge that the viewer–text relationship is complex and multilayered. The advantage of the ethnographic process is to provide the complexity of these interrelations between viewers' immediate social structures, their subjectivities and the text.

Most of the information discussed here was collected over a year-long period of formal and informal conversations, interviews, and participant observation. Over this time, I conducted several in-depth interviews with a select group of residents, thirty in total. That was an attempt to engage with telenovela viewers across class, gender, age, race, and education boundaries. Nevertheless, other residents with whom I maintained extensive contact, even if not through formal interviews, reinforced many of these in-depth accounts. Data from two surveys conducted in the community, as well as archival data, focus groups, and participant observation, were used in the weaving of this particular account of the engagement between the theme of adultery in the telenovela and the perception of adultery among local residents.

It is difficult to talk about data in an ethnographic project. The whole process, in a way, is part of the data, or, better yet, *is* data. Most of the time I talked about everything else, from the weather to local politics. As Barley (1983) said about his ethnographic endeavor among the Dawayo in Cameroon, 99 percent of his data was about everything but the point he was trying to research. But it is undeniable that all of this "other" information helped me to understand the way in which the community works and the values and attitudes that prevail.

The practicalities of ethnography

My entry into the community was facilitated by my contact, brokered by a University of Texas professor's daughter, with a young man from Caicó who worked in the mayor's office in Macambira. This entry point proved to be a double-edged sword. While this relationship helped smooth my way into the community, it raised concerns among members of the opposition party, who saw me as an ally of the mayor and his party. The fact that I conducted my research in an election year clearly affected my data collection in several ways. The animosity and divisive atmosphere reigning in the community due to political rivalries and the limited attention paid to other activities during the last few months of the political campaign certainly affected the attention given by many to the telenovela. The election of a new mayor in a small town like Macambira is a central event in the lives of community members, defining the new power structure and who will benefit from it. An election is also an event, with parties, rallies, dances, free food and drink, and an opportunity to get money or goods from the candidates who do not hesitate to barter voting intention for promises, goods or other forms of bribes. During the three to four months prior to the election in early October, the telenovela, and other forms of entertainment, became secondary to participation in the political campaign.

The house I rented was located at the entrance (or exit) to the city. It allowed me to see the movement of passers-by and encouraged people to stop to say hello and chat. My job as a substitute high school English teacher at the state school next door to my house served to establish ties with several younger residents who would become important sources of information. It also justified my presence in the community, and throughout my stay several people called me o professor (the teacher), even though I had taught only for three months.

For the duration of my fieldwork, with few exceptions, I ate at the home of the same family, paying weekly for my meals. Julião, Justina, and their four children became a family to me, caring for me when I got sick, and we enjoyed good times together. I also became a confidant for the wife about her troubled and unhappy married life. While the family helped to open doors to other families, more than anything they were a source of insight into the local lifestyle and culture. Participating in their household leisure activities, celebrations, and crises enabled me to experience the life of an extended local family in-depth.

There were several other key informants. Three young ladies who worked at the phone station befriended me early on and opened a channel to their families and friends. The health center staff provided vital information, particularly through Nilda, the head nurse, who helped me conduct a survey on the reproductive health history of more than sixty women in the lowest-income households. In the process, I gained access to a segment of the community that was disconnected from the main street life of the local elite and that had little participation in public debates or school, the sphere I was most closely associated with early in my stay.

The long-term contact with members of the community allowed me to ask personal questions and hear from friends about their private lives, musings, and dealings. Women would confide in me; men would share their escapades while we drank beer. I lived in the community. I heard in the morning about the fights the previous night, the cases of adultery that had reached the public ears. In the days following an event, I heard about some of them from those involved. Other stories I heard long after they had happened and were still under veils of secrecy. A short-term visit to this community may have led me to gain information about the lives of the residents and how they saw the characters in the telenovela, but it would have given me very little entry into the private domains and the everyday life of the community, the domain from which most of the information reported here pertains.

The immediacy afforded by my presence was another important benefit of the methodology. In the days after the telenovela scenes in which Leia was found committing adultery, or when she was the victim of domestic violence, I asked questions and listened to comments on the sidewalks and in small gatherings in the mornings and late afternoons. Similar to my experience with product placements (La Pastina, 2001), the immediacy of ethnography – the possibility of being in the living room when viewers are watching a particular scene, hearing their comments and engaging in conversation – provides material for a deeper level of analysis.

Macambira's mediascape and *The Cattle King*

In *The Cattle King*, traditional melodramatic elements of class ascension, love, and betrayal played a central role in the lives of the main characters. Adultery was one of the pivotal themes woven into the narrative from beginning to end. Adultery also was central to the lives of many residents in Macambira, where the continuous debate over mostly male adultery colored the discussions of the telenovela.

Of the 2,188 inhabitants of Macambira, 519 lived on small farms surrounding the urban core (FIBGE, 2000). Within the context of poverty that dominated the interior of the northeast, Macambira seemed to defy the images normally associated with the *sertão*. The paved main roads and white cinder-block houses gave first-time visitors the impression that it was a wealthy community. But a walk on the outskirts changed that perception. Close to 10 percent of the homes had no electricity, all used septic tanks and several had no running water (Rios-Neto et al., 1998). Until the mid-1980s the large majority of homes were made of *taipa*, a form of adobe. By the mid-1990s there were fewer than five *taipa* homes left, all owned by members of the opposition political party. Most of the 400 homes in Macambira were built in the previous ten years through federal government initiatives intended to eradicate *taipa* and to reduce the spread of illnesses such as *doença de chagas* (barber bug fever). Cinder-block homes represented better living conditions, but did not automatically improve sanitation or hygiene.

The housing developments and the availability of water and electricity dramatically changed the urban ecology of Macambira. The town was set in a grid with ten streets running east–west and five running north–south. The older neighborhoods were the downtown area and the *maloca*. The white families who traced their ancestry to the town's founders mostly owned the older, larger homes surrounding the church in the downtown area, around the main square and on the oldest street that starts in front of the church. The *maloca* was the neighborhood where the poor black population lived, until the recent past predominantly in *taipa* homes. A creek, which had been recently routed through a culvert, separated these two neighborhoods. With the building of cinder-block homes, the racial divide was undermined as families from different parts of town moved into the same neighborhood. Older residents got new houses and many multi-generational households, in which several married siblings lived together, were split, adding new homes to the structural make-up of the community.

As with many other small towns in the interior of northeast Brazil, Macambira suffers from periodic droughts that limit access to running water and undermine the ability to maintain a viable economy based on agriculture. The limited job pool for most males and the increased reliance in the 1990s on the income generated from women's embroidery subverted the traditional family structure in which men supported the house and women stayed at home, reproduced, and cared for the family. "Here in Macambira, women support most of the households." This statement, uttered by dozens of people throughout my stay, became a mantra to the understanding of the relationship between men and women in the community. The economic empowerment of women, I learned soon after my arrival, did not necessarily translate into their emancipation or into increased participation in the political process, which remained heavily controlled by men. Traditional patriarchal households and gender relationships were ingrained, and change was hard to come by. The perception that embroidering was an unmanly activity had profound ramifications for the power relationships between men and women. In many instances, people, including women, trivialized embroidery as a way of earning a living, saying one should not be proud of this as a profession. Consequently, the few men who worked peripherally in the embroidery industry had their masculinity questioned.

While limited local commerce, offering only the basic staples, helped generate and keep funds in the community, many residents went periodically to Caicó, the largest urban center in the region, to purchase staples and other consumer items. For most in Macambira, the dream of consumption was limited to a narrow range of items. Many longed to purchase a car. Residents without a refrigerator desired one. "We can save food and with this heat the children want ice on everything and the neighbors are always complaining if they keep asking for it," said Maroca (January 24, 1997).[3] But after basic household items, such as stoves and refrigerators, items associated with leisure activities were at the top of the list. For the few without television, that was their priority. The majority wanted a satellite dish, a videocassette recorder or a stereo. Young residents were appalled at the idea of having a home without a television and a stereo. Luzinha and Dezinha, two sisters in their twenties, could not conceive of it: "Life would be so boring without a television. Oh God! I could not live without a stereo either," said Luzinha, the older one (November 26, 1996).

Dezinha and Luzinha symbolized most residents I interviewed who saw mass media as the main source of entertainment and an important source of information. Of 203 households surveyed (Rios-Neto et al., 1998), 24 percent of the respondents said television was their preferred form of entertainment, followed by chatting (22 percent), strolling (15 percent), and listening to music (9 percent). Other self-reported leisure activities included religion (5 percent), partying (6 percent), and household tasks (3 percent). From these numbers, it is clear that for most residents television and radio dominated leisure opportunities, along with chatting and strolling, activities rooted in a pre-technological era that had been adapted to a new reality. Nevertheless, radio and television were not only forms of entertainment; they also represented a symbolic class ascension through the acquisition of knowledge. More than a passive way to entertain oneself, they represented access to the outside world. This exposure to other markets was underlined by the frustration that all the goods advertised at such bargain prices were in remote places. They could not see commercials from Natal, the state capital 300 kilometers away, where they could have some access to advertised consumer goods. In Macambira, unless the household owned its own satellite dish, the only station available was Globo, which was picked up by a satellite dish owned by the community directly from the national feed from Rio de Janeiro and then relayed to the households.[4] The signal came only with national advertisements and black spots where local advertisements should be inserted.

The public television set on the square close to the entrance to town was a relic of a time in which television wasn't so widespread. Unlike many other communities in which the public television set had been a part of the urban ecology since the late 1970s and early 1980s (or even earlier), Macambira did not get a public television set until the early 1990s. At that time a percentage of the households already had television sets and small viewing communities existed. In the mid-1990s, with inflation under control and consumer credit more widespread, the number of television sets increased dramatically, reaching close to 95 percent of the households. More residents owned a television set than a refrigerator (Rios-Neto et al., 1998).

Viewers in Macambira would tell me of the importance of following the first few weeks of a telenovela to master the characters and their relationships, and then one could relax. Even when not watching, viewers were aware of plot developments in the main telenovela through radio commentaries or chatting with friends. Few in the community had access to the Sunday television supplement in *O Poti*, the only daily newspaper from Natal, or weekly television gossip magazines such as *Contigo* or *Amiga*. But the popular program *Rádio Mulher*, a daily afternoon show on *Radio Seridó* in *Caicó*, provided between songs synopses of the telenovelas, gossip about actors and characters, and news about fashion trends.

O Rei do Galho[5]: adultery and gender roles in The Cattle King and Macambira

With its subplots on agrarian reform politics, cattle raising, and coffee farming, *The Cattle King* was perceived as a realistic text. Women enjoyed the rural subtext, but for them most telenovelas – and *The Cattle King* was no exception – were about romance. There was no need to find a reason to follow it, as males did, arguing that only telenovelas with historical, realistic, or rural themes attracted them. Women expected that telenovelas would provide a romantic text in which couples would slowly build a relationship through conflict, external opposition, and overcoming adversities to fulfill their love. Women viewers in Macambira perceived the melodramatic roots of the genre and expected them to be followed by the writers. The modernization of the genre in Brazil, which incorporated contemporary social and political elements, seemed to some viewers to be distancing it from its melodramatic roots, raising complaints among female viewers that Globo's telenovelas were no longer romantic. During this fieldwork, many women who had access to a satellite dish followed *Marimar*, the more "romantic" telenovela produced by the Mexican network Televisa, dubbed in Portuguese and broadcast by the SBT network (Almeida, Hamburger and La Pastina 1999).

For most viewers in Macambira, plots and situations in the telenovela resembled reality. However, there was also a perception that the reality represented in the telenovelas was remote and uncharacteristic of a small town. "Things like that only happen in larger cities" was a common allusion to images of sex and gender relations on telenovelas. The unstated reason why it could only happen in large cities – meaning urban centers in the South – was the conflictive nature of morals and values presented in the telenovelas. For many women, however, the distinction was ultimately located in the social control resulting from the lack of privacy in Macambira. Dinalva, in her late twenties with two children and no steady partner, felt that women in larger cities were more like the women in the telenovelas. "In the larger cities the rights [between man and woman] are more equal; there is no gossip. Here men and women have the same rights, but men have more freedom. The women are marked if they do anything; there is a lot of talk" (Fieldnote, November 6, 1996).

Prado (1987), conducting research with women viewers of telenovelas in Cunha in the interior of São Paulo in southern Brazil, found a similar pattern. Women in real life perceived women in the telenovelas and in urban centers to be freer, due to the lack of social controls, such as gossip, imposed on residents of the community. For Dinalva, gossip became a form of social control on women's lives in Macambira, while she perceived women in larger cities to be immune to the social pressures exerted by gossip. But for her, the fundamental distinction between men and women was much more dramatic than that between women in urban and rural communities. For her men were freer in both settings. Equal rights were assumed but qualified: men have more freedom. This theme was echoed by another viewer, Dete, a young single woman, who said that men and women have the same rights as long as men remain head of the household (September 20, 1996). The telenovela seemed to reinforce the perception of a gap between women's lifestyles in urban and rural centers but not the gap between men and women's roles, which seemed to be rooted in their experiences in a *machista* patriarchal society.

Patriarchal relationships with clear gender role definitions were still present in the local imagery. Younger men and women seemed to be more willing than older ones to reproduce perceived *machista* relationships. During focus group discussions with teens conducted in Macambira by Paula Miranda-Ribeiro with my help, it seemed that certain patterns that adults were moving away from were perceived to be valued and the norm among teenagers. Several teenagers of both genders perceived that violence against women was justified when the woman "disrespected" her male partner (Miranda-Ribeiro, 1997). Several older men and women whom I interviewed, many of them married with children, decried violence against women. In fact, during my stay in Macambira all the incidents of wife-beating or other violence against women were restricted to two couples who periodically had fights. These women were not respected by many of their peers because they remained in abusive relationships.

Machista households in Macambira were based on certain expectations regarding gender roles. There was a clear definition of male and female domains. The wife was supposed to care for the house and children, while the husband worked outside the house and supported the family. When the wife worked, she was helping support the household even when hers was the main source of income; the man, when he did any household chores, was only helping. *Machista* attitudes also defined clear sexual roles for men and women. Men's sexuality was not contained by marriage. Male escapades (or adultery) were perceived as wrong but not socially punished, while the wives had to remain loyal to their husbands. If a married woman committed adultery, she was ostracized by family and community, and might become the victim of violence, which in many cases would be perceived as justified by the couple's social peers.

The realization that a woman could bring more money into the household if she devoted more hours to embroidery led many couples to rethink the traditional male and female duties within the household. A growing number of men openly told me about cooking, cleaning, and caring for children. Many, however, were still reluctant to acknowledge caring for the household, concerned about their image, their authority, and ultimately their masculinity. There was reluctance among males to engage publicly in activities perceived to be feminine, such as washing clothes in public or embroidering.

The adultery

In *The Cattle King*, Leia betrayed her husband, Bruno, with Ralf, who, it turned out, was interested in her money. As the plot developed, it became clear that her betrayal was the result of her sense of solitude; she felt abandoned by her husband, whose only concern seemed to be his cattle and fortune. But Bruno also became more conscious of his faults as husband and father, and in this process appeased his anger and gave her a sizable portion of his fortune, to which she had lost her legal rights after he found her in bed with her lover. Leia's betrayal generated some of the most passionate comments about the telenovela. Her betrayal, her appearance, her demeanor, her lover, her lover's attitudes, his battering of her, and her children's behavior were mostly perceived to be her fault. In talking about her adultery, men and women in Macambira ended up discussing their views of adultery and male–female rights within the relationship. These viewers also talked about their perceptions of the gap in values and behavior between urban centers in the South and their community, as well as the influence of television in their society.

Thirty-year-old Anizio was married to Ina, who was younger and better educated. He had finished elementary school, but she had completed high school in Caicó and dropped out of college in Patos after the first year.[6] They had a two-year-old daughter and were raising Ina's baby sister because Anizio believed her mother's lifestyle was not suitable for raising a child. Her status as an abandoned wife – her husband left her with five kids to run away with a woman half his age – and her weekend outings to dance and drink were the marks of unsuitability in Anizio's eyes. They lived with his extended family and Ina embroidered and helped with household chores. When we talked about Leia's adultery Anizio focused on what he perceived to be the gap between what happens in Macambira and what happens in the telenovelas. He thought it was impossible that a man betrayed by his wife would befriend her after they separated. His wife was listening and at that point told a story about a couple in Macambira who separated and remained friends. He was fast to say that they were an exception and "besides she had not betrayed him." For him, the gap between telenovela and reality was also a gap between urban and rural, anonymity and community intimacy, private and public.

Anizio: In the telenovelas it is a mess; men date, women date. Here, whoever acts like that gets a bad reputation. There, it is their reality, the routine of their lives. . . . Not here. There is no such thing here. If there is anything like that here, everybody sees it, notices it and comments on it. In the telenovela everything happens. The woman dates someone else. That is a reality, and then they follow their normal lives as if nothing happened, they remain friends. . . . You see, Leia and Bruno remained friends. . . . Here, something like that would never happen. (January 7, 1997)

Early in his quote it seemed as if he posed that men dating women outside marriage also would get a bad reputation. Later he explained his views, arguing that adultery was wrong but reiterating the established mantra "*mulher fica mais marcada*" (women will be more marked).

Mariete, the mother of seven grown children, was a widow and an avid telenovela watcher. She was very critical of Leia and thought the adulterous wife was a bad influence on viewers. More than once she compared Leia to adulterous women in Macambira. She believed that telenovelas had an impact on women's behavior. "If the woman is not strong she will succumb to the temptations in the telenovelas" (Fieldnotes, June 29).

Corina, a young mother whose husband worked and lived in a neighboring state, thought that by showing the suffering of Leia and Liliana, these characters served as examples for women watching *The Cattle King*. For Corina, telenovelas had an impact in the community. She believed that images of adultery on the telenovela might promote the actual behavior. However, as others had mentioned, a telenovela's influence depended on the viewer. Apparently, there were some personal characteristics that determined how, or when, or what kind of person would be more susceptible to television's influence, but none of my informants delineated the characteristics that supposedly led to a greater susceptibility.

Corina: I am going to tell you, there were no cases like that [of adultery] before. But in the last few years, it started happening because they [women] see the telenovelas . . . the telenovelas influence a lot, but I think it also depends on the person. When a person doesn't like the other any more, they must get together and talk. To leave without giving an explanation, no, that is not the way to do it. (September 19, 1996)

Zé da Cana, a man who did not command respect in the community due to his drinking problem, summarized a view shared by many but rarely clearly articulated. He believed television and telenovelas were destroying families. According to him, telenovelas brought into the household images that led women to want their independence: "Telenovelas put lies in the minds of women." When I asked if it affected men as well, he said no, because women were weaker. His wife had left him and was working hard to support herself and her son. His wife's strength might have pushed Zé to arrive at this conclusion regarding the role of telenovelas, looking for an excuse to explain the changing attitudes among women.

Keila, a recently married woman who devoted much of her free time to reading romance novels, thought that television had an impact on its viewers and that showing adultery on the telenovela was "negative because it destroyed the family" (October 22, 1996). But her main concern was the lack of commitment in the relationships in the telenovelas. For her, the couples were emotionally and sexually involved too fast before having any kind of commitment.

Keila: There are no marriages [in the telenovelas]. They are all open relationships. I think that the most important thing would be for them [telenovela producers and writers] to think about preserving marriage. (October 22, 1996)

There was a clear sense from the interviews I conducted and the time I spent chatting with these viewers about telenovelas that most believed those programs had a role in promoting behavior that many deemed inappropriate. Ultimately, telenovelas seemed to be showing a society in which gender relations were challenging the established norms and, in doing so, promoting a subversion of established norms within the community of viewers. Maybe telenovelas were not responsible for any of the behavior changes that many viewers claimed, but it was undeniable that telenovelas were perceived to be responsible for promoting "new" and "urban" lifestyles. In this process, telenovelas were empowered among viewers who saw these texts as an oracle of images of a reality that even if distant seemed to be their future.

Augusto was eloquent; an elected councilman, he tried to find patterns and discuss issues in terms of local and national understandings. He liked telenovelas a lot, and had no problems talking about them. He never saw his desire to watch telenovelas as a threat to his manhood or his status in the community. Sometimes he watched at his place, but mostly he would go to the house of a friend or a co-religionist, since his wife worked the night shift as a nurse in Caicó. I saw the telenovela a few times with him, by chance, at the home of Marisa and Gere where I used to go quite often. For Augusto, *The Cattle King* provided examples for Brazil. While he saw pedagogical potential in Leia's adultery, the focus for him was on her relationship with Bruno, her former husband. While Anizio could not imagine a betrayed man befriending his ex-wife, Augusto saw a positive lesson for viewers:

Augusto: Let's look at Leia . . . at the beginning of the telenovela she was a well-married woman. After a while, she had a problem and separated from her husband and was living with another man. It was a big conflict. But as time progressed, she returned home, she saw her ex-husband, and they talked. He accepted her normally. So, the television is showing that even if the woman leaves him, it is not necessary to remain in that conflict, fighting, wanting to hit the wife. The scene is clear: there was a conflict, but it calmed down. And the telenovela shows to Brazil that it can happen within the Brazilian reality. It is a Brazilian reality because it happens in Brazil. It really happens because the telenovela is showing it. (December 23, 1996)

In this passage, Augusto proposed a role for television and telenovelas in Brazilian society. He saw the telenovela as showing the road to a behavior that was perceived to be more "modern" or "civilized." In another moment in the interview he argued that telenovelas were also influencing the way female adultery was perceived. He acknowledged that women's reputations were still more vulnerable than males', but he thought that was changing.

Augusto: The tendency is to evolve. Also, because if we look at television, we see the women leaving their husbands at work and going to other places, instead of going home to make love, to have sex. . . . As time goes by there will be no more discrimination, because it is something the society stops caring for. Look, here in a small town, once that happens it is very commented, but as time passes people forget and don't care anymore. . . . It is 40, 30 days, she is at the top of the gossip chain. After that people forget. She even becomes friendly with other women. They chat, and it is all over. . . . In the past it was different. If something like that happened, she would be practically isolated. Not today, now she returns to be a part of society. (December 23, 1996)

For Augusto, women in the telenovelas and, consequently, in larger centers were already liberated and engaging in practices that were still perceived to be wrong in a small town such as Macambira. And adultery was certainly wrong in Macambira, as the story of Edite seems to indicate. Seven years earlier, while she was still married, she had had an affair with another man. When the story became public her husband left her and moved to a *sítio* outside town. He had served twice as a councilman and their family was part of the so-called "society" of Macambira. Several people I talked to expressed sadness for what "she had done to him." However, she seemed to be an active part of the community, working at the school, selling embroideries, and attending college in Caicó. In 1996 she decided to run for councilwoman. Both parties were struggling to find women to run due to new federal legislation that required 20 percent of the total number of candidates per party to be women. Edite ran for the PMDB, the party in power. She received the lowest number of votes among more than twenty-five candidates scrambling for nine seats. It is hard, if not impossible, to establish causality between her adultery and her failure at the polls. However, what was clearly noticeable was that people had little respect for her. Most people I talked to said she had no chance of winning. When I asked why, respondents were vague.

Edite's betrayal without a doubt marked her and her family. Several years after they had separated, her husband still lived in a *sítio* and only came to town occasionally. Some people joked about his masculinity. I wondered many times if his virility was questioned not just because of her betrayal but also because he did not commit any violence against her. In chatting with other males in town, many times I heard comments that substantiated a view of a *machista* and male-controlled society and household. Uribe, a man in his late twenties with a wife and two children, said he had had an extra-marital affair and his wife did not know about it. He believed that if she knew she would leave him. He was obsessed with the idea of being a cuckold and said that if his wife betrayed him, he would kill her. Once, at a party that his wife did not attend, he told me he thought that men cannot treat women well. "Women of lowlifes do not cuckold. It is only the nice guys that get the horns" (Fieldnotes, June 27). Dvanir, a policeman married for the third time, once told me that "being married does not mean castrated," when I questioned his attitude that a married man should keep having sex with other women.

The local barber, Eusebio, was still in his twenties and had recently married. For him *The Cattle King* went too far. He liked the telenovela a lot until the betrayal. By that point he had begun to dislike it and then completely lost interest when the hero befriended the adulterous wife. The view of a man pardoning his adulterous wife, an image of a more sensitive, respecting, and understanding male shedding *machista* and patriarchal attitudes of male privilege, seemed to have little resonance among viewers in Macambira. Maurício was an exception. Most viewers perceived a woman's adultery to be a serious offense to male honor.

Gidião explained to me the difference between men's and women's adultery and the impact of betrayal on both genders.

Gidião: As an example, here, if a woman betrays a man (*bota chifre no homem*), for the rest of his life he will be marked. There are things no one can accept here, you see. And in the South it is not like that. I hear that there (in the South) it is common, the woman betrays him and the guy accepts her back.

Antonio: And here, if the woman betrays a man, she is marked forever?

Gidião: To the rest of her life!

Antonio: And he?

Gidião: Yes, he is marked as a *corno* (cuckold). And people talk about him.

Antonio: And the woman, if the man betrays her (*bota corno nela*), is she marked as well?

Gidião: No, she is not.

Antonio: And the guy who betrayed?

Gidião: (laughs) Here people are very *machista*, you see Antonio. A fellow who betrays the woman here is known as a goat . . . *machão*. And the woman doesn't get a reputation, you know. Nothing happens to her when the man betrays her. (January 16, 1997)

It seems that television was the source for this reading of different levels of acceptance of betrayal between the urbanized South and Macambira.[7] Gidião thought that Leia was a *safada* (a no good). He thought her role in the telenovela was horrible: first, because she betrayed her husband, and second, because she destroyed the family. The view that her betrayal was not only destroying her relationship but also destroying the family and placing her son in jeopardy was a recurrent motif in many interviews. There were several viewers who blamed

Leia for her son's behavior (getting involved in the death of her lover). She was seen as the cause for Marcos's downfall because he could not see his mother with another man. He had to vindicate his father's masculinity. It seemed, however, that more men presented this reading than women.

Everton and Maria Antonia had been married for more than twelve years. He was the secretary at the Municipal Council and helped his father-in-law to take care of his farm and cattle. Everton was traditional, well-educated, well-informed, interested in news, and always looking at magazine covers when he went to Caicó. He watched the telenovela almost daily and enjoyed it. We talked several times a week. But during an interview with him and his wife, a distinction between their views was noticeable. When I asked them about Leia, for instance, their views reinforced a certain pattern.

Everton: She is a vadia, a bitch, has a husband and does something like that. It ended up falling on Marcos . . . he kept his father's horns.
Antonio: But why do you think she betrayed?
Everton   I don't know.
Maria Jose: Solitude, her husband's absence. (January 18, 1997)

For Everton there was no possible explanation for Leia's behavior; there was no understanding of the motivation behind her actions. For Maria Jose there was a possibility of understanding Leia's situation based on her unhappiness in her relationship. This subtle distinction and Maria Jose's views on *machismo* clearly underlined her awareness about an unjust power imbalance between men's and women's rights and roles within relationships. While men seemed more prone to judge Leia responsible for the downfall of her son, women seemed more understanding and aware about Leia's motivations to commit adultery, even if they objected to her actions.

His betrayal is not as important

Leia's betrayal was seen as wrong, as a bad example. In a few cases, especially among women, there was a tentative justification that never materialized. These viewers said Bruno was also responsible for the failure of their marriage, but Leia's behavior was never justified. On the other hand, with few exceptions, male adultery was never an issue. In real life it was perceived as wrong, but accepted as part of male behavior with minimal consequences, or so it seemed to me. For many women, the reality of an adulterous companion was part of their existence. Several married women told me of threatening to leave their husbands. And some cases of violence against women were associated with the confrontation with their husbands when the women found they had been betrayed.

In *The Cattle King*, three male characters, Bruno, Zé do Araguaia, and the Senator, were closest to being perceived as adulterous, but no single viewer in the community saw a problem in their behavior. On the contrary, some felt the

141

Senator and Bruno should have committed adultery. The cases of Bruno and Zé do Araguaia were always justified. Bruno only stayed with Luana after he had found out his wife Leia was betraying him, and Zé do Araguaia had an affair with an Indian woman years earlier. The Senator, on the contrary, did not betray his wife. When asked about his relationship with his wife and the maid, some viewers laughed as if saying: "Well that wouldn't really happen for a man to reject a pretty woman like Chiquita." Another implication was that he was not manly enough to commit adultery. Few viewers saw his faithfulness as a sign of respect to his relationship with his wife.[8]

When I asked Gidião about the couples in the telenovela, he said he liked Zé do Araguaia and Donana. He said they had a great relationship. Like most people interviewed, he didn't see any problem in the fact that Zé do Araguaia had betrayed his wife in the past and had a child with another woman. He thought they were wholesome. Zé do Araguaia and Donana represented for several viewers in Macambira the relationship that closest resembled their own lives. Viewers noticed the instruments she used in the ranch kitchen as utensils they used in the past or still used. Viewers would comment on the couple's loyalty to their boss and Donana's devotion to her husband and later to his son. They represented traditional values many viewers espoused.

Emphasizing this view, Gidião said that Donana and Zé do Araguaia were not a typical couple in the telenovela. According to him, the telenovela used complicated relationships "to attract the viewer's attention."

Gidião: In this telenovela, *The Cattle King*, there is a couple with a good relationship, that one on the ranch, Zé do Araguaia and Donana. I think it is very beautiful, you see, Antonio. In the telenovelas there are only complicated relationships. It is part of the telenovela, you know? It's to attract viewers' attention. There is no perfect marriage, no. Constantly there are fights, aren't there? It is normal . . . In the telenovela it is one thing, Antonio, in real life it is a different thing. (January 16, 1997)

Zefa Nega, so named because of her black skin, was in her late twenties and married to Marcos, a white man who spent long periods as a construction worker in São Paulo. She was up front about the discrimination she suffered from his family, but also clear about her sexual desire for her husband. Marcos liked telenovelas and when in São Paulo he watched them at the dormitory provided by the construction company.[9] For Zefa Nega, Zé do Araguaia's betrayal was representative of reality.

Antonio: Do you think telenovelas resemble real life?
Zefa Nega: There are a lot of things that resemble real life. . . . There is the "cuckold queen:" Léia. . . . There is the example of Zé do Araguaia. And also Liliana, because when she got pregnant she was abandoned. When she needed him most, he left her. Zé do

Araguaia betrayed his wife. Léia betrayed the "king of cattle." Everything, one can say, is as if it was real life, because the majority of those things I've seen. (November 25, 1996)

Even though Zé do Araguaia's betrayal resembled real life, she saw no problem in him having a son because that had happened long ago and he and Donana had a good life together. Zefa Nega, however, had strong views about male–female roles. Even though male adultery in her view was less problematic than female adultery, she did not condone violence against women and saw those instances as an acceptable justification for a woman to betray a man. She was angry when Ralf hit Leia and enjoyed it when he was beat up "so he learns not to hit a women." For her nothing justifies a man hitting a woman.

When I asked Rosa, who was married with two children, about Zé do Araguaia, she saw no problem in his having had a son with another woman. When I asked if she saw a problem in him betraying his wife, she said, "I think it is wrong if he was already married, but I thought he had an affair before he got married." For some viewers there was a perception that his betrayal had happened long ago, probably before their marriage. Rosa thought betrayal was wrong for both men and women. She thought, however, that women's independence had led to more failed relationships. Rosa was much more lenient – engaging in a selective reading of the narrative – towards male betrayal than she was towards Leia's. Rosa's attitude seemed to reinforce the view that ingrained societal values about male and female adultery played a role in her reading.

Conclusion

In this chapter I have attempted to present a discussion of the ethnographic process grounded on an analysis of reception data of the telenovela *The Cattle King* among residents from Macambira, a small rural community in the interior of northeast Brazil. It seemed that *The Cattle King* allowed viewers to engage with their own sets of values and attitudes towards gender roles and practices. In this process, they questioned the validity of the images portrayed and their own reality. They shared their lived experiences while criticizing or praising the characters and situations. The inherent genre repertoire available to viewers, and their familiarity with it, allowed most male and female viewers to participate emotionally in the narrative at the same time as they were aware of its distance from their own reality. The telenovela served to remind viewers of who they were and where and how they lived. But it also served to tell them how people in urban centers live, a process that prompted them to question the lives of these "others." In a reversal of power roles, the underclass, the underrepresented, objectified the urban, modern upper classes represented in the telenovelas and consumed their lives to learn what they thought was good and discarded what they perceived to be bad. It seemed to me, however, that in this process most of what they perceived to be bad was also incorporated in their everyday lives.

Ethnography allows researchers to embody the fieldwork experience, living and feeling the daily routines that order the everyday lives of those in the field. My whiteness, my limited consumption of alcohol, my inability to dance, and even my digestive crises were markers in my relationship with the field. They defined who I was, and established my distance from the reality of those in the field, at the same time as they allowed me to discuss my not belonging. But these embodied experiences were also painful. My awareness of my privileged position sometimes made me painfully uncomfortable with my attempts to pry into participants' lives. There is a fine line in fieldwork between public and private and ethnographers are normally trying to cross that line and move into the private realm, to understand the idiosyncrasies of individuals' everyday lives, to understand patterns of values and attitudes. In discussing adultery I attempted to show how ethnography has the potential to provide a rich understanding of sensitive issues, allowing the researcher to delve into different layers of interpretation among different segments in the community.

Notes

1 Macambira, a plant found in the region that is not only beautiful but resourceful, is the name I assigned to the community in which I conducted this ethnographic work in an attempt to preserve informants' anonymity.

2 Fieldwork data reported in this chapter was collected as part of a larger research project entitled "The social impact of television on reproductive behavior in Brazil." This interdisciplinary research involved professionals from anthropology, sociology, demography, and communication from several institutions in Brazil and the United States (University of Texas at Austin, CEBRAP – Centro Brasileiro de Análise e Planejamento, University of Campinas, Federal University of Minas Gerais, and School of Communications at University of São Paulo). Hewlett Foundation generously funded the fieldwork.

3 Where I have used fieldwork and interview data I have included a reference to provide the reader with a sense of the kind of data used and the date on which it was collected. Fieldnote data is followed by (Fieldnote, [date]) and interview data is followed by the ([date]) on which the interview was conducted.

4 With a dish, the number increases to fourteen or sixteen stations depending on the size of the dish. Most of the open channels in the South became available, bringing in a wide choice. The reduction in the cost of a satellite dish, as well as the decline of inflation and the strengthening of the currency in the mid-1990s, gave many locals the chance to acquire larger consumer items, such as a dish, a video cassette recorder, or a stereo.

5 *O Rei do Gado*, as explained before, means The King of Cattle. In Brazil, when a person is betrayed, the derogatory word used is *chifre* (horns) or *chifrudo* (with horns). *Galho*, meaning tree branches, is also used as a synonym for *chifre*. In this way, The King of Cattle became The King of *Galho* (symbolizing horns, meaning one betrayed). This pun was used not only in Macambira, but throughout Brazil it was incorporated in comedic routines on television shows, on radio and in cartoons. In Macambira, people jokingly called each other *O Rei do Galho*. Slowly, however, calling someone *o Rei do gado*, maintaining the original name, become symbolic of calling someone a cuckold, undermining his masculinity. Many times the term *Rainha do Gado* (the Queen of Cattle) was used to refer to women whose husbands betrayed them often.

6   Patos is a city with a 100,000 people, about 60 miles from Macambira. There is a private college in that community with easier admission exams. Several people in Macambira went to night classes in Patos. There was a pick-up truck that took the students to the university three times a week. The monthly payment, during my field research, was close to US$80, more than the monthly income of many families in the community.

7   I failed to establish if there is a perception that men can betray as much in the South with impunity as is perceived to be the case in Macambira.

8   I wondered many times if their attitudes towards the Senator – being shy of saying anything about him – had anything to do with me. Supposedly in the community I was married and not willing to commit adultery. Few people commented on how rare my attitude was. But many were continuously trying to find out if I was having an affair with a local woman. Maybe the connection was never made, but I believe it to be pertinent to consider it a possible impact on my data collection.

9   Apparently younger men, in their thirties and married, had an easier time than older men acknowledging liking telenovelas. I wonder if this is related to their experience as migrant workers and the limited leisure activities on weeknights or to greater exposure to telenovelas at an young age. Several of the males who were more comfortable acknowledging that they enjoyed telenovelas were younger. Of the older men, several watched *O Rei do Gado*, but they normally said they liked few telenovelas, compared to younger males who acknowledged liking the genre.

References

Almeida, H., Hamburger, E. and La Pastina, A. (1999). The reception of imported telenovelas in three Brazilian communities. Paper presented at the II Colloquium on Communication an Cultural Industries in NAFTA and MERCOSUR, University of Texas at Austin, June 1–2.

Ang, I. (1991). *Desperately seeking the audience*. New York: Routledge.

Barley, N. (1983). *Adventures in a mud hut: An innocent anthropologist abroad*. New York: Vanguard Press.

D'Andrade, R. (1995). Moral models in anthropology. *Current Anthropology* 36(3), 399–408.

FIBGE (2000). *Sinopse preliminar do censo demográfico: Brasil*. Rio de Janeiro: FIBGE.

Giddens, A. (1979). *Central problems in social theory: Action, structure and contradiction in social analysis*. Berkeley: University of California Press.

Giddens, A. (1984). *The constitution of society*. Berkeley: University of California Press.

Katz, E., Blumler, J. G. and Gurevitch, M. (1974). Utilization of mass communication by the individual. In E. Katz and J. G. Blumler (eds), *The uses of mass communication*. Beverly Hills, CA: Sage.

La Pastina, A. (1999). The telenovela way of knowledge: An ethnographic reception study among rural viewers in Brazil. Doctoral Dissertation, University of Texas at Austin.

La Pastina, A. (2001). Product placement in Brazilian prime time television: The case of a telenovela reception. *Journal of Broadcast and Electronic Media* 45, 541–557.

Leal, O. F. (1986). *A leitura social da novela das oito*. Petrópolis, Brazil: Vozes.

Liebes, T. and Katz, E. (1990). *The export of the meaning: Cross-cultural readings of Dallas*. New York: Oxford University Press.

Lins da Silva, C. E. (1985). *Muito além do Jardim Botânico: um estudo sobre a audiência do Jornal Nacional da Globo entre trabalhadores*. São Paulo: Summus Editorial.

Lopez, A. (1991). The melodrama in Latin America: Films, telenovelas, and the currency of a popular form. In M. Landy (ed.), *Imitations of life: A reader on film and television melodrama*. Detroit: Wayne State University Press.

Marcus, G. and Fischer, M. (1986). *Anthropology as cultural critique: An experimental moment in the human sciences*. Chicago and London: University of Chicago Press.

Martín-Barbero, J. (1993). *Communication, culture and hegemony: From the media to mediations*. Newbury Park, CA: Sage.

Mazzioti, N. (1993). El estado de las investigaciones sobre telenovela lationo-americana. *Revista de Ciencias de la Informacion* 8 (special issue), 45–59.

McAnany, E. G. and La Pastina, A. C. (1994). Telenovela audiences: A review and methodological critique of Latin American research. *Communication Research* 21(6), 828–849.

Miranda-Ribeiro, P. (1997). Telenovela and the sexuality transition among teenagers in Brazil. Ph.D. Dissertation, Population Research Center, University of Texas at Austin.

Morley, D. and Silverstone, R. (1991). Communication and context: Ethnographic prospectives on the media audience. In K. Jensen and N. Jankowski (eds), *Handbook of qualitative methodologies for mass communication research*. London: Routledge.

Murphy, P. D. (1999). Media cultural studies' uncomfortable embrace of ethnography. *Journal of Communication Inquiry* 23(3), 205–221.

Prado, R. M. (1987). Mulher de novela e mulher de verdade: Estudo sobre cidade pequena, mulher e telenovela. Masters Thesis, Rio de Janeiro, Universidade Federal do Rio de Janeiro, Museu Nacional.

Rios-Neto, E. L. G., Miranda-Ribeiro, P. and Potter, J. (1998). I saw it on TV: Television and demographic change in Brazil. Paper presented at the Workshop on the Social Dynamics of Fertility Change in Developing Countries, National Academy of Sciences, Washington, DC.

Sanches, N. and de Lima, J. (1997). Entre a tela e a vida real. *Veja* 1482, February 12, 52–56.

Scheper-Hughes, N. (1995). The primacy of ethical: Proposition of a militant ethnography. *Current Anthropology* 36(3), 409–420.

Stoller, P. (1992) *The taste of ethnographic things: The senses in anthropology*. Philadelphia: University of Pennsylvania Press.

Tufte, T. (1995). Living with the rubbish queen: A media ethnography about telenovelas in everyday life of Brazilian women. Ph.D. Dissertation, Department of Film and Media Studies, University of Copenhagen.

9

METHODOLOGY AS LIVED EXPERIENCE

Rhizomatic ethnography in Hawai'i[1]

Fay Yokomizo Akindes

A rhizome has no beginning or end;
it is always in the middle, between things,
interbeing, *intermezzo*.

(Deleuze and Guattari, 1987, p. 25)

Rhizomes provide the necessary language – lines of flight – that frees me to be a "thinker of the outside" (Boundas, 1993, p. 1). The rhizome, as explicated by Deleuze and Guattari (1987), generates connections and has characteristics of heterogeneity, multiplicity, disjunction, difference, multiple entry points, and routes rather than roots. Such a figuration is particularly useful for my ethnographic study of music, identity, and tourism in a postcolonial site. More specifically, the rhizome invites an understanding of methodology as lived experience, as well as my subjectivity as a researcher, Hawai'i's positionality in a transnational context, hybrid identities and music, tourist discourse, and (auto)ethnography as a process and product.

Rhizomes blur the boundaries between ideological, scientific, and philosophical modes of thinking and promote an interdisciplinary epistemology by opening up an infinite number of entering points. In other words, rhizomes do not recognize borders; they connect ideas, things, people, places without biases and pre-judgments. Consequently rhizomes disrupt binary oppositions, unfixing the logic of either/or and replacing it with the possibilities of *both/and*. Graafland (1999, p. 3) writes, "This ambiguous spatial metaphor of the rhizome is comprised mainly of openings; it is not known whether these openings provide access to an inside or an outside, whether they are an entrance or an exit." Similarly filmmaker Trinh T. Minh-ha (1997) explains:

> The moment the insider steps out from the inside she's no longer a
> mere insider. She necessarily looks in from the outside while also

147

looking out from the inside. Not quite the same, not quite the other, she stands in that undetermined threshold place where she constantly drifts in and out.

(p. 418)

The ambiguity that Trinh describes echoes the rhizome and its propensity for conjunctions and composites, for unsettling binary thinking.

The rhizome creates a space where the "unexpected can occur, where change and transition are not only possible but necessary" (Graffland, 1999, p. 3), which makes it well-suited for interrogating postcolonial sites that dislodge totalizing Eurocentric thinking. Postcolonialism, as I view it, is not so much a chronological progression from colonialism but more of an epistemological stance that unsettles and de-privileges the colonial imagination. When understood in the context of Hawaiian-music radio and identity, rhizomatic music functions as a reflector of change through conjunctions and composites. Hawaiian music defies a tracing to origins and instead embodies what Hebdige (1990) calls the "cut 'n' mix" of hybridized voices and instrumentation in complex formations. Native Hawaiian rappers connect with African-American hip hop, for example, to produce *na mele paleoleo* (Hawaiian rap), a decidedly defiant articulation of resistance against colonizing forces (Akindes, 2001). Rhizomes also problematize the permanent anchorage of words and meaning, freeing them to multiple interpretations. This multiplicity of meaning could be viewed as a dilution of power, but from a post-colonial perspective it is liberating and empowering particularly for indigenous groups, such as Native Hawaiians, that are currently engaged in a nationalist movement for economic self-determination. Rhizomes, then, unleash identities from patrimonial (colonial) bonds. In terms of tourist discourse, rhizomes explain why the everyday lives of "living in Hawai'i Hawaiians" (J. Kaneshiro, personal communication, July 19, 1996) are always "in the middle, between things," serving the Other (tourist) while also being the Other. Perhaps most importantly, rhizomes explain why the tourist feels at home in Hawai'i while the Native is displaced. Multiple entry points for the tourist to feel at home also serve as exit points for the Native to feel displaced at home.

Auto-ethnography is rhizomatic in that it blurs the line between subject and object, researcher and research participants, in what Hastrup (1987) calls the "mirror of fieldwork." She questions fieldwork that is parallel-cultural as opposed to cross-cultural and suggests that:

[u]nder such conditions your fieldwork is likely to reflect the situation of the one-way mirror; *you* will see only yourself and you will identify "them" with your own image (of past and present conditions); *they*, on the other hand, will see through to "you", and talk to you as if you were a real person in their world, absolutely distinct from themselves.

(p. 104)

As a native ethnographer studying my home, my self was interpellated in the research process. What emerged was not only an understanding of the phenomena studied, but my-self as a subject. As Murphy (1999a) writes, "telling stories about the unfolding of the field experience is a useful way to explicate processes of self-destabilization, changing power relations, and *how one's own consciousness as an ethnographer is shaped and transformed*" (p. 481, emphasis added).

This essay explicates methodology as lived experience in the context of field/home-work in Hawai'i. Before I begin explicating methodological questions, I will historically contextualize Hawai'i in relation to its foreign colonizers and settlers.

Historicizing Hawai'i

The underlying assumption in dominant European and American discourse is that life in Hawai'i began with the accidental landing of the British Captain James Cook in 1778. In actuality Hawaiians were forming a meaningful existence even before "there existed an England, an English language, or an Anglo-Saxon people" (Trask, 1993, p. 4). When the Europeans first arrived, they were called *haole*, which literally means "without breath," because they could not speak the Native Hawaiian language. Today *haole* refers to white people. *Haole* also connotes a certain way of being, as reflected in the *Molokai Advertiser*, which in the mid-1990s headlined its police beat with "Report on *Haole* Activity" then explained that "[p]erpetrators of crime are acting *haole*."

Historically Cook is positioned as a great explorer, a benevolent man, whom the Native Hawaiians took to be the God Lono (Sahlins, 1995). Recently, however, the apotheosis of Cook has been rewritten as a European myth (Obeyesekere, 1992). There are several evidential examples that rebuke the likelihood that Cook was believed by Hawaiians to be their God Lono, the most striking being Hawaiians' behavior after Cook's death. The Hawaiians, for example, did not respond to his death as they normally would an *ali'i* (chief). Instead they demonstrated signs of disrespect including conch-blowing and parading in Cook's clothes and hat. In short, "they treated him as an opponent killed in a battle" (Obeyesekere, 1992, p. 187).

The arrival of *haole* triggered the violent genocide of Natives. Within 100 years, a population of nearly a million people was annihilated to less than 48,000, or a depopulation ratio of twenty to one, although many scholars consider this ratio to be too conservative (Stannard, 1989). Infectious diseases such as cholera, bubonic plague, measles, pneumonia, venereal diseases, and smallpox devastated the local population. The foreign imposition of capitalism (fur and whaling trade, sandalwood, cash crops), combined with Calvinist missionaries sent from New England, radically altered the material conditions of Hawaiians' everyday lives. The American invasion resulted in a state of "land, rule, and Christianity" (Kirch and Sahlins, 1992, p. 92). Practices that Hawaiians considered natural, normal, and sacred – sexuality, music, hula – were deemed abominable and sinful by the missionaries. The Hawaiian *ali'i* (chiefs) who converted to Christianity, in turn, banned such practices among their own people.

In the mid-1800s, American businessmen – many of them missionary descendants who commandeered the claiming of Native lands – capitalized on sugar and pineapple production for US export. They imported laborers from China, Portugal, Japan, Korea, Puerto Rico and the Philippines. The largest group of plantation workers originated in Japan; in 1920 Japanese workers constituted 42.7 percent of Hawai'i's population, compared to 16.3 percent of Native Hawaiians and 7.7 percent of *haole* (Lind, 1967, p. 28). Subsequently Native Hawaiians found themselves marginalized and displaced in their own home. In 1893 the Hawaiian monarchy was overthrown by American businessmen (some of whom were missionary descendants) with the armed support of the US Navy. Hawai'i was subsequently annexed and became a US Territory in 1900. This led to the colonial imposition of English as the official language and the silencing of the Native Hawaiian language – in short, the economic, political, social, and mental colonization of the Islands. Hawai'i was incorporated into the US as a state in 1959 followed by a dramatic economic shift from agriculture to tourism, which today is responsible (directly and indirectly) for 80 percent of the state's annual revenue (Hawai'i Visitors Bureau, 1993). During the 1960s a cultural revolution now referred to as the Hawaiian Renaissance revived an interest in the Native Hawaiian language, chanting, hula, and other cultural practices. This cultural awakening broadened to a political movement for economic self-sufficiency and self-determination among Native Hawaiians, currently called the Hawaiian Sovereignty Movement.

The term "Native" or "Native Hawaiian" is used to refer to members of Hawai'i's indigenous people as opposed to those living in Hawai'i of *haole* settler or immigrant genealogy. The use of "Native" by Hawaiians explains the importance of distinguishing the history and lived practice of immigrants and indigenous people. Trask (1990) writes:

> It is characteristic of American ideology to reiterate that "we are all immigrants." Capitalizing the word Native reminds the reader that some of us are not immigrants. Thus, my usage is political on a geographical level; we are Native to Hawai'i and not the United States. It is political on an ideological level: we are neither Western nor Eastern but Native to the Pacific Islands. And it is political on a cultural level: we're not transplants from somewhere else, but indigenous to our archipelago, Hawai'i.
>
> (p. 906)

As Trinh (1992) writes, "naming is always a political choice" (p. 183).

Tourist discourse

Discourse implicates power; those who have the power to create discourse – a way of seeing – also have the power to make it true. There is, therefore, no inherent "truth" but only constructed truth stemming from discourse. MacCannell (1973, p. 597) problematizes tourism based on Goffman's dichotomous theory of front region and back region. He claims that tourists seek an "authenticity" that is lacking in industrialized nations and that the demanding tourist gaze inevitably results in the host culture's constructing front spaces that resemble back spaces or "staged authenticity." He writes, "It is always possible that what is taken to be entry into a back region is really entry into a front region that has been totally set up in advance for touristic visitation" (p. 597). In contrast to this front region/back region dichotomy is the idea of "ethnicity-for-tourism" in which the tendency of tourists to "go native" is complemented by locals who "go-native-for-tourists" (p. 159). A good example of this phenomenon is the Polynesian Cultural Center located on the North Shore of Oahu and owned by the Church of Jesus Christ of Latter-Day Saints. The Center recreates seven "authentic" Polynesian villages complete with "Natives" (Polynesian students at the neighboring Brigham-Young University-Laie, also owned by the Mormon Church), constituting a human zoo where Island people are commodified as exotic specimens to be gazed at and fixed in photography. A promotional brochure for the Polynesian Cultural Center discursively situates the simulacrum as a continuity rather than a pre-tourist site, and promises tourists that the Cultural Center experience "will stay with you a lot longer than your tan."

Foucault's conceptualization of discourse as a system of knowledge helps to explain how tourist discourse functions in the lives of Hawaiians. For example, when Hawaiians who speak Pidgin English engage in the discourse of tourism, they are automatically positioned to speak the language of *haole*, in order to get a tourist job, to work more closely with *haole* (better tips), and to be rendered an "international sophisticate" able to traverse the universe. At the same time, however, speaking Pidgin is a means of excluding others (*haole*) and demonstrating working-class solidarity. It also represents the last remaining bit of authenticity left in Hawai'i among locals (Tsai, 1995).

Pidgin English is Hawai'i's lingua franca, which originated in ports of trade: Honolulu, Lahaina, and Hilo. It was the language of commerce between Hawaiians and *haole*. Later, during the plantation era, the language of workers – Chinese, Japanese, Filipino, and others – mixed with the language of the Native Hawaiians, the *haole* owners, and Portuguese *luna* (supervisors) to create a hybrid spoken language that incorporated non-verbal cues. What is commonly called Pidgin English in Hawai'i is theoretically Hawaiian Creole English, according to linguists. Sato (1985, p. 256) makes this distinction: "a pidgin is developed by speakers of different languages for use among themselves" whereas Creole is "a language spoken by native-born children of pidgin-speaking parents. It functions as the mother tongue of its speakers, not as a functionally restricted, structurally reduced second language."

An important aspect of discourse is how those who produce the discourse "also have the power to make it true . . . to enforce its validity" (Hall, 1996, p. 203). For example, during the 1970s and 1980s, when I still lived in Hawai'i, "word-of-mouth" stories circulated about tourist rental cars being vandalized at remote sites of the island or of *haole* tourists being beaten up by locals. Tourists were advised to avoid Waimanalo, Nanakuli, Waianae, Molokai – Hawaiian Homelands populated by Native Hawaiians – thereby keeping the "back region" doors shut to "guests." Fear-driven myths ensure that visitors are not exposed to the actual material conditions of Hawaiians, which contradict the tourist discourse of the "happy [and accommodating] Hawaiian" in paradise. Native Hawaiians parallel the lives of Native American Indians; both have the highest rates of alcoholism, homelessness, unemployment, and incarceration. Hawai'i residents who internalize the tourist discourse often adopt a similar degree of fear and distrust toward Native Hawaiians. This phenomenon under-scores how tourist discourse is the episteme that governs all public discourse, and raises questions regarding the various ways in which local residents negotiate discursive structures that position Hawai'i and Hawaiians both as a commodification of paradise and an internal threat to that paradise. How do locals reproduce "voices" (by this, I mean music, the spoken word, radio sounds) in negotiating their cultural identity? How do they negotiate conflicting "voices" in their everyday lives? How do they experience the "othering" of self?

Thinking research

This chapter is based on research that explored the function of Hawaiian-music radio in the identity of people living and working in a tourist habitus. During the course of twelve weeks in the winter of 1994 (December–January) and the summer of 1996 (June–July), I conducted thirty interviews with consumers and producers of Hawaiian-music radio, specifically two FM radio stations that broadcast 80–99 percent locally produced Hawaiian music. I also gathered documents from academic and popular discourse, and listened to Hawaiian music via radio broadcasts, CD recordings, and live performances. My research problematic was informed by cultural studies, auto-ethnography, and phenomenology, research methodologies that share paradigmatic assumptions of ontology and epistemology. Specifically these shared meta-theoretical ideas include the ontological assumption of free-will, as opposed to determinism, and the epistemological assumption that knowledge, both practical and theoretical, is constructed and inherently rhizomatic, rather than singular.

Doing research: trajectory

My rhizomatic ability to traverse borders, to be both inside and outside of academe and the working-class culture, much like my ability to speak Standard and Pidgin English, gives me multiple passports, multiple privileges. This constant shifting between insider and outsider, native and other, constitutes an in-betweenness that resists closure and classification. Du Bois (1993) perceived this concept of twoness or "double consciousness" as a curse, "this sense of always looking at one's self through the eyes of others, of measuring one's soul by the tape of a world that looks on in amused contempt and pity" (p. 179). Similarly Fanon (1967) recognized the doubleness of the black man's psychological alienation, specifically the economic inferiority and, more profoundly, the *internalization* of this inferiority. This hybridized position is, I believe, also a privilege. As Said (1998) writes:

> the essential privilege of exile is to have not just one set of eyes but half a dozen, each of them corresponding to the places you have been . . . There is always a kind of doubleness to that experience, and the more places you have been the more displacements you've gone through, as every exile does. As every situation is a new one, you start out each day anew.
>
> (p. 48)

The idea of *starting anew* is consistent with rhizomes; the field is always shifting, whether "talking story" or observing a particular habitus.

Research participants

In conducting interviews with consumers (listeners) of Hawaiian-music radio in Hawai'i, I was interested in discovering how listeners resist tourist discourse and how it positions them as Natives. The assumption that history does not emanate from tourist destinations, such as the Bahamas, Antigua, and Hawai'i, has dangerous leakages into the psychological sphere of people who live in these localities. Tourist discourse, as a form of colonialism, mutes the Native, who internalizes the assumption that his/her voice lacks any substantive value.

Mari, a 40-year-old housewife and mother, is a good example of how a local mutes herself as a (post)colonial subject. When I first met her, she questioned her suitability to be interviewed for my study because she said "local people have hard time expressing themselves." She was referring to her Pidgin English and suggested I talk to her local-*haole* husband because he speaks "better" English. This self-doubting and feeling of inferiority is characteristic of some Pidgin English locals, many of whom grew up in rural areas or in plantation towns where Pidgin is still the dominant language spoken and who equate English-language proficiency with intelligence. Yet Mari is someone who consciously clings to her Pidgin as a signifier of her local identity, something that feels comfortable, words that "come out like home" (Yamanaka, 1996, p. 13). While some parents disapprove of their children speaking Pidgin, Mari openly teaches her son and husband Pidgin expressions so that they can fit into local culture. She endures disapproving comments from her mother because, for Mari, it would be more shameful *not* to know a common Pidgin expression (Mari, personal communication, July 3, 1996).

When I first met Mari, I suspected her reluctance to speak was due, in part, to the presence of the tape-recorder, so I suggested we simply "talk story" without the recorder. We sat at the dining room table while our daughters played together in the adjoining living room. It was noon time and she was eating a "plate lunch" of miso butterfish with chopsticks. After a while she began to speak freely, sharing stories about her everyday life in relation to Hawaiian-music radio. Re-telling her experiences was clearly pleasurable. She took particular zeal in narrating an unexpected public encounter with "Uncle Sam Kapu," who is a Hawaiian DJ who speaks almost exclusively Pidgin English during his KINE-FM shift. When she recognized him, she said, "Eh, you Sam Kapu, eh?" and was stunned to silence when he responded in *Standard* English. She immediately labeled him a "fake" and thereafter resisted listening to his radio show since "he only talks Pidgin on the radio."

The next time we met, Mari gave me permission to use the tape-recorder. Her initial response to being interviewed is emblematic of women who, as gendered subjects in a patriarchal system, are positioned outside the realm of what constitutes legitimate experience and knowledge. Speaking out, though initially frightening, became self-validating and consequently empowering (Minister, 1991). Mari began "talking story" about her everyday encounters with a new sense of awareness by noticing the manifestations of identity in public spheres. For example, she went to a local eatery where her *haole* husband ordered a *mahi-mahi* (fish) sandwich and was asked by the waitress, "you like fries with dat?" Her husband, who wasn't listening, said "huh?" and the waitress quickly shifted her speech to "would you like fries with that?" Mari laughed at the memory and said, "I thought that was funny because I probably wouldn't have noticed it but all these questions you've been asking?" This kind of reflex is noted by Murphy (1999a): "after a period of incubation, individuals would return to ideas introduced in previous sessions to readdress them" (p. 499). This underscores the value of multiple "talk story" sessions as opposed to single sessions.

Interviewing Mari revealed to me the importance of being flexible in an interview situation and how "naming" the situation influences the nature of the exchange. "Interviewing" connotes a respondent who is learned and knowledgeable in the traditional sense; someone who is interviewed for televised news, for example, is usually a representative of official government discourse. "Talking story," on the other hand, describes verbal communication between locals. It is less hierarchical and suggests a balance of power, much the way removing one's shoes before entering a Japanese tea house normalizes social status among tea drinkers (this practice is emblematic of most households in Hawai'i, which makes for interesting analysis among Natives, locals, and *haole*). "Talking story" implies a spontaneous, casual, non-threatening exchange of ideas and feelings, and therefore precludes the necessity of a formal agenda or protocol.

Topical protocol

As Mari's struggle in becoming comfortable suggests, "talking story" sessions had to be "real" as opposed to the Uncle Sam Kapu "fake." Therefore, I designed a topical protocol with open-ended questions as a preliminary map of topics to be discussed rather than a preconceived sequence of questions. I engaged in the situation and the conversational logic of each person's narrative. My objective was to create a comfortable and non-threatening situation that was conducive to "talking story" about everyday experiences. Hawaiian-music radio functioned as a vehicle, a *medium* for talking about work, family, "small-kid time,"[2] pleasure – in short, their worldview. The everyday issues of incorporation were of equal, if not more, value to my study. I wasn't sure how music-radio interfaced with respondents' everyday life. I trusted that the meaning of Hawaiian-music radio would emerge in "talking story." As Trinh (1989) writes, "the heart of the matter is always somewhere else than where it is supposed to be . . . There is no catching, no pushing, no directing, no breaking through, no need for a linear progression which gives the comforting illusion that one knows where one goes" (p. 1). My topical protocol, then, served as a guide for numerous inter-actions, but was always interpellated differently.

Identifying/selecting participants

My criteria for "talking story" with listeners was that (1) they tuned-in to Hawaiian FM radio stations KCCN and/or KINE and (2) they had grown up in the Islands. At the start of the research process, I had established the criteria of interviewing only people born and raised in Hawai'i. While identifying research participants during my fieldwork, I met three *haole*, originally from the US continent, who listen to the station and offered to be interviewed. I awkwardly declined because of my initial criteria of "locals only." In retrospect, it would have added an important dimension to my study to probe their radio/music experiences and their adopted identity of Hawai'i as their new home. In other words, it would have been the rhizomatic thing to do.

In reflecting on my impulsive decision, I now realize that methodological issues that inform my research methods inevitably also implicate me on a personal level. Self-reflexivity holds a mirror up to myself, to see things whether I want to or not. What I see is not always admirable. Ironically, while I accuse others of essentializing, I have done the same. Moreover, I have excluded *haole* from my study as a means of denying their claim to Hawai'i as home. I have uncloaked my resentment toward "mainland" *haole* who have settled in Hawai'i while I live in exile in the US continent. By denying *haole* a voice in my study, I deny them the right to speak as Hawaiians. The subtext here is: "When are you going back to the 'mainland'?" This is the same attitude directed toward Asian Americans and other non-whites on the "mainland": "Where are you from/When are you going back?" (San Juan, Jr., 1994, p. 205). The underlying message is, of course: "You are not welcome here, you don't belong here, I don't

155

want to see you here." Denying *haole* a place in Hawai'i is the function of Hawaiian radio for John, one of my research participants. He works at the college gym where he sets the radio station to KCCN-FM, which plays contemporary Hawaiian music, including reggae-inspired "Jawaiian" music. John says, "The *haoles* don't like it. They always ask me to change. But there's always a bigger Hawaiian [laughs] so I say, 'oh, if you can tell them come and tell me change it' then I'll change it for you" (John, personal communication, July 10, 1996). John defers to the local students as "masters" of the radio dial, much the way male family members dominate the television remote control as a sign of power.

My assumption that "everyone" listens to Hawaiian-music radio was a hollow one. Soon after arriving in Honolulu, I began my search for research participants by describing my project to an informal network of three sisters, a brother, cousins, friends from high school and college, and former media colleagues (I formerly worked at the CBS-TV affiliate and Hawai'i Public TV). New technologies have made radio one of several entertainment choices in the car, where most radio listening takes place. As such, three to four people whom I spoke to prefer to listen to tape cassettes or compact discs in their car. Other people spend a limited amount of time in their car, do not have a car, or don't have a radio in the car. One person said she rarely listens to Hawaiian radio, but predicted that she would probably spend the entire next day listening to Hawaiian-music radio because she was about to leave for a ten-day vacation on the "mainland." Listening to Hawaiian music, then, was her preparation for coping with displacement, for anticipating homesickness.[3]

Inevitably someone knew of someone who listened to KCCN or KINE, or offered to ask around, and this resulted in an initial half-dozen persons to interview. I scheduled interviews throughout the week, but learned to expect change on a daily basis. Someone would reschedule, cancel, or simply fail to show up at the designated time and place. The resulting ambiguity was disorienting. Initially I expected a linearity in my research, a logic of control and predictability, which I eventually learned was an unrealistic expectation, particularly since my study was grounded in post-positivistic assumptions. I reverted to my child-laboring strategy of surrendering to the moment. This shifting presented an impossibility of using the traditional data-gathering technique called "snowballing," which assumes a certain clean order and more-over contradicts Hawai'i's tropical locus where it only snows high atop Mt Kilauea and Haleakala. Therefore, even though I may have practiced similar research techniques (asking participants for others to interview, new leads, etc.), the theoretical and metaphorical consequences were entirely different.

Rhizomes provide a theoretically grounded methodology for this study, as opposed to the epistemologically and geographically specific "snowballing" metaphor. The "snowball" metaphor emphasizes that all participants eventually merge into and are carried away by the larger project, which gathers momentum, speed, bulk, and power. The metaphor is flawed, in that it ignores the packing of data by someone onto the little snowball to make it bigger. Each new person interviewed was not isolated but part of the "middle," without beginning, without end. My interviews did not build one on top of each other in a progressive linear sequence (implied by the snowball method), but instead provided glimpses of experience from a variety of situated points of view. The experience was not without ambiguity, discomfort, and uncertainty, much the way nomads, exiles and hybrid identities experience home; "no sooner does one get accustomed to it than its unsettling force erupts anew" (Said, 1990, p. 366). As a methodological metaphor, then, rhizomes unsettle the illusion of rooted-ness that positivistic approaches to research convey. As Deleuze and Guattari (1987, p. 9) explain, "a rhizome may be broken, shattered at a given spot, but it will start up again on one of its old lines, or on new lines." Its chaotic nature enables me to be a "thinker of the outside," to consider new possibilities outside the dominant order of things.

Another way to describe my field experience is with the syncretic example of "zigzagging" or "tacking," which describes a researcher's movement between deliberate contact and deliberate distancing (Polkinghorne, 1983, p. 255). Just as a sailboat tacks alongside the wind and current, I tacked between Hawai'i and the continental US (winter 1993, summer 1995) then returned to the US continent with my stolen or borrowed bounty of empirical data: tape cassettes of personal interviews and radio broadcasts, CDs of Hawaiian music, magazines, newspaper clippings, and xeroxed copies of journal articles to consume and synthesize. My most recent tackings have been virtual, taking place in cyberspace on the World Wide Web. In addition to empirical data, I embodied the spatial distance from Hawai'i, in between visits, through regular phone conversations and e-mail correspondence with family and friends, subscriptions to *Honolulu* magazine and the *Honolulu Weekly* newspaper, and the internet. News of the death of musician Braddah Iz, for example, reached me through a phone conversation with my sister Lei, followed by news clippings of his stately funeral, and memoriam on the internet. My field research, then, did not stop when I left the Islands. Technological extensions (the telephone, mail, internet) were necessary, and proved to be essential, in continuing my research. In fact, my cyberspace habitus, which collapsed the distance between Hawai'i and Wisconsin, evinced the diaspora habitus and enabled me to access formerly inaccessible plateaus.

The first challenge in conducting interviews was scheduling meeting times; the second was ensuring that the meetings actually took place. I have identified several reasons why research participants chose not to meet with me: unfamiliarity with the research and researcher, intimidation by mention of the "Ph.D." or "dissertation," and the spontaneity of Hawaiian lifestyle which places priority on the "here and now" – if something comes up, *ain't no big t'ing braddah*. Other conceivable explanations focus more on my role as researcher: was my approach in inviting participants stilted? Were my assumptions unfounded? Everyone whom I interviewed had a close connection with me or someone close to me. Ontologically these are local people who value family and friendship.

Therefore, the tighter the personal relationship between the persons involved (research participant and referral), the more likely the interview would take place. One of my respondents is a banquet captain for a large Waikiki hotel where he works with my sister's best friend. His schedule changes weekly, which makes it difficult to schedule a time to meet. Three weeks of weekly phone calls transpired before we finally met for our interview. This example reveals not only the persistance necessary in scheduling interviews, but also the rhizomatic nature of the tourist industry and its implications for the lives of Natives. Tourists from around the world, and predominantly from the continental US and Japan, are constantly flying into the Islands and reconfiguring the landscape. In turn, Natives who service tourists live rhizomatic lives, reordering their everyday routines depending on the flow of tourists.

It is not surprising, then, that scheduled interviews were cancelled, both overtly (by calling me) or covertly (by not showing up). A woman who works in television programming with a former boss of mine cancelled her interview because of her second job as a hula dancer on a dinner-cruise for tourists. An escort for a tourist luau, who works from 3 p.m. to 10 p.m., missed our midday interview because he was sleeping in after a late night. Another woman, a working single-mother, cancelled to spend time with her daughter. These three persons who failed to keep appointments claimed to have conflicting engagements; I suspect they were also disinterested and perhaps wary of being interviewed by a stranger. The relationship that these three persons had with me or my contacts was more of an acquaintance than friendship, thus supporting my earlier stated theory that the degree of closeness between potential research participants and my contacts influenced their level of commitment to my project. These failed interviews make visible the obstacles in my research study that were out of my control and contributed to feelings of suspension.

Talking story and place

The physical setting where my "talking story" sessions unfolded were selected by the research participants. The place varied from a wooden picnic table near Makapu'u Beach to the living room floor at a walk-up apartment to a bench outside of an upscale shopping center. One session was scheduled for McDonald's but the noise level prevented our talk from being recorded, so we sat in my borrowed Toyota under a coconut tree. One participant suggested we meet for *pau hana* (after work) drinks and *pupus* (hors d'oeuvres). Another participant had her two-week-old baby sleeping in a bassinet nearby while we "talked story" at the dining table, drinking guava juice. The physical setting was important in putting the research participant at ease for "talking story" freely about everyday matters. As Gottschalk (1998) writes:

> Sites impact our senses, promote various insights, orient perception, nurture a variety of emotional responses, enable and limit different

kinds of interactions, summon diverse subjectivities, and thus should call for different approaches and writing styles. Site affects sight and site affects cite.

(p. 212)

The physical site or place/setting of sessions influenced the talk – the extensiveness in which the research participant revealed experiences and engaged in talk with me. My "talk story" session with Emma, a Native Hawaiian woman, took place at a beach near Makapu'u while fishermen reeled in their *papio* (fish). She talked of the *'aina* (land) and mentioned that the beach we sat on was Hawaiian Homes land. Eventually she "talked story" about her job in real estate and the emotional experience of observing the exchange of a sliver of Hawaiian land for millions of dollars to a foreigner from the "mainland." Emma says, "The Hawaiian people have had a lot of things taken away from them because of their lack of knowledge so I would really want to check and see what [the Hawaiian Sovereignty Movement] has to offer . . . I'm afraid to take that stand right now . . . I might not have a job. I have to protect my job" (Emma, personal communication, June 22, 1996). Her voice cracks; her sunglasses mask her tears. The wind sprays us with a mist of salt-water. *Site affects sight and site affects cite* (Gottschalk, 1998, p. 212, my emphasis).

Summary on doing research

For a long time, the "talk story" sessions I recorded in Hawai'i were foremost in my research, because they were new, original texts that I self-consciously produced. What I failed to consider was that they were one of several research texts to be synthesized into my study. Doing research, then, is a multifaceted practice that does not necessarily privilege one method over another, particularly in an interpretive study that constantly shifts and changes according to spatial and temporal contexts. At the same time, doing ethnography demands not only a convergence of theory and practice, but a certain vigilance to avoid slippage to "simulacrum ethnography, whereby ethnographic texts are produced by means of other texts rather than fieldwork" (Murphy, 1999b, p. 210). "Fieldwork, textwork, and headwork" remain critical nodes in rhizomatic ethnography (Van Maanen, 1995, p. 4).

Coda

In my mind's eye, I see a Hawaiian church on the Big Island of Hawai'i that was spared by one of Kilauea's multiple volcanic eruptions. Houses, trees, highways, even the famed Kalapana black-sand beach, were engulfed by lava, leaving just this simple wooden place of worship. Yet in a subsequent eruption it, too, disappeared.

When I envision a nature scene that exemplifies Deleuze and Guattari's concept of rhizomes, I think of the Big Island of Hawai'i and its active volcanic eruptions that, since 1983, have radically altered the island's landscape. Lava in the form of *a'a* (rough lava), *pahoehoe* (smooth lava), and *'ala* (water-worn lava) continually changes the surface of the lava fields while at the same time remapping the boundaries of the island as the lava converges with the sea. As Deleuze and Guattari (1987) explain, "The tree is filiation, but the rhizome is alliance, uniquely alliance. The tree imposes the verb 'to be,' but the fabric of the rhizome is the conjunction, 'and . . . and . . . and . . .'" (p. 25). In other words, the island is in a perpetual state of *becoming*. Similarly the surface appearance of my study had a destabilizing rhizomatic quality.

When I started this research project, I believed that I would enter easily into a linear ethnographic process. What I actually experienced, however, was a trajectory that was disjointed, destabilizing, and altogether messy. I was a "native Hawaiian" (with a small "n") no longer living in Hawai'i, returning home, asking questions about identity that were dormant in the minds of my research participants. As the research evolved into writing, and as I revised and re-arranged subsections and categories, it became clear that methodology is a continually shifting process, not only during the "data-gathering" stage, but more importantly in the hybrid reconfigurations of interpretation and identity-shifting of everyone involved. I am not the same person who visited the "homeland" as an indigenous ethnographer in 1994 and 1996. During the writing of this work, I lived in Wisconsin, surfed the internet, and found myself asking different questions, considering new sources of information and re-visions of interpretations. This hermeneutic spiral made visible the rhizomatic and hybrid nature of methodology and, more specifically, ethnography.

This chapter has traced the trajectory of thinking and doing ethnography. Rhizomatic shifts were constant throughout; new themes emerged while old themes receded. Just when I thought I had gained clarity, something or someone was introduced into the "mix" which caused me to rethink and question earlier assumptions and understandings. In other words, the research study constituted a multidimensional, dynamic, shifting rhizome with infinite points of entry. This rhizomatic characteristic of my study disrupted the neat sequence of field/home-work – travelling to Hawai'i, identifying research participants, scheduling "talk story" sessions, talking story, observing, note-taking, gathering literature, travelling back to the US continent, transcribing, etc. – by recon-figuring the imagined linearity to an unpredictable shifting rhizome.

Even now as I re-read, re-write, and re-think rhizomes, I re-vision my understanding of how rhizomes relate to Native Hawaiian identity in the context of the nationalist movement. While rhizomes may be liberating in dislodging Native Hawaiians from their colonial subjectivity, rhizomes also defuse their power by unfixing their inherent claims to the land. Rhizomes as a fluid line of conjunctions and composites expand my understanding of music, methodology, tourism, and ethnography, but it is problematic in the context of Native Hawaiian identity.

Rhizomatic concepts of displacement and homelessness complicate Native claims to Hawaiian land by suggesting that indigenous Hawaiians are rooted/ routed in the South Pacific, which negates the indigenous claims of Native Hawaiians and redefines them as "settlers" like the European and American capitalists and Christian missionaries. Although Native Hawaiians do share a common history of decimation, dispossession, and displacement with other sovereignty-seeking peoples in New Caledonia, West Papua, East Timor, Belau, and Tahiti (Trask, 1993), their assertions of sovereignty do not feature histories of travel and settlement, but "stress continuity of habitation, aboriginality, and often a 'natural' connection to the land" (Clifford, 1997, p. 252). As Clifford writes, "[t]ribal cultures are not diasporas; their sense of rootedness in the land is precisely what diasporic people have lost" (p. 252). In short, rhizomes de-root Native Hawaiians from the omnipotent land which gives and sustains life, incorporating them as perpetual colonial subjects. Ironically, to de-colonize themselves, Native Hawaiians must *fix* their identities in resistance to a globalized culture of rhizomes.

The postcolonial/postmodern concept of rhizomes re-positions my engagement with questions about power, identity, nationhood, and land – concrete issues with real consequences in the material lives of Native Hawaiians. What is the function of rhizomes in understanding the Native Hawaiian nationalist movement? How do we ground the figuration of rhizomes, in itself a rootless concept, in real-life contexts, particularly ones that resist rhizomatic exile? These questions cannot be answered here, but I offer a thought from Nancy Hartsock (1987) as a point of departure for re-thinking rhizomes:

> Somehow it seems highly suspicious that it is at this moment in history, when so many groups are engaged in "nationalisms" which involve redefinitions of the marginalized Others, that doubt arises in the academy about the nature of the "subject," about the possibilities for a general theory which can describe the world, about historical "progress." Why is it, exactly at the moment when so many of us who have been silenced begin to demand the right to name ourselves, to act as subjects rather than objects of history, that just then the concept of subjecthood becomes "problematic"?
>
> (p. 196)

In the process of problematizing rhizomes as an alternative way of perceiving the world, specifically in the context of studying music, identity, and tourism in Hawai'i, I find myself questioning the ethical relationship between theory and everyday lived experience. While rhizomes allow me to be "a thinker of the outside" (Boundas, 1993, p. 1), they also align me, to some extent, with the hegemonic ideology (Miyoshi, 1993) and that is unsettling.

Notes

Mahalo nui to Jenny Nelson and Patrick Murphy for their thoughtful comments on earlier drafts of this work.

1 An earlier version of this chapter appeared in *Diegesis: Journal of the Association for Research in Popular Fictions* 5 (Winter 1999), published by Liverpool John Moores University.

2 When locals "talk story" about "small-kid time," they are reminiscing about childhood experiences.

3 Similarly, whenever I'm taking long road trips into unknown territory, such as my inaugural 500-mile drive from Athens, Ohio to Kenosha, Wisconsin (from graduate student to college instructor), my chosen music is taped compilations of Hawaiian music. This did not occur to me until, perhaps, my third lengthy car ride. The music grounds me, making me feel a part of a physical space thousands of miles away, while outside my car window red barns and silos dot the flat exotic plains.

References

Akindes, F. Y. (2001). Sudden Rush: *Na mele paleoleo* (Hawaiian rap) as liberatory discourse. *Discourse* 23(1), 81–98.

Bhabha, H. (1994). *The location of culture.* London: Routledge.

Boundas, C. V. (1993). Editor's introduction. *The Deleuze reader* (pp. 1–23). New York: Columbia University Press.

Clifford, J. (1997). *Routes: Travel and translation in the late twentieth century.* Cambridge: Harvard University Press.

Deleuze, G. and Guattari, F. (1987). *A thousand plateaus: Capitalism and Schizophrenia* (trans. B. Massumi). Minneapolis: University of Minnesota Press.

DuBois, W. E. (1993). Double-consciousness and the veil. In C. Lemert (ed.), *Social theory: The multicultural and classic readings* (pp. 177–182). Boulder, CO: Westview Press.

Fanon, F. (1967). *Black skin white masks.* New York: Grove Press.

Gottschalk, S. (1998). Postmodern sensibilities and ethnographic possibilities. In A. Banks and S. P. Banks (eds), *Fiction and social research: By ice or fire.* Walnut Creek, CA: AltaMira Press.

Graafland, A. (1999). Of rhizomes, trees, and the Ij-oevers, Amsterdam. *Assemblage* 38, 28–42.

Grossberg, L. (1992). *We gotta get out of this place: Popular conservatism and postmodern culture.* New York: Routledge.

Hall, S. (1996). Discourse and power. In S. Hall, D. Held, D. Hubert and K. Thompson (eds), *Modernity: An introduction to modern societies* (pp. 201–205). Cambridge: Blackwell.

Hartsock, N. (1987). Rethinking modernism: Minority vs. majority theories. *Cultural Critique* 7, 187–206.

Hastrup, K. (1987). Fieldwork among friends: Ethnographic exchange within the Northern civilization. In A. Jackson (ed.), *Anthropology at home* (pp. 94–108). London: Tavistock.

Hawai'i Visitors Bureau (1993). *If we lose our visitors, we lose it all* [video]. Honolulu: KITV-TV.

Hebdige, D. (1990). *Cut 'n' mix: Culture, identity and Caribbean music*. London: Routledge.

Kirch, P. V. and Sahlins, M. D. (1992). *Anahulu: The anthropology of history in the Kingdom of Hawai'i*. Honolulu: University of Hawai'i Press.

Lind, A. W. (1967). *Hawai'i's people* (3rd edn). Honolulu: University of Hawai'i Press.

MacCannell, D. (1973). Staged authenticity: Arrangements of social space in tourist settings. *American Journal of Sociology* 79(3), 589–603.

MacCannell, D. (1992). *Empty meeting grounds: The tourist papers*. London: Routledge.

Minister, K. (1991). A feminist frame for the oral history interview. In S. B. Gluck and D. Patai (eds), *Women's words: The feminist practice of oral history*. New York: Routledge.

Miyoshi, M. (1993). A borderless world? From colonialism to transnationalism and the decline of the nation-state. *Critical Inquiry* 19, 726–751.

Murphy, P. (1999a). Doing audience ethnography: A narrative account of establishing ethnographic identity and locating interpretive communities in fieldwork. *Qualitative Inquiry* 5(4), 479–504.

Murphy, P. (1999b). Media cultural studies' uncomfortable embrace of ethnography. *Journal of Communication Inquiry* 23(3), 205–221.

Obeyesekere, G. (1992). *The apotheosis of Captain Cook: European mythmaking in the Pacific*. Princeton, NJ: Princeton University Press.

Polkinghorne, D. (1983). *Methodology for the human sciences: Systems of inquiry*. Albany: State University of New York Press.

Rosaldo, M. (1984). Toward an anthropology of self and feeling. In R. A. Shweder and R. A. LeVine, (eds), *Culture theory: Essays on mind, self and emotion* (pp. 137–157). Cambridge: Cambridge University Press.

Sahlins, M. (1995). *How "natives" think*. Chicago: University of Chicago Press.

Said, E. (1990). Reflections on exile. In R. Ferguson, M. Gever, M. Trinh and C. West (eds), *Out there: Marginalization and contemporary culture* (pp. 357–366). New York: New Museum of Contemporary Art.

Said, E. (1998). Edward Said: The voice of a Palestinian in exile. In *Third text* (pp. 39–50). London: Kala Press.

San Juan, Jr., E. (1994). The predicament of Filipinos in the United States: "Where are you from? When are you going back?" In K. Aguilar-San Juan (ed.), *The state of Asian America: Activism and resistance in the 1990s* (pp. 205–218). Boston: South End Press.

Sato, C. (1985). Linguistic inequality in Hawai'i: The post-creole dilemma. In N. Wolfson and J. Manes (eds), *Language of inequality*. Berlin: Mouton.

Stannard, D. E. (1989). *Before the horror: The population of Hawai'i on the eve of Western contact*. Honolulu: Social Science Research Institute, University of Hawai'i.

Trask, H.-K. (1990). Politics in the Pacific Islands: Imperialism and native self-determination. *Amerasia* 16(1), 1–19.

Trask, H.-K. (1993). *From a native daughter: Colonialism and sovereignty in Hawai'i*. Monroe, ME: Common Courage Press.

Trinh, T. M. (1989). *Woman, native, other: Writing postcolonialism and feminism*. Bloomington: Indiana University Press.

Trinh, T. M. (1992). *Framer framed*. New York: Routledge.

Trinh, T. M. (1997). Not you/like you: Postcolonial women and the interlocking questions of identity and difference. In A. McClintock, A. Mufti and E. Shohat (eds), *Dangerous liaisons: Gender, nation, and postcolonial perspectives* (pp. 415–419). Minneapolis: University of Minnesota.

Tsai, M. (1995). Pondering pidgin. *Honolulu Weekly*, 4 January, pp. 4–6.

Van Maanen, J. (1995). An end to innocence: The ethnography of ethnography. In J. Van Maanen (ed.), *Represention in ethnography* (pp. 1–35). Thousand Oaks, CA: Sage.

Yamanaka, L. A. (1996). *Wild meat and the bully burgers*. New York: Farrar Straus Giroux.

10

ON THE BORDER

Reflections on ethnography and gender

Heloisa Buarque de Almeida

In June 1996, I left my home in São Paulo, Brazil, to do fieldwork in Montes Claros, a city of approximately 250,000 inhabitants, in the north of Minas Gerais state, a droughtland region away from the main city centers of the country. In a larger research project,[1] I was supposed to watch the popular telenovela (around 50 percent of audience rates) *The Cattle King* (*O Rei do Gado*) with middle-class and working-class families. The program was aired on weekdays at eight o'clock on Globo, the largest Brazilian television network. The focus of this chapter is not the specific "findings" of the study, but rather the ethnographic work process with special attention to gender. My aim here is to reflect on traditional anthropological notions of participant observation via my own field experiences.

Many media reception studies in communication or cultural studies consider the need for ethnographic fieldwork, but conceptualize "ethnography" in a manner much more open than and thus quite distinct from anthropology's more rigid understanding. And while I find the work of some communication and cultural studies writers provocative, there seems to be a rather lose explication of what constitutes ethnography even as the importance of the social context is emphasized (see Ang, 1985; Brown, 1990; Morley, 1993; Seiter et al., 1989). Several reception studies by Brazilian anthropologists, on the other hand, demonstrate a commitment to the rigors of anthropology's notion of ethnographic inquiry (e.g. immersion, long-term participant observation, etc.) while also drawing on methods akin to those of communication researchers. For instance Leal (1986) and Prado (1987) both developed media ethnographies using in-depth interviews and focus groups without comprising the longer process of participant observation within a group or community. The experiences that I relate in this chapter can be considered an extension of this "anthropological" vision of what constitutes media ethnography.

A commitment to fieldwork can demand many months – in my case, seven. It was through such a commitment that I was able to draw from a rich experience of the day-to-day interaction of many individuals with television content. This is a point I want to stress, because the fruits of the field encounter were many. For example, first as an existential experience, the field process led me to deeper reflections about gender motivated by the constant perception of social inequalities between men and women and by a closer proximity to and identification with other women during fieldwork. Second, this immersion process was central to my grasp of the reality of people's everyday life and the place television and telenovelas take in this reality. Third, the field experience facilitated my understanding of both the social system in which my participants lived and their reading of televisual texts within that context. Finally, it also demanded that I consider my own interpretations of those readings because my status as "outsider" was a constant point of contention.

These field lessons frame the main focus of this chapter: the research dilemmas caused by the social place of women in the group researched and the social place of the ethnographer. As past research has made evident (Golde, 1986a), it can be difficult for the ethnographer to react and deal with behavior patterns that restrict the actions and movements of women. The ethnographer must deal with local gender constructions and the appropriate behavior for men and women, while also recognizing that those constructions and behaviors are in flux and heterogeneous as well. What is locally considered as appropriate femininity may vary among different social groups (age groups, for instance), but one has also to deal with the most dominant or hegemonic gender constructions. Those gender constructions often conflicted with my point of view and my experience of being a woman from São Paulo; they first restricted my action and generated a fear of expressing myself. Nevertheless, social heterogeneity and being an outsider also provide investigative opportunities for ethnographers (see Briggs; Codere; Freedman; Golde; Nader; and Weidman, all in Golde, 1986a).

The productivity of such field dilemmas is tied to another point of tension here: the contribution of so-called postmodern anthropology and its critique of the politics of fieldwork. In particular, Paul Rabinow's book *Reflections on Fieldwork in Morocco* (1984) haunts the pages of this chapter. Rabinow searches for a better understanding of the ethnographer's positioning in a liminal situation, trying to build bridges between cultures, but mainly constructed through an intersubjective and personal relationship with his or her informants. Considering this, fieldwork itself is a liminal intersubjective space of communication outside any specific culture, where both ethnographer and informant question their cultures and societies. The anthropologist rests in an unstable place, dealing many times with people who are also in liminal or critical situations in their society. Rabinow also stresses that the best informants are those not "well-fit" by social standards, for they might have a critical and reflective point of view even before meeting the ethnographer.

I propose here that this liminal space of fieldwork may allow the researcher to cross gender frontiers, dealing with both feminine and masculine universes – which may not even be so sharply distinguished as they seem at the beginning of fieldwork. According to many gender theories, feminine and masculine features are not necessarily attached respectively to women and men only – men can have feminine features and activities, and vice versa (see for instance Butler, 1990; Guttman, 1996; Louveau, 1996; Moore, 1997; Strathern, 1998; Strathern and MacCormack, 1980). The fact that the ethnographer is always an outsider makes it easier for a female ethnographer to break the restrictions imposed on most local women, and she may even be regarded as relatively "masculine" (or a-sexed) by her activity and work (Vale de Almeida, 1995). However, those acts of symbolic trespassing can create new problems, for people may distrust someone whose social status is not evident. My case exemplifies this productive but delicate tension between border crossing and trespassing.

Through my experiences in Montes Claros, I encountered at least three salient influences in gender constructions during fieldwork: a local heterogeneous context, television content and its multiple constructions, and finally the image of a "paulista" anthropologist ("paulista" is the word for those born in São Paulo). The image that people constructed of me (my "ethnographic identity") was influenced by what they saw on television and telenovelas about big city working women. Television images are pervasive in Brazilian society, and although there is a variety of readings, they also convey repetitive and dominant ideas. On the other hand, Montes Claros is not a small village or neighborhood. If it sounds coherent here, this is only a way of concisely showing some issues, looking for plausible generalizations.

Fieldwork experience

I begin this section with a personal citation from my field notes (re-written for this chapter). This citation reveals personal emotions and affective ties during fieldwork. But it also points to the matter of differences and distances between the ethnographer and community studied. It is common for ethnographers to be overwhelmed by mixed feelings and confusion like those analyzed here.

> Marcela sat on her bed and showed me the Bible: she had been praying when I arrived. I asked if everything was OK, and she said: "more or less." Why had she been praying so much? Because she had to get rid of many sins, she felt so guilty. She also prayed to protect their children, always asking God that they would not do drugs like her husband. She prayed in search of answers and to be more patient, to have peace. Her bad feeling could be something I would call anguish, but she never used this word.
>
> She told me she was very unhappy in her marriage. She had got married when pregnant (like many women I met there) at the age

of sixteen, and had two kids. She was tired of her husband, and thought she did not like him any more. But when she talked to him about divorce, he seemed to fall in love with her, and he would try to seduce her. Other times she thought she liked him, and then he did not treat her right. He drank, he did cocaine. Then I asked since she was so unhappy, why not leave him. She had no guts, she had no job, she had not even finished high school.

The talk was filled with long and uncomfortable silences. A deep sadness.

I heard it through the grapevine that they had a violent relationship. People said he abused her and she mistreated her children. It seemed she had been in a whirlwind of violent relations starting from the family in which she was born.

Then she talked again about her feelings of guilt. She felt guilty for not taking good care of her children, for not being a good mother, for not being a good housewife, for not having a job and being so messy. She was defining herself through negatives, through what she lacked. She did not know what to do about her older son and worried about him – a boy "too quiet." She repeated feeling guilty for her sins. I asked, which sins? She said that after her younger son was born she had taken "those pills that make your period come down." (That means she had taken an abortive medicine largely used in Brazil, where abortion is illegal. Saying she was "making her period come down" is also a common euphemism for abortion.) I told her that was usual; a lot of women had gone through one abortion in their lifetime. "No! I didn't say that! I mean . . . I don't like that word, it is too strong." She only took Cytotec[2] once; she had great pains, a terrible hemorrhage. It was only a way of doing . . . (the unspeakable) without her husband noticing it.

To get even with God, she would have another child – but not now, when she was thirty. She said she needed to be patient with everything, including her husband, in order to set her life in place again. She had already been patient with his unfaithfulness throughout these ten years.

It was so hard for me to be there with her, trying to show her she could change her life, there should be a solution for her pain. But her lost eyes, her feelings of a wasted life, her despair in face of such a great anguish. I did not know what to say.

And the silences.

Similar situations happened other times during fieldwork: I heard women's testimonials, long conversations sometimes filled with silences. But not often with that much pain or anguish. After those talks, I usually ran back to my boarding house bedroom, filled with anguish myself. To forget, I went to a public phone and called home in São Paulo. Then I could remind myself I had another life, far away from that place, where I would come back to after fieldwork was done.

Marcela's history was not a usual or typical one. The fact that she did not work – except helping her husband in his own business sometimes – distinguished her from most middle-class and working-class women I met in Montes Claros. All women I came to work with more closely had a source of income of their own – even if sometimes they worked at home with occupations like sewing or cooking for parties. The violence in Marcela's relationship was also untypical (although neither is it rare), but I was troubled by a general sense of inequality in the lives of the women I interviewed. Many middle-class women, and less frequently working-class younger ones, usually mentioned the matter of *machismo*.

I lived in Montes Claros in a boarding house close to downtown, which made my movements and transportation easier. Living in a boarding house with many students also helped me meet other people and establish a network of families and individuals to work with. My bedroom, a little apart from the house, seemed to be a metaphor for my sense of loneliness. According to Ruth Landes (1986), fieldwork hardships reside in the difficulty of "finding oneself" in a social context distinct from one's references. And ethnography, in the sense of a voyage to another social situation (even in my own country), usually generates an emotional fragility. Nevertheless, this is a central rite of passage in the disciplinary formation of anthropologists. During this process, a professional identity is constituted, as well as a personal change in the researcher.

But Montes Claros was not so far away, and television seemed to ease this passage, generating conversations, social relations and common references. I managed to establish a group of families with whom I watched periodically the eight o'clock telenovela, and who accepted my presence in their homes at this time of the evening. I established a network of people through personal contacts – each person introducing me to other people, sometimes friends, relatives, or neighbors. Some of those people watched *The Cattle King* regularly and took part in the reception study more directly. Others were just parts of the network; they perhaps did not enjoy telenovelas, but were nevertheless important for understanding the local context. People who were a little "marginal" (artists, homosexuals, outsiders) were great contacts who helped me understand many features in local social rules and values.

Besides watching television with people, visiting each family from time to time helped establish a sense of relative "naturalness" in my presence, and with time people felt free to say what they wanted about the telenovela, its characters, or television in general (I chose not to take notes at such moments). Often there were discussions about other subjects, like local politics or the Olympic games. While watching television with people one can observe the type of informal conversation, criticisms, face and body reactions which are not conscious or reflective information like that which can be derived from interviews. Finally, social life in general – in parties, working places, hairdressers, shops, and supermarkets – shows many aspects that reveal how television is pervasive in society in direct or indirect ways. Jokes about telenovelas, fashion, the way children sometimes try to imitate what they see on television – all these are precious sources of information for the ethnographer. They also reveal many other aspects of everyday life which people do not necessarily associate with television content, but could be analyzed as part of the television interaction with their everyday lives – sometimes related to family and gender relations, consumption and consumerism. This dynamic also expresses the importance of long-term participant observation.

Because my visits to each house became part of everyday life for participants, that made it easier for me to see people in a more relaxed way. My visits seemed normal, but everyone knew exactly what I was doing there – I certainly explained to each one that I was a researcher. On the other hand I know that my presence often heightened participants' interest in that particular narrative, and some people even told me they only watched that telenovela because of me. My presence also enhanced their reflection on this particular narrative, although people who are used to watching telenovelas also show a vast set of reflections and opinions on past narratives and on television content in general.

I also realized that being a woman made it easier to get into people's houses in the evening for telenovela watching. A man might have seemed more threatening. Furthermore, considering that telenovelas are seen as feminine and have a domestic setting, a female researcher seemed to fit the subject of study. This does not mean a man could not do the research; it only means I did not have to explain my interest in that subject – it sounded "normal." In this sense, behaving appropriately as a "family woman" was important for the first contacts – after people got to know me better and what I was doing there, they felt more comfortable with my presence. Being a "nice woman" with a constant smile – a gender training I grew up with – eased the way into people's houses, and it was a strategy of approaching them. I tried to go slow, step-by-step, and a certain type of intimacy was usually initiated with other women, particularly those about my age (usually, they were mothers in households with children and teens). Another important strategy was the network of kinship and friendship, and always making new acquaintances through those affective ties. If I was a friend of a friend, or a friend of a nephew, then I represented no harm.

Another unplanned situation also enhanced the image of a "good family woman." The boarding house owner's daughter, Miriam, was my first "little friend." She was ten years old and she often asked to come along with me to my evening visits when she found out I was visiting someone she knew, or someone with a girl her age. On one or two occasions I just could not deny her request, even though I was a little uncomfortable about taking her with me. Afterwards, though, I realized that walking around with a child turned me into an image of a respectable and caring woman (as Landes, 1947, also found out in her fieldwork in Brazil). Being an outsider who traveled alone (although married, and with no children) made me strange to Montes Claros residents. The keeping the company of a child, therefore, made me more traditionally feminine and even maternal. The research visits also seemed to be transformed into an ordinary visit – since I was taking the girl along, it looked like a normal family visit (Guttman, 1996, also mentions that the presence of his daughter helped him establish relationships during his fieldwork in Mexico City). Certainly, this only worked well because family relations constituted one of the main issues in the research.

Since this transformative dynamic in my ethnographic identity was very important, it warrants a bit more explication about local values and my "location" in the community. A woman on her own coming from São Paulo may seem threatening for local moral values – especially for people much older than me, and the more conservative Catholics who were a large group in the city. Local values concerning gender and sexuality are challenged by what people see on television, and consequently seem to apply to someone coming from a big city. Sometimes, these images even disturbed fieldwork. On one occasion, one man refused to introduce me to his wife, as if I were the other type of woman – in his mind, there were family women and prostitutes, no in-between. Coming from São Paulo and being associated with paulista girls' behavior in telenovelas, he probably saw me as having the type of sexual activity that did not fit his patterns of an appropriate family life. I now analyze a little further those local values, especially when they led people to compare me with what they saw on television or to make assumptions about my background. It was with those implicit comparisons in mind that the word *machismo* appeared more often.

Machismo and women's work

As mentioned earlier, people in Montes Claros are very guarded and often prejudiced. And the telenovela reality which they consumed presented a different model of life: a big city one, presenting the "reality" of Rio and São Paulo, where everything is more "natural." Values of that televisual world are of another time and place, an extreme contrast from the daily lives and practices of those in Montes Claros. Take, for example, perceptions about virginity and their circulation through generations of *machista* values – an example I am deliberately using here because it was a common theme in my fieldwork.

> "Ah, I want to date all of them." This is what boys say. "I want to date all girls, but I am going to get married only to a virgin, I won't get married to a girl that has already . . ." Can you believe it? . . . I heard those things from boys who are fourteen, fifteen, sixteen years old.
>
> (Laura)

Laura works in a public school and is the mother of two teenage girls. She often discussed the local *machismo*, criticizing it and showing how much she wanted to change the situation. To do so, she tried to raise her girls differently from her own upbringing. She got married at 18 and she said she wanted to give her daughters other options, so that they would be a little more mature when they got married. She wanted them to have some experience before marriage and regretted that she had got married so young. She told me she had to face many hardships at the beginning of her marriage and revealed a difficult relationship with her husband.

This *machismo* – the word was often used – was a recurrent theme when talking with women. For example, Graça worked as a manicurist, and was a working-class mother of four children. While watching the telenovela she was shy and did not talk much. I tried not to impose a rhythm or a way of speaking directly – a lot of people say things in an indirect way, through metaphors and examples, and, if the ethnographer is paying enough attention, even through silences. Those are difficult to interpret, but the ethnographer cannot force people into objectifying and expressing things directly (and that is also a reason why participant observation is fruitful in social research, for one can interpret and analyze data that come from actions and activities and not only words). After some time, Graça invited me for a beer in a bar just beside her house. In the bar, away from her husband and children, we had more intimate conversations. Considering her husband does not drink – a very atypical situation – the bar by her house became a place for our talk. Bars, in the evening, are usually masculine places, but up to a certain hour they are still a family setting, where we could stay and even meet her friends, who also complained about the *machismo* and repeatedly told me I was lucky to be a big city woman.

Like Graça's friends, other people often asked how come my husband had let me travel on my own and do this work. Many women told me my husband must be a very *good* man, who *allowed* me to travel, and that was possible because I had no children. (Men never discussed those matters in these terms, and some of them seemed to think my partner was weak or not a "real man.") They also mentioned that this could only be so because I came from São Paulo, where everything is more *modern*. Modern is also a local category which is permanently fed by media messages and content. Furthermore, they would say I was so *brave* for traveling on my own.

What surprised me is that I met many women who seemed to be very brave and did not fit exactly the traditional model – some of them had lived in larger cities for a while, and also were the target of gossips and jokes. Some of them needed another strong positive feature in order not to be ostracized – sometimes by being an artist, coming from an elite family, or a traditional family, or maybe just being an outsider. Quite often they were very good informants, sharp-witted, reflective about social rules and critically engaged. They even became good friends during fieldwork, secure in the knowledge that I was also "a little different" as they often expressed it. A special feeling of recognition and sometimes intimacy was developed.

Almost all women below 40, and many men as well, talked about *machismo* – a word that certainly has been diffused by the feminist movement. Women usually complained about men's unfaithfulness and jealousy. Those were usually criticizing the local tradition, but some people also were respectful of the tradition, stressing its Catholic values (but also criticizing *bad* men who are unfaithful or abusive with their wives). And almost everybody – both those in favor or against local tradition – stressed that Montes Claros was different from São Paulo. It was a backward, traditional, small countryside town – for those complaining about it, the adjective *machista* would come in the end. A constant opposition was revealed: one place which is here, Montes Claros, *traditional*, and another which is "there," São Paulo or Rio de Janeiro, *modern,* and site of the sort of behaviour witnessed in telenovelas. Modern, nevertheless, can be either positive or negative, depending on the point of view of who is speaking. Modern can mean the loss of family values, the immorality, sexual freedom, and chaos of a big city.

Very often the reference for this type of reflection was the family relations shown in telenovelas. Research participants would often say that families in *The Cattle King* were very different from the ones in Montes Claros.[3] For example, if in the story the hero's wife cheated on him, what happened most often in real life was the opposite – men cheat, women forgive. That is part of the *machismo*. Anyway, it seemed that the research situation was promoting an intense reflection about those types of subject. As Rabinow (1984) mentions:

> Whenever an anthropologist enters a culture, he trains people to objectify their life-world for him. Within all cultures, of course, there is already objectification and self-reflection. But this explicit self-conscious translation into an external medium is rare. The anthropologist creates a doubling of consciousness. . . . Consequently, the data we collect is doubly mediated, first by our own presence and then by the second-order self-reflection we demand from our informants.
>
> (p. 119)

Considering I represented a big city woman and also because of the types of questions I asked and the type of conversation I promoted, my presence encouraged participants' reflection on those subjects – family, gender, sexuality patterns. However, television and particularly telenovelas themselves raise those subjects – telenovelas tell stories about women, love, family relations and they show big city patterns, including a high rate of divorce and of sexual activity (as in the examples of Lia and Liliana mentioned in the above footnote). Television content and the habit of watching telenovelas and comparing characters' situations with their own lives also promotes reflection in telenovela viewers. It is also compared to telenovelas' content that the local machismo is constituted – it is a relative situation. There is a universe of mediations here, television being the subject of study but also a main reference and a space that constructs the gender and sexuality categories which people try to deal with. Certainly my presence and questions enhanced the process, but also implied a third comparison: with São Paulo, with me. Telenovelas were very often mentioned as representative of big cities' realities, values, behaviors, women, etc. Even when the telenovela refers to a rural situation – as in *The Cattle King* – family values, man–woman relationships, sexual behaviors are attached to big city patterns. Telenovelas are written and produced in Rio or São Paulo – those are the cultural references of their authors and producers.

Most women I interviewed had a job or worked and did not fit the submissive type described in Marcela's example. But the point they complained about and the sphere where inequality seemed to be greater was sexuality – also an example stressed when compared to telenovelas' characters. In telenovelas, "women are free" and are the main characters in the story. In Montes Claros, masculine sexual activity was seen as of an "uncontrollable nature," mainly outside marriage (which is consistent with women's complaints of men's unfaithfulness). Feminine sexual activity was supposed to be restricted to marriage – which also meant the ideal that girls should keep their virginity until getting married. This last point is a feature that is changing rapidly and that explains why older people stressed the "bad influence" that television and big city sexuality patterns have had on moral values.

Social change and crossing frontiers

Carlos and Fernanda have a relatively egalitarian relationship, both work, and he also takes care of the children. In fact, like many middle-class couples in their thirties, they reveal social and moral shifts. This model is interesting in part because Carlos told me that he had been raised very differently from his sisters – since being a teenager he had been encouraged to start having sex (mostly with prostitutes), while his sisters had been restricted. In his opinion, that control was useless, and two of his sisters got pregnant before the age of 18, got married and after a while divorced. This was a shock for his Catholic mother, but in his opinion it just showed that behavior changes were unavoidable, part of what was happening in Brazilian society at large.

Carlos and Fernanda were the owners of the boarding house where I lived, and it happened that they were also very critical of local society. We ended up developing a good friendship from the beginning of my stay in Montes Claros. In those seven months, I shared with them many events of their lives, and they took a part in my research. When they thought I was too lonely, they invited me to go out with them; when they were too busy, I helped with their kids; when I fell and broke my foot, they took me to the hospital; when Fernanda's sister died in a car accident, Fernanda came to cry and talk in my bedroom, and I helped her take care of her nephew. This was one of the most difficult situations in fieldwork, and work itself had to be left aside for many days.

As I have mentioned, I was very much defined by my place of origin: the "paulista" – a categorization that stressed my outsider status and my temporary

174

situation in the city, but a location that also granted me more freedom. Considering this, I started to enlarge the scope of the research by spending more time in the bar, sometimes in the company of men. I could have personal conversations with Carlos in his bar, where he also introduced me to some people. Sometimes the bar was also a feminine or familiar place – especially during the day, the beginning of the evening, and at weekends. But on weekdays, after 10 o'clock or so, it became a masculine place. I could stay there since I was behaving appropriately – I was not there trying to seduce anyone, and I was also in the company of men whose wives I knew and some were my friends. Sometimes, their wives also stayed longer in the bar with me, as long as I was there.

In the bar, I could also listen to men's complaints about women, and their thoughts about family relationships, gender, and television – again, such inter-actions are almost impossible without a long-term commitment to participant observation, as I never heard these accounts from men when in their home setting. In the bar, they only watched soccer games. But they also revealed through gossip how some women were criticized, and through this I understood better their moral values. In the bar, I came to realize there was also a type of women defined as "evil," usually those whose sexual life was not restricted to marriage or boyfriends. I had until then avoided this category by behaving as a "family woman," but I risked being categorized differently when I chose to use the space of the bar for participant observation as well. Staying longer in the bar with men in the evening also generated gossip about me – and people like Carlos warned me about that. He told me a man had asked him about his relationship with me, a question that in his opinion showed how "square" people could not understand that we were only friends. Interacting in the bar in a masculine time put me in the category of "streety" people, an adjective well fit for men, but "streety" women, women who stay longer on the streets, are not good family women – they are either prostitutes or "evil" girls.

Some ethnographic accounts (e.g. articles in Golde, 1986a) discuss the need for the ethnographer to go beyond the limits imposed by the researcher's gender. It is amazing how some authors stress, though, that this seems to be easier for women – whose movements are usually more controlled in most societies – than for men. Vale de Almeida (1995) insists that women ethnographers can sometimes easily take part in masculine spheres, but the opposite is harder to accomplish:

> Now that fieldwork experience belongs to the past, I realize everything would have been easier if I were a foreigner and had to learn the language, and also if I were a woman, not a man. My male status (and officially single) made it difficult to access the feminine world.
>
> (p. 22, my translation)

And in a footnote in the same page:

> in contexts of sharp sexual division there are few situations for inter-
> sexual contact. I would add: and when there are, informants do not
> necessarily "sexuate" the anthropologist. Field experience mentioned
> by some colleagues might indicate that female researchers are more
> easily "a-sexed" by informants, not to mention being "masculinized",
> what happens because of gender stereotypes associated to labor
> division and symbolic power of science.
>
> (p. 22)

His assertion that fieldwork is often "a-sexed" was consistent with some of
my own experiences, as my gender identity sometimes faded in relation to my
outsider status. And I did not feel I had to be particularly "a woman" all the
time when working in the field. Nevertheless, I do understand that to be "a-
sexed" is a difficult passage (from male to female worlds, or vice versa) in
fieldwork, and is contingent upon contextual factors. If I discussed the idea of
taking part in men's world, it is because that was possible in Montes Claros
where those worlds are not so strictly apart. Lila Abu-Lughod (1986) mentions
in her research among the Bedouins that, in order to be accepted, she had to be
adopted into a family and behave like a daughter. Any transgressions beyond
female behavior patterns would harm the honor of the family that had adopted
her. On the other hand, in the female and domestic world, there was a very
productive space for her research. Even acting according to very restricted social
standards for women, she had access to men's talk in a way no male researcher
would have to women's:

> My concentration in the woman's world might also be considered
> a limitation. In many ways, however, my access to both worlds
> was more balanced than a man's would have been. Except in rare
> instances, male researches in sex-segregated societies have far less
> access to women than I had to men. Not only was my host an
> extremely articulate and generous informant about himself and his
> culture, but his younger brother, sons and nephews, and the client-
> status men were all frequent visitors in the women's world with
> whom I could speak relatively freely. Furthermore, the structure of
> information flow between the men's and women's worlds was not
> symmetrical. Because of the pattern of hierarchy, men spoke to one
> another in the presence of women, but the reverse was not true. In
> addition, young and low-status men informed mothers, aunts and
> grandmothers, and (for the latter) wives about men's affairs, whereas
> no one brought news to the adult men. A conspiracy of silence
> excluded men from the women's world.
>
> (Abu-Lughod, 1986, p. 23)

Maybe Vale de Almeida's situation was a counterpoint for what Abu-Lughod discusses. However, he was studying masculinity in Portugal and his constant presence in masculine places could have taken him more and more away from the female world. Therefore, I consider one has to search for places and situations not so strictly marked by gender or even try to trespass across some gender frontiers in order to improve one's understanding of the social and cultural context. Nevertheless, in breaking local rules there are risks the ethnographer has to take into account.

Female strength and gender features

In Montes Claros, there was another pervasive gender construction related to family relations: the centrality of feminine and maternal figures. There is the idea that the mother is the person who keeps the family together, and a woman is someone who manages to take care of "everything" – in terms of family income, making ends meet, dealing with everyday life problems. Some women even stated that women are stronger than men – not physically, but emotionally. However, being stronger also means carrying the heaviest burden in life. Being the stronger sex is not necessarily better; it entails having to endure the hardships, deal with difficult situations and be everybody else's support. Strength – usually seen as a masculine feature – is therefore easily applied to women. This points to an important discussion in gender theory: feminine features and activities and masculine features and activities are not necessarily linked to women and men only. There is no direct assumption that femininity is only seen in women, as men like Carlos reveal when taking care of their children. This point is mentioned in many works of gender theory (e.g. Butler, 1990; Guttman, 1996; Louveau, 1996; Moore, 1997; Strathern, 1998; Strathern and MacCormack, 1980; Vale de Almeida, 1995).

It is also as strong women that telenovela heroines are mostly admired. This concept of female strength takes two opposite directions: on the one hand, it means a capacity to struggle through life, including a professional career and income independence; on the other hand, it may signify enduring whatever happens (like Marcela's example). Mainly for younger single women, this idea led them to think about their professional life and the relevance of their education.

"Struggling" – a common term women used – does not mean having a specific profession, but mainly it suggests the idea of "getting by" to make ends meet. Many women work in education, and those who do not have a profession often move from one job to another, including the informal labor market, trying always to earn enough income for their families. "To struggle" is the everyday effort to keep on going. In the category of a "struggler," I made sense – someone whose profession is so important she has even to travel and live away from her home. This also shows how the sexual division of labor is not so strict as it might seem in people's talk about what they see as male and female responsibilities in the home or in the family. Most couples revealed in their daily lives that women are also breadwinners, and men are also caring affective fathers who might assume many feminine tasks (such as cooking). Once more, such observations could only come from participant observations, because in discourse people do not reveal those daily activities as easily – men particularly deny doing activities that they fear are not seen as appropriately masculine.

If strength is a common feature that women feel they share with telenovela heroines, the issue of sexuality is a point of difference. Most people criticize morality on the television: there is too much sex and nudity, family values are lost, there is no respect for tradition. Even when criticizing its excesses, some people also see a positive aspect in the process of liberalizing and changing the traditional *machismo*. Some of those changes were also positive aspects in their life histories:

> I got married [pregnant] when I was 17, I had two kids, when Isadora [first child] was born I was 18. When I was 24 I had a tubal ligation, and then I got divorced. . . . Alberto [ex-husband] was the first man in my life, he was sure I would be his wife for the rest of my life, he never thought I'd have the guts to separate. I was always like that . . . with him, I was submissive. I didn't want to argue with him, because he was very rude. . . . I wanted to leave him when Isadora was born. I couldn't, because of my family. . . . I was 18 or 19, I couldn't . . . So one day I decided for myself, I thought: "No way, I don't want this, it's over. My mom won't live my life for me." I had to live my own life and leave behind the other . . . Because if I stayed with him, I was 27, if I stayed with Alberto longer, at 40 I would be dead. . . . I just wanted to be free, because he didn't treat me well, he was too jealous, possessive, he wouldn't let me talk to people, he wouldn't let me go out by myself, he wouldn't let me do anything. He was like that, *machista*.
>
> (Marta)

Marta's history is similar to Marcela's: she got married too young, when pregnant, but Marta always worked. Female strength can be useful to change one's situation, to struggle in search of a new life. Marta tells her history as a passage from a woman who bears a *machista* husband, to a woman who takes a decision and struggles for her life, even facing her family in the process. That process took almost ten years – not so easily as telenovelas show. Marta had doubts and anguish, but differing from Marcela and telling her history as if she were a telenovela protagonist, she decided to take action, fighting for her choices and freedom.

Intimacy

Generally, families who accepted me into their homes as a researcher were not experiencing any conflict in their family life. When I was still trying to establish a group of households to visit with frequency, I visited two or three families who displayed great discomfort at my presence. A certain initial sense of strangeness was normal, until people got used to my presence. But some people did not say a word while I was at their homes watching *The Cattle King*, and it was hard to develop a conversation afterwards, so I quit working with those families. If I was so disturbing – for whatever reason it was – I thought I was not going to accomplish a relatively "normal" setting of watching and talking, and taking part in their everyday lives.

Certainly, in the beginning I was a special visitor in most households. But progressively my visits became more normal. And this more comfortable situation made the ethnographic work run smoothly. People would tell me stories about their friends and families, about their personal lives, talk about local politics, the latest talk of the town (it was an electoral year), national politics and news that had the greatest coverage on the media, and so on.

But if families were not comfortable with me in moments of conflict, the opposite was also true – I could not feel comfortable in those places either. I also heard stories about violence, in cases similar to that of Marcela, but I never had direct contact with those couples. In fact, Marcela never told me directly anything about that matter; even when talking about *The Cattle King*, she never mentioned the violent relationship of Leia and Ralf. Many people talked about abusive husbands through Leia's case, but they were always mentioning someone else, not themselves. Marcela insisted I should go more often to her house to watch *The Cattle King* with her – she wanted a friend to talk to, but many other women also enjoyed that part of having an ethnographer at home. In her case, though, there was also a delicate matter: I could not feel comfortable with Marcela's husband, particularly at his home. He tried to be nice, and talked to me. But if I had to be seen as reliable in order to be welcomed into people's homes, the opposite was also true. What lacked in this case was a reciprocal empathy like that which I developed with most other families (even if not with everybody in the family). Maybe that is what Rabinow and other anthropologists call "rapport" – but even rapport is a subjective idea. In my fieldwork, considering the need to be in the private home setting, and the focus on personal and intimate issues like family relations, gender, and sexuality, rapport was fundamental for well-accomplished fieldwork.

Beyond a lack of rapport, there can even be dangerous situations for ethnographers. Fieldwork can sometimes involve unforeseen risky situations. Besides facing the distance from home, the lack of material goods, the change in food and housing, I also encountered innumerous misunderstandings, ironies and jokes I could not understand, and sometimes a lack of self-confidence or the feeling of having done something wrong that could ruin the work. To enter into another social situation also includes letting go – accompanying people to their whereabouts, accepting invitations to parties, visits, religious happenings, political rallies, etc. Often that leads the ethnographer to a sense of "where am I?" or "what am I doing here?," or "did I say anything wrong?" Nevertheless, after a while I started to feel at home in Montes Claros.

After a while, some people became really good friends, and this also meant sharing good and bad times with those friends. There were sudden deaths, like that of Fernanda's sister, which brought me even closer to her family and to share their grief. Sharing the grief and taking part in those affective moments also generated a sense of identification, a sense that happened more often with other women.

On the border

One can conclude that the liminal or intercultural place Rabinow describes for the ethnographer is similar to a certain liminality in terms of gender that is also generated in fieldwork. Those situations require from ethnographer and informants constant reflexivity and questioning. In my case, television content itself helped me in approaching informants, and it was also a mediation. Television worked as a passage, a space between big cities and local everyday life. By comparing me with television content informants could imagine who I was and I was also accepted as someone a bit different, an outsider. I was "sexuated" in many different aspects according to the situation (as a big city girl, as a "family woman," even maternal with Miriam, a-sexed or "evil" in the bar with different people) and had to deal with those and even use them in fieldwork.

There was also another paradox. If I had to "go beyond gender" to do the research and have better access to men's world, on the other hand I felt greater rapport with women. Considering the situations of gender inequality, my feminine identity was relevant, and I felt empathy for women's struggles or pain. I did not go to Montes Claros to do a feminist ethnography, but I came back feeling more and more like a feminist.

The attitude of trying to cross gender frontiers – or being a-sexuated by others, or even being masculinized – cannot erase completely our own gender identity (although it might be transformed). Some women approached me as a friend and confidante, as they wanted someone to talk to. And I didn't want to avoid those types of conversation – they were useful for my research as well. These women enjoyed the chance of having someone to talk to, someone who would listen carefully to their stories, complaints, anguishes, problems. This did not exclude me from developing good friendships with men at all. They were also good friends, and some of those were critical of local backwardness and "squareness," although they did not use the word *machismo* as often as women did.

However, one cannot erase other inequalities and differences in that process. On the one hand, being the researcher and having an idea of the total process I was doing there gave me more power in that process. On the other hand, men and women who became my friends were different from me: they were from a smaller town, there were social class, race, and everyday life differences. Being an outsider was sometimes a great relief, and Fernanda realized that when I was leaving Montes Claros for good:

> Heloisa, now you're going home. You're going back to São Paulo and you're going to write your dissertation, and you are going to forget about us. We are always going to talk about you and remember you in our conversations. But you will forget us.

In fact, I came back to São Paulo and her reality is far away from mine now. But the experience has left a mark. It was an unforgettable experience – particularly because my work requires that I reflect further about what I saw, heard and lived in Montes Claros. Coming back from fieldwork gives a sense of self-confidence to the researcher, because finally the traditional experience of fieldwork has constituted one as an ethnographer. Moreover, though, as many authors cited here mention, there is a personal and internal dimension in that process; the experience changes one not only as a professional. Unfortunately, "real life" does not fit neatly into the academic work; it vanishes under bibliographic reviews, theoretical issues, consistent arguments. When writing ethnographies, much of the real and intense life we shared is lost. This chapter is also an attempt to remember that behind methodological issues, there are real people struggling in their everyday lives.

Notes

1 "The Social Impact of Television on Reproductive Behavior in Brazil" included professionals from different fields (anthropology, sociology, demography, communication) and institutions (Cebrap, University of Campinas, Federal University of Minas Gerais, University of São Paulo in Brazil and University of Texas), and was funded by Hewlett, MacArthur and Rockefeller Foundations. My individual research project began on after the end of the collective one, in 1997. During this fieldwork I also elaborated my Ph.D. project, which aims to understand more about gender and consumption in telenovelas' production and reception. The Ph.D. project is funded by FAPESP, Fundação de Amparo à Pesquisa do Estado de São Paulo.

2 The name of the medicine, sold for gastric ulcers, but when taken in larger quantity it can cause abortion.

3 Written by Benedito Ruy Barbosa, the story of *The Cattle King* was aired for seven months in daily installments (from Monday to Saturday), comprising 205 chapters, and so it is not easy to summarize. Its main features surround the character of the cattle king himself, Bruno, a rich middle-aged farmer, very unhappily married with two kids, Lia and Marcos. His wife at the beginning of the story, Leia, cheats on him with the main villain, Ralf, who is a rascal and a male prostitute who only wants Leia's money. Bruno finds out about Leia's adultery and leaves her – she then gets married to Ralf, only to be unhappy and

abused by him. Sex scenes between Leia and Ralf, and between Ralf and his other lovers/clients, are seen as shocking and disturbing by most people in Montes Claros. Bruno then falls in love with a poor illiterate peasant, Luana, who happens to be his cousin, but she had lost her memory in an accident and cannot remember in the beginning who she is. He brings Luana to live with him, but his two spoiled kids do not accept her. His daughter (Lia) and son (Marcos) are portrayed as ex-drug addicts. Lia falls in love with a poor guitar player, and is one of the most loved characters in the story – she is seen as beautiful and elegant, and is the fashion promoter in the narrative. She makes sexual advances towards her lover, revealing that she has sexual experience in a way most criticized in Montes Claros. Nevertheless, sex scenes between Lia and her lover – as well as those between Bruno and Luana – are enjoyed as romantic love scenes by most people, only being criticized by older and more religious people. Marcos, Bruno's son, has an affair with a former teenage girlfriend, Liliana. Liliana is the daughter of a senator, who is also a close friend of Bruno, is unhappily married, and stays most of the time away from his family, in Brasília (the federal capital), where he works. Liliana gets pregnant, and the two families try to set a solution, but Marcos runs away on the day of the wedding. Marcos is seen as an irresponsible youngster who only changes when his father has an accident and he has to start working on the family farms. Liliana is also seen in Montes Claros as another bad example for girls and young women who might think that having sex before marriage is OK, promoting teenage pregnancy. She also seems to promote such behavior because she has a happy ending with Marcos when the baby is born – this is analyzed by Montes Claros viewers as even a worse example, because young girls might be deluded, thinking that early pregnancy is a solution with a happy ending.

References

Abu-Lughod, L. (1986). *Veiled sentiments: Honor and poetry in a Bedouin society*. Berkeley: University of California Press.

Ang, I. (1985). *Watching Dallas: Soap opera and the melodramatic imagination*. London: Routledge.

Briggs, J. (1986). Kapluna daughter. In P. Golde (ed.), *Women in the field: Anthropological experiences*. Berkeley: University of California Press.

Brown, M. E. (ed.) (1990). *Television and women's culture: The politics of the popular*. London: Sage.

Butler, J. (1990). *Gender trouble: Feminism and the subversion of identity*. New York and London: Routledge.

Codere, H. (1986). Fieldwork in Rwanda, 1959–1960. In P. Golde (ed.), *Women in the field: Anthropological experiences*. Berkeley: University of California Press.

Freedman, D. (1986). Wife, widow, woman: Roles of an anthropologist in a Transylvanian village. In P. Golde (ed.), *Women in the field: Anthropological experiences*. Berkeley: University of California Press.

Golde, P. (ed.) (1986a). *Women in the field: Anthropological experiences*. Berkeley: University of California Press.

Golde, P. (1986b). Odissey of encounter. In P. Golde (ed.), *Women in the field: Anthropological experiences*. Berkeley: University of California Press.

Guttman, M. (1996). *The meanings of macho: Being a man in Mexico City*. Berkeley: University of California Press.

Landes, R. (1947). *The city of women*. New York: Macmillan.

Landes, R. (1986). A woman anthropologist in Brazil. In P. Golde (ed.), *Women in the field: Anthropological experiences*. Berkeley: University of California Press.

Leal, O. F. (1986). *A leitura social da novela das oito*. Petrópolis: Vozes.

Louveau, C. (1996). Masculin/féminin – l'ère des paradoxes" *Cahiers Internationaux de Sociologie* 100, 13–31.

Moore, H. (1997). Understanding sex and gender. In T. Ingold (Org.), *Companion encyclopaedia of anthropology*. London: Routledge.

Morley, D. (1993). *Family television: Cultural power and domestic leisure*. London: Routledge.

Nader, L. (1986). From anguish to exultation. In P. Golde (ed.), *Women in the field: Anthropological experiences*. Berkeley: University of California Press.

Prado, R. M. (1987). Mulher de novela e mulher de verdade. Unpublished Master's Thesis, Federal University of Rio de Janeiro.

Rabinow, P. (1984). *Reflections on fieldwork in Morocco*. Berkeley: University of California Press.

Seiter, E. et al. (1989). *Remote control: Television, audiences and cultural power*. London: Routledge.

Strathern, M. (1988). *The gender of the gift*. Berkeley: University of California Press.

Strathern, M. and MacCormack, C. (1980). *Nature, culture and gender*. Cambridge: Cambridge University Press.

Vale de Almeida, M. (1995). *Senhores de si: Uma interpretação antropológica da masculinidade*. Lisboa: Fim de Século.

Weidman, H. H. (1986). On ambivalence and the field. In P. Golde (ed.), *Women in the field: Anthropological experiences*. Berkeley: University of California Press.

11

RADIO'S EARLY ARRIVAL IN RURAL APPALACHIA

A harbinger of the global society?

Jacob J. Podber

In the 1960s, Marshall McLuhan (1964) predicted that we were at the dawn of a new era of global communications where electronic technology would bring mankind into a "seamless web of kinship and interdependence." In the 1990s, the rapid expansion of the internet seemed to suggest that this vision has already been realized. Certainly, the internet has provided an immediate global forum for the access to new information and the exchange and diffusion of ideas, and may well be the most significant phenomenon of the new millennium (see Lowe, 1998; Gates, 1999). However, while traveling around rural Appalachia, I recognized that for many elderly residents, it was the inception of radio in the 1920s that brought a genesis of belonging to a national community to this region of the country. As Hilmes (1997) observed, "radio seemed in its early days to lend itself to association with ideas of nation, of national identity, to the heart and mind of America" (p. 1).

In the following pages, I attempt to show how radio affected the lives of people in this mountainous region of the United States. Through oral histories, residents of four Appalachian Ohio counties[1] recall how this "new" medium enhanced their lives. Using their own words, I examine how their use of radio has informed their identity and included or dis-included them. As participants recalled their histories, I attempted to record their lived and reconstructed past while looking at participants' memories of radio, how they used it, and the social impact this medium had on the region.

If one traces back the origins of the words community and communication, one finds that they share the same Latin root: "communis," meaning common. Because of their isolation, rural communities appeared to have much to gain from early electronic media. With the arrival of radio, especially in the 1930s with high-powered clear channel stations that broadcast from the "big city," listeners in the most isolated regions of the country could gain a feeling of connectedness with the rest of the world. By listening to newscasts, they learned how others coped with the Great Depression, and shared the pain, losses, and victories of World War II with other listeners around the country (Smulyan, 1994). Daily soap operas allowed radio listeners to learn "of critical values, of themselves, and of their fellow citizens. The premise of all soaps was the commonness of the American experience" (MacDonald, 1979, p. 239).

Although much has been written on the coal-mining communities of Appalachia (see Eller, 1982; Fisher, 1993; Yarrow 1990), and on ethnicity within the region (see Billings, Norman and Ledford, 1999; Cunningham, 1980; Klotter, 1980; Snyder, 1982; Turner and Cabbell, 1985), there is a dearth of literature on electronic media usage within the Appalachian community. An important distinction should be made in that there is a body of work that examines print media's effect on Appalachia (see Stephens, 1972; Maggard, 1985). In addition, Newcomb (1979) examines how Appalachian stereotypes are perpetuated on television, Williamson (1994 and 1995) points out how the Appalachian is portrayed in motion pictures, and some alternative media sources, such as Appalshop Film and Video in Whitesburg, Kentucky, produce works on Appalachian culture and history (see *Mountain Vision: Homegrown Television in Appalachia, and Strangers and Kin*).[2] None, however, address *electronic* media usage *by* Appalachians. Therefore, I hope the oral histories collected in this study will contribute to the understanding of the impact radio had on the residents of rural Appalachia, especially from a social historical context.

I see a great value in a human diary that documents how early listeners chose their programs, how, where, and with whom they listened, and perhaps most importantly, how radio affected the lives of the people I met in Appalachia.

Appalachia on my mind

Appalachia is many things to many people. Novelist Jesse Stuart once said, "Appalachia is anywhere there's coal under the ground" (Garrett, 1972). Perhaps one cannot define Appalachia except in geo-political terms. In 1965, the Appalachian Regional Commission (ARC) simply defined the Appalachian region as consisting of 360 counties in eleven states from Alabama to Pennsylvania. Two years later, it changed its mind. In 1967, the ARC broadened its definition of Appalachia to include 397 counties and thirteen states ranging from as far north and east as New York to as far south and west as Mississippi. In 1990, an additional county was added along with yet another in 1991, bringing the total to 399 counties. In 1998, seven more counties were added for a grand total of 406 counties comprising the Appalachian Region of the United States. Given the broad geographical region of Appalachia (approximately 6 percent of the country lies within the ARC boundaries), pinning down the term has always been problematic. Within the region, there are plateaus, ridges, valleys, piedmonts, several mountain ranges, tiny "hollers," and major metropolitan areas such as Appalachian Cincinnati. There are also poverty, vast welfare programs, isolation, coal mines, and a distinctive culture.

Defining what makes up Appalachia continues to be elusive in nature. As Whisnant (1980) asserts, "Appalachia's boundaries have been drawn so many times by so many different hands that it is futile to look for a correct definition of the region" (p. 134).

Euroamericans began settling in the region in the eighteenth century. As Salstrom (1994) notes, "Between 1714 and 1775 . . . thousands of rent-racked flax and linen producers abandoned their tiny leaseholds in Northern Ireland and flooded across the Atlantic to America, where many or most of them lit out for the territories of that day" (p. 1). By 1790 approximately 250,000 Scotch-Irish had settled in America, at least three-fourths within Appalachia (Keller, 1991). In addition, thousands of Germans and immigrants from other European countries settled within the area. Although many landed in New York, the majority of these transatlantic immigrants arrived in Philadelphia. Later arrivals were directed to the ports of Wilmington and Charleston. Given that coastal areas were comparatively well-developed and land further west was considerably cheaper, many immigrants chose to settle inland. The diagonal flow patterns of the region's river system (e.g. the Roanoke and James) also facilitated the movement of these settlers. As reason would dictate, early settlers chose the more fertile land adjacent to the Great Valley and only later did they move further inland where the soil was of lesser quality, the slopes steeper and the area more isolated (Rehder, 1992).

Geology and geography may have determined the original focus of the Appalachian Region, but political and cultural influences continue to reshape its characteristics.

Methodology

Using oral histories to record a community's history is often fraught with challenges, particularly when the interviewer is viewed as an outsider by the interviewees. Some participants, uncomfortable with an interviewer entering into a region where many are burdened by low education levels, were reluctant, at first, to be recorded. Given the way the media often depict Appalachians in movies (*Deliverance*), television (*The Beverly Hillbillies*), and comic strips (*Snuffy Smith*), their reluctance is not surprising. John Kennedy and Hubert Humphrey's "political pity and piety" during the 1960 West Virginia presidential primary "were mythologized by enough television and print media to transform 'Appalachia' overnight from a previously antique folk culture, on the periphery and therefore vaguely threatening to urban America, into a liberal cause, a social problem just begging to be solved and solvable given enough federal cash and volunteers in service" (Williamson, 1995, p. 251). In fact, Williamson argues that the media's coverage of Lyndon Johnson's 1964 visit to the front porch of a poor coal miner in Inez, Kentucky, forever established that "starving, dirt dumb" coal miner in front of his "tumbledown" porch as representative of Appalachia in the American psyche.[3] In "The Appalachian inheritance," Cattell-Gordon (1990) describes the Appalachian region as a "culturally transmitted traumatic stress syndrome" (p. 41). Yet, Banks, Billings and Tice (1996) suggest that

> this account of the effects of history as social trauma bred in the bones of the people of the region is flawed because it constitutes Appalachians solely as "victims" and obscures the potentiality of diverse subjects' making history . . . thereby minimizing the possibilities for agency and empowerment. Such an account leaves unquestioned paradigmatic views of Appalachia that have the effect of either marginalizing and excluding Appalachians as fully human beings or else treating them as a monolithic category.
>
> (p. 82)

It is therefore my intention to allow the participants who were interviewed to express themselves using their own words. Doing this, I hope, will lead to a better understanding of early radio usage in rural Appalachia and its connection to the formation of Appalachian culture.

I recognize that as a white urbanite male doing interpretive research within a rural community, I might raise some eyebrows. There is some discussion within the academy as to whether it is even possible for an "outsider" to effectively record a community's history. Gluck and Patai (1991, p. 2) address "research by, about, and for women." African-American Studies departments often have few majors who are not of color. Today, there may be a danger of swinging towards a totally inclusive expectation for research. In *The English Flag*, Kipling wrote, "What should they know of England who only England know?"

Fine (1994) examines the importance of the relationship between the researcher and the informant as she refers to working the "hyphen" between insider and outsider, while Collins (1991) addresses conditions related to being an "outsider within." Throughout my research in Appalachia, I always felt like an insider in outsider's clothing. Although I was born and raised in Atlanta, Georgia, I lived most of my adult life in London, New York, and Los Angeles. Upon first moving to Appalachian Ohio, to pursue my doctorate degree, I was surprised by the ease I felt sharing yarns with my new neighbors. Even though most had accents different from those I heard growing up in Atlanta, many reminded me of my childhood neighbors. It is perhaps for this reason that I always felt somewhat like an insider while recording the oral histories of rural Appalachians. As several of my colleagues began to travel to Africa and Asia to pursue their media research agendas, I recognized that members within my own community had important stories to share about early radio's impact on rural communities in the United States. Furthermore, I recognized how under-represented rural Appalachia was in the media literature and hoped this work would make a contribution.

As I began exploring the impact of radio on rural Appalachia, fifty-one residents (seventeen males and thirty-four females) from Morgan, Vinton, Meigs, and Athens Counties in southeastern Ohio were interviewed. Desiring a group old enough to recall the inception of radio into this region of the country, I actively sought elderly residents for discussions in community centers, nursing homes, retirement communities, and senior citizen centers. I was sometimes aware of suspicious looks I received when first entering a center. However, after informally chatting with the residents, most would let down their guard within a few minutes.

After meeting with the first group, a snowball effect occurred where participants suggested individuals and social clubs they felt might be interested in participating in the discussion. In addition to interviewing Appalachians at community and retirement centers, I began to be invited into some inter-viewees' private homes. This broadened the age group of the participants in the study from twenty-two years of age to eighty-eight. Three interviews were conducted by telephone, and one occurred at a neighborhood potluck dinner party. Occasionally, I would bump into some of the interviewees at community events such as dances and conferences, or while shopping. These casual meetings often led to introductions to other participants interested in sharing stories about the early arrival of radio into rural Appalachia.

Depending on the age of the participants, the period discussed was from 1920 to 1960. Female participants outnumbered male participants two to one. Given that the majority of interviewees were in their seventies and eighties, this statistical demographic was not surprising.

The initial interviews at the various community centers included all members who attended. Groups over four and as large as nine necessitated the use of videotape as the primary recording tool. The videos proved invaluable in identifying speakers in the transcription process, especially when more than one participant spoke at once. Before starting my recorder, I would ask interviewees to sit in a semi-circle facing the camera. The use of a story-circle, whereby each question was posed and participants responded in order, helped trigger memories of other interviewees in the group. This proved particularly helpful with elderly participants. Bruchac and Morin (1997) describe the story-circle as a metaphor for the Native American circle of life, whereby each phase of life is represented in the interview procedure. The "child" represents phase one, where we listen to stories. The "adolescent" represents phase two, where we observe the context of a story. The "adult" represents the third stage where we recall stories from our youth. Lastly, the "elder" represents phase four where stories we have learned are shared with others. Banks (1997) calls attention to the impact of the four phases upon the interviewer in an oral history setting. He argues that phase one represents the collection of data by the interviewer; phase two, the placing of data into various contextual frames; phase three, the comparison of current data with other data from a similar period; phase four, the sharing of compiled information with an audience. As with much qualitative research today, the interrelationship between the interviewer and the interviewee is of great importance. However, within story-circle group dynamics, the interrelationship amongst the interviewees is of equal importance. For example, with subsequent interviews, where a large number of participants were available, I asked interviewees to break up into smaller groups for recording. This seemed to defuse the anxiety of some who watched the first group being interviewed. Once comfortable with the topic, many onlookers were eager to join the second group being recorded. Others remained off-camera but would interject comments or suggest words for a stumbling friend. When invited into the group by myself or other interviewees, most chose to remain on the sideline. As mentioned above, this could have been for many reasons: fear of speaking on camera; fear of speaking in front of others; concern for not appearing "smart enough"; or simply feeling their stories were of little interest to others.

In addition to the formal, structured interview sessions, either in story-circle groups or individually, there were many times when I was without my recorder and simply had casual conversations with members of the community. These conversations usually occurred spontaneously. As I did not record these conversations, I would try to jot down notes in a small notebook whenever I was alone. Lindlof (1995) tells of how some researchers in these situations record their notes during frequent visits to the restroom. During my unstructured conversations, new questions came to mind that I would later use during structured/recorded interview sessions. More importantly, perhaps, these conversations gave me a truer insight into the lives of the people I would be writing about.

Traveling around Appalachia, I would stop to interview someone in his or her home, and without fail I would be obliged to stay for supper. Schwandt (1997) described participant observation as including "activities of direct observation, interviewing, document analysis, reflection, analysis, and interpretation" (pp. 110–111). Although I was surprisingly successful in finding respondents with stories they were eager to share, I was also mindful of the region's "code of the hills" addressed in Trillin's (1972) "A stranger with a camera."[4] The author tells of a film crew working in the mountains of Kentucky who had gone onto private property without permission. Seeing strangers with camera equipment on his land, the landowner pulled a gun and shot one of the filmmakers for trespassing. While interviewing for the story, Trillin was told by a local resident, "Now, that's the code of the hills. . . . I wouldn't have gone on that old man's land to pick me a mess of wild greens without I'd asked him" (p. 201).

When I first arrived in Appalachian Ohio, I befriended my neighbor who had been living in the same house for the past fifty years. Although he was always happy to chat with me, he would never set foot onto my yard without an invitation. He would stand at the edge of his well-manicured garden and shout to be heard, rather than move closer without permission.

Interestingly, whenever I was given the name of someone to interview, I was often told simply to "go over to his or her house, knock on the door, and introduce yourself." Given "the code," I was always a little reluctant to pursue anyone without an introduction. Once, I was given the name of someone with whom to speak. When I arrived unannounced at the man's business, his sons told me that their father was at home and they gladly gave me directions. Driving up to the man's house, I recognized his car coming towards me and turned my vehicle around to give chase. As we passed his place of business, his sons enthusiastically waved me on. I finally caught up with him in town. After introducing myself, the man excused himself saying he was too busy to speak to me and went into Hardee's for lunch. This event reiterated the fact that I was still a stranger with a tape recorder.

There are, however, some advantages to being viewed as an outsider. For example, various authors have addressed the "sometime" benefits of being an outsider when recording oral history, not the least of which being the ability to view the situation from a neutral perspective (Guy, 1997; Thompson, 1978; Yow, 1997). "The outsider can ask for the obvious to be explained; while the insider, who may in fact be misinformed in assuming the answer, does not ask for fear of seeming foolish" (Thompson, 1978, p. 117). "Merely having rapport," observed Jackson (1987, p. 68), "is no guarantee you'll be able to record anything."

Certainly interpretive researchers have been criticized for attempting to speak "for" a group of people. One must ever be sensitive to issues of power, class, identity, gender and race. Research should be approached as a discourse: a coordinated process of socially constructed meaning (Tyler, 1986).

"[C]ritical ethnographers," writes Stacey (1991), "eschew a detached stance of neutral observation, and they perceive their subjects as collaborators in a project the researcher can never fully control. Moreover, they acknowledge the indispensably intrusive and unequal nature of their participation in the studied culture" (p. 115). I have always felt that telling one's story can be cathartic in nature and hope that some respondents in this study benefited from telling their stories.

Orality

Larson (1992) examined how the twentieth century witnessed an explosion of the "electronic word" in many forms, while Ong (1982) looked at how this explosion of orally based media transformed our society in ways that resemble primitive oral cultures. Specifically, Ong observed that radio (along with other electronic technology) "brought us into an age of 'secondary orality'. This new orality has striking resemblances to the old in its participatory mystique, its fostering of a communal sense, and even its use of formulas" (p. 136). Given the importance of the oral conveyance of information via the radio, it stands to reason that an oral history approach would be a natural methodology for exploring the evolution of radio. In addition, the importance of the oral tradition in Appalachian culture should not be overlooked. On a few occasions, participants, especially elderly Appalachians, would get caught up in telling tales from the past. Having always loved stories, I can only assume that the pleased expression on my face must have encouraged the storytellers. Although I would try my best to allow the interviewee to go in any direction the story would take him or her, I often found myself telling stories about my own early memories of television.[5] This give and take, I believe, helped put the participant at ease and facilitated the flow of information that led to this oral history of radio in rural Appalachia.

Although the use of oral history has been quite effective in the past, there are relatively few works using oral history to examine radio's inception. In *Listening to Radio, 1920–1950*, Barfield (1996) uses oral histories to trace the birth of radio by letting what he calls "veteran listeners" speak for themselves. As Thomas Inge writes in the foreword, "rather than trace the history of radio through the usual route of the development of technology, radio stations, broadcast systems or popular shows and programming, [Barfield] has sought out a body of oral history from those who grew up with and listened to radio" (p. ix). In other words, Barfield unveiled a social history of radio. Other scholars, such as Keith (2000), examined the history of American radio through oral history interviews with authors, scholars, and industry figures who recall the central events surrounding the rich beginnings of radio. Still others, such as Skutch (1998) and Corwin and Bell (1994), explored radio's early years based on interviews with radio producers and directors.

Although others have explored radio's general development through the use of oral histories, this project looks specifically at the development of radio within rural Appalachia: an area often overlooked in the literature.

Interviews

Lindlof (1995) says that "[i]nterviews are especially well suited to helping the researcher understand a social actor's own perspective" (p. 167). Although my spontaneous interviews helped gain the trust of many respondents, I attempted to structure my formal interviews, where I used a tape or video recorder, in as relaxed a manner as possible. I would often chat casually with the participants before turning on the recorder. When I sensed that the interviewee was beginning to settle down, I would announce that I was about to start recording. After recording, I would again make casual conversation for another minute or two. I also paid careful attention to microphone placement. I would try not to place the microphone in the sight line between the participant and myself. This helped insure that the interviewee would be looking at me and not the microphone when he or she spoke. Often, this allowed the participant to forget that his or her words were being recorded and made for a more relaxed interview.

My recordings generated more than 100 pages of transcripts, each ranging from three to twenty-six double-spaced pages. After completing the interviews, I began "living with the data" (Nelson, 1989). I listened to (or watched) the tapes, and read the transcripts and my notes repeatedly until I began to recognize patterns. Often, while re-reading the transcripts, images of the participants would appear in my mind's eye. While listening/watching tapes, careful attention was paid to voice inflections. The way in which a speaker's voice gained excitement at a certain point or became softer at another added insight into the person's feelings on the topic being discussed. To take account of these tone/tempo variations, I would make parenthetical notes in the transcript. If, for example, a person giggled while speaking, I would simply write [giggle] before his or her statement.

The recollections of many of the participants I interviewed were so rich that I feel fortunate to have been able to record them and am eager to share them. I attempted to keep quotes as close to the original as possible. Some oral history purists feel that the transcription of the recorded interview is sacrosanct. Many feel that editing out pauses distorts the participant's message. Others feel that such a concession is a small price to pay for easier readability. I did remove some "uhs" to facilitate the flow of the statements unless they contributed to the feeling or meaning of the quote.

I also felt it imperative to maintain the vernacular of the region whenever it occurred. Although some may view mountain speech as characteristic of an illiterate person, Hendrickson (1993) finds its roots in Old English. For example, the use of an "a" before a present participle as in "I'm a-comin'," was used by Shakespeare in *Hamlet* when he wrote, "Now might I do it pat, now he is a-praying." As a Southerner, I have always felt that modern English suffers from the lack of the collective second person or plural you. The use of "you-uns", often ridiculed in Southern speech, can however be traced to the "ye ones" of Chaucer's time (see Dillard, 1985; Hendrickson, 1993; Wolfram and Christian, 1976). A statement like "I've been a-knowin' these people since childhood" conveys feelings of ongoing familiarity (continuing from past into present and perhaps into the future), which is not quite as well conveyed in the more standardized "I've known these people since childhood." The use of the vernacular should be seen as contributing to the interpretation of the respondent's feelings and "informed by the unique context in which they live" (Rabinow, 1977, p. 103).

As in most oral histories, I use the respondents' names since I do not want those who were interviewed to feel that I am speaking for them or taking away their voice. However, the analysis and interpretations are mine. Given that I was on a first-name basis with most of the people I interviewed, after using a participant's full name the first time I refer to them, I will use only their given name on subsequent reference or citation.

Interview questions

Throughout the interview process, I tried not to rely too heavily on my prepared questions and allowed the interviewee to follow any unexpected path he or she chose to take. Of course, my initial questions did shape the direction in which I felt I could derive the most raw material (memories), and I tried my best to guide participants in the direction which best served my scholarly aim. As the author of this work, I also recognize that I chose the quotes that are included herein. Frisch (1990) addresses this dilemma of voice and authority, noting that while the interviewer may feel more responsible for the creation of a work, the interviewee is the greater partner. It is in the interviewees' stories that the greatest value of an oral history resides. Furthermore, the interviewees also participate in the interpretation of the stories since they constantly analyze their own motives while recalling them (see Ritchie, 1994).

Areas of discussion revolved around the inception and use of radio in rural Appalachia and began with inquiries into each participant's earliest memories of radio. "Where were you when you first listened to radio?" was one of the first questions asked. This allowed the participants to place their memories within a location, thus helping to center the participant (Henige, 1982). In addition, where people gathered to listen gave clues to the social aspects of radio listening. If they listened to the radio in their home, this might indicate a level of wealth, as many participants within this rural Appalachian region were too poor to afford a radio. As a result, these participants said that they went to a neighbor or relative's house to listen. Further inquiry focused on how listening habits changed once respondents acquired a radio at home.

Access to electricity seemed to have determined how people listened to radio. Given electricity's late arrival into the region (in some cases, as late as 1960), questions focused on how the coming of electricity changed habits. With the advent of electrical power, did people develop different listening habits from when they listened to battery-powered radio? Did people still listen as a community or did radio simply become background noise as they went about doing their daily activities? In addition, was electricity responsible for the elimination of communal gatherings centered around the radio? And finally, what programs did the community listen to? Did participants use the media as a news source or was it valued more as an entertainment medium? My interests lie in how media contributed to the social fabric of the participants' lives.

Research question

Much has been written on the effects electronic media and new technology have had on our sense of community. Riesman's (1950) "lonely crowd" theory of the individual living in a modern technological society yet existing in seclusion seems to echo the belief that electronic media, starting with radio, were isolating catalysts on society. Given the strong feelings of community and family within the Appalachian region, would participants indicate that the inception of radio into the region disrupted rather than enhanced their community?

Radio in rural Appalachia

In 1936, the United States Department of Agriculture's Chief of Radio Service wrote: "during the early days of the development of radio, farm families were among the leading investors in receiving equipment" (Salisbury, 1936). However, this was not necessarily the case within distressed areas of Appalachia where many families could not afford the cost of a radio. "You know times was hard," commented Dulcie Reinhart. "Everybody worked hard at that time. I don't remember anybody back then who had a radio where we lived. I enjoyed it, yes I would have liked to have a radio, it's just we couldn't get it. Mom and Dad was lucky to have stuff on the table, there were nine children."[6]

However poor the region was, residents were resourcefully determined to join the radio revolution. Ida Mae Stoneburger recalled, "I remember when I was married in 1931. We was very poor and we traded five hens and roosters for a radio."[7] Buying a radio during this period was considered a major purchase. During the 1930s, the average yearly salary in the United States was $1,368 (Gordon and Gordon, 1990). However, in a region where most were farmers and miners, income levels were considerably lower than the national average. For example, a coal miner's yearly income for 1933 was $900 (Derks, 1994). Of course, the cost of living during the 1930s was considerably less than it is today. A new Ford automobile could be purchased in 1930 for $495 and a movie ticket was $0.35–$0.50 (Gordon and Gordon, 1990). In 1930, the average radio cost $78. As set production increased to meet the demands of more radio-owning households, the average cost of a receiver dropped to $55 in 1935 (Sterling and Kittross, 1990). Still, $55 to $78 for a radio was a considerable amount to spend for a non-essential commodity and many within the region simply could not afford to purchase their own sets. Some, like Paul Weaver, made their own sets:

> The first one we owned was the one I made out of an oatmeal box and you'd wrap a wire around it so many times, and it was called a crystal set. I copied it out of the *Popular Mechanics* magazine. The reason that I didn't keep making radios, after the three tube come out with a speaker on it [is because] by that time I'd have had maybe $8 to $10 in it and I didn't have that. We never was without food nor clothing but we didn't have any money to jingle in our pockets either.[8]

Crystal radios required no power source and were unable to amplify incoming signals, thereby requiring the use of headphones. What followed were tube radio sets that required a power source, usually a wet cell battery. Later models were powered by dry cell batteries and electricity.

Not all crystal sets were homemade. Some participants, like Frank Frazel, had pre-fabricated sets. "I had a manufactured crystal set that I got from my dad

194

and it was the type that you would hook to the bed springs in the bed. By the time I got it, it was an antique. The springs worked as an aerial."[9] Besides needing a bedspring (or some other aerial), there were definite limitations to crystal sets. Edger Smith remembered the early crystal sets. "You had the earphones, the headphones on your ears. And I'd use them too, but there was ten of us kids, five girls and five boys and it was busy all the time. Someone was listening on it all the time. I wasn't very old, I was five or six years old at most although I really enjoyed listening to it."[10] Ida Mae recalled her brother getting a crystal set. "You had to put the earphones on to listen to it and we had to fight over the earphones to see who got to listen."[11] Clyde Pinney spoke of visiting his grandparents. "My grandfather, who was a Baptist minister, was also an avid fight fan. The first radio they had was a crystal set with earphones, and Grandpa and my dad would share the earphones and the rest of the people would talk while Grandpa and Dad listened to the prizefight on the radio."[12] Given the expense of tube or console radios, it was understandable that many within this poor region of the United States first listened to crystal radio sets even as late as the 1930s.

In 1933, at the age of sixteen, Henry Shaffer went to work in the coal mines for $13 a week. "Of course Dad dealt with the company store so he never got no pay check. So in order to get any money, I started working at the mine. Then we'd use my money to go buy things that we wanted."[13] The establishment of the company store by coal-mining corporations exacted powerful social controls over miners and led to economic exploitation. If miners wished to draw on their pay before their monthly or bi-monthly payday, scrip was issued. Printed by the coal-mining company, scrip could only purchase goods from the company store. Given that the miner paid the company for his housing, mining explosives and tools, there was often little left for purchasing anything other than bare essentials (Shackelford and Weinberg, 1977). As Henry put it, "We had to buy our own powder, we had to buy the carbide lights, we had to buy the tools to work with. The company furnished the coal for us to dig out."[14] Only with Henry's second paycheck were the Shaffers able to be the first family in the "holler" to get a console radio.

Although Ong (1982) describes radio as an orally based medium that "has brought us into an age of 'secondary orality' [with] its fostering of communal sense" (p. 136), it is interesting to note that he was presumably speaking of radio transmitted over a speaker that could be listened to by a group. Yet, these early radio enthusiasts listening to broadcasts on headphones were in fact isolated from those around them because of their immersion in their own auditory experience. In effect, these headphone-wearing listeners were as isolated and closed off as readers of printed text. Ong might have described them as members of "the individualized introversion of the age of writing" (Ong, 1971, p. 285). Unlike the communal experience participants often cite in listening to radio, these early examples seem to be antithetical to communal listening.

Powering the radio

It is important to recognize that during this period, when people spoke of listening to radio within this area of the country, they were speaking of battery-powered radio. Since most people in this region were without electricity during the 1920s, 1930s and 1940s, a battery was needed to power their radios.

In the 1930s, the Rural Electrification Administration (REA) began bringing electricity to rural areas of the nation (Parker and Hudson, 1992). But for many people in rural Appalachia, electricity didn't reach their homes until the 1950s or later. According to the Ohio Rural Electric Cooperatives (1985), "Ohio cities had enjoyed the benefits of electricity for several decades prior to 1935. But only two Ohio farms out of ten were electrified by 1935 and, for the most part, those were farms close to towns and existing power lines" (p. iii). Although rural electric cooperatives started to appear in Ohio in 1935, much of the four high distress counties within the Appalachian region of the state was not wired. Only tiny northeastern and southwestern corners of Athens County were served by the Rural Electric Cooperative that provided electrical power to the area. Approximately 50 percent of Meigs and Morgan County was electrified (Ohio Rural Electric Cooperatives, 1985). Although Vinton County was included in its entirety within the Buckeye Rural Electric Cooperative Service Area, not all residents within the county had electric power in their homes. Reasons for not having electricity ranged from economic barriers to residents' concerns over electricity's safety. As Edna recalled:

> When electricity first came to our area, the people were told of all the dangers . . . that lightning could run in on it, and they told people they needed a lightning rod for their house. So, the neighbors had a meeting and they got together and discussed whether we should have electricity or not because it was so dangerous. They said if you're even putting a bulb in, you could get shocked. So, we were a little scared about it. So when we finally got electricity I remember my dad the first time he had to change a light bulb. All of us went into the kitchen; we had to get way back and here's about seven or eight of us with our heads stickin' around the door watching to see if dad got electrocuted whenever he changed the bulb. You know, it was a scary process. I never will forget that.[15]

In the 1940 Census, only 26.7 percent of rural farm homes in Meigs County had "electric lighting." (One must assume from the "electric lighting" category that this meant electric service to the house rather than a gasoline powered generator or a battery-powered home plant. Censuses earlier than 1940 made no mention of this category. Because most participants lived on farms, the "rural farm" category in each census was chosen for this comparison. Although some participants spoke of living in coal towns, those locations were often as isolated as rural farm districts.) There were 39.2 percent of Athens County rural farm homes with electric lighting and just 12 percent in Morgan County. Interestingly, Vinton County, the only county included in its entirety within a rural electric cooperative service area, had only 17.1 percent of its rural farmhouses electrified in 1940 (*Sixteenth Census of the United States*, 1943). This is in contrast to 36.6 percent of all Ohio farm dwellings that were electrified by June 1937 (Ohio Rural Electric Cooperatives, 1985) and 78.8 percent of all dwellings in the United States with electric service by 1940 (*Historical Statistics of the United States*, 1975).

By 1950, these numbers had increased dramatically. Rural farm houses in Meigs County were 88.2 percent electrified, Athens County had 84 percent of its rural dwellings electrified, Morgan had 77.9 percent, and Vinton had risen to 78.8 percent (*Census of Housing: 1950*, 1953).

Given these limitations, participants' first radios, regardless of the decade, were most likely battery-powered. However, as some in the region started to purchase or trade for radios, many could not afford the wet cell battery that was required to operate it and were forced to use the one from their automobile. Edna told of some of the difficulties in removing the car battery when they wanted to listen:

> My dad bought a radio and he would take the battery out of the car to run it. When we used it on Saturday nights, my dad would park the car up on the hill so when he put the battery back in the car we could shove the car down the hill to get it to run and re-charge the battery. You had to be careful where you were or you couldn't get the car started after using the battery for the radio. If you couldn't push the car to get started with the dead battery, you would have to get the mule to pull you.[16]

Participants were quite ingenious in devising ways of listening to the radio. Before getting a radio at home, Edna recollected going to listen at a neighbor's house. "The first radio I can remember was at a good friend's house, which was powered by a windmill on top of their house, and that charged the battery and kept the radio going."[17] Others built homemade generators. John Williams "rigged up a battery charger with a washing machine gasoline engine and a Model-T Ford generator."[18] Because of economic reasons, the radio was used only sparingly. Golda recalled, "Of course you couldn't hear it for everything. You'd play it and then you shut it off to save your battery."[19] Clyde added, "If there was anything important coming along that we wanted to watch [*sic*], why the battery would be charged and we would keep it charged for that particular event. It wasn't just turn it on like we do today with our television and let it run all day. We took care of the amount of battery power that we had."[20]

When households were electrified, radio had become such an important part of people's lives that some had an electric set waiting. As Clyde recalled, "We bought an electric radio and had it sitting on the shelf waiting for the electricity to be turned on. Whenever the electricity arrived, the radio was there waiting for it."[21]

Distant stations

During radio's early years, the most powerful AM broadcasters were the clear channel stations that were authorized to broadcast at high power levels and granted exclusive use of their frequency at night (Foust, 1994). These stations enabled radio listeners to pick up programming from hundreds of miles away. This was especially important for people living in isolated, rural areas of the country. In 1962, *Broadcasting* magazine wrote:

> From 1930 to 1950 – give or take a few years on either side – the clear channel stations reigned supreme. They were the big voices of the air. . . . Their programs and commercials rang loud and clear during the day, and rose to a roar at night. . . . It was these stations that carried the most popular programs, the national advertising – both network and national spot – that brought to millions of listeners in rural America their only nighttime service.
>
> ("Clear tops for 20 years", p. 29)

Clear channel stations had frequency signal protection at night from 700 to 750 miles and southeastern Ohio's geographical location placed it within the frequency protection zone of several clear channel broadcasters. The Federal Radio Commission's 1928 frequency allocation plan was the first to allow a handful of stations to broadcast on AM frequencies at the highest power available: first 25,000 watts and later 50,000 watts. Other stations could use these frequencies during the day but were forced off the air at night to prevent interference with the clear channel stations. The purpose was to provide service to ensure good reception for rural and remote radio listeners. The Federal Radio Commission and later the Federal Communications Commission agreed that this policy should be among their most important concerns (Foust, 1994).

Owners of clear channel stations formed the Clear Channel Broadcasting Service (CCBS) to lobby for the protection of clear channel policy. After the start of World War II, CCBS members wrote a letter to President Roosevelt affirming the group's interest in keeping rural and small town radio listeners informed:

> As the nation's independently owned clear channel stations, ours is a doubled responsibility in radio during this crisis. Our audiences comprise not only city listeners, but also the millions of Americans living on farms and in small towns across the country. The principal radio voice reaching some 50,000,000 rural and small town listeners must promote the unified effort needed to win this crucial struggle.
>
> (Foust, 1994, p. 129)

Because of their isolation, rural communities may have had the most to gain from these high-powered radio stations. Yet, living in rural Appalachia had its own quirks. Roy Cross remarked, "Down here you were so restricted, you couldn't get the Columbus [Ohio] station like BNS but you could get Atlanta [WSB], loud and clear."[22] Archie Greer also remembered listening to clear channel stations. "You didn't get a lot of radio back then in this area. You got WLW out of Cincinnati, that was a clear channel you could get on a good night. Also WJR out of Detroit. Of course, at night you could pick up a lot of stuff. You could pick up New York, Nashville, Boston, Atlanta."[23] Some spoke of the mountains as an aid to radio reception. As Cecil Webb recalled: "My daddy was interested in prizefights, but we couldn't pick up the station that broadcast those prizefights at home, so me and my dad would drive up to the top of the mountain and sit there in the car and listen to the fights."[24]

Programming

If there was one program that most participants mentioned listening to, it was *The Grand Ole Opry*. Before electricity came into the region, participants spoke of how they planned their radio usage to guarantee that the batteries would be charged on Saturday nights so they could listen to *The Opry*. As Irene Flowers recalls:

> Saturday night was the only time we listened to radio. Daddy never went anywhere on Saturday. We only had a Model-A Ford and he would take the battery out on Saturday night and hook it up to the radio so he could hear *The Grand Ole Opry* and that was the only music we had, the only couple of three hours we could listen. We never did it no other night, just Saturday night.[25]

The Grand Ole Opry went on the air in 1925, broadcast from Nashville's WSM radio station. (Interestingly, seventy-five years later, on June 17, 2000, *The Grand Ole Opry* went online, when the program was first webcast on the internet.) Modeled after the WLS *National Barn Dance* from Chicago, *The Grand Ole Opry* was originally launched as the WSM *Barn Dance*. Radio stations across the South and Midwest had been broadcasting live country music since the early 1920s. Many attribute WSB in Atlanta with starting the trend and WBAP in Fort Worth, Texas, with originating the first radio barn dance. Before government regulations, WBAP's early barn dance programs out of Fort Worth were picked up as far west as Hawaii and as far south and east as Haiti (Malone, 1985). The huge broadcast footprints of these clear channel stations allowed country music programming to gain popularity throughout most of the nation.

In 1927, the WSM *Barn Dance* followed NBC's *Musical Appreciation Hour*. When WSM's country music program went on the air, the announcer said, "For the past hour we have been listening to music taken largely from grand opera, but from now on we will present *The Grand Ole Opry*" (Hay, 1953, p. 1). The name stuck and *The Grand Ole Opry* is now the world's longest running live radio program.

The Grand Ole Opry's predominance as the leading country music program was solidified in 1939 when NBC agreed to carry a thirty-minute segment each Saturday night on its national network. NBC affiliate stations across the country broadcast the show, thus allowing listeners outside of WSM's reception area to tune-in to the program. By being carried on a network, the show gained national status. However, the thirty-minute segment was only a portion of the four-and-a-half hour program. True *Opry* fans who were able to receive WSM listened to the full program. Ivan Tribe recollected that "here in southeastern Ohio, just about everybody listened to WLW out of Cincinnati. At night, they did network shows. And we listened to WSM in Nashville a lot, and the *Grand Ole Opry*. People also listened to WLS in Chicago."[26]

Variety shows featuring country music, sometimes referred to as "hillbilly music," were among the most popular regularly scheduled programs on early radio. However, when John Williams joined the Navy, he quickly found out that there were radio variety hours featuring something other than "country" music:

> When I went into the navy in 1943, about half of our group was from this part of Ohio, Kentucky, and Tennessee. The other half was from Chicago and Michigan and large cities. We had one radio in boot camp and *The Hit Parade* and *The Grand Ole Opry* were on at the same time and that caused a terrible fight because fifty percent wanted *The Hit Parade*, which played popular music and the other half wanted *The Grand Ole Opry*. I heard that someone purposefully damaged the radio so that it would put an end to the fighting.[27]

Participants living in southeastern Ohio did listen to musical shows other than *The Grand Ole Opry*. Those interviewed spoke of listening to the WLS *National Barn Dance* from Chicago, the WLW *Barn Dance* out of Cincinnati, WWVA's *Wheeling Jamboree* from West Virginia, and WNOX's *Midday Merry-Go-Round* from Knoxville. Given that most of these stations were clear channel stations, these programs could be heard over a large portion of the country. At night, for instance, *The Grand Ole Opry* could be heard all over the southeast and as far west as Texas. WWVA's *Wheeling Jamboree* blanketed the northeast as far as Canada and WLS's *National Barn Dance* covered the Midwest (Malone, 1985).

In addition to country music on the radio, many participants spoke of the importance of news programming. As with *The Grand Ole Opry*, Edger spoke of his father saving the radio battery to insure being able to listen to informational programming. "My dad liked to listen to the weather report because he was a farmer. He wouldn't let anyone else take the radio. We kids couldn't listen to anything cause we had to save the battery for that report."[28]

Interestingly, few mentioned Roosevelt's fireside chats, except in passing, although listening to news reports of America's war efforts during World War

II was a top priority. Rather than mentioning specific events, many participants spoke of the broadcasters who brought the news into their homes. Lowell Thomas, H. V. Kaltenborn and Gabriel Heatter were often mentioned. Edger, however, spoke of how his mother became the newscaster in his family. "My mother always listened to the news, you know, and when my dad would come in he'd ask her if there was any news of the day and she could quote him everything just word for word what she'd heard on the radio, you know. What news was happening."[29]

Sporting events, especially the "big fight," seemed to be the perfect vehicle for early radio broadcasting. Legendary boxers such as Jack Dempsey and Gene Tunney came to fame just as radio began to make inroads into American homes. As special event radio broadcasts, championship prizefights were not to be missed. John and his uncle, however, were not so lucky:

> Boxing or prizefights was another big thing around [the Ohio towns of] Hope and Zaleski. I remember my uncle taking me, when we didn't have a battery, into Zaleski to hear some of the Joe Lewis fights. I remember Max Schmeling of Germany was a top fighter at that time. And there were quite a separate group that wanted Schmeling to win and others Joe Lewis. I know my uncle took me to a local store in Zaleski to listen to it but Lewis knocked Schmeling out before we got there.[30]

Baseball games were also mentioned as participants spoke of trying to pick up ball games, mainly from Cincinnati. Of course, early radio not only carried musical and sporting events, it captured the listeners' imagination with drama, soap operas, comedy, adventure, and religious programming. Seventy-year-old participants recalled their youth when they ran home from school to listen to soap operas such as *Stella Dallas*. Others, like Mary Rouch, spoke of "sitting on the floor with all the kids listening to *Amos n' Andy*, *The Lone Ranger*, *The Green Hornet*, and of course *Jack Armstrong*, you didn't miss 'Jack Armstrong,' he was [giggle] the All-American-Boy!"[31]

Social effects

Many participants who didn't have radio at home spoke of going elsewhere to listen. Retired coal miner Henry Shaffer recalled: "The first memory I have is tuning in the Jack Dempsey fight. It was between 1925 and 1927, down there in Millfield, Ohio. There was a guy that lived there that had a radio, so I suppose there was forty or fifty people sitting out in the yard, he had the radio on the porch."[32] Golda Hart recollected going to a neighbor's house:

> I remember back when we went to our neighbors; we wanted to hear what was going on in the world. That was back in the '30s, after

201

I got married. I was just a farm girl you know. I married a farm boy, and we'd go to an older couple – they were such good friends of ours – and we'd listen to *The Grand Ole Opry* on Saturday night. And that was our Saturday night deal. She was a good pie maker and of course there would be snacks and pies. We didn't have a radio at home at that time.[33]

Getting together with neighbors and family to listen to the radio was an important social event and food was often mentioned when recalling these get-togethers. Snacks such as pies and popcorn were often brought up.

Many participants spoke of putting the radio on the porch to listen, although Bridget Marsh told of how her porch was not large enough to accommodate all her friends and relatives who wanted to listen to the first radio in the neighborhood:

We had one of the first radios in our neighborhood, if you want to call it a neighborhood, because our nearest neighbor was like a half a mile out. But my dad cleared out the front yard and put the radio out and all the neighbors would come on Friday and Saturday evening to listen because we were the only ones that had a radio. . . . We had lots of relatives, probably sometimes twenty to thirty people would come. We didn't put it on the porch, no, we stayed outside under the trees. We wanted to be comfortable. It was like going to a drive-in almost, only under the trees.[34]

Like so many others, Bridget spoke of how family members had a specific job at these gatherings. Some would bring food and drink while the youngsters had a more onerous responsibility:

Because we were related to everyone, of course, it was very friendly and lots of time my aunt would bring something, maybe a cake or something or a jug of tea or something. . . . We also had giant mosquitoes and stuff like that. We would always have to get the cow patty things to make a smoke for the night. That used to be my younger sister's duty. It's not offensive at all. My little sister would gather the thin dry ones, you know, we would light them and the smoke would keep the mosquitoes away. It always worked.[35]

During an era before air-conditioning, sitting outside under the trees or on the porch during the summertime was quite common. It not only kept one cool, it helped bring people together. As Bob Cole recalls:

I remember listening to radio, playing in the street and listening to news about the war. My parents, we didn't have air conditioning, so my parents would sit on the porch. The neighbors walked along the street and would stop and listen to the radio and then they'd discuss the news about the war or listen to the programs. The kids would play in the street while the adults sat on the porch, so there was a lot of interaction of people and everybody knew everything that was going on in the neighborhood.[36]

Certainly, people sat on their porches before radio, but listening to the radio on the porch, especially during a national crisis such as World War II, seemingly brought people together, allowing them to voice their feelings and concerns about the war.

Just as most participants spoke of listening to *The Grand Ole Opry* every Saturday night, many spoke of listening to news broadcasts about the war each evening. Wanda Rose told of how it became a routine. "I remember back during World War II that at 9:00 at night we always listened to the news, you know, on the war, the war news. That was really important because there were so many people in service. We listened every night."[37]

By this time, radio had already begun to have a great impact on how people scheduled their time. In an area where outdoor activities were an integral part of social life, radio seemed to encroach upon that lifestyle. Lenora recalled how radio programming had an impact upon her father. "My dad was a foxhunter, he had a foxhound. And he and my brother would go fox hunting. At that time they used to call boxing prizefights, so if there was gonna be a prizefight my dad would stay at home, he wouldn't go fox hunting, he would stay at home and listen to the fight."[38]

Listening to prizefights on the radio may have brought men indoors, but it still allowed for male bonding. Lloyd Porter recollected memories of his father and uncle:

I don't know, it must have been about '30 or '32, something like that, I was about five years old or six, and a big fight was comin' on. I remember my uncle had a radio in the neighborhood. I don't know if anybody else had a radio or not. But my dad, and I guess maybe ten men in the neighborhood, was gathered around in this room around that radio and I went down to listen with them. Well, it was a show. I observed all of these old men, chewin' tobacco, sittin' around and spittin' and smokin' and it was a show when that fight came on. They were doin' this and that in their seats, you know, "ooh wowee," but the radio was fadin' in and fadin' out, you could hear something every now and then. And they were enjoying it. I didn't know what was goin' on, but I remember that stuck in my mind.[39]

Dancing to the radio was another cheap form of entertainment, even if it meant dancing in the streets. Henry tells of how "people went to the company store to listen to radio. The company store was open on Saturday night. People used to come down and they would try to dance in the road or do this or that, whatever they could do, 'cause on Saturday night there was no place to go anyhow."[40]

With "no place to go anyhow," and little cash, Saturday nights were usually spent listening to the radio. As Edna recalled, "You went to church on Sunday and prayer meeting on Wednesday night and that was the only time you went out. So going to the neighbors on Saturday to listen to the radio was a big event."[41]

The coming of electric power into the region dramatically changed the listening and consequently the social habits of rural Appalachians. With battery-powered radios, the entire family and visiting friends and neighbors would gather around the set to listen. As Lloyd recalled, "you couldn't listen to it, you couldn't turn the radio on unless everybody was there in the family."[42] The arrival of electricity into the region, however, allowed for a more casual interaction with the radio. Mendelsohn (1964) wrote that "generally speaking, radio functions as a diverting 'companion' and helps to fill voids that are created by routine and boring tasks" (p. 242). Only with the arrival of electricity was the radio relegated to a secondary position. It no longer was the center of attention as listeners turned it on for music while dusting furniture or snapping beans for canning. Virginia Miller told how her uncle ran an electric wire down to his barn so he could "put on the radio while he was milking so there would be music for the cows, plus he could catch the news broadcast while he was milking. They said it would soothe the cows so they would give more milk and everything."[43] Electricity permitted the listener to turn on the radio whenever he or she wanted. There was no longer the need to save the battery for Saturday night and *The Grand Ole Opry*. It was perhaps electricity more than the medium itself that changed people's listening habits. Lenora recollected:

> I remember when my brothers went to the service during World War II. My mom was always trying to get what was going on because she was concerned with their welfare. At that time we didn't turn it on [the radio] whenever we wanted to because, like I said, you had to save that battery. But now you just push a button and it comes on. So it's entirely different. I think you listen to it more now. Sometimes I'll just turn it on for the music while I do my work like dusting but not with the battery radio because you saved it for important things. Back then, after everything was done, you'd gather around the radio. It was real serious. You had to be quiet. My dad wouldn't let us laugh or giggle. It was serious business. They were really interested in what was going on.[44]

With the coming of electricity, participants, particularly women, began to mention doing housework while the radio was on. When asked how electricity changed her life, Marian Dees compared her electric radio to the old crystal sets. "Sure it changed our habits 'cause it was there available all the time. It wasn't like that crystal set that somebody else had to handle. You could do it yourself, you could turn it on, it played a lot. My mother played it a lot. She would take her sewing basket and sew and we'd all gather around and listen to 'the stories'."[45] The "stories" or soap operas became an important diversion for many. Rhea Boring spoke of how they would "bring the green beans in, snap off those beans and get them ready for canning the next day while listening to the 'the stories' on the radio."[46] Although many participants spoke of doing work while the radio was on, some, like Pearl Borne, would give their full attention to the soap. "There was a soap at about two o'clock in the afternoon and I would quit work, whatever else I was doing, I'd quit everything to watch [sic] my soap."[47]

Others, like Bennie Lawson, didn't get electric power in their homes until the 1950s and used gasoline-powered generators to run the few electrical appliances they owned:

> Our electric lights and iron was probably the only electric appliances we had because we didn't have electricity until I think about 1951 in the house I grew up in. We were real conservative about it. Mother had an electric iron so in order to listen to *Stella Dallas* there was no problem with me ironing in the afternoon so I could run the generator and listen to the radio. . . . I would iron so I could listen to the radio.[48]

Although the radio was battery-operated, both it and the generator were used sparingly because of economic concerns. Like many others without electricity, Bennie found ways to listen to her favorite programs.

Female use of radio in the home seemed greatly to influence the course media took in America as women started to use radio to eliminate some of the tedium of housework. In addition, radio may have alleviated women's feelings of isolation and loneliness, as most were secluded at home while their husbands, sons, and brothers were in the field. Broadcasters recognized this domestic economy opportunity and aimed many daytime programs at this female audience.

Radio, arguably, was the first medium that connected rural Appalachia to the rest of the nation and to the world at large. In *The Radio Diary of Mary Dyck*, Pamela Riney-Kehrberg (1998) found that "radio connected rural people to the world beyond their farms in ways that no other medium of communication could" (p. 70). Clyde agreed:

> I would say radio broadened our horizons. You knew things that were happening all over the world rather than just in your immediate neighborhood. Even with the local newspaper, you're more or less limited to a small geographical area. When radio came

into being in this part of the country we could hear things from all over the world.[49]

Of course, motion pictures brought the world to residents of even the most rural communities. Because of their isolation, however, getting to a town that could support a theatre was a big event. There were also concerns over cost, as taking a family to the movies was often prohibitively expensive for many within this region.

So, it was the radio that brought the world into the living rooms of rural Appalachia. As Smulyan (1994) observed, by listening to radio, especially distant stations, rural people gained a feeling of connectedness to the rest of the world.

Conclusion

From the very beginning, rural Appalachians faced obstacles while embracing the arrival of radio. The widespread poverty in the area during the 1920s and 1930s made it difficult to purchase radios. When funds for a radio were available, often the listener could not afford the battery to power it. If batteries borrowed from the car or truck expired, getting the vehicle to start with a dead battery caused other logistical problems requiring mules or strategically positioned automobiles.

Poverty within the region had an impact upon the social usage of radio in many ways. Many participants simply could not afford social activities that were costly. Gatherings at a family member's house for a potluck dinner or dancing in the street while the radio played were not only inexpensive forms of entertainment, they also brought family and community together.

In an area in which isolation fostered independence, strong family and community values were very important. Contrary to the popular "lonely crowd" theory, where electronic media was sometimes looked upon as an isolating force in society, the inception of radio into rural Appalachia appeared to enhance rather than disrupt family and community unity. No longer was church the major unifying factor. In addition to getting out of the house to attend church on Sundays and prayer meetings on Wednesday nights, going to a friend or neighbor's house on Saturday night to listen to *The Grand Ole Opry* on the radio became a "big event" in the lives of most participants who were interviewed.

The coming of electricity into this distressed region of the country also had a dramatic impact upon the ways in which people experienced radio. It could be argued that electricity's arrival, more than the evolution of the medium itself, changed people's listening habits. The ability to turn on the radio while dusting furniture or canning beans placed radio into a secondary position and allowed for a more casual interaction with the medium. No longer did people have to "take care of the amount of battery power" that they had. Electricity assured that the radio could be turned on whenever the listener liked. As Mendelsohn put it, radio began to "function as a diverting companion."

It is important to mention, however, that there were some participants who spoke of windmill chargers or jerry-rigged gasoline engines that were used to recharge spent radio batteries. Although there were problems with these devices, people with the ability to charge their own batteries (before getting electricity) spoke of listening to their favorite programs more often than those who either purchased new batteries or paid to have them recharged.

The popularity of soap operas with women during this period greatly contributed to the recognition of the domestic economy and to this day influences the daytime broadcast strategies adopted by executives in the electronic media industry. These serials introduced issues that were common to all Americans, regardless of what region of the country they inhabited.

In addition, the establishment of clear channel stations and networks further contributed to the common national experience brought about with radio. In some cases, participants in southeastern Ohio were able to receive stations from Atlanta (approximately 575 miles away) more clearly than from the state capital of Columbus (approximately 75 miles away). Clear channel radio reception brought news and ideas from different regions of the country, which certainly contributed to the nationalizing force of radio.

Looking towards the future

Today, with the advancement of cellular telephone technology, many under-developed areas of the world are now better able to take advantage of telephone access, which may not have been as readily available if traditional wiring of the regions was required. In the future, Web radio could bring news and entertainment into underprivileged regions of the world not already within the receiving area of traditional broadcast stations. Just as the arrival of radio into rural Appalachia precipitated communal listening, the arrival of Web radio could result in the increase of communal listening habits in underdeveloped regions without radio stations. Residents could gather at community centers, or even listen to the news while riding on a bus, thereby creating an opportunity whereby issues of the day could be discussed with other members of the community. Of course, Web radio could also complement areas with established broadcast stations by bringing alternative voices into a region.

In spite of the obstacles of limited resources and isolation, Appalachians found ways to join the electronic media revolution that began with the advent of radio. It is therefore important to recognize, as we catapult into the next millennium, digitally powered by the computer, that radio paved the way that led us to the information super-highway.

Notes

1 These Appalachian Ohio counties were: Athens, Morgan, Vinton, and Meigs Counties.

2 Created in 1969 as a War on Poverty program to train young people in media production, Appalshop is a media arts center located in central Appalachia where it continues to produce and present works on social, economic, and political issues concerning Appalachian culture.

3 It could be argued that the "Hillbilly" icon was well established in the American psyche (for example, in nineteenth-century literature and newspapers) long before these images appeared on television news programs in the 1960s.

4 *Stranger with a Camera* is also a recently released Appalshop documentary on the same subject.

5 Given the age differential between myself and most of the interviewees, some participants' stories about early radio triggered my own memories of early television and its impact on my life.

6 Interview with Dulcie Reinhart, 17 June 1998.

7 Interview with Ida Mae Stoneburger, 17 June 98.

8 Interview with Paul Weaver, 19 June 1998.

9 Interview with Frank Frazel, 19 June 1998.

10 Interview with Edger Smith, 17 June 1998.

11 Stoneburger interview.

12 Interview with Clyde Pinney, 25 June 1998.

13 Interview with Henry Shaffer, 17 June 1998.

14 Ibid.

15 Interview with Edna Norris, 11 May 1998.

16 Ibid.

17 Ibid.

18 Interview with John Williams, 25 June 1998.

19 Interview with Golda Hart, 16 June 1998.

20 Clyde Pinney interview.

21 Ibid.

22 Telephone interview with Roy Cross, 24 February 1998.

23 Telephone interview with Archie Greer, 20 January 1998.

24 Interview with Cecil Webb, 20 May 1998.

25 Interview with Irene Flowers, 13 May 1998.

26 Telephone interview with Ivan Tribe, 3 February 1998.

27 Williams interview.

28 Smith interview.

29 Smith interview.

30 Williams interview.

31 Interview with Mary Rouch, 16 June 1998.

32 Shaffer interview.

33 Hart interview.

34 Interview with Bridget Marsh, 18 June 1998.

35 Ibid.

36 Interview with Bob Cole, 11 May 1998.

37 Interview with Wanda Rose, 22 June 1998.

38 Interview with Lenora Pinney, 18 June 1998.

39 Interview with Lloyd Porter, 22 June 1998.

40 Shaffer interview.

41 Norris interview.

42 Lloyd Porter interview.

43 Interview with Virginia Miller, 19 June 1998.

44 Lenora Pinney interview.

45 Interview with Marian Dees, 30, June 1998.

46 Interview with Rhea Boring, 19 June 1998.

47 Interview with Pearl Borne, 19 June 1998.
48 Interview with Bennie Lawson, 20 May 1998.
49 Clyde Pinney interview.

References

Banks, A., Billings, D. and Tice, K. (1996). Appalachian studies and postmodernism. In M. Rogers and G. Ritzer (eds), *Multicultural experiences, multicultural theories* (pp. 81–90). New York: McGraw-Hill.

Banks, D. (1997). The impact of oral history on the interviewer: A study of novice historians. Paper presented at the Annual Meeting of the National Council for the Social Studies, Cincinnati, OH, November 20–23.

Barfield, R. (1996). *Listening to radio, 1920–1950*. Westport, CT: Praeger.

Batteau, A. (1990). *The invention of Appalachia*. Tucson: University of Arizona Press.

Billings, D., Norman, G. and Ledford, K. (1999). *Confronting Appalachian stereotypes: Back talk from an American region*. Lexington: University Press of Kentucky.

Bruchac, J. and Morin, P. (1997). *Lasting echoes: An oral history of Native American people*. San Diego: Harcourt Brace and Co.

Cattell-Gordon, D. (1990). The Appalachian inheritance: A culturally transmitted traumatic stress syndrome? *Journal of Progressive Human Services* 1, 41–57.

Census of Housing: 1950 (1953). Taken as part of the Seventeenth Decennial Census of the United States. Volume I – General Characteristics, Part 5. Washington: United States Government Printing Office.

"Clears tops for 20 years." (1962). *Broadcasting*, October 15, p. 29.

Collins, C. (1942). Nineteenth century fiction of the southern Appalachians. *Bulletin of Bibliography* 17, 186–90.

Collins, P. H. (1991). Learning from the outsider within: The sociological signifi-cance of black feminist thought. In J. Hartman and E. Messer-Davidow (eds), *(En)Gendering knowledge: Feminists in Academe* (pp. 40–65). Knoxville: University of Tennessee Press.

Corwin, N. and Bell, D. (1994). *Years of the electric ear*. Metuchen, NJ: Scarecrow Press.

Cunningham, R. (1980). Scotch-Irish and others. *Appalachian Journal* 18(1), 84–90.

Derks, S. (ed.) (1994). *The value of a dollar: Prices and incomes in the United States 1860–1989*. Detroit: Gale Research.

Dillard, J. (1985). *Toward a social history of American English: With a chapter on Appalachian English*. New York: Mouton.

Eller, R. (1982). *Miners, millhands, and mountaineers: Industrialization of the Appalachian South, 1880–1930*. Knoxville: University of Tennessee Press.

Eller, R. (1999). Foreword. In D. Billings et al., *Confronting Appalachian stereotypes*. Lexington: University Press of Kentucky.

Fine, M. (1994). Working the hyphens: Reinventing self and other in qualitative research. In N. K. Denzin and Y. S. Lincoln (eds), *Handbook of qualitative research* (pp. 70–82). Thousand Oaks, CA: Sage Publications.

Fisher, S. (1993). *Fighting back in Appalachia: Traditions of resistance and change*. Philadelphia: Temple University Press.

Foust, J. C. (1994). A history of the clear channel broadcasting service, 1934–1980. Unpublished doctoral dissertation, Ohio University, Athens.

Frisch, M. (1990). *A shared authority: Essays on the craft and meaning of oral and public history*. Albany: State University of New York Press.

Garrett, B. (1972). An Appalachian author describes his life style. *Appalachia* 6(3), 25–28.

Gates, B. (with Hemingway, C.) (1999). *Business @ the speed of thought: Using a digital nervous system*. New York: Warner Books.

Gluck, S. and Patai, D. (1991). *Women's words: The feminist practice of oral history*. New York: Routledge.

Gordon, L. and Gordon, A. (1990). *American chronicle: Seven decades in American life 1920–1989*. New York: Crown Publisher.

Guy, R. (1997). Down home: Perception and reality among Southern white migrants in post World War II Chicago. *Oral History Review* 24(2), 35–52.

Hay, G. (1953). *A story of the Grand Ole Opry*. Nashville: Hay.

Hendrickson, R. (1993). *Whistlin' Dixie: A dictionary of southern expressions*. New York: Facts on File.

Henige, D. P. (1982). *Oral historiography*. New York: Longman.

Hilmes, M. (1997). *Radio voices: American broadcasting, 1922–1952*. Minneapolis: University of Minnesota Press.

Historical statistics of the United States: Colonial times to 1970. Part 2. (1975). Washington: Bureau of the Census.

Jackson, B. (1987). *Fieldwork*. Urbana: University of Illinois Press.

Keith, M. (2000). *Talking radio: An oral history of American radio in the television age*. Armonk, NY: M. E. Sharpe.

Keller, K. (1991). What is distinctive about the Scotch-Irish? In R. Mitchell (ed.), *Appalachian frontiers: Settlement, society, and development in the preindustrial era*. Lexington: University Press of Kentucky.

Klotter, J. (1980). The Black South and White Appalachia. *Journal of American History* 66(4), 832.

Larson, C. (1992). *Persuasion: Reception and responsibility*. Belmont, CA: Wadsworth.

Lindlof, T. R. (1995). *Qualitative communication research methods*. Thousand Oaks, CA: Sage.

Lowe, J. (1998). *Bill Gates speaks: Insight from the world's greatest entrepreneur*. New York: John Wiley and Sons.

MacDonald, J. F. (1979). *Don't touch that dial! Radio programming in American life, 1920–1960*. Chicago: Nelson-Hall.

Maggard, S. (1985). Cultural hegemony: The news media and Appalachia. *Appalachian Journal* 12(3), 67–83.

Malone, B. (1985). *Country music, U.S.A*. Austin: University of Texas Press.

McLuhan, M. (1964). *Understanding media: The extensions of man*. New York: McGraw-Hill.

Mendelsohn, H. (1964). Listening to radio. In L. A. Dexter and D. M. White (eds), *People, Society, and Mass Communications*. New York: Free Press of Glencoe.

Nelson, J. (1989). Phenomenology as feminist methodology: Explicating interviews. In K. Carter and C. Spitzack (eds), *Doing research on women's communication: Perspectives on theory and method* (pp. 221–241). Norwood, NJ: Ablex Pub. Corp.

Newcomb, H. (1979). Appalachia on television: Region as symbol of American popular culture. *Appalachian Journal* 7(1), 155–164.

Ohio Department of Development. (1997). *Ohio's Appalachian region: By the numbers.* Columbus: Office of Strategic Research.

Ohio Rural Electric Cooperatives (1985). *The light and the power: Commemorating 50 years of electricity in rural Ohio.* Columbus: Ohio Rural Electric Cooperatives, Inc.

Ong, W. (1971). *Rhetoric, romance, and technology: Studies in the interaction of expression and culture.* Ithaca, NY: Cornell University Press.

Ong, W. (1982). *Orality and literacy: The technologizing of the word.* London: Methuen.

Parker, E. and Hudson, H. (1992). *Electronic byways: State policies for rural development through telecommunications.* Boulder, CO: Westview Press.

Rabinow, P. (1977). *Reflections on fieldwork in Morocco.* Berkeley: University of California Press.

Rehder, J. (1992). The Scotch-Irish and English in Appalachia. In A. Noble (ed.), *To build in a new land: Ethnic landscapes in North America.* Baltimore: Johns Hopkins University Press.

Riesman, D. (1950). *The lonely crowd: A study of the changing American character.* New Haven: Yale University Press.

Riney-Kehrberg, P. (1998). The radio diary of Mary Dyck, 1936–1955: The listening habits of a Kansas farm woman. *Journal of Radio Studies* 5(2), 66–79.

Ritchie, D. A. (1994). Foreword, In J. Jeffrey and G. Edwall (eds), *Memory and history: Essays on recalling and interpreting experience.* New York: University Press of America.

Salisbury, M. (1936). Radio and country life. *Rural America* 14(2), 17–18.

Salstrom, P. (1994). *Appalachia's path to dependency: Rethinking a region's economic history, 1730–1940.* Lexington: University Press of Kentucky.

Schwandt, T. A. (1997). *Qualitative inquiry: A dictionary of terms.* Thousand Oaks, CA: Sage.

Shackelford, L. and Weinberg, B. (Eds). (1977). *Our Appalachia.* New York: Hill and Wang.

Shapiro, H. (1978). *Appalachia on our mind: The southern mountains and mountaineers in the American Consciousness, 1870–1920.* Chapel Hill: University of North Carolina Press.

Sixteenth Census of the United States: 1940. Housing – Volume II. General Characteristics. (1943). Washington: United States Government Printing Office.

Skutch, I. (ed.) (1998). *Five directors: The golden years of radio, based on interviews with Himan Brown, Axel Gruenberg, Fletcher Markle, Arch Oboler, Robert Lewis Shayon.* Lanham, MD: Scarecrow Press.

Smulyan, S. (1994). *Selling radio: The commercialization of American broadcasting 1920–1934.* Washington: Smithsonian Institution Press.

Snyder, B. (1982). Image and identity in Appalachia. *Appalachian Journal* 9(2), 124–133.

Stacey, J. (1991). Can there be a feminist ethnography? In S. Gluck and D. Patai (eds), *Women's words: The feminist practice of oral history.* New York: Routledge.

Stephens, L. (1972). Media exposure and modernization among the Appalachian poor. *Journalism Quarterly* 49(2), 247–257.

Sterling, C. and Kittross, J. (1990). *Stay tuned: A concise history of American broadcasting* (2nd edn). Belmont, CA: Wadsworth Publishing Co.

Thompson, P. R. (1978). *The voice of the past: Oral history.* Oxford: Oxford University Press.

Trillin, C. (1972). A stranger with a camera. In D. S. Walls and J. B. Stephenson (eds), *Appalachia in the sixties: Decade of reawakening*. Lexington: University Press of Kentucky.

Turner, W. and Cabbell, E. (1985). *Blacks in Appalachia*. Lexington: University Press of Kentucky.

Tyler, S. (1986). Post-modern ethnography: From document of the occult to occult document. In J. Clifford and G. E. Marcus (eds), *Writing culture: The poetics and politics of ethnography*. Berkeley: University of California Press.

Ulack, R. and Raitz, K. (1981). Appalachia: A comparison of the cognitive and Appalachian Regional Commission regions. *Southeastern Geographer* 21(1), 40–53.

Whisnant, D. (1980). *Modernizing the mountaineer: People, power, and planning in Appalachia*. New York: Burt Franklin.

Williamson, J. W. (1994). *Southern mountaineers in silent films: Plot synopses of movies about moonshining, feuding, and other mountain topics, 1904–1929*. Jefferson, NC: McFarland.

Williamson, J. W. (1995). *Hillbillyland: What the movies did to the mountains and what the mountains did to the movies*. Chapel Hill: University of North Carolina Press.

Wolfram, W. and Christian, D. (1976). *Appalachian speech*. Arlington, VA: Center for Applied Linguistics.

Yarrow, M. (1990). Voices from the coalfields. In J. Gaventa, B. E. Smith, and A. W. Willingham (eds), *Communities in economic crisis: Appalachia and the South*. Philadelphia: Temple University Press.

Yow, V. (1997). Do I like them too much?: Effects of the oral history interview on the interviewer and vice-versa. *Oral History Review* 24(1), 55–79.

Part IV

ARTICULATING GLOBALIZATION THROUGH ETHNOGRAPHY

12

"ASK THE WEST, WILL DINOSAURS COME BACK?"

Indian audiences/global audience studies

Vamsee Juluri

What drives global audience studies? The recognition in media ethnography of the rapid growth and proliferation of media across numerous national contexts in recent years may be usefully attributed to a number of forces and developments that may be said to constitute globalization in a broader sense. These include not only the succumbing of partially protected national markets and audiences in post-colonies to transnational economic forces, new media technologies, and a deluge of media programming, but also the rise of new challenges in the academic formation of media studies brought on by curricular recognitions, student and publishing needs, and the driving force of fragile but committed communities of scholars.

It is the last of these factors that I wish to acknowledge at the outset in this chapter, given the particular relevance of the question of intellectual community formation in the context of the goals of this volume and the wider pursuit of self-critique in ethnography and issues of constituency and representation in postcolonial cultural studies. This is clearly not to endorse any overwhelming sense of agency or individuality (or self-indulgence) on the part of those who are engaged in critical media audience studies in transnational contexts. It is, however, an attempt to stake a claim for this "us" as "us" given what seems to be the sheer disjuncture between the urgency and intensity of the questions that bring such academic formations together and the somewhat modest size and resources of such formations in comparison to media studies, global studies, academics in general, and of course the commercially convoluted social formation as a whole. In other words, as Arjun Appadurai (2000) argues, the pursuit of "knowledge of globalization" needs to be tempered by an understanding of the politics of the "globalization of knowledge" as well.

The historical moment that has led to the particular work I discuss in this chapter begins for me with the advent of satellite television and economic liberalization in India in 1991. At that time, like others of my generation, I was caught up in all the intensities of competitive entrance examinations and career choices. In journalism school in New Delhi, our shared feeling seemed to be one of urgency, of breaking free from what seemed like oppressive old Nehruvian social goals and rusty print-oriented mores. With Star television and even the Indian state television network Doordarshan's slick world news program *The World this Week* as our guiding lights, ambitions were at a high pitch. Even as some journalism majors switched to the lure of advertising and producing television serials, some of the old sensibilities remained. The advanced journalism course our institute offered for reporters from Non-Aligned Movement (NAM) nations kept a sense of an earlier, perhaps fading, international, anti-colonial perspective aloft. Despite the rising tide of anti-Muslim feelings in Hindu middle-class India, the destruction of Iraq during the Gulf War was widely condemned for what it was.

The spread of satellite television in India may thus be located at the confluence of two forms of internationalism: a development and state-centered one, and a newer, commercial one. In the popular imagination, though, there was little doubt that it was the new satellite television delivered one that would take hold. In the months that followed the Gulf War, its immediate horror seemed to be quickly replaced by a new form of connection to the rest of the world for many middle-class Indians. The possibilities of satellite television had become known during the war when five star hotels had set up dishes to receive CNN. However, when the Hong Kong based Star television began broadcasting across Asia later that year, a ground level storm of enterprise and enthusiasm followed. By the late 1990s, India had gone from none to over 15 million cable and satellite television households.[1] While the early months of satellite broadcasting featured mainly Western programming, such as *The Bold and the Beautiful* on Star and music videos on MTV (one of the few channels available at that time), dozens of international, national, and local language channels had entered orbit by the middle of the 1990s. The early global culture was exactly what one would assume it to be: American programs. The global culture that began to appear in India later in the decade, though, was far more complex: it was marked by foreign channels localizing furiously; films, music videos and advertisements celebrating a new form of Indian national identity in an explicitly global context; and the rise of curious hybrid cultural forms and products such as "Hinglish" (Hindi and English) and Kellogg's Basmati Flakes.

Given the disparity in terms of investment and resources between this media phenomenon and the efforts of scholars and commentators to critically make sense of them, it is perhaps no surprise that even the proliferation of studies about media and cultural globalization in recent years seems to pale in comparison. Within and despite this tension, though, the urgency of one particular concept in media and cultural studies would seem hard to deny – that of the audience. While the notion of the audience does not exhaust our understanding of media or globalization, there is no doubt that in the context of the rapid proliferation of satellite television in India (and, of course, the changing equations of the already preeminent Indian film culture) the stakes surrounding questions about media audiences have assumed greater proportions than ever before. To put it figuratively, what does the fact that tens of millions of people in India have now begun to watch dozens of new television channels, sometimes at the same time as millions of people in other nations as well, say about the power of media – particularly in the context of the rapid social and economic changes entailed by liberalization – and the role of media students in engaging with this? In other words, I would like to situate this chapter not only in terms of a personal narrative of seeking to understand an intensely experienced social moment through concepts returned home by virtue of travel, struggle, and situation in the US academy, but also in terms of how the theoretical lens of audience studies is itself being recast in its turn to non-Western contexts and questions.

Making audience studies global

As Lewis and Cruz (1994) argue, questions about the audience have been at the center of academic and commercial research about the media in the United States, and the particular sense of power and powerlessness attributed to the audience has also been related to broader political interests on the part of both academic and market researchers. For instance, even as early mass communication research in the US academy may have presumed audience passivity to facilitate psychologistic propaganda studies, the commercial interest always held aloft the banner of consumer sovereignty. Moreover, the conceptualization of audiences in mass communication research was also subdued within the mandate of social science at that time merely to empirically verify the American dream, as Stuart Hall (1982) says. Audience research and theories at that time were also somewhat independent of international communication research, both in its critical aspects represented in the cultural imperialism discourse (Tomlinson, 1991) as well as in the more normative "press-systems" approach of international communication that Hanno Hardt (1988) bitingly calls the pursuit of a "world according to America."

The rise of British cultural studies in the 1960s and 1970s challenged all that, making a critical engagement with social and historical power its central issue and the study of audiences an important aspect of such an engagement. While the conceptualization of media audiences since and in cultural studies has been widely discussed elsewhere (Gibson, 2000; Nightingale, 1996), what is more relevant to this essay is the specific commonalities and contradictions that emerge when audience studies with a critical cultural studies commitment meet the concerns of international communication, and more recently, post-colonialist approaches to global media and cultures. At the outset, it is worth noting that audience studies and international communication, particularly the cultural imperialism thesis, have been positioned as opposing traditions (Roach, 1997). Despite the somewhat inaccurate conflation of audience theories as unilaterally celebratory in this move, it is worth spelling out the complexities and tensions that arise in this debate. While a critical political-economy approach to international communication (Schiller, 1991; Herman and McChesney, 1997) has clearly identified the growing monopolization of media, the highly unequal terms of cultural exchange laid down within the one-way structures of information flow, and the broader social costs of privatization and deregulation, this approach has been criticized for sometimes failing to recognize the complexities of the notion of culture. In particular, it has been pointed out (Buell, 1994) that cultural imperialism theorists have tended to assume that the Third World lacks even a trace of agency, as audience members, or as subaltern subjects capable of resisting cultural imperialism. Audience studies, on the other hand, have been faulted for overstating the ability of audiences to resist media discourses. However, the limitations of this criticism may be appreciated by noting that audience theorists have themselves frequently sought to isolate the "resistive" strain as only one small component of this line of work, and restore the centrality of questions of determination by emphasizing the unequal terms on which media power and audience activity meet (Gray, 1987; Morley, 1993).

In addition to the audience resistance debate, the recent rise of postmodernism in audience studies also has particular relevance for the task of global audience studies. As Jensen (1995) argues, the rise of postmodernist criticism in the social sciences and humanities has led to a very valid questioning of the presumptuousness of modern and Western ways of knowing. Such a valid critique is found in audience theories in the work of Ien Ang (1991), who argues that the audience constructed through ratings discourses by media institutions is but a "fiction" and only a partial representation of the complex world of real media audiences. Beyond this context, though, postmodernist criticism in audience studies has culminated in what may be called a notion of "elusive audiences" which seems to deny the usefulness of any empirical audience study. One cause of this tendency may be the conflation of the terms "globalization" and "postmodernization," which seems to confront global audience theories, for instance, in the later work of Ang (1996). In other words, what does it mean for us as scholars to bow to postmodern recognition of the impossibility of total knowledge precisely at that moment when millions of people all across the non-Western world have only begun to become global television audiences?

This particular question, and the project of contestation it entails against the less enfranchising tendencies of postmodernism and its location in the Western academy, have been raised in a number of disciplinary contexts. Radhakrishnan (1994), in his important essay "Postmodernism and the rest of the world," argues that even a call to openness, which is what postmodernism can be in its expression as an epistemic critique of Western modernist thinking, translates into a disempowering abandoning of all issues of representation and constituency for postcolonialist scholarship. The internal recognition (without discounting the "external" factors that have facilitated such a recognition) of the failure of Western modernity's universalist promises, in other words, does not imply that other universalisms, or better universalisms, are impossible. In the context of audience studies, as I have argued elsewhere (Juluri, 1998), the task of engaging with audiencehood as a condition in the context of globalization and emerging globalisms is one that must challenge the assumptions and constraints imposed on scholarship of non-Western audience studies by the logics of the Western academy. To put it simply, the project of global audience studies need not apologize or become paralyzed by the impossibilities of globalist projects only because the globality of the West and modernity is under challenge. In addition, the voices of audiences and audience scholars coming from non-Western and marginal contexts need not confine themselves to narrow niche constituencies dictated by the relativism of postmodernism. Instead, such voices should be explored for their location within the possibilities of their own universalisms and globalisms.[2]

It is also important to note that global audience studies, in this context, must be seen not only in terms of their location in Western academic institutions, but more importantly in terms of their own geo-historical locations. As Natrajan and Parmeswaran (1997) argue, the rise of "everyday life" as an area of study in media studies and ethnography makes this, "rather than the academy . . . the primary site for political struggle" (p. 37). Their argument highlights the dangers of reducing critical engagement with the academy to internal struggles mostly of a "textual" nature, and calls instead for the pursuit, in media ethnography, of "alternative knowledge" in the broadest sense. The strategies for such a goal is summarized by them as follows:

> Alternative knowledge may be better produced if Third World ethnographers write about the everyday lives of Third World people with an awareness of the political need for claiming legitimacy as Third World scholars.
>
> (p. 53)

Global audience studies, in other words, may be seen in terms of these dual demands. The defining issue is, on the one hand, the engagement with the nitty-gritty of media audiencehood and everyday life in non-Western contexts, and on the other, the negotiation of the constraints that the location of the non-Western scholar in the Western academy may place on his or her engagement with such work. In the following sections, I elaborate how such a task has unfolded in my own studies of film and television audiences in India in the post-liberalization decade of the 1990s, and outline some possibilities for audience studies as a globalist project.

Television and film cultures in post-liberalization India

A feeling of inadequacy during one's engagement with the immensity of the transformation in the media environment in the 1990s even in one particular national context may be excused in the light of the rather large scope of phenomena the study of the "global" in general entails. In the Indian context, the historical continuities between liberalization and commercialization of state television in the 1980s and the explosive growth of markets and media in the 1990s may be important, but the suddenness and sheer pervasiveness of these changes after 1991 have made the task for media and audience studies far more challenging.[3] However, for the theoretical reasons outlined above, it is important not to subsume the methodological challenges of conducting audience research in a context of richness and complexity under a more rigid declaration of the impossibility of the fruitfulness of any such research. My own research on Indian audiences has engaged with what I believe are two important moments: the rise of music television channels and programs across cable and satellite television in general, and the immense popularity of one Hindi film, *Hum Aapke Hain Koun* (Who am I to you?) in the immediate context of liberalization in India.

In the summer of 1994, the Star television network launched a youth music television channel called Channel V to replace its earlier transmission of MTV Asia. Channel V, however, was so focused in its localization strategy that it rapidly became synonymous with satellite television and youth culture in India. Although the presence of VJs with American accents, generic "attitude" and an altogether new fashion aesthetic together with the inevitable hip-hop music videos translated into a constant 24-hour grinding of bodies and sexuality that seemed to simultaneously tantalize, trouble, but also not deeply offend anyone, what was more important was the clever audience-building strategy followed by Channel V. It positioned itself in generational terms as being "a youth channel in attitude, and a family channel in demographics" because of the constraints on niche audience-building in India at that time.[4] It would be appealing enough for the young, but not necessarily offensive to adults (it is noteworthy that in a decade of rising religious intolerance and attacks on artists, historians, and intellectuals in India, Channel V and MTV have hardly ever been criticized by the Hindu right-wing). In addition, Channel V also inaugurated the "Indian inside, Western outside" approach, localizing its content but presenting it in an attractively global package. In programming terms, this has meant, basically, a turn to Indian film music and the nascent Indian pop music culture as well. As Channel V's General Manager at that time put it, "We took the gamble of telling kids, look at film music, it's really cool."[5]

Film music thus became "cool" for the young urban middle-class audiences of post-liberalization India. The Indian film industry, which had once worried about satellite television, now found a new mandate. It was obvious that there could be no television in India without cinema, and while television has largely depended on film-based programs, the culture of Indian cinema has been transformed under the spell of televisual culture as well in the post-liberalization years. For the first time, the audience base of the Indian film industry has been broadened to include the urban upper class as well. In the process, a new cinematic idiom has emerged along the lines of what one critic has called the "Riverdale" culture of Archie comics.

The first substantial response of the Indian film industry to the advent of global culture, however, preceded many of these changes. In late 1994, an unusually simplistic film called *Hum Aapke Hain Koun* was released by Rajshri Productions, a family-owned group famous for its family-oriented pictures. *Hum Aapke Hain Koun* (*HAHK*) had a rather simple story, extended over three hours and many songs: a wedding, family fun, romance, a tiny bit of tension (in the last quarter of the film), and a wedding again. For one year after that, *HAHK* became the reigning cultural phenomenon in India. It broke all earlier box-office records, and brought people back from in front of their televisions into theaters. Young and old, rich and poor, all seemed to enjoy this "glorified wedding video" as it was sometimes called. It said very little about everything that had changed in India since liberalization and satellite television, but it obviously found some profound popular resonance.

If *HAHK* brought Indian audiences back from a fleeting and fragmented spell of globalization into an idyllic domesticity, a new music video in 1995 took the global/national question head on. Indian pop singer Alisha China's *Made in India* was not only the first ever Indian pop music album to achieve commercial success on a par with Indian film music albums, it also marked a spectacular beginning to the era of Indian music videos. More importantly, the music video, directed by Ken Ghosh, told a story that seemed very appropriate, especially given its broad cultural resonance, to the emerging context of globalization. The video features a fairy-tale setting in which a Princess turns down suitors from different countries and finally chooses a man "Made in India." This story, combined with the onslaught of music videos and advertisements that followed celebrating a new form of Indianness attuned to the emerging global context, may be seen as one of the first popular (and commercially created) statements about Indian national identity in the post-liberalization era.

Although the complexity of media developments in India since 1991 exceeds these two examples, these two moments in popular culture arguably represent a rich point of investigation for media scholars. My own engagement with these issues took place over two visits to India, and two independent audience study projects. The first of these, a reception study of *HAHK*, was conducted in 1995 rather spontaneously as it were because of the enthusiasm of the graduate students I was teaching as a guest lecturer at the University of Hyderabad. Our goal was basically to get a sense of why this film was so immensely popular, particularly in the context of liberalization and satellite television. The second project, which was conducted in 1997 as a part of my doctoral research, sought to understand the reception of music television as an important part of the experience of globalization from the standpoint of the television audience. In this case, my goals were somewhat broader, and included discussions with participants not only about "Made in India," but about music television programs in general, including the prolific and pervasive genre of the countdown show on Indian television.

In both these projects, I encountered a number of questions of access, authority, and representation pertinent to audience studies in a global context – including the all-important theoretical question of how a particular field experience in a national context could be situated as a theory of globalization rather than one strictly of national and/or cross-cultural issues. In the following sections, I address these questions with the aim of both identifying problems and constraints in conducting such a line of work, and outlining, through a brief discussion of my conclusions in these projects, how some of the basic questions about media determination and audience agency may be addressed and reconfigured in the terms of a postcolonialist mandate in the present global media context.

Reception study and audience access

Media ethnography in general, and reception study as a subset of that with a textual predilection, presuppose a well-informed faith in magnification given the fact that the limited engagement with the real (and methodologically constructed) audience must be imagined into larger and deeper arrays of social conditions and consequences. Although the relative valences accorded to media "texts" and "contexts" (Jensen, 1991; Morley and Silverstone, 1991) may qualify the form such a project could take, the particular focus on texts in reception study invokes one central issue. Contrary to the perception that intertextuality and the relative autonomy of audience readings mitigate the determinative capacity of texts or media in general, it is more important to see these as characteristics that produce a certain kind of guarantee for the specifics of audience readings of particular texts to be legitimately interpreted as concrete manifestations of broader social and historical phenomena (Jensen, 1995). In other words, rather than seeking to essentialize the exteriority of audiences to the readings of specific media texts in terms of their possession of certain kinds of cultural capital or certain "traits"[6] with the aim of arguing their agency as audiences, it is more helpful to appreciate these readings, in the light of the widespread dissemination of these texts (which may be expressed in terms of commercial success or "popularity" in a certain sense), as being guaranteed a certain value in the social formation at a given moment. For instance, the reading of "Made in India" as an authentic expression of Indian identity by some of the participants in this study may be seen, in relation to the specific discourses in this music video, as evidence of a certain kind of meaning being ascribed to "Indian identity" both as a cause and an effect of globalization taking form in certain historically constrained ways.

My real encounter with participants in the course of these studies, however, posed many immediate challenges. Although access was somewhat uncomplicated in the case of the *HAHK* study, finding the "music television audience" was far more challenging.[7] My first sense of how people responded when asked to participate in a study on *HAHK* (mostly by my students at the University of

Hyderabad) was that there was a pattern to the ways in which people volunteered (or refused) to become "audiences." This pattern, it may be argued, also corresponds in some ways to the role that certain kinds of television discourses seem to play in positioning real viewers as "audiences": in other words, it may be argued that one kind of normalization that a certain body of televisual discourses have enabled in India is that of constituting one's self as an audience and speaking as an audience. For instance, the widespread presence of vox pop or "public" programs on Indian television has made it quite conventional to watch other "ordinary" people speaking before the camera about film and popular culture (usually outside cinema halls and shopping plazas). It seemed that some of the people who participated in the *HAHK* interviews were happy to join in, but their expectation of the situation was that the interview would be along the lines of the vox pop shows (the presence of cameras led some to ask when and on what channel the interview would air). The thought of a one-hour interview, however, perplexed some of them, although I find in most of the videos of the interviews a shift in the conversation from the first five minutes when most people responded with summaries of their overall assessment of the film loaded with current popular discourses ("number one," "family picture," etc.) to the rest of the interview when people began to talk in depth about issues like marriage, tradition, and Indian identity. A related issue on this note also was the mixed perception among participants about "opinion" and "knowledge." Although most interview questions leaned towards the former, there were also some questions aimed at eliciting participants' reconstruction of the film. For example, the question "where do you think the story was taking place?" opened up discussion not only of the possible geographical location of the story but also about the class, ethnic, linguistic, and religious identities of the characters. The reconstruction of "knowledge" about the story and its characters revealed not only a sense of the cultural competence of participants in decoding sometimes subtle cultural cues in the text, but also their varied levels of interest and investment in these features.

While the popular resonance of *HAHK*, and perhaps its more widespread appeal in demographic terms, allowed for keen participation by a broad range of people, the opinion/knowledge tension was far more prevalent in the relative reluctance of people to participate in the music television study – the most widespread statement made by people who declined to participate was that they didn't "know" enough about music television (even if they watched some of these programs, by their own admission). In addition to the logistical difficulties of conducting interviews around video screenings (as opposed to the *HAHK* study where the film had already been seen numerous times by most participants and did not require a screening at the time of the study), it was obvious that even people who watched a fair amount of music-based television programs would not always identify as music television viewers. This pattern corresponds to the broader constitution of music television audiences. On the one hand, "music television" in India refers not only to music television channels (like the international MTV India and the more national Music Asia) but also to the predominant presence of music-based programs in widely watched channels as well (like Doordarshan's weekly countdown *Superhit Muqabla*). On the other hand, exclusive viewers of any channel, including MTV, are very few. A similar pattern was evident from the participants in this study as well, with most participants being regular viewers of national and local language channels and film music programs (among other things) rather than international channels like Channel V and MTV. However, it is useful to note that being local channel viewers did not preclude access to discourses about globalization for many such participants, even as predominantly MTV viewing did not imply any less involvement with Indian music or nationalist discourses for the more upper-class youth participants.

In other words, despite the class correspondences to audiencehood (which I will elaborate upon shortly), and despite the qualitatively different content and experiences of a film like *HAHK* and those of global, national, and local music television programs, it is instructive that participants in both these studies were for the most part involved in discourses about identity, nationality, family, selfhood, and globality in general. This involvement may also be located, at the outset, in terms of the location of this study in the city of Hyderabad. My aim in these studies, in some ways, was to cast these participants as audiences of film and television in certain ways that would on the one hand be generalizable to other Indian, urban, middle-class people of a certain age and disposition, but also retain the specificities of the experience of the local and the global in this city. As a multilingual and multi-religious city with a rich media environment, Hyderabad offered a good case for exploring the various levels of cultural globalization (and a continuing sense of personal investment for me as a "home" site). On the one hand, Hyderabad is increasingly globalized not only in terms of media access, but also in terms of its emerging significance as one of India's premier information-technology bases. On the other hand, at least at the time of these studies, Hyderabad was not perhaps as visible a market for foreign consumer goods as Mumbai or Bangalore. In addition, I was also told by music retailers and local television producers that they sometimes felt Hyderabad does not get the attention it deserves from marketing executives controlling budgets from another city.

If the place afforded a certain kind of context to the constitution of "audiences" in these two studies, what is equally important is the demographic complexities of the "people." The *HAHK* study was somewhat more successful in finding participants from a wider range in terms of class and age than the music television study, although participants in both studies were fairly representative of the linguistic diversity of Hyderabad as a metropolis. While the largest number of participants in both studies were native Telugu speakers (the regional language of the state of Andhra Pradesh, of which Hyderabad is the capital), there were speakers of at least five other languages in these studies as well. The interviews, however, took place in combinations of English, Hindi, and Telugu, which are the three languages commonly spoken in Hyderabad (in addition to Urdu).

The question of language, and what people actually said in the course of these interviews, raises an important issue that is pertinent not only to factors of access, but also to broader questions of analysis and authority that I will discuss in the subsequent sections. Despite the emphasis in reception studies on speaking, it is important to note the pattern of silences in interviews as well (Lewis, 1991), for these silences may constitute the boundaries of not only what people would like to say, but perhaps what they are capable of saying as well. In other words, what is not said points out the "limits of intelligibility" of certain discourses. In the case of both selecting what is said and speculating about what is unsaid, the role of the researcher becomes all the more important – including the question of how he or she negotiates, in the interview and later in the academic institutional context, questions of authority and representation. In other words, with what kind of sense of constituency and authority do the fragments of interviews become positioned within broader discourses about media, audiences, and globalization, for instance, even as these discourses are sought to be constructed as oppositional to both mainstream discourses and certain dominant Western academic discourses about globalization? What enables a researcher to constitute the knowledge coming out of field experience in a manner that may be justified not solely in terms of his or her authority (or qualifications of the same using arguments for relativism), but as nothing more or less than a yielding to the totality such knowledge evokes?

Authority and audiencehood in global context

At a descriptive level, the reception of *HAHK* and music television as seen in these two projects may be summarized in the following manner. *HAHK* was almost universally seen by participants as a lively and entertaining evocation of Indian family life and values, especially in opposition to the present context of globalization, fragmentation of families, and pervasive "sex and violence" in both Indian cinema and global television.[8] Despite their cultural and demographic diversity, most middle-class and upper-class participants (of both genders, notably) sought to identify with various themes and marriage customs depicted in the film as pan-Indian, despite the rather culturally specific Hindu, upper-caste, North Indian context of the characters in the film. However, some of the working-class participants – who also expressed their investment in the relational and familial elements of the film – made no such attempt to identify across regional cultural lines as it were. From the researcher's interested perspective, though, what was important about this study was the clear ability and interest among participants of various backgrounds in talking about the film and their own lives in relation to it to some extent. For instance, as the following quotes show, both upper-class and working-class participants identify with the family in *HAHK*, in this case in a somewhat nostalgic way:

[*HAHK*] represents the Golden Age of the family, not necessarily a
dream, but a Golden Age.
(Upper-class participant, retired public official)

Our families used to be like that. I was reminded of those days.
(Working-class participant, domestic worker;
translated from Telugu)

In the case of the music television study, the difference in terms of class and
access to cultural competences about music television was not only evident in
a larger group of working-class participants but essentially resulted in some
interviews where the terms of the questions, and some of the discourses that were
sought to be examined through video screenings, failed to produce the kind of
discussions that had arisen with other participants. While it was clear that
working-class participants had less access to satellite television programs than
middle-class participants, by their own admission they watched music television
genres common to both. For instance, one of the most widely watched programs
among all participants was the DD film countdown *Superhit Muqabla*. However,
it was only the young middle-class participants who seemed interested and
arguably invested in all the conventions that music television entails such as the
discourse of rankings. Older middle-class participants and working-class
participants said that they did not know (or care) what all the fuss between the
songs was about. At the same time, these participants were not altogether
disinterested in music on television. Their main interest, however, seemed to
be the film songs themselves, which they engaged with in terms of the
expression of sentiments and relational values.

To illustrate, the "meaning" of music television for middle-class participants
may be summarized in the three following points[9]: (1) the normalization of
various music television discourses such as the presence of VJs and their chatter
("we cannot go directly into a song, it looks odd"); (2) the acceptance of the
premise of rankings in countdown shows even if the veracity of these charts are
sometimes questioned ("I do need to know what the rankings are") that leads to
a broader perception of private, satellite television as being more representative
of the "public" than state-run Doordarshan ("we used to feel the distance
of Doordarshan [a pun on 'door,' meaning 'distant'] . . . now we feel we can
approach ETV people or Gemini people"); (3) the reading of Alisha China's
"Made in India" as an authentic representation of Indian identity and its
recognition in a global context that is connected to a broader perception of
globalization as the "export" of Indian culture rather than an "import" of Western
culture ("we get the feeling that they are showing our programs to Europe, US,
everywhere it's being shown . . . we are part of the international audience").

As an audience researcher, these findings presented a number of challenges
and temptations. On the one hand, there is certainly a need to validate participants' own sense of who they are in relation to media, especially given the

tendency in traditional cultural imperialism discourses to assume a dumb passivity for Third World audiences in general, as described earlier. On the other hand, though, it is equally important not to slide into an easy celebration of audience resistance to globalization or media, given that the structural and cultural realities of globalization are only partially accessible from the position of audiencehood. The move towards characterizing media determination in particular, or cultural imperialism in general, is of course further complicated given the empirical geo-cultural realities that need to be taken into account in formulating audience reading positions a propos the encoding-decoding model (Hall, 1993). For instance, a class-based encoding-decoding analysis of global media imperialism would have to establish "encoding" as a Western process, and the preferred meaning of the text in question as pro-Western and anti-local or national, and the various decoding positions seen then in relation to these factors. However, in the case of both these studies, such an easy fit is hard to accomplish. "Encoding" in the case of *HAHK* is domestic. Even in the case of music television, despite the Western ownership of parent companies like News Corporation and Viacom (which own Channel V and MTV India respectively), programming has been largely localized. Furthermore, the "preferred meanings" of *HAHK* and music television are far from pro-Western and anti-national. In *HAHK*, the "West" hardly ever figures in the film, except in the domesticated form of consumer goods like Pepsi and so on. In music television discourses, the West figures, when it does, merely as a point of reference for exerting Indian greatness, for instance, in music videos like "Made in India."

Domestication and determination

Given the domestication, in some senses, of the "foreign" in these media examples, would evidence of media determination be a good thing or a bad thing for critics of imperialism? In addition, how would the advancing of a thesis about media determination by the researcher be constrained or enabled by the lay perceptions of determination sometimes expressed by participants themselves? In both these studies, my conclusions sought to affirm what I believed were the important aspects of reception to participants without slipping into a necessarily celebratory position about their resistance or agency. Despite all the disheartening conclusions about popular culture that one may be led to given the rather shallow, crass, and socially unrepresentative aspects of current media discourses, what was genuinely surprising to me in the course of both the studies was the extent to which the noblest sentiments and values about family, identity, and nationality were being expressed. I saw little personal, ethical, or methodological justification in devaluing these sentiments as an outpouring of false consciousness, but at the same time, what was truly puzzling was what seemed like the growing disjuncture between these values and the poverty of imagination in the media discourses around which such values were being expressed. In other words, it seemed that a model of media determination would have to be advanced that saw audience agency not as a form of resistance to media, but as something that was being gradually appropriated by media, and particularly within a changing trend within media discourses that increasingly set the terms for definition within these discourses rather than those of everyday life and the popular.

In particular, it is useful to note the interested and invested role of the researcher in drawing conclusions from the rather limited set of what participants are able and willing to say in relation to media. During the course of both these studies, there were moments of interrogation by participants, although I was somewhat surprised (and relieved in some ways), by the time of the music television study, by the perceived legitimacy and normalcy being accorded to the whole process of being interviewed as television viewers (the hesitations described earlier notwithstanding). In the *HAHK* study, though, there were a number of observations that have remained instructive in my efforts as a researcher, and particularly in terms of my strategies for analysis. While at least two other participants asked me during the interviews what I thought of family life and values in the US (in relation to the *HAHK* model), one participant was especially articulate in his expression of a certain kind of anti-intellectual populism (despite his own reputation as a renowned civil servant and public intellectual) combined with a deep-rooted suspicion of the determinative capacities of media.

Despite clearly enjoying the process of being interviewed about the film, this participant made numerous observations about the inability of "our intellectuals" to understand the popularity. In fact, he uses this fact as a touchstone of the film's popularity, defining *HAHK* as a film that is so popular that "our intellectuals would never understand." I took this to mean that while he was according me some legitimacy in interviewing him about a mere movie, I would have to be cautious about attributing more importance to it than necessary. In response to my question about whether he thought the film had had any "impact," he wittily retorted, "ask the West, will dinosaurs come back?" in a reference to the film *Jurassic Park* and how ludicrous it would be to ask its viewers such a question.

If the clearly articulated expression of the popular over the intellectual in this case provided one guideline for global audience studies, an even stronger understanding of what exactly the popular entails in the Indian context became clear to me in the course of my discussions with working-class participants in the music television study. Despite what can be described in all candor as a feeling of almost reeling from the way the interviews with these participants went off (or did not go off), what seemed evident was the clear presence of a cinematic, melodramatic form of reception among these participants in the context of their viewing of music on television. Was it only the unfamiliarity with the interview setting and the particularly rigid structure of a reception study that precluded their talking about music television in the same manner as other participants? Perhaps not, for what was also clear during the same conversation was the obvious importance that these participants accorded to film songs in their own lives (see Dickey, 1996). Judging from the way in which film songs were talked about, it seemed that what was "natural" or commonsensical for them was the relational and emotional aspects of these songs. For instance, one working-class participant, a mother and a domestic worker, referred to one song during the interviews merely as the one that "a mother sings to her child" (rather than referring to it by the title, the film, or the performer's name). These instances, admittedly, do not exhaust the complexities of working-class reception of television under globalization, but raise further questions considering the fact that these participants are indeed beginning to encounter discourses (such as the global nationalism of "Made in India") which are a presence in their lives but are perhaps not yet being consciously made sense of in the same manner as the more familiar film songs.

At the same time, it is also clear that the aspects of reception that are meaning-fully articulated by working-class participants – the relational and emotional values – are also present in the reception of music television by young middle-class participants. Without necessarily overstating the question of whether, for instance, middle-class tears and working-class tears are the same thing, it is worth noting that the "popular" in one sense extends across classes in this particular context (see Martín-Barbero, 1993). However, the key difference, and an instrument of hegemony, is the fact that young middle-class participants inhabit a world of discourses that, perhaps by definition, devalues the core values of the popular. In other words, for MTV audiences, the popular enters their world not within the ambit of the sentiments of music videos alone (which are evidently important to them) but through the larger meta-discourse of rankings, ratings, and so on. Theirs is a world in which they are privileged to have a greater self-consciousness as audiences, and by extension, global and national audiences and subjects in some contexts. Their sentiments about character and relationships cannot occupy the same centrality in terms of knowledge about their own selves and television as would be the case for working-class participants.[10]

Conclusion: learning from global audience studies

My conclusions from these studies may therefore be seen as favoring a critique of media hegemony rather than an affirmation of audience resistance. In the case of both *HAHK* and music television, it is apparent, from audience study, that there is a cohesive expression around issues such as family ties and personal relationships of what matters to audiences in reception. It is possible to charac-terize these values as constituting the popular – and remain true to the terms on which participants would perhaps like to see themselves represented. However, the appropriation of this popular sensibility by the media remains too important a social and political force to warrant any posing of this as resistive. In the context of the emerging social relations under globalization in general, or under the domestic name of liberalization in India, the specific stories and images employed to convey these feelings by media – whether domestic or international – support a model of media appropriation and global hegemony through the national rather than anything else. It may be praiseworthy that *HAHK* is seen as representing Indian family values, but its easy and shameless equation of consumption with tradition in a real context of rapid and growing consumerism (which also impinges increasingly on weddings and marital politics as well) shows that it is also ultimately the latter that is normalized. Similarly, it may be equally commendable that young MTV viewers see music television and music videos like "Made in India" as representing Indian character in a global context in authentic, egalitarian, and universal terms. However, in a media context of growing self-exoticization and a broader political context of rampant and aggressive cultural nationalism, these commendable, universal, humanistic values ultimately become secondary to the sloganistic display of one's national (and yet modern and global) credentials. To illustrate, once a culture has been established in which saying "I love India" is perceived as "normal", not to advertise this supposed love (on T-shirts, for instance) becomes tantamount to treason, and all the positive sentiments that seemed to have informed this sense of being Indian in the first place become marginalized.

For these conclusions to inform a project of global audience studies, it is important not to think of them in absolute terms of national-cultural specificity. Instead, what is required is a more globalist, and by implication universalist understanding of how media and audiences are implicated under the changing social relations of globalization everywhere. It is not difficult to see the parallels of these developments in perhaps a far more rigorous scale in the regimes of representation presented for instance in the US media, although what is indeed far more challenging is conveying such a critique within the US media studies classroom. In the past, I have often been the only "international" person in the undergraduate classes that I teach, and short of sequestering my research into a parallel "research" life shared with colleagues rather than students, I have had to find ways of making an international research perspective meaningful in this very domestic context as well. For instance, in a large introductory course I used to teach, I often discussed four examples to illustrate the encoding–decoding model: two from the United States, and one each from the UK and India. Despite the responsiveness of those students who seemed to gain by this, I cannot also deny the fact that there would always be some students who were troubled by the last example.

In fact, it would not have mattered if the next round of examples in the semester mentioned China or Latin America; it would all be the "Indies" to those whose resistance to the global is guaranteed by the full strength of their implication as Americans in it (Nandy, Davies and Sardar, 1993). Perhaps the next question for global audience researchers to examine is how it is not only the institutional imperatives negotiated with canons and colleagues that constitute the politics of representation in media ethnography, but those imperatives which raise generational and pedagogical issues as well. In other words, what happens when global audience studies are taught, for instance, in US classrooms? Is there even a chance for a critical globalization in the face of the immense nonchalance with which the global figures in the lives of privileged First World "consumers" of education? After the events of September 11, though, neither this nonchalance nor the past experiences of teachers can remain the same as a new interest in global perspectives born out of tragedy enters the American classroom. Perhaps now, more than ever, the globality of an alternative, counter-hegemonic "common-sense" can be demonstrated, through audience studies and other approaches, and is worth struggling for.

Notes

1 "Couch potatoes on the rise" (1998).
2 This distinction may be usefully appreciated by contrasting the claims made for an exceptional Western universalism by Samuel Huntington (1993) against the alternative, multiple universalisms professed by Gandhi as discussed in Nandy (1987).
3 See McDowell (1997) for a discussion of the political economy of telecommunications in India. Kurien's (1994) overview of the Indian economy in a global context is very useful in this context as well.
4 Hussain (1997).
5 Ibid.
6 Appadurai's (2000) distinction between "trait" and "process" geographies is also useful here.
7 The *HAHK* study, conducted in 1995, consisted of nine group interviews with thirty-three participants in all. Two groups each consisted of upper-class and working-class participants, while the rest consisted of middle-class participants of various ages and professions. Each interview lasted nearly one and half hours and was videotaped. Questions ranged from preliminary ones about the viewing context (who they watched it with) and the story, to broader ones about tradition, marriage, and family. The music television study, conducted in 1997, consisted of nine groups with forty-two participants in all. Nine participants could be classified as "working-class" while the rest were middle-class or upper-class in terms of their or their parents' incomes/occupations. Each of these interviews was structured around four video segments, and each interview lasted about one hour. The interviews began and ended with open-ended questions on music, television, and cinema. Directed questions were also asked around each clip, particularly around VJs, the countdown format, and nationalistic music videos. The interviews were transcribed, coded, and analyzed for broad patterns in terms of responses to key questions.
8 A more detailed discussion of these findings may be located in Juluri (1999).
9 This study is explored in depth in Juluri (forthcoming).
10 Purnima Mankekar's (1999) discussion of the notion of "bhaav" ("feeling"/"meaning") in her ethnographic study of female state-television viewers in India is useful here.

References

Ang, I. (1991). *Desperately seeking the audience*. New York: Routledge.

Ang, I. (1996). *Living room wars: Rethinking media audiences for a postmodern world*. New York: Routledge.

Appadurai, A. (2000). Grassroots globalization and the research imagination. *Public Culture* 12(1), 1–19.

Buell, F. (1994). *National culture and the new global system*. Baltimore, MD: Johns Hopkin University Press.

"Couch potatoes on the rise." (1998). *Screen* [online] available http://www.expressindia.com/screen.

Dickey, S. (1996). Consuming utopia: Film watching in Tamil Nadu. In C. Breckenridge (ed.), *Consuming modernity: Public culture in a South Asian world* (pp. 131–135). Minneapolis: University of Minnesota Press.

Gibson, T. (2000). Beyond cultural populism: Notes toward the critical ethnography of media audiences. *Journal of Communication Inquiry* 24, 253–276.

Gray, A. (1987). Reading the audience. *Screen* 28, 24–35.

Hall, S. (1982). The rediscovery of ideology: Return of the repressed in media studies. In M. Gurevitch, T. Bennett, J. Curran and S. Woollacott (eds), *Culture, society, and the media* (pp. 56–90). London: Methuen.

Hall, S. (1993). Encoding, decoding. In S. During (ed.), *The cultural studies reader* (pp. 90–103). New York: Routledge.

Hardt, H. (1988). Comparative media research: The world according to America. *Critical Studies in Mass Communication* 5, 129–146.

Herman, E. and McChesney, R. (1997). *The global media: The new missionaries of global capitalism*. Washington: Cassell.

Huntington, S. (1993). The clash of civilizations? *Foreign Affairs* 3, 22–49.

Hussain, S. (1997). V'Jaying on. *Economic Times*, August 6–12, p. 8.

Jensen, K. (1991). Reception analysis: Mass communication as the social production of meaning. In K. Jensen and N. Jankowski (eds), *A handbook of qualitative methodologies for mass communication research* (pp. 135–148). New York: Routledge.

Jensen, K. (1995). *The social semiotics of mass communication*. Thousand Oaks, CA: Sage.

Juluri, V. (1998). Globalizing audience studies: The audience and its landscape and living Room wars. *Critical Studies in Mass Communication* 15, 85–90.

Juluri, V. (1999). Global weds local: The reception of *Hum Aapke Hain Koun*. *European Journal of Cultural Studies* 2, 231–248.

Juluri, V. (forthcoming). *Becoming a global audience: Longing and belonging in Indian music television*. New York: Peter Lang.

Kurien, C. (1994). *Global capitalism and the Indian economy*. Hyderabad, India: Orient Longman.

Lewis, J. (1991). *The ideological octopus: An exploration of television and its audience*. New York: Routledge.

Lewis, J. and Cruz, J. (1994). Introduction. In J. Cruz and J. Lewis (eds), *Viewing, reading, listening: Audiences and cultural reception* (pp. 1–18). Boulder, CO: Westview Press.

Mankekar, P. (1999). *Screening culture, viewing politics: An ethnography of television, womanhood, and nation in postcolonial India*. Durham, NC: Duke University Press.

Martín-Barbero, J. (1993). *Communication, culture, and hegemony: From the media to mediations* (trans. E. Fox and R. White). London: Sage.

McDowell, S. (1997). *Globalization, liberalization and policy change: A political economy of India's information sector*. New York: St Martin's Press.

Morley, D. (1993). Active audience theory: Pendulums and pitfalls. *Journal of Communication* 43, 13–19.

Morley, D. and Silverstone, R. (1991). Communication and context: Ethnographic perspectives on the media audience. In K. Jensen and N. Jankowski (eds), *A handbook of qualitative methodologies for mass communication research* (pp. 149–162). New York: Routledge.

Nandy, A. (1987). From outside the imperium: Gandhi's cultural critique of the West. In A. Nandy, *Traditions, tyrannies and utopias: Essays in the politics of awareness* (pp. 127–162). Delhi: Oxford University Press.

Nandy, A., Davies, M. and Sardar, Z. (1993). *Barbaric others: A manifesto on Western racism*. London: Pluto.

Natrajan, B. and Parmeswaran, R. (1997). Contesting the politics of ethnography: Towards an alternative knowledge production. *Journal of Communication Inquiry* 21, 27–59.

Nightingale, V. (1996). *Studying audiences: The shock of the real*. New York: Routledge.

Radhakrishnan, R. (1994). Postmodernism and the rest of the world. *Organization* 1, 305–340.

Roach, C. (1997). Cultural imperialism and resistance in media theory and literary theory. *Media, Culture, and Society* 19, 47–66.

Schiller, H. (1991). Not yet the post-imperialist era. *Critical Studies in Mass Communication* 8, 13–28.

Tomlinson, J. (1991). *Cultural imperialism: A critical introduction*. Baltimore, MD: Johns Hopkins University Press.

13

WHERE THE GLOBAL
MEETS THE LOCAL

South African youth and their experience
of global media

Larry Strelitz

This chapter is part of a larger study conducted between 1999 and 2002, which explored how a sample of South African youth on the Grahamstown campus of Rhodes University[1] responded to texts produced internationally but distributed locally (Strelitz, 2002a).[2] Recognizing the profound rootedness of media consumption in everyday life, the research examined the way these youth, differentially embedded in the South African economic and ideological formation, used these texts as part of their ongoing attempts to make sense of their lives. In particular, the study investigated the complex individual and social reasons that lie behind media consumption choices, and the diverse socially patterned reasons why local audiences are either attracted to or reject global media. Using a combination of quantitative and qualitative research methods, the research sought to highlight the interplay between agency and structure, between individual choice and the structuring of experience by wider social and historical factors.

The range of responses to global media expressed by local youth, this chapter argues, highlights the deficiencies of the media imperialism thesis with its definitive claims for cultural homogenization, seen as the primary, or most politically significant, effect of the globalization of media. As such, it should be read as a dialogue with those schools of thought that take a more unequivocal point of view on the impact of globalized media culture. The notion that cultural imperialism is a penetrating, monolithic force that wipes out diversity and homogenizes all cultures must be abandoned. What must be substituted, Mattelart asserts, is "analysis that illuminates the particular milieux that favour [or hinder] this penetration" (Mattelart quoted in Morley, 1994, p. 72). In line with this call, I will next outline some of the key characteristics of the current South African socio-political milieu in order that we may locate the responses of different groups of students to global media.

The South African social and political context

Despite the transition to democracy that followed the elections in 1994, the social effects of apartheid are very much still in evidence. South Africa, with Brazil, tops international tables of Gini coefficients and other measures of inter-household income inequality (Seeking, 2000, p. 53; Leibrandt et al., 2000, p. 31). Statistical indicators show the racial dimension of poverty and inequality in South Africa: 95 percent of the very poor are African and 5 percent are coloured. Poverty has a rural dimension, with 75 percent of the poor living in rural areas. Poverty also has an age dimension, with 45 percent of the poor being children below the age of 15 (Jennings et al., 1997, p. 8). Some 49 percent of African youth live in households that at some point during 1994/95 were unable to feed their children. This applies to 35 percent of coloured youth, 11 percent of Indian and 6 percent of white youth (Jennings et al., 1997, p. 23). Similar ratios are borne out by life expectancy rates amongst the different population groups. For the years 1996 to 2001, the average life expectancy for Africans is 64.5 years, for Indian 70.2 years, for coloureds 64.4 years, and for whites 73.6 years (SAIRR, 1998).

However, the inequalities in South Africa correspond largely, but not exclusively, to racial divisions, and among Africans huge disparities have opened. Marais (2001, p. 106) points out that the mean income of the lowest-earning 40 percent of African households declined by almost 40 percent between 1975 and 1991, while that of the richest 20 percent of African households rose by 40 percent. African professionals, skilled workers and entrepreneurs benefited from the collapse of apartheid, making them the most upwardly mobile 'race' group. As a result, South Africa is currently witnessing the emergence of a differentiated class structure among the African population, which includes a strong middle-class and professional stratum, and a tiny economic elite. In other words, the country's income maldistribution is increasingly shifting from being 'race'-based to class-based (Marais, 2001, p. 106).

The post-apartheid state is a modernizing state, strongly influenced by conventional neoliberal wisdom, and thus closely allied to the institutions of global capitalism (the World Bank and the International Monetary Fund) (Bond, 2000, p. 216; Mangcu, 2001, p. 9). Marais (2001) argues that the basis for the transition from apartheid to democracy in South Africa rested on "the dire need to modernise and reinvigorate the processes of capital accumulation, on the apartheid state's simultaneous inability to manage the expansive forms of restructuring that were required, and on the democratic opposition's ability to challenge and veto the haphazard 'modernization' attempts of the state and capital" (p. 3). The neoliberal features of the African National Congress (ANC) government's macro-economic strategy, which include bowing to the demands of capital and the building of a black "patriotic bourgeoisie," are not surprising. Marais (2001) notes: "By 1996 . . . the ANC government's economic policy had acquired an overt class character. It was geared to service the respective prerogatives of domestic and international capital and the aspirations of the emerging black *bourgeoisie* – at the expense of the impoverished majority's hopes for a less iniquitous social and economic order" (pp. 123–124).

Modernity and tradition

Besides the racial and class divides in South Africa, another fundamental cleavage is that between "modernity" and "tradition," with some authors arguing that it ranks as the most fundamental, unresolved contradiction in much of post-colonial Africa (Marais, 2001, p. 303). In South Africa, for example, millions of rural inhabitants continue to live under the rule of local chiefs operating within the ambit of customary law (Marais, 2001, p. 3).

Marais (2001) sees a schism between the democratic movement, which framed its struggle against apartheid in Enlightenment terms (hinging on civil and political liberties), and the tribal chieftaincies, which see themselves as protecting traditional African customary law. According to Marais, "At the root of the chiefs' power is an admixture of ethnicized tradition, inherited authority and clientelism that fits uneasily with the principles of individual rights and democratic processes that underpin the new political system. The severely diminished status of women under traditional authorities is emblematic of this contradiction" (p. 303).

This tension is reflected in the ongoing disputes between the ANC-led government and the Congress of Traditional Leaders of South Africa (Contralesa) over the place of traditional culture, norms, and customs, and the role of traditional (non-elected) leaders in post-apartheid South Africa in their traditional rural strongholds (see, for example, Gevisser 1996, p. 14). The President of Contralesa, Patekile Holimisa, writes: "the present struggle [with the ANC-led government] is not about the retention of power for its own sake, it is for the retention of power so that it can be used to safeguard the African value systems which are the bedrock of society" (Gevisser, 1996, p. 14). Thus, for example, at the 1992 Convention for a Democratic South Africa (Codesa) negotiations at the Johannesburg World Trade Centre, Contralesa's delegations insisted on exemptions for customary law and from the gender equality clause in the Bill of Rights (Gevisser, 1996, p. 14).

As we can see from the above discussion, South African is a deeply divided society. Samir Amin has recently characterized the divisions thus:

> There is the overwhelmingly white section of the population whose popular culture and standard of living seem to belong to the "first" (advanced capitalist) world . . . Much of the urban black population belongs to the modern, industrialising "third" world, while rural Africans do not differ much from their counterparts in "fourth" world Africa.
>
> ("Foreword" to Marais, 2001, p. vii)

South African youth

These structural inequalities are reflected in the lives of young people, the focus of my research, in contemporary society.[3] Writing on the social and educational inequalities that exist amongst South African youth, Van Zyl Slabbert et al. (1994, pp. 56–60) have noted that the country's social dynamics have placed white South African youth in areas where housing is readily available. Almost all whites have electricity, water and water-borne sewerage in their homes, refuse removal, tarred roads and street lighting. White income levels are relatively high and poverty is minimal. Whites have access to adequate schooling with high enrolments. Retention levels at school level are good and white youth dominate tertiary education institutions. The white population growth is low. White people as a group are largely urbanized and relatively unaffected by unemployment (Van Zyl Slabbert et al., 1994, p. 56).

While Van Zyl Slabbert et al. (1994, pp. 57–58) distinguish between poor rural and urban middle-class Africans, they feel that on the whole, African youth live in a different world compared to white youth. It is a world of unemployment, poverty, high population growth rate, inadequate schooling and largely unavailable basic social amenities. Coloured and Indian youth in South Africa appear to be positioned between African and white youth. Population growth and urban/rural ratios among the coloured and Indian communities are similar to those of the white community (Van Zyl Slabbert et al., 1994, pp. 57–58). While I accept this, given the rapid changes in class composition that have occurred since the 1994 elections, as discussed above, it is no longer possible, as my interviews indicate, to identify clear "racial" identities. As a result, in many instances black middle-class youth have more in common with white middle-class youth, in some areas of their identities, than with black working-class and peasant youth.

Locating myself

My interest in the relationship between local youth and global media is rooted in my own youthful immersion in American popular culture. In the early 1970s, as a 12 or 13 year old, I forged a strong identification with the American counter-culture. Haight-Ashbury signified communal living, sharing, personal freedom, and experimentation, and contrasted strongly with the isolation, conservatism and restriction I experienced growing up in a white middle-class nuclear family, in a small South African town, during the apartheid years. Significantly, my knowledge of this distant culture was mass mediated. It came to me through magazine images, and increasingly through the music of American West Coast bands – the Grateful Dead, the Quicksilver Messenger Service, and the Jefferson Airplane – whose songs celebrated these counter-cultural values, and against which my own lived "reality" was judged, and was found wanting. My local 'reality' had been shaped by the discursive practices of South African "ideological state apparatuses," including my family, the militaristic all-white boys' school I attended, the state-controlled radio I listened to, and the local newspaper I read. All of these institutions generated the discourses appropriate to the maintenance of the deeply conservative political consensus of white South Africa prevalent at the time. Mass mediated global culture provided me with a degree of "symbolic distance" (Thompson, 1995, p. 175) from the conditions of my day-to-day life, and alerted me at an early age to the complex, and often unanticipated, role that global media can play in local lives, the subject of this study.[4] Reflecting on these processes in later life spurred my curiosity about the impact of global media on South African youth in general.

The uneven penetration of global media into local cultures

In his study of media consumption practices in Latin America, Straubhaar (1991, p. 51) coined the term "cultural proximity" to describe the desire of the "lower classes" to consume nationally or locally produced media that are more reinforcing of traditional identities. He further observed that this desire for "cultural proximity" may not be as strong for elites, who seem much more internationalized, as dependency theory would predict (also see Abu-Lughod, 1995).

Straubhaar (1991, p. 151) fails to clarify what constitutes "cultural proximity" for local audiences. While it could refer to the use of language, the narrative construction, or the thematic concerns of the text, the concept is, at a descriptive level, reflected in South African radio and television consumption patterns (Strelitz, 2002b). For example, local music content averages for the public broadcaster radio services in South Africa indicate that the urban-based, English-language stations play a much lower percentage of local music than do the rural, indigenous language stations (IBA, 1999). Two radio stations, 5 FM and Ukhozi FM, provide cases in point. Some 74 percent of 5 FM's listeners are white, while 99 percent of Ukhozi FM's listeners are black. According to the Independent Broadcasting Association's Monitoring and Complaints Unit, during 1998, 15 percent of the music played on 5 FM was local. By contrast, 71 percent of the music played on Ukhozi FM was of local content (IBA, 1999).

The South African Advertising Research Foundation (SAARF) has divided the South African population into eight different Living Standard Measures (LSMs). LSM group 8 is the most highly educated, with most of this group in white-collar jobs. They are better educated than the other LSM groups, have low unemployment and have the highest representation of professionals and self-employed across all groups. At the other end of the continuum we have LSM 1. Two-thirds of this group have no more than "some" primary school education. Literacy levels are below average, with one in every three people being illiterate. Almost 41 percent of this group are unemployed. The LSM categories were created by the advertising industry as a means of getting away from racial classification, but because of the historical legacy of apartheid, one finds that whites (and some blacks) tend to occupy the higher LSM categories, while the lower categories are mostly occupied by blacks.

If we examine the LSMs of the audiences of the two radio stations, we find that over 50 percent of 5 FM's listeners fall into LSM 8, while 34 fall percent into LSM 7, and less than 3 percent fall into LSMs 1, 2, and 3. By contrast, 47 percent of Ukhozi FM's listeners fall into LSMs 1, 2, and 3, with just 6 percent falling into groups 7 and 8. Similarly, 75 percent of 5 FM's listeners earn R4,000 or more a month, while this is true for only 7 percent of Ukhozi FM's listeners. In fact, nearly one-third of Ukhozi FM's listeners earn less than R500 a month. If we look at occupation, 45 percent of 5 FM's listeners can be classified as white-collar, compared with 21 percent for Ukhozi FM. Some 56 percent of 5 FM's listeners list English as their home language, with just 7 percent listing an indigenous African language. Ukhozi has no English home-language speakers, and 94 percent listing Nguni (SAARF, 1997). Of 5 FM's listeners 74 percent have a Standard 10 or further qualification, while the corresponding figure for Ukhozi FM is 9 percent, and 35 percent of Ukhozi FM's listeners have either no schooling or some primary schooling. While there are no figures for the urban/rural split in listenership, we can get some indication if we take into account that 89 percent of 5 FM listeners live in communities of 40,000 or more, while the corresponding figure for Ukhozi FM is 37 percent. In fact, over half (56 percent) of Ukhozi FM's listeners live in communities of less than 500 in size. What these figures indicate is that *for rural, black, relatively poor and ill-educated South Africans, local music has a strong resonance, while for white, urban, well-educated and relatively affluent South Africans, the opposite is true.*

These statistics indicate that the penetration of foreign cultural forms into local cultures is a far more complex process than the media-cultural imperialism thesis allows for. In some sectors of society the global media resonate with local audiences (although this still begs the question of the meanings audiences make of these media), while in other sectors of society global media are less popular than local forms.

The "Homeland" students

Interviews with African students from rural working-class or peasant backgrounds confirmed these national trends. The research revealed that many of them relied on an "empiricist" understanding of "realism" (Ang, 1982, p. 36; Ellis, 1982, pp. 6–7) – in that at the level of denotative meaning they sought a literal resemblance between the fictional world of the text and the "real" world as they experienced it – in rejecting global media. This antipathy towards foreign television and film productions, a result of their lack of empirical realism, is evidenced in following extract from a focus group interview.[5]

Andile: My personal response to *Isidingo* [a South African soap opera] is one that is informed by my background. The very fact that our fathers and brothers were working on the mines . . . they used to come back and talk and relate these stories to us. So now what is happening in *Isidingo* is the confirmation of that. So every time I see that setting I reflect back on those things they used to tell us . . . working at Iscor [steel refinery], things like that. Tribal conflicts, faction fights . . . within that setting. So it's a confirmation of those things that I used to hear.

Duminsani: When I watch South African dramas, these are realistic to me. They speak about what is happening, what I know. I understand why this guy is doing this. Sometimes not understanding someone's culture is a problem. For example, these alien things . . . seeing these aliens on television. When I see these funny people that don't look like us I don't know what the person producing had in mind.

Thikhithiwi: I prefer local programmes. For me I think it's just getting in touch with my roots, to feel at home, something that you know.

This rejection of foreign media is reflected in a more general opposition to the "modern" Western middle-class values they feel pervade the institution of Rhodes University. The majority of these students come from the rural areas, having attended rural and township schools under the control of the Department of Education and Training (DET).[6] Coming to Rhodes University has provided them with their first close contact with urban, middle-class African, white, Indian, and coloured students, and with white lecturers and administrators. Furthermore, the majority of them were initiated traditionally into manhood ("been to the bush"[7]) and thus find themselves at odds with what they regard as the infantile behaviour, such as excessive drinking and prank-playing, of other students in residential accommodation.

Andile: Because of my background I experience it [Rhodes University] as a white institution. Because I've already gone to the bush, I don't involve myself with some of the activities there. If I did, I would be compromising my manhood. I can give an example of the students water-bombing each other during exams. I don't like that. So instead of changing me, it has reinforced my sense of being a black South African.

These students believe that the majority of African middle-class students are no different from their white counterparts. They refer to them as "coconuts" – black on the outside but white on the inside. One of the most obvious signs of the perceived assimilation of middle-class African students into white culture is their preference for the English language.

Andile: You meet someone here [at Rhodes] and you greet him in your own language, and he responds to you in English. These are things which make us say that these people are fake.

To be fake is thus to deny your traditional black culture. This is their perception of many South African black middle-class students, and also many black Zimbabwean students. As Michael noted, everything African middle-class and (African) Zimbabwean students do "is something that is done by whites . . . I've never seen them being proud of their (African) culture."[8]

The lack of African content in the courses is also a source of much frustration for these students.

Michael: The identity of the courses is still largely white. I did politics for example and we did Utopia and Saint-Simone. It was really hard. It's core European history and it's really hard for us. First of all we don't have the interest, and secondly, we don't have the background. We meet those things for the first time here in university, and it's certainly very difficult for us to master such subjects. Blacks who master these subjects come from Model C or private schools. They have the background and maybe they gained their interest while they were at school. So the content is very white.

Their cultural isolation from the black and white middle-class students on campus is reflected in the fact that a number of the students from African working-class or peasant backgrounds prefer to watch television in their own viewing space, attached to one of the university residences, which they have named the "Homeland" (Strelitz, 2002b).[9] Every evening, with the regularity of the ritual it has become, fifteen to twenty of these students gather to watch their favourite programmes. The viewing sessions start at 18.30, when they gather to watch *Isidingo*, a local African drama set on a goldmine. At 19.00 they disperse for supper in the residences, returning at 19.30 for the African language news. At 20.00 they view a local black drama *Generations*, set in an advertising agency. At weekends they often meet to watch South African soccer. *Missing from their daily television diet are any foreign productions.*

The "Homeland," where only Xhosa is spoken, allows these students to interact with each other confidently, free from the ridicule of the better-educated, more urbane, middle-class "modern" students. In this space their traditional cultural identities are confirmed. It provides a haven from the threat of the "modern." Thus, faced with an institutional culture in which they feel white and black middle-class norms dominate, they have felt the need to consolidate and signify their difference from such a culture and to reconfirm their traditional African identities. The nightly ritual of local television consumption in the "homeland" is one of the means of achieving this. As Thompson notes (1995,

p. 204), migrant populations – these students have "migrated" to Rhodes University – often display a strong quest for roots.[10]

Andile: Whenever I meet with my friends we discuss things from where we've come. So people tend to say that we are traditionalists. That perception gives us the spirit to stay together to share this one vision. They don't see traditionalism as positive, they talk about it as a negative thing . . . you're backwards. We don't see a reason why we have to change because we are at Rhodes. If we can tolerate them, why can't they tolerate us? When we are sitting with these people watching television, they'll make a silly comment about someone who can't speak English. We understand that in our places we were never exposed to many things and we didn't get a good education . . . so how can you laugh at someone who can't speak good English? So we said, let's not sit with them because we'll always be angry. Rather sit with these people because we share the same perception of things.

Of significance is the fact that many of these students, before entering the "alien" space of Rhodes University, were consumers of global media. Interviews revealed that in many cases, within a rural context of reception, such media conveyed the "promise of modernity." Now, in contrast, within the context of Rhodes University, these students indicated a preference for local dramas which, they pointed out, raised issues of cultural concern for further discussion, which in turn helped solidify an identity rooted in traditional African culture.

Andile: When watching *Isidingo*, it's quick for us to select a particular aspect of what is happening and talk about it. But when it comes to these white soapies, I find it very difficult. In *Isidingo* there's this guy on the mine who doesn't want to go underground because he had this dream which said he shouldn't. Those are things that happen in our culture and they reflect the way we think.

The existence of the "homeland" students provides not only an example of the rejection of global media by a sector of South African youth, but also lends some support to Ang's claim that we need to understand the media's meanings for its audiences within the context of the "multidimensional intersubjective networks in which the object is inserted and made to mean in concrete contextual settings" (1996, p. 70). This approach, Ang argues, entails a form of "methodological situationalism," which recognizes the importance of context – from the macro-context of South African to the micro-context of Rhodes University – in trying to make sense of how people interact with the media in everyday life.

Global subjects

As Morley (1994, p. 145) reminds us, "foreign" is a problematic category in that "what is 'foreign' to whom?" needs to be posed as an experiential question. In other words, sometimes "foreign" productions have a "local" relevance which renders them empirically real. As I noted earlier, what unites the different understandings of "empiricist realism" is that at some level a similarity is found between the realities "in" and "outside" a text. Thus, one of my interviewees, Zukile, an African student who grew up in the rural Eastern Cape, noted that when he was growing up he was drawn to the American soap opera *Dallas* precisely because its representation of white affluence on an American rural homestead reflected his lived reality on a white-owned South African farm better than anything he had seen in local productions.

Other interviews provided me with further examples of how foreign media can, in certain instances, accurately reflect local lived conditions. One of the interviewees, Mandela, grew up in the black urban township of Soweto during the 1980s at the height of the armed resistance to the apartheid regime. His parents were members of the then-banned ANC. In his interview extract, he discusses the resonance that American rap music had for him during these turbulent times.

Mandela: There used to be a lady living in our street who was an MK [Umkonto weSizwe, the armed wing of the African National Congress] cadre. In fact, there used to be quite a lot [of MK operatives] because they used to come to our home and ask if they could sleep over for two days. I used to see these guys and my mom used to say, "That guy can fire an AK" [the Russian-made rifle most often used by members of Umkonto weSizwe and synonymous with liberation struggles around the world] and I used to say like "damn!" The thing is that Ice-Cube [a rap artist] and those guys from America wrote about AK 47's. And here was a guy in my house with a trenchcoat and he's sleeping under the table, or some woman and she can fire an AK 47.

For many white students, their identification with Western/European culture (in South Africa the term "European" is often applied to whites as a way of denoting their historical roots in Europe rather than Africa) means that it is foreign rather than local productions that are experienced as being more empirically "real." In a course assignment I set for second-year students in which I asked them to reflect on their preference for local or global media, Loren, who comes from a white, middle-class family, wrote that her favourite television programme was the American series *Ally McBeal*:

Monday nights in the Olive Schreiner [female residence] common room are always full when *Ally McBeal* is on, and one has to arrive

243

early to get a seat. It is a programme I watch religiously because it gives me an hour in which to laugh at familiar characters, and essentially, at myself. Also, much of the appeal lies in the opportunity to interact socially with peers of the same outlook, backgrounds and spheres of reference. The next day the plot, the court cases, Nelle's latest outfit and the romantic mishaps of the characters are analysed and debated around the lunch table, each girl contributing her own opinion on the episode.

The characters in *Ally McBeal* enjoy a First World lifestyle in a capitalist, consumer-driven society in which male and female colleagues enjoy the same legal status. Although not applicable to all South Africans by virtue of their vastly differing cultural and socio-economic status, I, as a white, educated and middle-class female, identify with the context of the show, and can draw many similarities with the programme and my present environment. I dress similarly, aspire to be similarly successful in my career, use the same products and seek out the same forms of social entertainment. The group of heterosexual colleagues and friends working closely together for a common objective and sharing in each other's daily life experiences relates particularly to my university experience wherein females and males mix together comfortably in classes, social situations and residence.

As in *Ally McBeal*, there is a degree of sexual tension between me and friends as many of us are engaging in our first relationships with members of the opposite sex. There is jealousy and rivalry amongst competing individuals, both in my sphere of reality and in the show. Similarly, there are the same miscommunications that arise between the sexes which are, more often than not, humorously addressed in the show. It can be said that this factor is a strong motivation for the popular viewership amongst my colleagues. It is a frame of reference by which we construct meaning for ourselves in our daily environment.

As Loren indicates, there is a degree of "fit" between the issues dealt with in *Ally McBeal* – for example, sexual rivalries and tensions, career aspirations, dress, and so on – and the concerns of modern white, middle-class, heterosexual subjects in South Africa.

However, not only white students identified easily with the values carried by global media. The next focus group interview with African middle-class students, who had attended private schools, demonstrates a similar identification. These students, unlike the "Homeland" students, showed little ambivalence to Western culture. They perceived themselves as modern subjects for whom traditional cultural values had little purchase. Unlike the "Homeland" students who had grown up in a rural environment and who had attended primarily DET schools, these African students were urban and middle-class and had made an unproblematic transition to Rhodes University.

Siyanda: I think, most of us we were in private schools and we were tended to be sheltered from everything, and what's happening now, is very much something I grew up with. So, I'm pretty much used to it, it's not a huge change, it's not like I have to get used to white people, sitting with white people, eating with them and that, you know. I've always been able to interact, as from young, like these guys.

This particular group of students felt that they had more in common with white students than with African students who had attended DET schools. They stated that their identities were now more strongly shaped by class than by "race" and as such they felt distant from many aspects of traditional African culture. As one middle-class African student noted, "We have KFC [Kentucky Fried Chicken] and I'm not into 'pap and vleis' [a traditional African diet of maize meal and meat]." Another noted, "You just don't relate to [the tradition of] traditional customs such as the paying of *lobola* and stuff."[11] As a student who comes from the rural areas but went to a private school in Johannesburg succinctly put it, "I love going back home . . . but at the end of the day, herding cattle ain't my thing."

Unsurprisingly, these students related strongly to the modern cultural values carried by primarily foreign media. For example, in the following focus group extract these students discuss the attraction of an American series set in New York, *Sex in the City*.

Mooketsi: Like I say, it's the way of life around us. *Sex in the City* depicts what we are now. I would say it's more like cosmopolitan . . . you know that type of thing going on.

Siyanda: It's different from the normal [local] programming.

Twcu: Ja, it's very truthful.

Tafadzqa: I mean they show a whole lifestyle, not just the sex thing, and certain topics a lot of programmes choose not to cover because of censorships or whatever. They tend to cover everything, regardless.

Siyanda: I think we relate more with that because personally, I can see myself doing that once I've started working. That's the way it's going to be.

Mooketsi: Just the whole lifestyle . . .

Siyanda: Everybody tries to find the perfect relationship, going out with a range of people.

Twcu: With my folks you meet a person, you stick with that person, you have kids, you die. With us it's more like . . .

Mooketsi: Like I say, it's the way of life around us. *Sex in the City* depicts what we are now.

Siyanda: Like with movies, it helps you notice that there are other people like you out there.

Mbuso: It's the same with [American] Hip-Hop music. It just makes you see that, ah, there are people across the world that are like that.

Here we witness the role of mass mediated popular culture as a "carrier of modernity" (Berger et al., 1973, p. 43). Both Tomlinson (1991, p. 140) and Drotner (1992, p. 44) believe that the attraction of Western media has to be seen in the context of the attraction and subsequent spread of capitalist modernity. However, we must not forget that the journey from tradition to modernity does have an imperialist dimension. As Berger et al. (1973, p. 119) point out, an essential difference between Third World societies today (which includes most of South African society) and the process of modernization in Western societies is that in Third World societies the impulse to modernization comes from outside the local culture. Thus they write: "To a large extent, modernisation in the Third World has been tantamount to Westernisation, both in objective social fact and in the subjective perceptions of the people affected. In these countries the economic and political carriers [are] alien importations" (p. 119).

The hybrid intersection of global and local

While the students I have discussed so far saw themselves as either "modern" or "traditional" subjects – reflected in their media consumption preferences – the final group of students I will discuss occupied a hybrid space, articulating their identities at a juncture between these two competing discourses. This hybridity of identity is reflected in a deep ambivalence towards global popular culture.

Kraidy (1999) describes a similar phenomenon in his research into the ways in which cultural identities are reconstructed by Christian Maronite youth in Lebanon at the intersection of global and local discourses: "[a]n overriding concern among my interlocutors was their inability and unwillingness to exclusively belong to one or the other of what they saw as two irreconcilable worldviews" (p. 464). Identifying the Arab world with tradition and the West with modernity, "young Maronites articulated both discourses with the cultural matrices permeating their consumption of media and popular culture" (p. 464). The consumption of American television in the local cultural space of Christian Maronite youth both reflected and helped these young people to construct hybrid identities – caught between "the West" and "the Arabs," modernity and tradition.

The process of simultaneous identification with two very different cultural traditions was strongly evidenced in my interviews with Indian students on campus. For many of these youth, the student culture of Rhodes University contrasted strongly with their more traditional and conservative family values and as a result they felt they had to move continuously back and forth between two very different sets of cultural expectation. This was clearly expressed by Amichad, a second-year pharmacy student from KwaZulu-Natal:

Amichad: I do go overboard when my parents are not here, but when I go back home, I'm back to being the mummy's boy that I am. Rhodes has got to me. When I came here I had everything that I learnt at home and I embraced all my culture. In the first day that I came here I was faced with every single situation that went against everything that I believed in. But over the years I've learned to actually make a blend between what I believe in and what is here. . . . I've made a negotiation. Everyone on campus . . . they try to enhance the Western style, but we try and keep some of the Eastern stuff. Basically, like I've said, we've drawn that line. We stick to our culture. So we do our ritual prayers in our room and we go to the temple on Sundays, fasting at the appropriate time . . . and come to fun days, we take a break from our work and we go for it.

"Going for it" includes drinking at the Victoria Hotel on a Friday night with other Indian students, something many of them would never do at home.

Kirti: It's something you just do here, it's not part of you. Because I know, like with me, when I go home it's fine to stay at home and not go out on a Friday night. It's not a major issue, but like when I am here I do go out and it's just a pastime.

Depending on the dictates of their family cultures and religious traditions, students found it easier or more difficult to move between what they perceived to be two irreconcilable sets of cultural expectations. An example of the latter was Amina, who comes from a strict Muslim family background, and has accepted the choice of marriage partner made for her by her parents.

Amina: I don't think the two can overlap at all. I mean, when I'm on the plane back home [to Zimbabwe] I have to totally psych myself mentally, because I mean if you do some things at home . . . Like here I will wear track suit pants and a shirt because I am cold, and that's fine, but if I did that at home both my parents would freak out totally.

Other students found the transitions easier to deal with.

Kirti: You learn to adapt, to balance your life. Because like at home I don't usually go out but like here we do . . . my parents know about it and stuff, but at home I just wouldn't. It wouldn't be okay.

It is because their family cultures are so strong that they find themselves caught between the modern and the traditional.

Amina: That's the whole idea of keeping us close to them, so that their values are passed on to us. It's the way we were brought up. Like I was brought up in a very strict family so I've got very strong feelings of right and wrong . . . like with dressing I shouldn't wear trousers or tight clothing.

Despite many of these students staying "within the traditions" of their family cultures, many admitted to enjoying American teenage drama series, such as *Friends*. They were interested in the clothing the characters wore and the fact that it centred on the lives of young people – "we can identify more because it's a young crowd . . . the things they speak about are things that we as teenagers can identify with."

Multiple identities

Indian students' simultaneous identification with traditional parental values and the Western youth values of youth-oriented American television dramas echoes Kraidy's (1999) finding that Maronite youth displayed an inability and unwillingness to belong exclusively to one or other irreconcilable worldviews. Their experience reminds us that we are composed of multiple identities, that our subjectivities are "nomadic" in that, as Fiske (1989, p. 24) has observerd, we realign "[our] social allegiances into different formations . . . according to the necessities of the moment." (Also see Hall, 1991, p. 57.)

This tension was reflected in the television consumption practices of the Indian interviewees, as many admitted to being drawn to programs which promoted values at odds with those of their parental culture. A recurrent response was to deny the cultural significance of these programmes by dismissing them as "mere entertainment" (and therefore, culturally insignificant). However, as the following interview extract illustrates, this neat separation of "entertainment" from "cultural significance" was often difficult for the students to sustain.

Khavita: It's entertainment, I mean it's television . . . it's not something you're going to live by . . . it doesn't affect our lifestyle.
Amina: It's another world . . . it's entertainment . . . half an hour of it and it's over.
Neeta: · But I like the independence . . . like *Friends* you know . . . being away from home, working . . . you don't have to get married straight after you finish your education . . . things like that.
Khavitha: Freedom.
Seema: I think a lot of times it's freedom to be yourself and that's still OK.
Khavitha: Yeah, whereas in our culture it's a bad thing to be different you know. Like you shouldn't stand out in a crowd . . . like we come from such a conservative community that I think being different is a bit difficult for our parents to accept.

Lukrisha: In American programmes there's lots of focus on women's lib that I find very appealing.

Kirti: It's nice to look. Just see like them wearing the short skirts or not wearing anything . . . like just covering the bare necessities. It's just nice to see the different ideas people have . . . Like I've been to a fashion show and it's nice to see the different ideas people have . . . yeah, how ridiculous people can be.

The simultaneous attraction and rejection of Western values expressed in Kirti's final statement – attracted to different expressions of fashion while at the same time rejecting such displays as "ridiculous" – reflects the difficulty students face in attempting to reconcile the opposing pulls of tradition and modernity.[12]

Ambivalence towards American cultural values

As Kraidy (1999) found with his Maronite youth, the Indian students admitted to being "entertained" by American media, and attracted to certain of the values espoused, while simultaneously remaining critical of the lack of strong values they felt was evidenced in American culture. These included what they viewed as excessive materialism, and disrespect towards parents and the institution of marriage: "they don't have a strong set of values"; "like once you're 18 your parents are nothing"; "to them marriage is a joke"; "they just think that money grows on trees"; "It's just that in America they have less values, less ethics, less principles as compared to us." This general antipathy towards American culture (when compared to their own traditional cultural values) by Indian students often translated into criticism of the values conveyed by American mass mediated popular culture (which, however, they continued to consume). As Shakti, one of my respondents pointed out, while he didn't personally follow what he referred to as "America's propaganda stories," he would still watch American big budget movies – "If there's this guy and he spends R200 million on making that spaceship fly in a film, I'll think 'ah, let's just watch it.'" What emerged in numerous interviews is that part of the attraction of American film and television to students is their perceived "superior" production values (hence the reference to the R200 million spent on production) and the lack of availability of media which could speak more directly to local cultural concerns.[13]

Global media and the process of "symbolic distancing"

This ambivalence towards Western culture as carried by the mass media also emerged in a number of interviews I conducted with urban African middle-class students. For example, Machemo and Lebo claimed that one of their favourite programmes was *Ally McBeal*, but they remained highly critical of some of the values they felt it promoted.

249

Machemo:	The thing I find when I watch *Ally McBeal* and stuff like that is the way there's no such thing as morality any more . . . you know what I mean. Like if you've got morals like there's something wrong with you. In African culture there are strong morals and rather, if you don't agree with them, there is something wrong with you.
Lebo:	I mean people do all sorts of things.

In explaining this seeming tension, these students, like the Indian students, distinguished between the "entertainment" offered by these programmes and the cultural values they espoused. They felt that their African culture provided a screen against unwanted Western cultural influence.

Lebo:	I think it's because we have somewhere to go back to. You watch the Western culture but you still have to compare it to African culture. If we were born in a Western culture we would have nothing else to compare it to.
Machemo:	And also it's kind of like out there because it's on television and you're thinking that when you see something on television it's like a story . . . things like that don't really happen, you know what I mean . . . and everyday life is not like that so it's quite easy to relate to it.
Lebo:	But I mean it's OK because it's on television . . . but I mean in real life it's not OK. It's just how I feel.
Machemo:	I feel they are acting and that's fine. But if it were in real life, I wouldn't find it that amusing.

At the same time there were Western cultural values which these students found attractive. This is a reminder that Western culture does not constitute an indivisible package that is either adopted or rejected by local cultures. Rather aspects of this culture are adopted while others are found irrelevant and are resisted (Tomlinson, 1991, p. 74). This differentiation is a feature of both hybrid cultures and hybrid identities. For example, Marshall and Phila were two of many African students who, in interviews, pointed to the lack of communication between parents and children. These students said that Western values, as carried by Western media, provided an alternative, more attractive model of the child/parent relationship. Marshall and Phila claimed that exposure to foreign television was partly responsible for African children having the confidence to engage verbally with their parents in times of disagreement:

Marshall:	I find that black people, their relationship with their parents is very based on respect and obedience and knowing who your elders are. Whereas I find with the white friends that I have, it's like they are more like friends with their parents. They talk to their parents a lot easier than we do. In a way I think sometimes there's

Phila: a sort of slight fear of my parents . . . you know there's a gap. With white people it's more integrated.

Phila: The white culture is more direct. There are certain things I couldn't dream of going to talk to my father about, no way.

Interviewer: Would you prefer that kind of relationship with your own parents?

Marshall: I actually would and I think with age I have acquired it.

This final interview, which highlights the role played by Western media in providing local consumers with access to cultural difference, has been explored by a number of writers. For example, in his critique of the media imperialism thesis, Thompson (1995) points out that part of the attraction of global media for local audiences is that their consumption often provides meanings which enable "the accentuation of symbolic distancing from the spatial-temporal contexts of everyday life" (p. 175). The appropriation of these materials, he further notes, enables individuals "to take some distance from the conditions of their day-to-day lives – not literally but symbolically, imaginatively, vicariously" (p. 175). Through this process, Thompson writes, "individuals are able to gain some conception, however partial, of ways of life and life conditions which differ significantly from their own" (p. 175). Thus, as Thompson indicates, and as many of my interviews revealed (see Strelitz, 2001), global media images can provide a resource for individuals to think critically about their own lives and life conditions.[14]

Conclusion

As I have argued in this chapter, the identities of South African youth are often deeply shaped by their structural location within the socio-political landscape and it is this location which mediates their relationship and response to global media. Such a position implies a critique of the claim that the media are the primary shapers of identity (see, for example, Kellner, 1995, p. 1; Bly, 1996, p. vii; Willis, 1990, p. 13), an assumption that the media imperialism thesis draws on when arguing that we are currently witnessing the spread of a global culture (see, for example, Schiller, 1998).

Such an approach draws on Tomlinson's (1991) caution against the "media-centeredness" of media theory, which refers to "the tendency of people working in this area to assume the cultural and ideological processes they study are at the centre of social reality" (p. 58). The result is, as Tomlinson points out, that media theorists see the media as determining, rather than mediating, cultural experience. As he reminds us, media messages are themselves mediated by other modes of cultural experience. Thus, in contrast to those theorists who collapses the distinction between "media" and "culture" (see Kellner, 1995), Tomlinson urges us to view their relationship as a "subtle interplay of mediations" (p. 61). On the one hand, we have the media as the dominant representational aspect of modern culture, while on the other we have the "lived experience" of culture (see also Warde, 1996, p. 305).

This study has described a range of responses from local youth to global media. In all cases we have seen the need to locate these responses within the context of the cultural complexity of the South African "reality."

The research findings discussed in this chapter also remind us – in contrast to the claims made by the media imperialism thesis – that the penetration of foreign cultural forms into local cultures is an uneven process. In some sectors of society the global media resonate with local audiences (although this still begs the question of the meanings audiences make of these media), while in other sectors of society global media are less popular than local forms.

Notes

1 Rhodes University has two Eastern Cape campuses, one in Grahamstown and a smaller one in East London. The Grahamstown campus, where this research took place, is largely residential. It takes its name from the British imperialist Cecil John Rhodes, after the Rhodes Trustees donated £50,000 pounds towards the establishment of Rhodes University College in 1904 (Currey, 1970). In 1951 it was converted to a university.

2 I decided to use students on the Grahamstown campus of Rhodes University as the subjects of this study. In 1998 (the start of this study) the majority of students on campus were white (55 percent), although there were also significant numbers of students from other "race" groups. Fortunately, as a result of the availability of study loans to financially needy students from the Tertiary Education Fund of South Africa (TEFSA), the campus was home to students who came from a range of class backgrounds. I thus had access, in one space, to a cross-section of South African youth. I was aware that these students did not represent the full range of South African youth and that this would raise the issue of the generalizability of my research findings to the rest of the population. However, in line with the position taken by qualitative researchers on this issue, I believed that the critical issue would be the cogency of my theoretical reasoning, couched in terms of generalizability of cases to theoretical propositions, rather than to populations or universes. In other words, I was using my findings amongst a particular group of youth, to reflect on the debates within media studies concerning the relationship between texts and audiences in the age of globalization. I was not setting out to provide a comprehensive picture of media consumption patterns amongst South African youth.

3 In South Africa, the problems of the definition of youth are especially acute. According to Van Zyl Slabbert et al. (1994), the unstable socio-political conditions in South Africa have made any attempt at gaining conceptual clarity when talking about youth "a frustrating and enigmatic exercise" (p. 12). They write:

> Whilst it is trite to say that life itself is a process and not an event, this observation gets specific meaning when one tries to pin down youth as a social category. Infancy, adulthood, old age, marriage, birth, death are concepts that enable us to identify clear patterns of social interaction and institutional organisation. In relatively stable societies, organised education provides the best arena in which to explore the transient characteristics of youth; but in unstable, unequal and deeply polarised and divided societies, problems in educational organisation very often add to the difficulties in coming to grips with youth as a social category.
>
> (p. 12)

Because of these considerations, these authors advocate adopting the broadest possible definition of youth, namely South Africans of all population groups between 15 and 30 years of age. The authors admit that this conceptual definition of youth is much more one of operational convenience than of any philosophical substance (p. 13). However, as they note, this broad definition "enables us to cluster and clarify research results which relate to young people who fall in this age category and who, from different points of view, and for varying purposes, are referred to as 'youth'" (p. 13). The broad definition of youth is echoed in the National Youth Commission Act (no. 19 of 1996), which takes into account the fact that people between the ages of 25 and 30 bore the brunt of the recent political struggles in South Africa in the 1970s and 1980s. The National Youth Commission therefore defines the range of youth from 14 to 35 (NYC, 1997, p. 7). In my own research I interviewed students aged between 18 and 24.

4 On the role played by global media in providing cultural meanings which transcend the confines of local meanings also see Davis and Davis (1995, p. 578); Appadurai (1990, p. 7); Deswaan (1989, p. 720).

5 According to Ang (1982, p. 36), "empiricist realism" is cognitively based and works primarily at the level of denotative meaning, in which a literal resemblance is sought between the fictional world of the text and the "real" world as experienced by the audience member. Judgments are made accordingly, and as Ang explains, ". . . a text which can be seen as an 'unrealistic' rendering of social reality (however that is defined) is 'bad'" (1982, p. 36).

6 After 1954, "Bantu" education was administered by the Department of Education and Training (DET). The Eiselen Commission (1949–51) had recommended schooling for African children which, in accordance with apartheid ideology, would strengthen their roots in African culture and society, and prepare them to take up their "places" in the South African economy. From about 1960 onwards, secondary schooling for Africans was concentrated in the "Bantustans." Bantu education sought to retribalize Africans with a heavy emphasis on teaching in the African mother-tongues. The Homelands policy was supported by the establishment of Black Tertiary Institutions. Prior to 1994, all Coloured and Indian education was administered by the provincial governments. The Coloured Affairs Department (CAD) was established by the Nationalist Party government after 1948 to serve the special social and welfare interests of the Coloured people. In 1964 the CAD assumed control of Coloured education. According to the De Vos Malan Commission their education had to make them conscious of their separate existence and readiness to work. Indian education followed a similar route. After 1948, the government promoted Christian National Education for white schools. White education was comparatively generously funded for the provision of buildings, amenities, teachers and so on to accommodate the Compulsory Schooling Act. In 1992 the National Government issued an Education Renewal Strategy which established Model C schools. After 1994, all schools became non-racial but fee structures ensured that Model C schools were mainly white.

7 This takes place any time after the age of 17 and consists of various rites of passage (amongst others, circumcision) towards becoming an adult.

8 Because the Zimbabwean students are not eligible for bursaries at South African universities, the majority tend to come from middle-class families who can afford the fees.

9 Apartheid was premised on the classification of people into different race groups and their segregation into different residential areas, educational systems and public amenities. Under this policy, the reserves, known as Bantustans or the Homelands, saw land which had been set aside in 1913 and 1936 (by the 1913

Land Act and the 1936 Native Land and Trust Act) consolidated into ten ethnic geo-physical units. These "national states" were the only places where Africans were allowed to exercise political and economic "rights" (Stadler, 1987, p. 34). Disenfranchised from the South African state, it was here that Africans were supposed to express their political, economic and cultural aspirations – no longer as South Africans but as citizens of these independent states. However, since the first national democratic elections in 1994, the African National Congress-led government has promoted the idea of a unified South African national identity (Steenveld and Strelitz, 1998). The voluntary return to a symbolic "Homeland" by these students, and their rejection of foreign television, therefore signifies the students' continuing sense of "disenfranchisement" on the campus of Rhodes University.

10 As Thompson (1995, p. 204) points out, the appeal of the quest for roots is that it offers a way of recovering and, indeed, inventing traditions which reconnect individuals to (real or imaginary) places of origin.

11 *Lobola* refers to bridewealth and is a key institution around which traditional African societies in Southern Africa are organized at the level of the family. As Ross explains: "A woman moved away from the family in which she was born to that of her new husband, where she would labour in the fields, cook, keep house and, hopefully, give birth to children. In return for this loss of labour and reproductive potential, her husband, aided by his family, would transfer cattle to his wife's father and brothers, in part at once, in part only when she had demonstrated her fertility by having a child. From then on she was a member of her husband's family, even if he died. In such circumstances, one of his brothers would take her over, but any children she had would nevertheless be considered the legal heirs of the dead man" (1999, pp. 12–13).

12 See Fiske (1987, p. 175) for a discussion of the process of simultaneous attraction and rejection of Western values by non-Western audiences.

13 For a discussion of the importance of production values in explaining why Israeli, Danish and French youth are attracted to American media, see Lemish et al. (1998).

14 Other writers who have explored this theme include Davis and Davis (1995); Appadurai (1990); Deswaan (1989); Hannerz (1996); and Schou (1992).

References

Abu-Lughod, L. (1995). The objects of soap opera: Egyptian television and the cultural politics of modernity. In D. Miller (ed.), *Worlds apart: Modernity through the prism of the local*. London: Routledge.

Ang, I. (1982). *Watching Dallas: Soap opera and the melodramatic imagination*. London: Routledge.

Ang, I. (1996). *Living room wars: Rethinking media audiences for a postmodern World*. London: Routledge.

Appadurai, A. (1990). Disjuncture and difference in the global cultural economy. *Public Culture* 2(2), 1–24.

Berger, P., Berger, B. and Kellner, H. (1973). *The homeless mind*. New York: Penguin Books.

Bly, R. (1996). *The sibling society*. New York: Vintage Books.

Bond, P. (2000). *Elite transition: From apartheid to neoliberalism in South Africa*. London: Pluto Press and Petermaritzburg: University of Natal Press.

CSS (Central Statistical Services) (1997). *October household survey 1995: Eastern Cape*. Pretoria: Central Statistical Services.

Currey, R. F. (1970). *Rhodes University 1904–1970*. Cape Town: Rustica Press.

Davis, S. S. and Davis, D. A. (1995). The mosque and the satellite: Media and adolescence in a Moroccan Town. *Journal of Youth and Adolescence* 24(5), 577–593.

Deswaan, A. (1989). Platform Holland: Dutch society in the context of global cultural relations. *International Spectator* 43(11), 718–722.

Drotner, K. (1992). Modernity and media panics. In M. Skovmand and K. C. Schrøder (eds), *Media cultures: Reappraising transnational media*. London: Routledge.

Ellis, J. (1982). *Visible fictions*. London: Routledge and Kegan Paul.

Fiske, J. (1987). *Television culture*. London: Methuen.

Fiske, J. (1989). *Understanding popular culture*. Boston: Unwin Hyman.

Gaganakis, M. (1992). Language and ethnic group relations in non-racial schools. *English Academy Review* 9, 46–55.

Gevisser, M. (1996). That other Holomisa. *Mail and Guardian*, 13 September, 14.

Gevisser, M. (2000). Ubukhosi the bedrock of African democracy. *Mail and Gaurdian*, 11 February, 29.

Hall, S. (1991). Old and new identities, old and new ethnicities. In A. D. King (ed.), *Culture, globalisation and the world-system*. London: Macmillan.

Hannerz, U. (1996). *Transnational connections: Culture, people, places*. London: Routledge.

IBA (Independent Broadcasting Authority) (1999). *SA music monitoring report PBS and private radio samples: 1998*. Johannesburg: IBA.

Jennings, R., Evaratt, D., Lyle, A. and Budlender, D. (eds) (1997). *The situation of youth in South Africa*. Johannesburg: Community Agency for Social Enquiry (CASE).

Kellner, D. (1995). *Media culture: Cultural studies, identity politics between the modern and the postmodern*. London: Routledge.

Kraidy, M. M. (1999). The global, the local, and the hybrid: A native ethnography of glocalization. *Critical Studies in Mass Communication* 16, 456–476.

Leibrandt, M., Woolard, I. and Bhorat, H. (2000). Understanding contemporary household inequality in South Africa. *Studies in Economics and Econometrics* 24(3), 31–51.

Lemish, D., Drotner, K., Liebes, T., Maigret, E. and Stald, G. (1998). Global culture in practice: A look at children and adolescents in Denmark, France and Israel. *European Journal of Communication* 13(4), 539–556.

Mangcu, X. (2001). Liberating race from apartheid's yoke. *Sunday Independent*, 6.

Marais, H. (2001). *South Africa limits to change: The political economy of transition*. London: Zed Books and Cape Town: University of Cape Town Press.

Morley, D. (1994). Postmodernism: The highest stage of cultural imperialism. In M. Perryman (ed.), *Altered States: Postmodernism, politics, culture*. London: Lawrence and Wishart.

NYC (National Youth Commission) (1997). *Youth policy 2000*. Pretoria: National Youth Commission.

Ross, R. (1999). *A concise history of South Africa*. Cambridge: Cambridge University Press.

SAARF (South African Advertising Foundation) (1997) *AMPS 97: Technical Report*, vol. 1 (Jan–Jun). Johannesburg: SAARF.

SAARF (South African Institute of Race Relations) (1998). *South African Survey 1997/98*. Johannesburg: South African Institute of Race Relations.

SAARF (South African Institute of Race Relations) (1999). *South African Survey 1999/2000*. Johannesburg: South African Institute of Race Relations.

Schiller, H. I. (1998). American pop culture sweeps the world. In R. Dickenson, R. Harindranath and O. Linne (eds), *Approaches to audiences: A reader*. London: Arnold.

Schou, S. (1992). Postwar Americanisation and the revitalisation of European culture. In M. Skovmand and K. C. Schrøder (eds), *Media cultures: Reappraising transnational media*. London: Routledge.

Seeking, J. (2000). Visions of society: Peasants, workers and the unemployed in a changing South Africa. *Studies in Economics and Econometrics* 24(3), 53–71.

Stadler, A. (1987). *The political economy of modern South Africa*. Cape Town: David Philip.

Steenveld, L. and Strelitz, L. (1998) The 1995 rugby World Cup and the politics of nation-building in South Africa. *Media, Culture and Society* 20(4), 609–629.

Straubhaar, J. D. (1991). Beyond media imperialism: Asymmetrical interdependence and cultural proximity. *Critical Studies in Mass Communication* 8, 39–59.

Strelitz, L. (2001). Global media/local meanings. *Communication* 27(2), 49–56.

Strelitz, L. (2002a). Where the global meets the local: South African youth and their experience of global media. Unpublished doctoral thesis, Rhodes University.

Strelitz, L. (2002b). Media consumption and identity formation: The case of the "Homeland" viewers. *Media, Culture and Society* 24, 459–480.

Thompson, J. B. (1995). *The media and modernity: A social theory of the media*. Cambridge: Polity Press.

Tomlinson, J. (1991). *Cultural imperialism*. London: Pinter Publishers.

Van Zyl Slabbert, F., Malan, C., Marais, H., Olivier, J. and Riordan, R. (eds) (1994). *Youth in the new South Africa*. Pretoria: HSRC.

Warde, A. (1996). Afterword: The Future of the Sociology of Consumption. In S. Edgell, K. Hetherington and A. Warde (eds), *Consumption matters*. Oxford: Blackwell/The Sociological Review. Willis, P. (1990). *Common culture*. Milton Keynes: Open University Press.

14

CHASING ECHOES

Cultural reconversion, self-representation and mediascapes in Mexico[1]

Patrick D. Murphy

In *Local Knowledge*, Clifford Geertz (1983) argued that ethnography is not about perceiving what one's "informants" perceive, but rather seeking out symbolic forms (words, images, institutions, behaviors) "in terms of which, in each place, people actually represent themselves to themselves and to one another" (p. 58). When viewed through the lens of the emergence of hybrid cultural forms charted by researchers in recent years (Bhabha, 1994; Fiske, 1996; García Canclini, 1990, 1993; Kraidy, 1999; Kumar and Curtin, 2002), I think Geertz's provocation has special, perhaps even unavoidable implications for ethnographers of media and globalization. This is especially the case when framed in reference to how mediated images and narratives, the products of corporate media which serve as the ideological tools to deepen global capitalism, are drawn on and used by historically situated social agents to shape those hybrid forms and transform popular culture.

The trouble is, how do we recognize moments of symbolic self-representation in popular culture? Are they obtrusive and easily recognizable displays of aesthetic preference and emerging "global" practices? Do they crystallize in the quiet but culturally productive "poaching" (de Certeau, 1984) of hegemonic cultural capital? Or, are they marked by more salient and antagonistic articulations of counter-hegemonic activity? Indeed, much of the findings from transnational audience studies positions reception as a politically and culturally emancipatory activity (Fuenzalida and Hermosilla, 1989; Liebes and Katz, 1990; Parameswaran, 1999; Schou, 1992; Yang, 2002). But while globalizing mediations may encourage culturally resistive tactics and alternative subjectivities, do such demonstrations of agency sever the ideological threads that corporately produced and controlled media bind together through mediascapes? That is, does audience activity truly work against the grain of hegemonic culture?

With such questions in tow, my reaction to a Geertzian ethnographic task for media global studies is to pursue the articulation of self-representation through two interrelated foci. First, how does hegemonic culture "speak through" popular culture via historically situated social agents? Second, how does the articulation of self-representation in cultural hybridity exhibit residues of local, traditional cultural memory? Together these foci direct attention to how hegemonic ideology is naturalized, transmuted and/or challenged through everyday life practices. Such a research objective requires the study of collective ways of knowing, and an analysis of how the worldview expressed in popular culture reveals ideological fragments (e.g. value system and moral direction) from varying institutional sources (Geertz, 1983). But within this collectivity, it also means looking at how individuals assert creative agency over meaning construction and media use, and how those activities reflect, challenge or customize popular memory and local practice.

Through a narrative account of fieldwork conducted in central Mexico from 1989 to 2001, this chapter presents three points for analysis through which I address the above concerns. These are:

1   the presence of "multitemporal heterogeneity" in culturally mundane, collective practices;
2   processes of "cultural reconversion" that demonstrate the creative interplay between mediascapes, local culture and hegemonic culture;
3   the articulation of "common sense" that suggests how the local, national and global converge.

The tales from the field put forward were selected because they represent ethnographically thick moments in my research on media and culture with members of popular-class communities, suggesting that the formation of complex localized identities and practices surface less as a measure of specific content than method. Moreover, they underscored that researching self-representation in popular culture is contingent upon the embodied experience of being in the field so that ethnographers can connect to how social agents demonstrate the reflexive properties for creating, performing and revealing the tonalities of cultural life and media's place within it. This means that "proximity, not objectivity, becomes the epistemological point of departure and return" – a commitment that instantiates a closeness to culture punctuated by "exposing oneself to a hermeneutics of experience, relocation, co-presence, humility and vulnerability" (Conquergood, 1995, p. 149). I believe that this is a way of knowing and understanding cultural transformation that is perhaps unique to ethnography as a disciplined methodology (Murphy, 2002) and, returning to Geertz, presents ethnographers with the possibility of talking with an informed sensitivity about the way people actually represent themselves to themselves and to one another.

In this chapter I strive to present the complexity, indeed the paradoxical dynamic of self-representation, community and social power, and media's place within that dynamic. As such, these tales from the field are not media-centric accounts, but rather illustrations of how media narratives and aesthetics surface and confront everyday life practices and expose the conflictive forces at work within culture. Mediascapes – what Appadurai (1990, p. 331) defines as "image-centered, narrative-based accounts of strips of reality" – are not only seen as penetrating social life through active and creative appropriation by highly reflexive social agents, but as being deliberately extracted from as means through which to stimulate "authenticating practices" and identity formation. Rather than being suggestive of resistance or emancipation, however, these cultural negotiations reveal a limited opposition in that the negotiation of mediated cultural capital presents a muted sense of hegemonic culture and so serves to extend its range.

Media, cultural capital and multitemporal heterogeneity

A few years ago I attended a conference on ethnography where I had the pleasure of hearing social-worker-turned-doctoral-student Marcelo Diversi talk about his interactions with street children in Campinas, Brazil. Working with shoe-less, technologically deprived street kids, Diversi (2000) found that the symbolic currency of *his* self-presentation (specifically, the wearing of Nike shoes and ball cap) served, quite by accident, to reveal their level of consumer sophistication and media "literacy."

> "So how come you are wearing these old-fashioned Nike Shoes" he said opening a big smile.
> "But I just bought them before I came to Brazil three months ago!" I reacted, somewhat surprised, looking down at my black Nike cross-training shoes.
> "And you bought this old model anyway, huh?" Lico said, now rolling backwards with laughter.
> Two boys who had been kicking cans around a few yards away walked towards us smiling and looking at me.
> "Why didn't you buy an Air Jordan?" said one of them.
> "What's the difference?" I asked.
> The three of them were soon, all at once, saying things like having better cushioning, jumping higher, protecting joints, enhancing performance, and moving really fast. I felt like I was in a Nike commercial.
>
> (Diversi, 2000, p. 2)

Diversi's experience with street children who owned neither shoes nor televisions suggests the pervasiveness of media's cultural capital and the extent to which people can access and make use of that capital in newly industrialized societies (e.g. Brazil, Mexico, Turkey). His presentation also underscored the importance of the embodied field experience to encounter and extract the layers of "common sense" that reverberate how the mediascapes and ideoscapes of global culture (Appadurai, 1990) reside in the life worlds of even the most marginalized groups.

Admittedly Diversi's comments, while not so much directing my attention to consider such connections of self-representation and cultural capital, pushed me to revisit the sort of "invisible" cultural connectivity instantiated above in my own field experiences. In fact, much of my interest in ethnography as a tool for inquiring about media's relation to culture was stimulated by my early research experiences in San Miguel Canoa, an indigenous community undergoing rapid modernization and technological saturation (televisions, video recorders, camcorders, etc.) where I had "broke my teeth" as an ethnographer in 1989 and 1990. There I had learned to respect the wisdom of tradition when a *curandera* (traditional healer) set my broken ankle (see Murphy, 2002). But it was also there that I came to see the birthing of composite cultures through the interplay of consumer modernity and tradition, and by extension what García Canclini (1990) means by *multitemporal heterogeneity*.

The mixing of temporal matrices is often most salient in big, loud forms, such as in themes parks or Hollywood films where the "history" and "myth" are pliable capital for the consuming present. However, as I learned from my ethnographic encounters in San Miguel Canoa, multitemporal heterogeneity also resides quietly in daily activities and practices. Some of these are so seamless in presentation and form as to appear almost invisible. Take, for instance, the drinking of Coca-Cola – a definitively "American" product that paradoxically epitomizes global mass culture – poured, warm, into a plastic bag *para llevar* ("to go"). This mode of consumption suggests at least three intertextual layers of meaning, articulating pre-Columbian, capitalist and "postmodern" culture. The drinking of warm *refresco* (soda pop) is common among Canoans and members of communities in rural areas throughout central Mexico, even when refrigeration is available. Drawing on indigenous/pre-Columbian concepts of existence, many Canoans associate warmth with life and health, while cold is associated with sickness, death, and even witchcraft. Thus, most refreshments are taken at room temperature. The drink is put into a plastic bag so that the vender can guard his/her investment and claim the refund on the returnable bottles, while the plastic bag, along with a straw, allows the drink to be taken in transit. This exchange is a product of capital investment and monetary profit, but it is also a consumer "service" suggestive of Western (US) temporal divisions of work and leisure. Moreover, the drinking of soft drinks has been positioned by local mediascapes (television, radio, billboards and sporting events) as a "modern," sexy and festive thing to do, and is often consumed in preference to more nutritional or traditional drinks.[2] The popularity of a modern product such as Coke in regions not particularly "modernized" speaks of its "pre-post modernity" and underscores how difficult it is to determine unified meaning.

What both my example from San Miguel Canoa and Diversi's experiences with the street children of Campinas point to for media ethnography is that there is often a certain abstractedness between meaning construction and media consumption; that is, the "where" (consumption spaces), "what" (texts consumed) and "how" (access to media technology) of media consumption are sometimes more ethnographically evocative than transparently performative (e.g. domestic rituals of viewing a favorite text). What this means for the media ethnographer, then, is that he/she must look for mediated ideas and narratives through everyday life practices and common-sense assumptions that expose "the complicated and interconnected repertoire of print, celluloid, electronic screens and billboards" (Appadurai, 1990, p. 330). After all, media's cultural capital is transmitted through images and narratives rather than the sort of direct material exchange, social obligation and public rituals that have provided the basis of so many anthropological studies. Or is it?

Cultural reconversion

As I had found through my field studies in Querétaro (1993–94; 2000–01), it is often precisely in non-reception circumstances that mediated narratives and images surface to direct and even channel research. This data is not always conveniently marked in domestic viewing rituals or presented in pre-planned topical interviews, but is rather often revealed as a quick turn or an allusion in the flow of a conversations, as accents of self-presentation, or as common-sense utterances of political and social knowledge. Ethnography is, after all, a commitment to be "surprised, to be caught off-guard, and to be swept up by events that occur in the field as a result of which even the original directions of the inquiry may significantly change" (Gille, 2001). But one must first be in the field, or more precisely, in the flow of people's everyday lives for this to happen.

Elsewhere I have explicated in depth my entrée into the field in Querétaro, my connection to Mexico, and the productive discomfort and pleasures of extended fieldwork (Murphy, 1999 and 2002). Suffice it to say here that I chose Querétaro as the site for a reception study because in many respects the city was a microcosm of contemporary Mexico: a provincial population with roots in the city's colonial past (Calderón, 1993), unskilled laborers from rural areas and neighboring states, a diversity of indigenous peoples,[3] middle-class and upper-class immigrants from Mexico City, and "new money" industrial elites (Secretaría de Desarrollo Económico, 1992). But unlike many other cities in Mexico, where geographic proximity to the US border, patterns of labor migration, international tourism, or the presence of large indigenous populations strongly influence the transformation of culture, Querétaro's changing cultural terrain was less immediately discernible. Apart from the rapid industrialization, Querétaro's chief outside influences were the transportation system (one of Mexico's major highways connects Querétaro and Mexico City) and the mass media. What this socio-economic and geo-political structure suggested was that Querétaro's ongoing cultural transformations were the product of influences operating more through abstract articulations of cultural capital (industrial production of culture, entertainment and leisure) than through territorialized and concrete "cross-cultural" experiences (e.g. migration, refugees, expatriates, and tourism).

Upon arrival I initiated my field studies in San Francisquito and La Cruz – two of Querétaro's oldest and most culturally rich neighborhoods (Calderón, 1993; Moreno Pérez and Barrera, 1994; Whiteford, 1990). I set up residence in La Cruz and explored the two neighborhoods, trying to establish links to community members early in my research (see Murphy, 1999). From almost the beginning the two communities presented their layered histories, which were literally painted on the walls. Old logos of now non-existent brandy, low-grade brews and cantina monikers emerged from beneath weathered and peeling paint. The corridor at the edge of La Cruz and moving into San Francisquito was evidently Querétaro's old "red light" district where *pulquerias* (*pulque* bars) and brothels once ruled the day. As I walked into San Francisquito I was met with "Los Ramones" spray-painted on various walls – territorial reminders that I was entering the turf of a Querétaro gang that took its name from the US punk group "The Ramons." These were foreshadowing signs of the multi-temporal and heterogeneous cultural motifs and iconography that I would find throughout my fieldwork.

The depth and vitality of these layers sprung to life one day when I began a discussion about drum-making with Eladio Rodríguez, a leader of a *conchero* dance group located in the barrio of San Francisquito.[4] Eladio told me that after he selected a proper section of trunk from a tree for a drum, he would hollow it out to where it would produce a nice sound. Upon achieving acceptable sound quality with the instrument, he then would turn his attention to decorating its exterior. Many of his drums he would decorate with Aztec icons like Huitzilopochtli, Tezcatlipoca, and Quetzalcoatl – pre-Hispanic symbols to mark a psychic and artistic territory that he wished to inhabit and celebrate. He said, without hesitation, that he copied them from anthropology books he bought at one of the local bookstores, noting that they were good sources for indigenous authenticity.

Eladio's candor struck me with a sense of cultural and political purpose that I was perhaps not originally prepared for. Indeed, somehow his "confession" left me a little disheartened as I struggled to come to terms with the fact that a captain of conchero dancers noted locally for their indigenous authenticity was drawing on anthropological sources to recreate "authentic" living culture. And in fact, more than with any other relationships, my experiences and discussions with Eladio, don Antonio (Eladio's father) and others from San Francisquito stripped away my presuppositions and lingering romantic notions of cultural fidelity, and in their case, indigenous identity based purely on popular memory. My interactions with them revealed in very plain terms the constant state of flux and invention between tradition and modernity, and the ambiguous but often deliberate line between culture and politics. Thinking about his own experiences of trying to balance tradition and change, don Antonio told me early on in my research:

Before, nobody took it [*conchero* dance] seriously; nobody thought it was important. If you went to dance, nobody came to watch. Nobody. But we were Indian and we couldn't deny it, so why would we question it? Our traditions are indigenous, are authentic. What we've had we've had for five or six generations. But culture is becoming weaker every day. And if we can teach our children to value it, then, well, there's a trajectory for growth for something that's beautiful. And people can see that, as much the government as with the people. We can look at something that happened centuries ago and those people have disappeared, but we still have their traditions. We can talk, like I did with my wife's father, and involve ourselves in its continuation. And so I adopted the dance as well, and we do it the same as her father did it. It's tradition.

(Personal interview, November 1993)

Don Antonio's memories are at once both romantic and defensive. This short excerpt from his memory of cultural commitment and struggle does not include divergent histories, such as the way that the traditional art form he inherited from his father-in-law transmuted considerably under his own leadership. For example, another senior resident of San Francisquito, don Luis Felipe, explained to me that the use of drums was a relatively new introduction to their dance rituals. Traditionally, the musical instrument that accompanied ceremonial and other dance occasions was the armadillo- or tortoise-shelled guitar. These instruments are actually the source of the concheros' name (*concha* meaning shell in Spanish). Such alternative histories suggested that don Antonio's memory was somewhat more selective and directive than the very indigenous roots he claimed to have been preserving under his stewardship – a conclusion that grew only stronger during my fieldwork as I began to find even more visions of tradition presented by Eladio and others in San Francisquito.

As we continued to talk, Eladio pulled out a box of old photographs and other articles that documented in one way or another the concheros' story, and proceeded to explain some of the challenges he faced with what he understood as the "politics of culture." He showed me a photograph of himself covered in jaguar and coyote skins embracing the Governor of Querétaro. One of Eladio's brothers, Jamie, had stopped by and, pointing to Eladio in the picture, said to me "Look how Indian Eladio is! He's really Indian." Eladio was aware, however, what such posturing translated into for the *barrios* and *pueblitos* of popular/marginalized peoples such as San Francisquito. The concheros, and thus the community of San Francisquito as a whole, were being courted precisely for their cultural identity, and the fact that Eladio and company dressed in "traditional" garb made this identity a visible fund for local media. The Governor of Querétaro appeared at their local ceremonies so he could tap into this fund, inviting newspapers and television cameras to confirm his dedication to *la cultura* and sensitivity to the marginalized underclass. This posturing,

Eladio recognized, was not only a necessary strategy for elected government officials, but for himself and the concheros as well. What Eladio was getting was exposure for San Francisquito and its tradition, which in turn added legitimacy to its own existence, assuring, to some degree anyway, continued interest in its actuality (e.g. new recruits for the dance). Eladio asserted that, as with other "products," indigenousness had to be marketed if it was to be maintained within the neoliberal currents of modernizing Mexico.

Eladio asked me if I thought he was selling his culture. The question was asked rhetorically, and we continued to search through the pile of documents and photos. One document, a certificate from the State of Nayarit, proclaimed his dance group as winner of the 1992 indigenous festival of *Mexicanidad* (Mexicanness). He didn't seem to mind the inherent contradiction of an award administered via the state for indigenousness. Another document was a letter from a German politician exalting the indigenous style of Eladio's Chichimeca concheros. This accumulation of "official" documentation of indigenous authenticity was telling, yet it was a series of newer photographs that told a related but more interesting story. He thumbed through a stack of color photographs of a recent dance festival that his group had attended, pausing on a photo of an attractive young dancer in customized regalia. Here Eladio began to comment on what he perceived to be the influence of television on traditional conchero dance. The dancer, in her late teens, had "modern" make-up and adopted some styles that reflected what Eladio called the "Thalia look." Thalia is a sexy singer-dancer and telenovela star of various productions of the Mexican television giant Televisa. The blond Thalia often showcases her talent via music videos, advertisements and variety show dance numbers in which she appears clad in skimpy outfits garnished with sequins and feathers. According to Eladio, the young Chichimeca dancer had appropriated Thalia's style, incorporating yellow feathers into a low-cut top, placing her hair (dyed blond) into a Thalia-type pony tail, and painting on thick, dark eye-liner. "This is not traditional," commented Eladio.

Such customizations of tradition were tolerated because Eladio knew that through the creative interpretation of the art, new dancers felt as though they were more fully participating by contributing. He explained "How long do you think they would keep dancing if I told them exactly what to do?" Over time, I found that his acceptance of the ideas of other dancers actually increased the appeal of being part of the concheros for many of San Francisquito's youths. In addition, through long-term interaction with community members, I began to see in more immediate and concrete terms how they were reinterpreting and building on tradition, and how the flow of ideas and images was drawn upon creatively to stimulate cultural investment that also reified dominant discourses. Eladio, via don Antonio's teaching and anthropological texts, reinterpreted tradition through his relationship with myth and scholarship, whereas the girl, among other younger conchero dancers, drew on the sources of ideas and images that were most readily available, such as telenovelas and music video. So while from a distance the concheros appeared to have mounted a highly conscious effort to resist the interferences of modern consumer culture by reinvesting in traditional modes of cultural expression via hand-crafted costumes and traditional instruments, the art form is in fact being elaborated in reference to multitemporal motifs.

These adaptations exemplify García Canclini's (1992) concept of *cultural reconversion*. As he notes, old and new symbolic forms offer broad opportunities for cultural investment. "Instead of the death of traditional cultural forms, we discover that tradition is in transition, and articulated to modern processes. Reconversion prolongs their existence" (p. 31). Along these lines, the attractive young dancer was doing exactly what Eladio's group needed to persevere in the current consumer climate where modern logic can work in the service of tradition. Objectified, her beauty and "modernity," ironically, were powerful tools in highlighting the group's tradition. Eladio and other male dancers performed in what he continually referred to as "traditional Chichimeca" cultural garb (jaguar, coyote and mountain lion skins, bones, hawk feathers and claws of various animals, etc.); the young woman (and other young dancers) contradicted their "authenticity" through the material adaptation of televisual aesthetics.

These self-representations underscored a dialectical elaboration of authenticity that works both to reify tradition's local currency and to underscore its "legitimacy." That is, the concheros' perceived fidelity to the past (via the teachings of community elders), when coupled with the incorporation of anthropologically validated iconography, maintained its sense of history and appeal to state officials and other indigenous groups. However, the inclusion of the aesthetic preferences of younger community members works to extend the tradition's future. While given less prestige by Eladio and the other elders, these newer adaptations were accepted because they understood that the rejection of modern/commercial forces would ultimately undermine the tradition's future. Such compromises are what Eladio called the "cultural embrace." What this embrace seemed to translate into for the concheros was a highly strategic process of cultural reconversion that worked interstitially through traditional practices, an imagined past and a tactical negotiation of modernizing hegemonic discourses. Thus the process of reconversion speaks to both the evolving nature of culture and the penetration of hegemonic culture into the popular through active agents.

Common sense and resisting resistance

I returned to Querétaro in December 2000 and stayed until July 2001 as part of a sabbatical leave. I found the city had transformed. San Francisquito and La Cruz had remained largely the same, preserving, ironically, their respective marginality from the economically vibrant parts of the city (although now in La Cruz there was a new statue commemorating the concheros). But as a whole Querétaro had undeniably achieved the status of tourist destination – a status evidenced by its inclusion in tour packages of central Mexico, with buses leaving Mexico City and snaking their way through Querétaro, San Miguel de Allende and Guanajuato as part of a Bajío tour of "colonial Mexico." Bus-loads of foreign travelers are now regularly deposited to wander about the beautiful, renovated and award-winning ("Cleanest city in Mexico") Centro. My old friend Juan Alonso told me, and not without a sense of irony, that now that the *gringos* (a term that most Queretanos apply to Europeans as readily as Americans) had discovered El Centro it had become fashionable for the Querétano elite. New restaurants, artisan shops, outdoor cafés and Trova bars sprung up where there were formally paper shops, candy stores, small service businesses and cantinas. In the evenings, especially Friday nights, literally hundreds of Querétaro teenagers took over the Plaza de Armas, one of the city's oldest and most highly regarded historical landmarks. Armed with cell phones, leather jackets and exposed belly buttons, the young and the conspicuously consuming cruised the manicured Centro as if posing for MTV or Televisa cameras. The "new" Querétaro indeed seemed a neoliberalist's dreamscape, and was definitely on the map for *la gente de la onda* (the beautiful people).

It was also apparently on the map for *los de abajo*, as I learned that Querétaro was scheduled to be a stop for the *caravana zapatista* (Zapatista caravan), a political consciousness raising tour of the Ejército Zapatista de Liberación Nacional (ELZN). The "Zapatour," as dubbed by the popular press in Mexico and elsewhere, was to take Subcomadante Marcos and company through central Mexico beginning on February 25 and culminate in Mexico City's Zócalo on March 11. As far as the caravan's selection of cities was concerned, aside from the expected end of tour showdown in Mexico City (where the Zapatistas would be joined by Oliver Stone, Robert Redford, and Nobel prize winner Jose Saramago), Querétaro was probably the most anticipated stop because of the inflammatory remarks made by the state's Governor, Ignacio Loyola, against the EZLN days prior to their arrival. In the face of positive political energy generated in Mexico from the first fraud-free election since 1929 and the potential to capitalize on that energy to create progress, Loyola had publicly questioned Marcos's patriotism, and even suggested that he receive the death penalty for his treasonous activities.

I saw the March 1 rally as an excellent opportunity to experience the complexity and sophistication of organized resistance for social change. I was also interested to see how it would be covered by the local, national and international presses, and to get an up-close and personal look at the Zapatistas. Once I arrived at the rally location, I tried to locate the stage and wandered into the sea of youths in Che Guevara T-shirts and Zapatista ski masks and sweating, camera-toting journalists. Both groups began to take to the trees and cling to the walls near the rally stage, and I couldn't help but envision Marcos showing up with the Grateful Dead. For hours we waited, but the Zapatistas didn't show. The mixture of more people, more heat and more waiting began to increase tensions, and the open space around the front of the stage began to implode. A man moved on to the stage and grabbed a microphone, announcing with authority, "Please move away from the stage so that the media personnel can have access." I was struck by the blatant pandering to the press in an atmosphere that was ostensibly designed to give voice to the downtrodden and forgotten, which for me included the people surrounding the stage. Yet I also knew that the Zapatour was, after all, part of Subcomadante Marcos's "rebellion of words" and he was keenly aware that the press was necessary for those words to serve as weapons (see *The Nation*, July 2, 2001; *Proceso*, March 11, 2002). The man with the microphone repeated his request. Behind him stood ten indigenous Querétano leaders dressed in traditional grab. The crowd pushed back to reveal a hundred or so camera operators and reporters from various news services from around the world. We all waited, watching the press watching the indigenous leaders watching us.

After a few hours, my exposed white skin was now bright red, and so I took refuge under a tree far from the action at the stage. Rumor had it that one of the Zapatour buses had hit a pedestrian, and so they were indefinitely delayed. By early afternoon the Zapatista caravan began to arrive. Finally, Marcos and some of the Zapatista Comadantes took their place on the stage. The crowd became electric.

The next day I wanted to see what Queretanos had made of the Zapatour, so I wandered over to El Centro looking for the local paper, *Diario de Querétaro*. Despite covering almost all of the news kiosks, I couldn't find any copies. I even went to the *Diario de Querétaro*'s main office. "Sold out," the man at the desk told me. So much for the thesis of the passivity of news consumption and the dominance of the television news audience, I thought. With my hope of finding a newspaper dashed, I decided to walk over to Eladio's house, hoping he would be home and looking forward to his interpretation of the Zapatista visit. I knocked on his big steel garage front door and he welcomed me in. He was covered with animal hair and asked me to forgive the mess. We walked over to his workbench where he had some new skins laid out for curing.

"I am working on a new piece for my conchero costume. It's a cougar's paw. Look at the size of it!" Eladio said, showing me the severed limb.

"Are you sure that's a cougar, Eladio? Looks more like an African lion's paw to me," I said speculatively, while wondering how he would have obtained such an artifact.

"No, it's a cougar's. You'd be surprised how big they get. Why are you so red?," he said, changing the flow of our conversation.

"I went to the Zapatour rally. I was in the sun for hours and forgot to wear a hat."

"Oh, yeah. I heard that Marcos and his tour showed up a little late. I guess they hit a policeman that was directing traffic with one of the buses. Want something to drink? You know, I was going to go down there, but after I heard about the delays, crowds, and roadblocks and stuff, I just came home to see if I could watch it on television. What did he have to say?"

"Well, mostly he poked fun at the Governor, which the crowd seemed to like. But he also spoke about the sort of thing that he has been saying at all of the Zapatour stops: that the Mexican government needs to recognize the rights of indigenous peoples throughout the country, that marginalized people need to organize and demand respect and inclusion, that the aim is peace but that there is dignity in rebellion. These kinds of things."

"Hmmm," Eladio responded. "That's what I heard on television, too. I like that he is saying these things, and that the media are carrying these messages to people throughout Mexico and the world, but . . ."

"But what?," I probed.

"Did you see how they had the Otomí leaders lined up on stage for the cameras? These leaders come and join these manifestations looking for respect, hoping people will take their needs and hopes seriously. And what happens? They become props, background scenery to frame an indigenous insurrection with Marcos doing all the talking and the foreigners hanging on to every word. And now Televisa and TV Azteca are putting on a concert for 'Peace in Chiapas.'[5] Seems like everybody's getting in on this, but I see very little indigenous presence in all of this. I am for getting the media involved, but now when we see or hear about Chiapas, we see video and photos of indigenous people in the background while priests, politicians and rock stars talk about the issues. And the international press loves it. I sometimes wonder who this is all for."

Eladio put his attention to the lion's paw. Eladio's brother, Hector, a local taxi driver, had showed up with some beer and soon he entered the conversation.

"You know, Tricho [what Hector called me]" he said, "to me the whole Zapatista thing has transformed into some sort of international movement and looks very similar to what happened in the Spanish Civil War. Just look at the role of foreign enthusiasts. Like in the Spanish Civil War, they are having a profound affect on our politics. For instance seems like more than half of the 'Zapatistas' aren't Mexican. At least they're certainly not indigenous. And if you've been watching closely it seemed as though the most active or politically strident participants have been the foreign contingent of the caravan. I think they are Italian. Every time things seem to settle down a bit they get people worked up again, whether here or in other parts of the Zapatour. Their impact is interesting but also troubling to me, as if they don't have anything to get politically active about in Italy now so they are here to show us Mexicans the way to do it."

"And that bothers you?", I asked.

"I don't know that it bothers me", he responded "There is something to be said for the energy, the belief in political participation or action in Mexico that we didn't have even a few years ago. But what I find difficult to take is what seems like the hypocrisy of 'radical' political activity. First, I hear people say: 'Fox used to work for Coca-Cola,' implying that he is going to turn Mexico into one big global supermarket. But when we see television images of the

Zapatistas drinking Coca-Cola in the Lacandon jungle and no one says a thing.
. . . What I don't really understand is Marcos's agenda. If I could ask him, I'd
say 'Why do you always attack the "marketing" of Fox?' 'Why do you hate a
"regime" that just took office.' Isn't that precisely what Marcos himself is doing
through all of these interviews on television and in newspapers and magazines?
And for what? He says he wants an inclusive Mexico, but does that include
business opportunities? So where does he plan to take the people of Chiapas: to
progress or to war?" (Fieldnotes, March 2, 2001).

I left Eladio's place with our conversation about the Zapatour echoing in my
mind. Eladio and Hector's deconstruction of the Zapatour rally suggested a
multilayered local-national-global critique of the Zapatista movement punctuated by personal investments and common-sense assumptions reflective of
national mainstream politics. And for my part, even in light of their criticisms,
I couldn't help but think that I too felt an attraction to the Zapatour even with,
or perhaps especially because of, its postmodern feel: an insurrection of words
not bullets; its complex caste of characters from around Mexico and the globe;
a movement worthy of the attention of politicians, peasants and intellectuals
alike. So was I, too, guilty of being an adventure-seeking foreigner?

Feverish quests and acts of agency in popular culture

García Canclini (1996) has argued that popular culture acts as the "depository"
for both official discourse and popular narratives, creating a space where the
modern and traditional converge through the practices of everyday life. For Latin
American cultural theorists (see Murphy, 1997; Rodriguez and Murphy, 1997),
these practices reveal not only intrusions of power and persistence of tradition,
but underscore social tensions, conflicting local, national and transnational ways
of life, and the interplay between cultural memory and economic opportunities
and pressures. My field studies in Querétaro and elsewhere in Mexico have
supported this characterization of the complex qualities and multilayered
texture of popular culture.

In the case of my experiences with the concheros in 1993–94, the symbolic
and material expression of cultural negotiation exposed how high (anthropological texts), popular (cultural memory), and mass (e.g. telenovelas, advertising,
music video) culture are reconverted to nourish community life. Among other
things, this reconversion instantiates the importance of mediascapes in shaping
how active agents invest in community, and thus collective identity, implying,
to use the classical social dichotomy elaborated by Ferdinand Tönnies, a merging
of the "organic" family/village/folk community ontology (*Gemeinschaft*) with
the industrially organized and mass mediated underpinning (*Gesellschaft*) of
modernization. The connection can be understood in a more individual form if
we look at different ways in which Eladio and the young woman dancer, both
of whom are practicing members in conchero dance and therefore collective
culture, selectively poached cultural capital to extrapolate their distinctiveness

and their personal interpretations of tradition. Innovation and appropriation in terms of self-representation are marked by how the currency of symbols from mediascapes and the social capital of popular memory are valuated and applied as mechanisms to invest in *and* refashion community life. These tactics underscore what Martín-Barbero (2002) suggests are, drawing on Manuel Castells, "feverish quests" for "social and personal identity which, based on images of the past and projected onto a utopian future, allow them to overcome an intolerable present" (p. 622). In short, the privileged community status of conchero dance culture is based on authenticating practices and cultural heritage. But its ability to maintain this status of privilege is elaborated through an imagined cultural fidelity that also provides a space for creative "autonomy" that assures a place for the expression of individuality.

The dual, intertwined processes of negotiating culture at the community and individual levels demonstrated by the concheros are key, I think, to understanding the ideological dimensions of globalization and media's place within it. For instance, if cultural reconversion presents the process through which both collectivity and individuality can be pursued and, ironically, reveal how traditional, authentic culture is established, understood and animated to carry cultural capital in community life, it must also been seen as a creative activity that serves to echo the power and social currency of modern-transnational hegemonic culture. In other words, hegemonic global culture takes on an organic quality and so is reified as members of the collective community invest in local, self-validating practices.

Additionally, localized investments of cultural identity also articulate some semblance of national myth and politics consistent with the state's own modernizing rhetoric of progress and democracy. That is, local cultural identity reveals how national identity (in this case, Mexicanness) also resides in the common-sense assumptions of the popular classes. As my later field experiences with the residents of San Francisquito demonstrated, when global politics appeared too near, threatening and "foreign" to the local, a defensive posture was assumed even when the global may resonate with a community's own local interest. Here the ideological aspect of mediascapes (what Appadurai (1990) calls "ideoscapes") is presented through the contradictory nature of popular culture. For instance, despite their location of subalternity and connection to "deep Mexico" (Bonfil, 1990), Eladio and Hector seemed unconvinced that the Zapatour was a sign of social emancipation or counter-hegemonic activity by and for Mexicans. Instead they saw it largely as a political intrusion from the "outside," framed by an elite and detached global press and shaped by foreign interests that subverted its potential to truly speak for the indigenous experience or, more broadly, for the Mexican disenfranchised. As such, the Zapatour was disassociated not only with the everyday reality and cultural identity which participants in my research lived and understood as their social struggle, but with the ideological references that ground them such as "representation," "progess" and "democracy" (Appadurai, 1990). For Eladio, the Zapatour had the right vision for indigenous gains and social welfare, but that vision was compromised by the tokenization of indigenous peoples and their concerns in their own movement. Thus Eladio's experiences with the Zapatour, framed through local media and gossip with friends in the community, coded the tour negatively in terms of representation. For Hector, it was an event embedded with historical significance, but its mediacentrism (Marcos's international stardom, foreign "radical" protestors, huge press corps, etc.) seemed superficial and disconnected from his hope for the new, democratically sanctioned Mexican government and its promise of progress. For both, Marcos's use of media, while politically astute and appealing to the outside world, was seen as a means in which the popular classes that the Zapatour sought to represent were ultimately displaced.

These "reads" of the Zapatour mediascape resonated with commonsensical, local understandings of social struggle, and emerge as organic. But it is precisely the commonsensical, organic articulation of these interpretations that reverberate the Mexican states' own neoliberalized and convenient nationalism, which might be summed up as: culture and history are important when something impedes the free market version of "democracy" and "progress" (see Monsiváis, 1996). Government officials questioned the patriotism, indeed the Mexicanness of the Zapatour, and the local and national press pretty much echoed these sentiments. What comes through Eladio and Hector's brief but telling interpretation of the Zapatour is a recomposition of nationalism, articulated in reference to non-representative "others" which Marcos and the non-indigenous face of the Zapatista tour constituted. "Otherness," therefore, allows for the Zapatour to be interpreted as a non-Mexican event, which in turn allows the states to continue to maintain control over the ideological domains of democracy, progress and representation. That Che circulated as the icon of resistance and revolution over Mexico's own Emiliano Zapata – a Mexican revolutionary who defined himself and his movement during the first part of the twentieth century via an unwavering fidelity to peasant rights – perhaps then becomes symbolic of Eladio's and Hector's own suspicions of the Zapatour's purpose and relevance in their lives.

Conclusions

When taken together, my 1993–94 and 2000–01 field experiences with the residents of San Francisquito question the deterministic potential of globalization, at least as a blanket homogenizing force. That is, rather than just being constituted as unconscious bearers of interest calculation, contaminating local culture with camouflaged ideas and images from the culture industries, individuals actively engage and reconvert the symbolic capital of mediascapes. These engagements, however, are processed through local common sense and collective interpretive communities that are temporally situated. These modes of negotiation, which at some levels may appear as tactical raids against global strategies (de Certeau, 1984), actually place into question the emancipatory potential of transnational discourses, and "cast doubt that localistic or nationalistic fundamentalisms can be overcome by new global technologies of communication that also encourage creativity" (García Canclini, 1992, pp. 32–33).

We need to be careful where we go with these conclusions, however, as this research also shows, to quote from Martín-Barbero (1989), that the popular sectors are "continually redefining their modes of acceptance . . . in which they go about appropriating an economy that harms them but which has been unable to suppress or replace the particular way that these cultures mediate between memory and utopia" (pp. 21–22). The tales from the field presented above provide powerful illustrations of how popular culture's heterodox mixtures of commercial mass culture, global-national politics and local common sense are the stuff of everyday life that define and give texture to what we might more intimately see as globalization.

From warm Coca-Cola in plastic bags *para llevar* to self-styled indigenous dancers questioning the sincerity of the Zapatour via the local press and national politics, these examples of multicultural heterogeneity and cultural reconversion represent shades of both cultural resistance and accommodation, but rarely do they provide testimony to transparently empowering or debilitating cultural negotiations or media's place within them. Rather, what they show is that aesthetic preferences and common-sense assumptions are conditioned through their presentation and practice, a transmission that seems to blur the distinction between their cultural and ideological currency. The resulting self-representations retain a strong identification with local notions of authenticity and places of origin, but to celebrate them for their resistant qualities or merely cast them aside as signs of compromised cultural authenticity is to miss their significance. Rather, the presence of conflicting expressions of "locality" and "globality" should be seen as complex entanglements which underscore "feverish quests for authenticity" and cultural adaptation as readily as they do the intrusions of power. But while not automatic or deterministic, that hegemonic power *does* emerge through these entanglements of common sense, aesthetic dispositions, and consumption modes should not be lost as they evidence not only that hegemonic culture is echoed in local cultural life, but how that power is legitimated and customized through local-contextual practices and frameworks of belief. In short, these forms mark how people exercise control over their socio-cultural environment, but their tonalities instantiate a troubling limited opposition to hegemonic culture.

Lessons for media ethnography

To understand more fully how self-representation articulated these processes, researchers must continue to search for how memory and ideology coalesce in the forms of popular practice and common sense, processes that prolong traditional knowledge as it re-inscribes the hegemonic within the practices of popular culture. Cultural authenticity, or perhaps more precisely the idea of the authentic, remains an important mooring in the negotiation of cultural identity for subaltern communities. However, researching how various influences foster the transformation of culture as well as its preservation should not be a romantic quest for resistance nor a search for modernization. Rather, asking questions about how mediascapes surface through the common-sense utterances and practices of everyday life requires attention to the equilibrium of past and present and between self and community because it is the circulation of mediascapes' cultural capital and its incorporation into everyday practices that tell us most about the way culture is being transformed, and more critically, in whose interests.

As this chapter gives testimony, the "being in the field" part of ethnographic inquiry forces us to represent people in various global contexts as "part of the same cultural worlds we inhabit – worlds of mass media, consumption, and dispersed communities of imagination" (Abu-Lughod, 1997, p. 128). It also shows how ethnography is "entrained in the flow of contemporary history" and "enacted via the uncertainty of the eddies and flows" of larger social structures and trends (Willis and Trondman, 2000, p. 6). This investigative dynamic cannot be substituted for in the quest for cultural self-representation. To make the mistake of finding the field in the ethnographic poetics of the pen or the computer is to cheat popular culture of its transformative energy and the adaptive qualities of human agency that researchers strive to understand.

Notes

1 Segments of this chapter originally appeared in Murphy (1999).
2 Soft drinks have become the standard drink in Mexico among the popular classes, often replacing fruit juices, sweet coffee, and *atole* at meal times or as refreshment; and beer has all but replaced the consumption of *nectli* or, as it is called in Spanish, *pulque*.
3 According to the 1992 annual report of the State of Querétaro's Secretary of Economic Development, the largest indigenous group in the city is Otomí, but there are also smaller populations representative of other linguistic groups such as Náhuatl, Zapotec, Mazahua, Maya, P'hurepecha and Huasteco.
4 In Querétaro there are various community-based groups which practice *conchero* dance, an indigenous stylistic form associated with the Chichimec and Aztec culture. The centerpiece of most costumes is the headdress, especially those worn by men, which are most often embellished with long feathers that accentuate movement. Querétaro is host to a national conchero dance celebration every September.
5 On March 3, 2001 Mexican television giant Televisa joined forces with television Azteca to organize "Unidos por la paz," a fund-raising concert in Mexico City's Aztec Stadium featuring mega-groups Mana and Jaguar to promote peace in Chiapas.

References

Abu-Lughod, L. (1997) The interpretation of culture(s) after television. *Representations* 59, 109–33.

Appadurai, A. (1990). Disjuncture and difference in the global cultural economy. In P. Williams and L. Chrisman (eds), *Colonial discourse and post-colonial theory* (pp. 324–339). New York: Columbia University Press.

Bhabha, H. (1994). *The location of culture*. Routledge: London.

Bonfil, G. (1990). *México profundo*. Mexico, D.F.: Editorial Grijalbo.

Calderón, V. M. (1993). *Monografía histórica de Querétaro*. Querétaro: Archivo historico de gobierno del estado de Querétaro.

Conquergood, D. (1995). Of caravans and carnivals: Performance studies in motion. *Drama Review* 39, 141–167.

de Certeau, M. (1984). *The practice of everyday life*. Berkeley: University of California Press.

Diversi, M. (2000) Street kids in Nikes: In search of humanization through the culture of consumption. Paper presented at the Society for the Study of Symbolic Interaction Annual Symposium, January 28.

Fiske, J. (1996) Hybrid vigor: Popular culture in a multicultural, post-Fordist world. *Studies in Latin American Popular Culture* 15, 43–59.

Fuenzalida, V. and Hermosilla, M. E. (1989). *Visiones y ambiciones del televidente*. Santiago: CENECA.

García Canclini, N. (1990). *Culturas híbridas*. Mexico, D.F.: Grijalbo.

García Canclini, N. (1992). Cultural reconversion (trans. H. Staver). In G. Yúdice, J. Franco and J. Flores (eds), *On edge: The crisis of contemporary Latin American culture* (pp. 29–43). Minneapolis: University of Minnesota Press.

García Canclini, N. (1993). The hybrid: A conversation with Margarita Zires, Raymundo Mier, and Mabel Piccini. *Boundary 2*, 20(3), 76–91.

García Canclini, N. (1996). Popular culture: From epic to simulacrum. *Studies in Latin American Popular Culture* 15, 61–71.

Geertz, C. (1983). *Local knowledge*. New York: Basic Books.

Gille, Z. (2001). Critical ethnography in the time of globalization: Toward a new concept of site. *Cultural Studies/Critical Methodologies* 1(2), 319–334.

Kraidy, M. (1999). The global, the local, and the hybrid: A native ethnography of glocalization. *Critical Studies in Mass Communication* 16, 456–476.

Kumar, S. and Curtin, M. (2002). "Made in India": In between music television and patriarchy. *Television and New Media* 3(4), 345–366.

Liebes, T. and Katz, E. 1990. *The export of meaning: Cross cultural readings of Dallas*. New York: Oxford University Press.

Martín-Barbero, J. (1989). Repossessing culture: The quest of popular movements in Latin America. *Media Development* 36(2), 21–24.

Martín-Barbero, J. (2002). Identities: Traditions and new communities. *Media, Culture and Society* 24(5), 621–641.

Monsiváis, C. (1996) Will nationalism be bilingual? In E. McAnany and K. Wilkinson (eds), *Mass media and free trade* (pp. 131–141). Austin: University of Texas Press.

Moreno Pérez, E. and Barrera, G. (1994). *El barrio de San Francisquito*. Querétaro, Mexico: Talleres Gráficos de Gobierno del Estado.

Murphy, P. D. (1997). Contrasting perspectives: Cultural studies in Latin America and the United States: A conversation with Néstor García Canclini. *Cultural Studies* 11, 78–88.

Murphy, P. D. (1999). Doing audience ethnography: A narrative account of establishing ethnographic identity and locating interpretive communities in fieldwork. *Qualitative Inquiry* 5(4), 479–504.

Murphy, P. D. (2002). The anthropologist's son (living and learning the field). *Qualitative Inquiry* 8(3), 246–260.

Nation, The (2001). A Zapatista reading list. July, 2, pp. 36–37.

Parameswaran, R. (1999). Western romance fiction as English-language media in postcolonial India, *Journal of Communication* 49(3), 84–105.

Proceso (2001), La entrvista insólita. March 11, pp. 10–16.

Rodríguez, C. and Murphy, P. D. (1997). The study of communication and culture in Latin America: From laggards and the oppressed to resistance and hybrid cultures. *Journal of International Communication* 4(2), 24–45.

Schou, S. (1992). Postwar Americanisation and the revitalisation of European culture. In M. Skovmand and K. Christian Schrøder (eds), *Media cultures: Reappraising transnational media* (pp. 142–158). London and New York: Routledge.

Secretaría de Desarrollo Económico (1992). *Anuario económico 1992*. Querétaro, Mexico: Gobierno del estado.

Whiteford, A. H. (1990). *Two cities of Latin America*. Prospect Heights, IL: Waveland.

Willis, P. and Tondman, M. (2000). Manifesto for ethnography, *Ethnography* 1(1), 5–16.

Yang, M. M. (2002). Mass media and transntaional subjectivity in Shanghai, In F. D. Ginsburg, L. Abu-Lughod and B. Larkin (Eds), *Media Worlds* (pp. 189–210). Berkeley: University of California Press.

15

GLOBALIZATION *AVANT LA LETTRE?*

Cultural hybridity and media power in Lebanon

Marwan M. Kraidy

A few years before the outbreak of the 1975–90 war in Lebanon, Hudson (1968) wrote:

> The Lebanese Republic is one of the most unusual states in the world. It is a conglomeration of paradoxes and contradictions. Since it became independent of France in 1943 it has struggled from one crisis to another, avoiding disaster by the narrowest of margins. Lebanon as a polity is archaic, inefficient, and divided; it is also liberal, democratic and – in general – orderly. It is Arab and Western, Christian and Muslim, traditional and modern. Its precarious survival is a fascinating subject . . .
>
> (p. 3)

Unfortunately, in the 1970s Lebanon could no longer avoid disaster and descended into violent protracted conflict, lasting from 1975 to 1990, which fragmented this small country into minuscule enclaves controlled by paramilitary militias.[1] Otherwise, Hudson's assessment applies to Lebanon in the early twenty-first century, with the exception that when his *The Precarious Republic* was published in 1968, Lebanon had only one television station, Télé-Liban, whose ownership the state shared with private individuals. During the war, the total collapse of state authority prompted feuding confessional[2] factions to establish unlicensed radio and television stations as mouthpieces, culminating in the early to mid 1990s with more than 50 television and 100 radio stations (Kraidy, 1998).

Created in 1956 and on the air since 1959, Télé-Liban's fortunes have ebbed and flowed with Lebanon's political mis/fortunes (Boulos, 1996; Kraidy, 1998). It was the only television witness of Lebanon's golden era in the 1960s and early 1979s. During that period, Télé-Liban was a creative laboratory for how to operate a national television in a pluralistic nation. Dramatic productions eschewed characters with names that were clearly Christian or Muslim, such as "Joseph" or "Muhammed," opting instead for neutral Arabic names, such as "Ghassan" and "Ziad." In the golden years of the 1960s and the first half of the 1970s, several dramatic series such as *Ad-Dunia Hayk* and *Abou Melhem* explored inter-confessional coexistence and traditional methods of conflict resolution. A second era stretches from the launch of the Lebanese Broadcasting Corporation (LBC) – the first commercial television station in the Arab world – in 1985 to the Audio-Visual Media Law (AVML), the first legislation of its kind in the region, passed in 1994. During this time, Télé-Liban was unable to compete with LBC, whose new and pirated programming was highly successful with Lebanese audiences. As a result, Télé-Liban went through a protracted decline precipitated by political interference, rolling ownerships of the private shares and technical deficiencies (Kraidy, 1999b; 2003 forthcoming). By revoking Télé-Liban's legal monopoly over broadcasting without proposing a viable solution for the ailing station, while at the same time legalizing private broadcasting, the 1994 AVML launched the third era of Lebanese television, which continues to this day.

The wartime rise of private broadcasting, then, occurred at the expense of Télé-Liban. First on the airwaves in 1985 was the LBC, launched by a Christian paramilitary formation, the Lebanese Forces, as both a commercial company and propaganda tool. LBC's inaugural programming grid relied heavily on imported – mostly pirated – programs such as British comedy, French drama and US sitcoms and soap operas. I distinctly remember the excitement generated by the launch of LBC. As teenagers confined indoors by indiscriminate shelling and bombing, we were glued to the television set, watching *The Benny Hill Show*, *Zora La Rousse*, *Santa Barbara*, the *Cosby Show* and others. These were decisively more attractive than Télé-Liban's stodgy diet of older US police series, German documentaries, French Vaudeville theatre, and the occasional local dramatic series. I vividly recall the growing popularity of LBC's local game shows, a format "adapted" by LBC director Simon Asmar from US and European originals, where participants won consumer goods from the programs' sponsors, ranging from cars to the winner's weight in soap. Numerous other stations followed, creating a mediascape as pluralistic and fragmented as Lebanon's political landscape. Nonetheless LBC played a historic role in introducing US-style commercial television to the Middle East, several years before other Lebanese terrestrial stations and half a decade before it was emulated by the explosive growth in the 1990s of the pan-Arab satellite industry (Kraidy, 2002b).

Lebanon's media and identities: beyond the global–local divide

Lebanon's media landscape has challenged the view that media privatization in developing countries is largely a top-down process triggered by neoliberal reforms. Indeed, media "liberalization" in the Arab world has largely been a top-down process: in Egypt, the state retains editorial control of media; in Qatar, a liberal emir allows the birth of al-Jazeera by decree; Saudi royals finance a private news channel broadcasting in Arabic, first from London, and later from Dubai. In contrast, Lebanon's media sector was radically "privatized" by the war, reflecting the country's religious pluralism and wartime political fragmentation. Therefore, the media privatization in Lebanon has been a bottom-up process. The war that launched private television, however, was from the beginning an entangled web of global, regional and local issues, such as Cold War superpower rivalry, the Arab–Israeli conflict, and Lebanese intercommunal tensions (Khalaf, 2002). As I have argued elsewhere (Kraidy, 2001), the Lebanese television landscape is deeply enmeshed in a local-to-global continuum of political, economic and cultural forces.

Understanding media and culture in contemporary Lebanon thus requires a focus on the local scene, not as a counterpoint to globalization, but as an ethnographic field that invites intricate engagement with a local-to-global continuum. "[T]o write about television in Egypt, or Indonesia, or Brazil," wrote Abu-Lughod (1999), "is to write about the articulation of the trans-national, the national, the local and the personal" (p. 129). Agreeing with this principle, my central research concern is not to examine how the global has influenced the local. Rather, I explore locality in all its complexity – and Lebanese locality is extremely complex – and draw on the early stages of an ongoing research project, examining the multiple forces that shape the construction of locality. Critical to this chapter is an attempt to articulate ethnographic audience research to the political economy of Lebanese media. This entails re-evaluating the meaning of central concepts such as *local* and *field* at the conjunction of ethnography and global media studies.

Modernity has reconstituted identities on a large-scale basis, with the rise of nationalism, for instance, and also by transforming subjectivity at a more intimate level. This process, as García Canclini (1989), Giddens (1990) and many others have argued, has disembedded social practices and spawned hybrid cultures. Modern media technologies play a crucial role by intensifying the incorporation by local cultures of foreign cultural elements, some visibly, others more surreptitiously. It is this phenomenological experience of hybridity that I examine in this chapter through a retrospective analysis of fieldwork, inter-views, and media texts gathered in Lebanon between 1992 and 2001, in ongoing research on Lebanese television and culture. Elsewhere (Kraidy, 1999a) I focused on the strategies used to enact hybrid identities by young, middle-class Maronites living in the central Mount Lebanon *mohafaza*, or province. How was the mass media's "cultural capital appropriated by Maronite youth? How did they deploy it in their daily lives as they made sense of an unstable cultural identity in a country whose history has consisted of a perpetual identity crisis?[3] My main interest continues to lie in the relation of hybridity to power (Kraidy,

2002a), and in the affective articulations that young Maronites establish between media texts and cultural identity.

Public television and the rise of private broadcasting

The anarchic mediascape of the 1975–90 preempted the emergence of a national public sphere, enshrining *de facto* fragmentation into a collection of warring public sphericules (Kraidy, 2000). Even four years after the official end of the war, when the AVML – passed in 1994 but implemented in 1996 – reduced the number of television stations to five (four private stations plus Télé-Liban, as I will subsequently explain), the licensed stations were politically affiliated and confessionally typed. The multiple identity discourses I had experienced while growing up in Lebanon were evident in my fieldwork. Maronites – members of an Eastern branch of Catholicism who historically lived in the Lebanese mountains and were allied to France (Chabry and Chabry, 1987; Gemayel 1984a and b; "Réfléctions sur," 1994; Tabar, 1994) – clearly positioned themselves between different worldviews. For them, these worldviews represent stronger and better defined "Arab" and "Western" identities, roughly equivalent to the realms of "tradition" and "modernity." "Arab" and "Western" identities were articulated as dialogical counterpoints, setting the boundaries of a discursive field where young Maronites constructed a third, hybrid, Lebanese identity. In other words, the "Arab" and "Western" categories were first-order identifications, while "Lebanese" was a second-order identity. This identity, as I have found elsewhere (Kraidy, 1999a), carries progressive elements of identification with both Arab and Western values, in addition to stereotypical statements about Arabs and Westerners, and even some hegemonic perceptions of Arabs. Manifest in the articulation of this hybrid identity is a staunch refusal to belong fully and exclusively to the Arab or Western worldviews, coupled with strong identification with aspects of both Arab and Western culture. As I was told by a 24-year-old medical student (to whom I will give the pseudonym Peter) whom I interviewed in a fast-food restaurant overlooking the Mediterranean sea:

> In some ways, we resemble Arabs. In other things, we resemble Europeans. Nothing makes you distinct as a Maronite Lebanese . . . you have falafel and you have hamburger. What is Lebanon? . . . a creative mixture of the hamburger and the falafel . . .

Peter's perspective, his colorful metaphors – perhaps inspired by the setting – notwithstanding, is very typical among young Maronites. The majority viewed themselves as Arabs or "similar to Arabs" in terms of language, location, and values such as hospitality, social compassion and tightly knit families. But they spurned the social conservatism and anti-Western attitudes that they saw as Arab values. At the same time, they identified with perceived Western values such as freedom but dismissed others such as individualism and sexual promiscuity. These positions, which suggest a degree of cultural categorization, were formulated in conjunction with a vast and eclectic field of media and popular culture consumption including Lebanese, Arab, French and American cultural fare.

Media texts and hybrid local identity

The abundance of inexpensive and accessible foreign programming, the bilingualism (and in many instances, trilingualism) of Lebanese audiences, and the lack of investment in local programming, have impacted Lebanese television production.[4] Local programming in Lebanon consists mainly of current affairs, variety and game shows, while dramatic productions have remained relatively sparse. A notable exception was a dramatic series produced in 1994 by Télé-Liban called *The Storm Blows Twice*. It depicted contemporary Lebanese society caught in the social and cultural dilemmas of the transition between tradition and modernity, with characters struggling to keep their balance between two competing, even clashing sets of values. *The Storm Blows Twice* aired on Wednesdays during prime time, and was remarkably popular among the young Maronites who shared their viewing experience.

The Storm Blows Twice's "in between" social and cultural position was enacted in formal and stylistic choices. These include the clothing style of the actors mixing simple Lebanese middle-class attire with fashion accessories in tune with international style, what Fuad, a 27-year-old hospitality professional with whom I had several long conversations, described as "a mixture of classical clothing with avant-garde fashion." Audience members also liked the production style, characterized by fluid camera movements, dynamic editing, high-quality acting and overall sophisticated creative execution. Besides its attractive production values, the series was praised for its "realistic" and "sincere" depiction of Lebanese society. Whereas Peter, the medical student with a proclivity for culinary metaphors, told me that the *The Storm Blows Twice* "carries a chunk of the problems of Lebanese society and its anxieties," Hala, a 25-year-old development worker whose house I often visited, offered a more detailed description. After praising the "excellent acting" and the "wonderful story," she said:

> It is the life of a woman who got divorced. You know, in Lebanon, *divorce is a taboo*. A woman who divorces is regarded negatively. Anyway, she lived around twenty years with her husband, bearing him . . . She cooks for him and pampers him. But whenever he feels like it, he fools around with other women.

In Lebanon, divorce is indeed taboo. Besides being negatively looked upon, it is very difficult to achieve through the courts. Matters such as divorce, marriage, birth and death fall under the jurisdiction of religious authorities. For instance, civil marriage is legally non-existent in Lebanon, because marriage is outside the prerogatives of the state: it is the exclusive domain of the church or mosque. In the Maronite community, where conservative Catholic values dominate, divorce is virtually impossible. Couples with compelling reasons are granted permission to separate, but unless there are exceptional circumstances, separated couples remain legally wedded. These legal practices have proven to be resilient as a proposal to establish civil marriage sponsored by then President of the Republic Elias Hrawi failed throughout 1998 to overcome a concerted opposition campaign spearheaded by Christian and Muslim clergymen.

The young men and women – there were no significant gender differences, although women tended to be more forthcoming in raising this issue – with whom I spoke admired the female characters for daring to take controversial action to improve their lives. They also praised the writer and director of the series for treating controversial issues thoroughly, and for presenting unconventional solutions. Both male and female participants mentioned the difficulty for some women in Lebanon to strike a balance between their professional and personal lives. Other attractive features of the program were the sincerity of actors in discussing controversial issues such as pre-marital sex, drugs and gender relations. As Serge, a 24-year-old engineering student from a rural, conservative background, summed it up, the series was "refreshing" because it showed "a mixed cultural reality."

As I have already mentioned, *The Storm Blows Twice* addresses the dilemmas of Lebanese society torn between tradition and its strictures on one hand, identified by the audience as typically Eastern, and on the other hand modernity and its promise of freedom from social and religious restrictions, identified as Western. As a young university student aptly described it to me, the series represented "that tearing apart between Western and Eastern values." Interestingly, what viewers appreciated the most was the fact that *The Storm Blows Twice* showed that breaking taboos was not impossible, as long as it was not done in a confrontational manner. Also, they admired the fact that the characters only defied some traditional conventions, while adhering to other social norms. In doing so, they picked from both tradition and modernity, but did not completely embrace either of the two, enacting a hybrid identity.

Audience members' propensity to position themselves between worlds became even clearer when they shared with me their musical preferences, including favorites they identified as typically Lebanese: the music and songs of Lebanon's most famous family of musicians, composers and singers, the Rahbanis. The popularity of the songs and music of the Rahbanis marked a peculiar exception to the preponderance of television in the life of the young people involved in this project. The Rahbani brothers Assi, Mansour and Elias enjoy a mythical status in Lebanese culture. Their music, a mixture of European (classical) music, classical Arabic music and Lebanese folk melodies, was popularized by the equally mythical Fairuz, whose unique voice has mesmerized audiences across the Arab world, in addition to prestigious Western concert halls such as Bercy in Paris and the Royal Festival Hall in London. Fairuz sings mostly in colloquial Lebanese Arabic, and her music is seen as a mixture of Western and Eastern influences, which to young Maronites is "typically Lebanese," hence their unabashed enthusiasm for her music.

Fairuz and Assi's son, the musician, composer, singer, actor, writer, director, satirist and leftist social critic Ziad Rahbani, is credited by some in Lebanon with introducing jazz into Arabic music. He too was greatly popular. Elham, a 25-year-old videographer with a tendency to express herself in French, expressed a fascination with Ziad's music and songs. She said of him:

> Ziad Rahbani makes great music. I love straddling two cultures [à cheval entre deux cultures]. He . . . mixed jazz with Eastern music. He mixed blues guitar scales with the *taqassim* [Arabic scales] of the *oud* [traditional Arab instrument]. He mixed Charlie Parker with Sayyed Darwish . . . He rendered "Round Midnight" with the *oud* and the *qanoun* [another string Arab instrument]. *The result is unique, special. It is not Western, but not Arabic. It is more Lebanese than anything else. It is in between. It is more Lebanese than the cedar.*
>
> (emphasis mine)

Young Maronites lavished praise on Ziad Rahbani's music, songs and plays. Beyond his artistic accomplishments, Ziad Rahbani and his work were significant to the people I spoke with on another, more important level. For them, like his mother, he was "typically Lebanese" due to his "mixing" and "blending" of cultures. In the discussion I will argue that Ziad's vision of Lebanon was completely different from, even antagonistic to, that of his parents. But the young Maronites I spoke with did not make that distinction. To them, Ziad mixed both Western and Arab elements in a way that transformed both, producing a music which was, to repeat Elham's words, "more Lebanese than the cedar." Fuad's rendition of that theme was even more exalted:

> Fairuz and the Rahbanis sing us! They sing Lebanon at its best. *They sing Lebanon the mixture, Lebanon the mélange, Lebanon East and West and neither of them, Lebanon Christian and Muslim and both of them, Lebanon the in between.*
>
> (emphasis mine)

The political economy of mediated hybridity

How do the affective articulations that young Maronites establish with media texts relate to the structural form of Lebanese media and cultural industries? How do the performed identities I have observed in fieldwork relate to the media programs that young Maronites watch? How do local political circumstances mediate the cultural capital brought to this audience by television? In short, how does the ethnography of a Lebanese audience articulate the political economy of Lebanese media? In the remainder of this chapter I will attempt to elucidate these questions. Following Abu-Lughod's (1999) observation that "for a truly thick description, we need to find ways to interrelate [the] various modes of the social life of television" (p. 114), what Martín-Barbero (2000) called "cultural mediations," I will draw on the Lebanese context to explore the nexus of audience ethnography and political economy in global media studies.

In 1996 all Lebanese television stations were forced to close, except four private television stations (plus Télé-Liban) that obtained licenses under the auspices of the 1994 AVML. LBC, which was awarded a license after a reshuffling of its board of shareholders to include influential politicians, remains Lebanon's leading station. Murr Television (MTV), opened in 1991, belonged to the brother of the Deputy Prime Minister, and was initially oriented towards entertainment programming, forgoing a news department for the first three or four years of its existence. Since 1997, when government officials attempted to ban an interview with an exiled opposition figure, MTV has increasingly become the voice of the opposition, leading to its forced shutdown on September 4, 2002 (Kraidy, 2002d). At the time of its forced closure, I was told by Lebanese media sources that MTV approached LBC's domestic audience ratings, due to a large extent to its oppositional stance towards the regime. Future Television (FTV), affiliated with Prime Minister Rafik al-Hariri, has a pro-business, pro-Saudi message, in line with Hariri's neoliberal economic agenda. The National Broadcasting Network (NBN), controlled by Speaker of the Council of Deputies Nabih Berri, is the smallest of the stations and does not really compete at the national level. NBN followed a niche approach, focusing on cultural and current affairs programming. Later, two religious stations, Télé-Lumière, affiliated with the Maronite clergy, and al-Manar, owned by Hizbollah, the fundamentalist Shiite formation leading anti-Israeli guerrilla resistance in South Lebanon, were also allowed to continue broadcasting, but without being granted official licenses like LBC, MTV, FTV and NBN.

These four stations reflected Lebanon's confessional landscape. LBC was *the* Maronite Christian station, FTV *the* Sunnite Muslim station, NBN *the* Shiite Muslim station, and MTV *the* Greek Orthodox Christian station, in which the Druze community was rumored to have some influence. MTV was less confessionally typed than the other stations, because its owner and the Greek Orthodox community in Lebanon did not have a predictably confessional political discourse. Consequently, MTV and Télé-Liban could have become television stations with a national discourse transcending confessional affiliations and loyalties. Unfortunately, this potential was squandered, as MTV became increasingly associated with the mostly Christian opposition, while Télé-Liban was appropriated by politicians who did not own television stations, and was eventually stripped of much of its resources, forced in late 2002 to re-broadcast old series from the 1960s and 1970s in order to maintain a primetime presence. After nearly fifty years of existence, the lack of political cover and confessional affiliation have reduced Télé-Liban to a shadow of its former self.

Beyond cultural proximity? Texts, audiences and institutions

What articulations exist between these structural aspects of the Lebanese media and the results of the ethnographic study discussed earlier in this chapter? Young Maronites have unequivocally gravitated towards domestic productions that they claimed to be typically Lebanese, illustrating the predicament of inhabiting cultural crossroads. Does this resonance between hybrid television programs and popular music on one hand, and an existential experience of cultural hybridity on the other hand, merely constitute an example of what Straubhaar (1991) and others have called "cultural proximity"? Or is there something more to be read in the fact that the two most popular texts (as will be explicated shortly) among young Maronites are not compatible with the political orientation usually ascribed to the Maronite community?

What appears to be a lack of compatibility between audiences and texts is noteworthy. Ziad Rahbani's vision of Lebanon is markedly different from that of his parents. The plays created and executed by Assi and Fairuz became central events at the International Baalbeck Festival in the 1950s and 1960s, putting Lebanon on the global cultural map. These were lavish folkloric celebrations of the history and culture of a Lebanon basking in glory. In sharp contrast to this patriotic romanticism, Ziad's plays and songs, in which he often parodies his parents' creations, are a mixture of deep disappointment and cynicism, rendered in the biting sarcasm that is Ziad's landmark. In the elder Rahbanis' productions, the Arabic spoken is a Lebanese lingua franca reflecting Lebanon's pride as a unified, sovereign and green nation. Ziad's plays and songs, however, are hetero-glossic reflections of Lebanon's fractured ethnic and class landscape, as enacted by the different accents of his actors: a working-class Bastawi accent mixes with a middle-class spoken Lebanese peppered with French, in addition to broken, gender-confused Arabic spoken by Armenian characters. While his parents were not politically active beyond composing and singing both for Lebanon and, in a more limited fashion, the Palestinian cause, Ziad Rahbani is a known leftist activist who during Lebanon's civil war left Maronite-controlled East Beirut to live in predominantly Muslim West Beirut. Ziad's take on Lebanon's descent into chaos is expressed in his song " 'Oum Fout Nam" (Get Up and Go to Sleep):

> Get up and go to sleep . . .
> and dream . . .
> That our country has become a country
> Get up and go to sleep . . .
> These days
> A child can shut down a *hara* [neighborhood]
> This, a country?
> No, not a country!

A gang of people added/united,
Added/united? No!
Subtracted/proposed? No!
Hit/multiplied? No!
Divided . . .
Get up and go to sleep . . .
and dream . . .

The song's resigned disappointment and bitter statement about the Lebanese polity has a powerful resonance, albeit ironic, with Lebanese youth. Ziad fully exploits the polysemy of the Arabic language, in which words for the mathematical operations *addition, subtraction* and *division* also mean, respectively, *unity, posing* (of an option or a problematic) and *division*. Ziad's bitterness about the war is also clear when he sings about a "child shutting down a hara," a reference to the armed thugs, domestic and foreign, who terrorized the Lebanese population during the war. This is in contrast to Fairuz's declaration of undying love to her country, regardless of shortcomings, in the song "Bhebbak Ya Loubnan" (I love you, Oh Lebanon):

I love you, oh Lebanon
My nation I love you
In your North, In your South
In your plains I love you
You ask what is wrong, and what is not
I love you, oh Lebanon
My nation I love you . . .

If you were to leave me
Dearest of lovers
The world would become a lie

I love you, oh Lebanon
My nation I love you . . .

They asked me what is happening
My country surrounded with fire and rifles
I told them our country is being reborn
Lebanon is dignity
and a resilient people

Whereas Ziad sees fragmentation as a proof that Lebanon may not be viable as a country, Fairuz sees the destruction of the war as an opportunity for rebirth. That young Maronites perceive both Fairuz and Ziad to embody Lebanon's character reflects an ambivalence about its identity. On one hand, there is the romantic view of Lebanon, replete with epithets such as "green," "beautiful," "proud," sung indefatigably by Fairuz, which is counterbalanced on the other hand with a harsher but more realistic acknowledgement of Lebanon's predicament, rendered in Ziad's acerbic but ultimately sad songs. There is an uncanny parallelism between the two repertoires and the metaphors used for Lebanon, from "Paris of the Orient" and "Switzerland of the East" in its pre-war days to "Precarious Republic" and "Improbable Nation" during conflict.[5]

The *Storm Blows Twice* is also trapped in a contradiction. The series elaborates a secular, ostentatiously progressive ideology, but is popular with members of a community often labeled as socially conservative and politically Christian. What does this apparent paradox tell us about the dynamics between audiences and media content in a pluralistic, multi-confessional country like Lebanon? *The Storm Blows Twice* was produced by Télé-Liban at a time when the half state-owned, half private station was attempting to become a public television in the European, mostly French tradition. Under the leadership of Fouad Naim, who at that time was the director of the station, Télé-Liban initiated an ambitious plan to become a public, national television, headlined with the slogan "The Nation's Imagination." As a dramatic series addressing social issues between and beyond Lebanon's confessional dynamics, *The Storm Blows Twice* was one of the main components of that plan. This move was reminiscent of the station's golden years of the 1960s and early 1970s, when dramatic productions earnestly tried to engage and illustrate the uniqueness of Lebanon's identity as a small, pluralistic, fragile democracy.

As carriers of different worldviews articulating a hybrid positionality, Ziad Rahbani's work and *The Storm Blows Twice* take a predominant cultural position in the Lebanese mediascape, exceeding in importance all other global and local media and cultural products. On the surface, they appear to be textbook examples of "local" productions whose cultural "proximity" makes them popular with Lebanese audiences. However, the local – identified as "typically Lebanese" – character of these texts is ontologically dubious. In international communication research, the "local" often connotes cultural authenticity, the expression of local identity in its historical and cultural dimensions. This notion of the local as unadulterated is foundational to the concept of cultural proximity, whose premise is that audiences tend to prefer local productions because they are proximate to their life experiences. Proximity reduces culture to the idea of tradition, understood as a set of practices performed in a locale with relatively clear spatial demarcations, embodied in a local identity.

A closer reading, however, suggests that rather than being "local," in other words being typed with a distinct and particularistic cultural belonging, these cultural products in fact carry inherent contradictions. The hybridity that emerges as a result of the contextual cohabitation of different cultural forms thus suggests that proximity need not be understood in terms of being close to a well-defined, relatively distinct, cultural sphere. Rather, it may be useful to re-conceptualize the idea of cultural proximity in terms of *relevance* to an existential experience lacking a clearly defined identity because of multiple cultural and ideological forces that bear upon a community like the Maronites. Relevance, writes Fiske (1988), is when "[t]he viewer makes meanings and pleasures from television that are relevant to his or her social allegiances at the moment of viewing" (p. 247). There is a significant difference between "proximity" and "relevance" since proximity is the result of deeply rooted cultural preferences, while relevance is a more contingent manifestation of a connection between media texts and personal identities. It is noteworthy that the idea of cultural proximity can be traced back to the US Foreign Service Institute in the 1940s, where anthropologist and cross-cultural trainer Edward T. Hall emphasized *proxemics*, or use of personal space, as an important dimension of cross-cultural communication (Leeds-Hurwitz, 1990). For Hall, culture consisted of stable, observable, and therefore predictable patterns of behavior. It is this assumption of a synchronic predictability of culture that, in my opinion, distinguishes proximity from relevance. Whereas, according to Fiske, "the criteria for relevance precede the viewing moment," relevance occurs in a "moment of semiosis" which comes to be "when social allegiances and discursive practices are personified and held in *relative stability on a point of relevance*" (1988, p. 247, emphasis mine). In spite of the fact that relevance is not as predictable as a narrowly defined proximity, Cohen (1991) suggests that the issue of relevance has been a recurring, albeit latent, theme in media studies.

Like Ziad Rahbani's music and plays, *The Storm Blows Twice* carries a message that attempts to transcend confessional sensibilities. However, this is not an ideology-free national/ist discourse, but rather a recasting of Syrian Nationalist ideology. One of three political ideologies to have laid claim to Lebanon (see Firro, 2003; Khalaf, 2002; Salibi, 1988; Zamir, 2000), Syrian Nationalism (or Syrianism) calls for the unification of Lebanon, Syria, and parts of historic Palestine into Greater Syria. The other two ideologies are Lebanese nationalism (or Lebanism), which has a Christian undertone (see Phares, 1995) and calls for Lebanon as an independent and fully sovereign nation, and Pan-Arabism, calling for the integration of all Arab countries, from Morocco to Iraq, in one Arab nation. In fact, the series' writer, Choukry Anis Fakhoury, comes from a prominent Lebanese family of writers and journalists known for their Syrian Nationalist political beliefs. This is one of the reasons why *The Storm Blows Twice* was criticized in some Maronite circles for carrying a pro Syrian Nationalist political message. In this context, the concept of "storm" is highly symbolic, since the Syrian Nationalist Party's symbol is the *zawbaa*, a star with jagged edges connoting revolutionary political action. Other signs can be read in that direction, such as a party leader referred to as the *zaim*, or chief, the nickname given by his followers to Antoun Saadé, the founder and ideologue of the Syrian Social Nationalist Party.

The admiration for *The Storm Blows Twice* expressed by young Maronites, whose mainstream political leaders have historically advocated a Lebanese nationalism antagonistic to Syrian Nationalist ideology, raises important questions about the relationship between audience interpretations and television ownership and programming strategies in Lebanese television. As discussed earlier in this chapter, broadcasting licenses were awarded largely according to confessional considerations, in tune with Lebanon's system where resources are distributed under an obsessive formula of "confessional balance" rather than according to merit or competence. The philosophy underscoring this allocation of media holds that each station will cater to its community, so LBC would have a Christian, predominantly Maronite audience, FTV a Sunnite following, and NBN Shiite viewers. While I do not purport to generalize from a study of admittedly limited scope focusing on the youth of one of Lebanon's confessional groups, this chapter nonetheless suggests that the Lebanese state's confessionalist approach to media policy may not correspond to Lebanese audience realities.

The persistence of the confessional formula in the Lebanese polity is a formidable challenge to the establishment of a national public television station, as Télé-Liban's fate painfully demonstrates. The carve-up of the audience on confessional lines by the political elite who negotiated and passed the 1994 AVML ensures the continuing networks of political patronage that constitute the power base of Lebanon's political leaders (see Khalaf, 1987). More importantly, it insures that television would not contribute, as it should, to a *national* public discourse whose existence is essential for Lebanon to move into real civil peace. Now that militia rule has been replaced by *Pax Syriana* – a Lebanese security state under Syrian control – the Lebanese media and political landscape, once pluralistic, is turning monochromatic. The state apparatus exercises a large degree of control over media institutions through indirect and increasingly direct pressure. In late 2002, a growing – and imposed – homogenization of political discourse is palpable in television newscasts and talk-shows.

In the current conjecture, privately owned television stations are unable to contribute to building and strengthening a sense of national citizenship that could over time mitigate the political influence of confessional identities. However, the experience of a segment of Maronite youth with *The Storm Blows Twice* intimates that the right programmes will lead audience segments to "move" out of their traditionally predictable confessional lines. The popularity of a text with a decidedly secular message does not constitute a decisive crossing of confessional boundaries; nonetheless, it is teeming with potential, especially if it indicates, as I think it does, that the Maronite community itself is not monolithic, but is rather diverse across generational and ideological lines.

Historical precedents of programming strategies that aim to cross the Lebanese confessional divide do exist. Since the 1980s, LBC, owned by Maronites, has scheduled special programming during the Muslim Holy month of Ramadan, such as Egyptian *Fawazir Ramadan*, or Ramadan quiz-shows, and Arabic dramas, in order to attract Muslim audiences. A more intriguing example of "cross-over" programming is the serial drama on the Virgin Mary, an Iranian production, that al-Manar, Hizbollah's station, has aired during Ramadan in 2002. Driving on Lebanon's coastal highway during Ramadan in November 2002, I was struck by the numerous billboards promoting this series in predominantly Christian

East Beirut and elsewhere. Surely the broadcast of a drama on the Virgin Mary by a Shiite fundamentalist television station should make media scholars ponder the multiple religious, political and economic considerations that affect programming policies in diverse nations, and renounce simplistic explanations of such phenomena.[6]

Conclusion: ethnography and the "field" in/of global media studies

What conclusions can be drawn from this chapter? To what extent has my attempt to articulate audience ethnography to the political economy of the media been heuristic? By suggesting that young Maronites gravitate towards a program that does not cater to the traditional political concerns identified with the Maronite community in Lebanon, ethnographic fieldwork illustrates some of the fractures of the confessional logic that permeates Lebanon's polity. The structure of Lebanon's media serves the interests of the elites by consolidating their power over their communities. However, this chapter suggests that when presented with well-crafted programs, viewers will watch television programs (and listen to music) that do not cater to the particularistic ideologies of their confessional group. This propensity to cross confessional lines, however, remains fragile in the context of a system whose *raison d'être* has been hijacked by a deeply rooted political confessionalism. Notably, the current media system in place in Lebanon is hard-pressed to contribute to the growth of inter-confessional dialogue. When privately owned media attempt to reach across the lines, it is mostly for commercial considerations, as the Lebanese audience is one of the smallest in the world, and breaking it down into confessionally defined segments reduces it even further, bringing advertising rates to non-viably low levels.[7]

In light of this study's objective to articulate audience ethnography with political economy, focusing on audience interpretations of media texts while at the same time scrutinizing media ownership structures, can we continue with our traditional understanding of the ethnographic field? If we are, as I have proposed, to reformulate the "local" as mixed and hybrid, and not pure and insular, then we also need to re-think the ethnographic "field." If knowledge, as Geertz (1983) famously wrote, is "ineluctably local" (p. 4), and if the local, as I have been arguing, is connected to extra-local forces, and therefore always already hybrid, then the ethnographic field should be understood as a space of articulation. The pristine locales of traditional anthropology where time is frozen and space is bounded by a warped epistemological imagination have been washed over by that phenomena we, with trepidation, call globalization. If the ethnographic field is not a narrowly defined locale where human interaction is observed, but rather a contextualized landscape where we study an entire constellation of political, economic and symbolic forces, on the local, national, regional and global level, what are the field's ontological and epistemological boundaries?

The field is not a text, even if it is conceptualized as a con/text. By exploring an entire field of relations among an audience composed of young, middle-class Maronites, a national historical and political environment, and a media structure controlled by interlocking economic and political elites, this study did not initially focus on a specific media text. It rather investigated media consumption as a bundle of connections between identities, texts and institutions. Had I oriented my fieldwork and designed my interviews in such a way as to focus on one text, it is highly probable I would have failed to grasp the importance of *The Storm Blows Twice*. In all likelihood, I would have focused on *Beverly Hills 90210*, the Fox network series about an upper-class Californian young community, which was also highly popular among young Maronites who told me that its treatment of some youth problems was "relevant to our personal lives." It took a prolonged period of fieldwork, an extended quotidian presence with groups of young Maronites, for *The Storm Blows Twice* to emerge as a paramount text. Hence the importance of focusing on an ethnographic field of relations with popular culture, letting important texts emerge in the course of naturalistic inquiry. The field should therefore be seen as a node of what Tomlinson (1999) calls "complex connectivity."

The field is not a place one visits and leaves, but a space ethnographers remain enmeshed in long after the *in situ* stage of ethnographic observation and composition. As I reflect on my work with young Maronites, the importance of long-term involvement in an ethnographic project dawns on me with full force. In this particular case, my experience with the Maronite community has been lifelong, since I myself am a member, albeit from a distance, of that community. My long-term involvement with the community was since 1972 primarily as a brother, son, friend, relative, neighbor, student. As I moved to the United States twenty years later to become a media scholar, the "blood" ties remain (I am still a brother, son, etc.) but other social ties one develops in quotidian interactions have weakened, some broken – I surely am not a neighbor in Lebanon any more. While I do not wish to revisit the thorny issue of "native" ethnography (Kraidy, 1999a) here, since 1992 I have returned to Lebanon for several extended stays of several months and numerous shorter visits of several weeks, each time conducting research on media and audiences. Quicker, more instrumental ethnographic snapshots would have most probably taken me in a different direction, because they would have involved research designs that focused on one predetermined media text, or one foregone issue, thus skewing naturalistic inquiry.

The field is a space of cultural translation. Obviously border-crossing ethnographic work requires the ability to render words, puns and jokes into the familiarity of (an)other language(s). On a second level, translation involves being able to establish connections between disparate hinges of meaning, connecting audience self-representations *vis-à-vis* media and popular culture with texts and contexts that their narratives elide. In other words, translation entails *the articulation of presence and absence*. For example, perceptions of individual freedom and sexual promiscuity as "Western" values, and of conservatism and repression as "Arab" themes, are in themselves troubling, for they contribute to placing "cultures" into artificial categories that at best trivialize cultural differences and at worst promote intolerance. It is therefore the ethnographer's task to contextualize these perceptions by interpreting the reasons for their elaboration and the dynamics of their use.

The field is also a personal choice, albeit influenced by forces beyond individual ethnographers. The boundaries of this ethnographic field of relations have been to a large extent drawn by my own political and epistemological sensibilities. Numerous times since undertaking this project I have asked myself about my "field selection." At the same time, I keep imagining what it would be like, in postwar Lebanon's highly charged confessional atmosphere, to gain entrée and establish rapport with members of other confessions, customary ethnographic concerns from which my "native" status among Maronites somewhat liberated me. Even further, how would my experience be different if I were to move to other, less evident fields, to which I have no ties except my ethnographic research? My reaction to these questions is grounded in my belief that depth and not breadth should be the hallmark of ethnography.

Although I am tempted to conclude here, to reach the closure that all ethnographers know to be only too ephemeral, I must address the issue of the import of the phenomenon of globalization, which I have hitherto in this chapter resisted addressing directly. In other words, I want to move from the field as the site of ethnography, to global media studies as an emerging field of theory and research (Kraidy, 2002c). The interplay between the political economy of Lebanese media and the narratives of Lebanese audience members proffer that media power is oblique and diffused, which intimates that a model of *articulation* is preferable to a model of *determination* in global media research. The intricate connections between what Appadurai (1996) calls ethnoscapes (in this case the confessional identity of audiences), ideoscapes (ascribed "Western" and "Arab" values), and mediascapes (on the local-to-global continuum) suggest that we can understand a lot more about power if we do not explore it according to predetermined research designs. This chapter is thus an attempt to address social (as opposed to individual) and structural concerns in media ethnography (see Morley, 1992; Willis, 2000). Naturalistic inquiry, because it is epistemologically pliant, is an adequate methodology for excavating the workings of power in culture and communication.

The oblique powers of globalization are manifest to the observer of Arab television. I mentioned earlier that the rise of LBC in 1985 was a harbinger of things to come on Arab television: commercial stations with myriad advertisements, scantily clad women hosting shows, introducing programs, or reporting on the weather, corporate sponsorships, etc. As such, the rise of private television in Lebanon constituted a kind of media globalization *avant la lettre*, a precocious gesture towards neoliberalism that was to find its fulfillment seven years later with the regional media forces unleashed by the Gulf War in 1991. Since then

Arab television has gone increasingly commercial, with a diet of sensationalism, titillation and verbal jousting, while at the same time remaining subject to a degree of political control, with the noteworthy exception of al-Jazeera. At the same time, pan-Arab television has emerged as an arena where taboos are broken, orthodoxies questioned and kings and rulers challenged. More importantly, the rise of the pan-Arab television industry has challenged the dominance of Western news media, as was most spectacularly demonstrated during the March–April 2003 Anglo-American invasion of Iraq. The result is the entrance of the "Arab Street" into the arena of international politics, an ironic statement about audience agency that ethnographers can perhaps appreciate more than others.

Notes

This chapter has benefited from conversations with several Lebanese media professionals. The contribution of Joe Khalil, television director and producer, is especially appreciated. All translations from Arabic and French are mine, unless otherwise indicated.

1 In 1989, under Saudi sponsorship, the Document of National Understanding, better known as the Ta'if Agreement, put an official end to the conflict. However, more than a decade later, there has still not been meaningful national reconciliation. Confessional tensions are running high, and the country's most divisive issue remains relations with Syria, which enjoys full hegemony over Lebanese public life.
2 I prefer the term "confession" to "sect" when writing about the more than eighteen religious groups represented in the Lebanese population. Recent estimates (there has not been a census in seven decades) put the population at slightly under 4 million and the Muslim to Christian ratio at 6 to 4. The main groups are Shiite Muslims, Sunni Muslims, Maronite Christians, and Greek Orthodox Christians. For more in the issue of confessionalism or sectarianism, see Makdisi (2000).
3 Lebanon's civil upheavals in 1958 and 1974 brought to the surface Lebanon's fundamental identity dilemma: is Lebanon a unique country with Phoenician ascendance, Western affinities, distinct from its Arab environment, as some Lebanese nationalists argued? Or is Lebanon an integral part of the Arab world, inseparable part of a whole, sharing the history, cultural values and national identity of its neighbors (see Salibi, 1971)? This question has ensnared Lebanon in a permanent identity crisis, imbricated in regional politics, as the Arab–Israeli conflict has upset the country's delicate demographic balance and its fragile political equilibrium (see Salibi, 1988). The Arab identity issue has been settled in Ta'if, which proclaimed Lebanon to be a sovereign Arab country.
4 Access to television in Lebanon is indeed inexpensive. There are no licensing or subscription fees and the only expense for the viewer is the cost of the television set and the electricity to power it. Private neighborhood cable networks constitute a peculiar phenomenon. Enterprising citizens pay satellite subscription fees and establish their cable network that can include hundreds, even upwards of a thousand subscribers. While illegal, these businesses are ubiquitous in Lebanon, and promote their services through printed flyers and word of mouth. In late 2002, a household linked to such a network enjoys an excess of 90 channels, including all the Arab satellite channels and the major American and European

cable and satellite channels, ranging from al-Jazeera to ESPN to Canal Plus. This "package" typically costs around US $10 per month!

5 While "Switzerland of the Middle East" and "Paris of the East" were propagated in the international press, metaphors of decay were captured in titles of books about Lebanon: e.g. Hudson's (1968) *The precarious republic* and Mackey's (1989) *Lebanon: Death of a nation.* See Khalaf (2002) for more on this issue.

6 Hizbollah-owned al-Manar's satellite broadcasts are highly popular with Arab audiences, especially in the Levant. While adhering to an Islamist discourse inspired by the Iranian revolution, the station's overt focus is the resistance to Israel. In the early to mid-1990s, al-Manar dispatched cameramen with commandos executing operations against the Israeli army occupying southern Lebanon. Vivid, "reality" footage was replayed on the nightly newscast to great effect. Also, al-Manar has challenged the stereotype of the veiled, subservient Muslim woman by employing articulate women, in Islamic dress, as program hosts.

7 This was one of the main forces leading to the 1994 Audio-Visual Media Law. With numerous media outlets vying for a national audience of a couple of millions, media proliferation brought Lebanon's once thriving advertising industry to the brink of collapse. For a systematic analysis of the political, economic and technical forces leading to the establishment of Lebanon first broadcasting law, see Kraidy (1998).

References

Abu-Lughod, L. (1999). The interpretation of culture(s) after television. In S. Ortner (ed.), *The fate of "culture": Geertz and beyond.* Berkeley: University of California Press.

Appadurai, A. (1996). *Modernity at large: Cultural dimensions of globalization.* Minneapolis: University of Minnesota Press.

Berger, R. A. (1993). From text to (field)work and back again. *Anthropological Quarterly* 66(4), 174–186.

Boulos, J. C. (1996). *La Télé: Quelle histoire!* Beyrouth: Fiches du Monde Arabe.

Chabry, L. and Chabry, A. (1987). *Politique et minorités au Moyen-Orient: Les raisons d'une explosion.* Paris: Maisonneuve et Larose.

Cohen, J. R. (1991). The "relevance" of cultural identity in audiences' interpretations of mass media. *Critical Studies in Mass Communication* 8(4), 442–454.

Firro, K. M. (2003). *Inventing Lebanon: Nationalism and the state under the mandate.* London: I. B. Tauris.

Fiske, J. (1988). Meaningful moments. *Critical Studies in Mass Communication* 5, 246–250.

García Canclini, N. (1989). *Culturas híbridas: Estrategias para entrar y salir de la modernidad.* Mexico City: Grijalbo.

Geertz, C. (1983). *Local knowledge.* New York: Basic Books.

Gemayel, N. (1984a). *Les échanges culturels entre les Maronites et l'Europe: Du Collège Maronite de Rome (1584) au Collège de Ayn Warqa (1789).* Beirut.

Gemayel, N. (1984b). *Les échanges culturels entre les Maronites et l'Europe, Deuxième partie: Les contributions des élèves du Collège Maronite de Rome à l'essor du mouvement culturel au Liban.* Beirut.

Giddens, A. (1990). *The consequences of modernity.* Palo Alto, CA: Stanford University Press.

Hudson, M. (1968). *The precarious republic*. New York: Random House.

Khalaf, S. (1987). *Lebanon's predicament*. New York: Columbia University Press.

Khalaf, S. (2002). *Civil and uncivil violence in Lebanon: A history of the internationalization of communal conflict*. New York: Columbia University Press.

Kraidy, M. M. (1998). Broadcasting regulation and civil society in post-war Lebanon. *Journal of Broadcasting and Electronic Media* 42(3), 387–400.

Kraidy, M. M. (1999a). The local, the global and the hybrid: A native ethnography of glocalization. *Critical Studies in Media Communication* 16(4), 456–477.

Kraidy, M. M. (1999b). State control of television news in 1990s Lebanon. *Journalism and Mass Communication Quarterly* 76(3), 485–498.

Kraidy, M. M. (2000). Television and civic discourse in postwar Lebanon. In L. A. Gher and H. Y. Amin (eds), *Civic discourse and digital age communications in the Middle East* (pp. 3–18). Stamford, CT: Ablex.

Kraidy, M. M. (2001). National television between localization and globalization. In Y. Kamalipour and K. Rampal (eds), *Media, sex and drugs in the global village* (pp. 261–272). Lanham, MD: Rowman and Littlefield.

Kraidy, M. M. (2002a). Hybridity in cultural globalization. *Communication Theory* 12(3), 316–339.

Kraidy, M. M. (2002b). Arab satellite television between globalization and regionalization. *Global Media Journal* 1, 1, available http://www.lass.calumet.purdue.edu/cca/gmj/submitted documents/kraidy.htm

Kraidy, M. M. (2002c). Ferment in global media dtudies. *Journal of Broadcasting and Electronic Media* 46(4), 630–640.

Kraidy, M. M. (2002d). State–media relations in Lebanon: National, regional and global dimensions of the shutdown of MTV. Paper presented at the convention of the Middle East Studies Association, Washington, DC, November 23–26.

Kraidy, M. M. (2003, forthcoming). Emerging Arab media legal frameworks: Lebanon's national television between the state and the market. In Y. Haddad and B. Stowasser (eds), *Arab Legal Frameworks in Transition*.

Leeds-Hurwitz, W. (1990). Notes on the history of intercultural communication: The Foreign Service Institute and the mandate for intercultural training. *Quarterly Journal of Speech* 76, 262–281.

Mackey, S. (1989). *Lebanon: Death of a nation*. Chicago: Congdon and Weed.

Makdisi. U. (2000). *The culture of sectarianism*. Berkeley, CA: University of California Press.

Martín-Barbero, J. (2000). The cultural mediations of television consumption. In I. Hagen and J. Wasko (eds), *Consuming audiences? Production and reception in media research* (pp. 145–162). Cresskill, NJ: IAMCR and Hampton Press.

Morley, D. (1992). *Television, audiences and cultural studies*. London: Routledge.

Murphy, P. D. (1999). Doing audience ethnography: A narrative account of establishing ethnographic identity and locating interpretive communities in fieldwork. *Qualitative Inquiry* 5(4), 479–504.

Nightingale, V. (1996). *Studying audiences: The shock of the real*. London: Routledge.

Phares, W. (1995). *Lebanese Christian nationalism: The rise and fall of an ethnic resistance*. Boulder, CO: Lynne Rienner.

Réfléctions sur la crise de la communauté maronite. *Les Cahiers de L'Orient*, 1993, third trimester/ 1994, first trimester, 221–251.

Salibi, K. S. (1971). The Lebanese identity. *Journal of Contemporary History* 6(1), 76–86.

Salibi, K. S. (1988). *A house of many mansions: The history of Lebanon reconsidered.* Berkeley, CA: University of California Press.

Straubhaar, J. (1991). Beyond media imperialism: Asymmetrical interdependence and cultural proximity. *Critical Studies in Mass Communication* 8(1), 29–38.

Tabar, P. (1994). The image of power in Maronite political discourse. *Beirut Review* 7, 91–114.

Tomlinson, J. (1999). *Globalization and culture.* Chicago: University of Chicago Press.

Willis, P. (2000). *The ethnographic imagination.* Cambridge: Polity Press.

Zamir, M. (2000). *Lebanon's quest: The road to statehood 1926–1939.* London: I. B. Tauris.

Part V

AFTERWORD

16

MEDIA ETHNOGRAPHY

Local, global, or translocal?

Marwan M. Kraidy and Patrick D. Murphy

"The task of ethnography," Appadurai (1991) wrote, is "the unraveling of a conundrum: what is the nature of locality, as a lived experience, in a globalized, deterritorialized world?" (p. 196). In media studies, ethnography's potential to make the local experience of globalization intelligible remains to be fully exploited. To be fair, this is a challenging task, which requires an inter-disciplinary commitment to theoretical and methodological creativity. For how else can ethnography, with its fundamentally *local* ethos, illuminate the experience of *globalization*, albeit manifested at the local level? Ethnography's commitment to depth clashes with the epistemological breadth that is necessary to comprehend the multifaceted complexity of globalization. This book has taken up the challenge to articulate ethnography and globalization at a nexus where we think many people living in late modernity experience the global in their local life: mediated cultural consumption.

The chapters we have selected for inclusion in this book address globalization with varying degrees of depth. Some, like Juluri's chapter (Chapter 12) on Indian audiences and global audience research, have directly put globalization at the heart of the analysis. Others, such as Podber's chapter (Chapter 11), have taken a resolutely local path to raise important questions about global society. Strelitz directly frames his chapter (Chapter 13) within the local–global encounter. While they may differ in approach, all contribute to the debate on the local–global nexus in its multiple dilemmas and implications: the position-ality of the researcher is dissected in the chapters by Darling-Wolf (Chapter 7) on Japanese notions of beauty, by Yokomizo Akindes on the lived experience of being an ethnographer in Hawai'i (Chapter 9), and by Buarque de Almeida on "genderization" pressures in the field in Brazil (Chapter 10). Couldry (Chapter 3), Clua (Chapter 4), and Kraidy (Chapter 15) attempt to re-locate the ethnographic field at a time when mobile populations, deterritorialized media, and postmodern theory have dislocated the sites of inquiry. At a time when the debate on globalization is replete with hyperbole on new, post-broadcast media technologies, the chapters by Algan (Chapter 2), Law (Chapter 5), Yokomizo Akindes (Chapter 9), and Podber (Chapter 11) remind us that radio, this supposedly antiquated and blind medium, constitutes much of people's mediascape in Turkey, rural Appalachia in the United States, Hawaii, and India.

Hybridity and the global/local nexus in media studies

The orientation of individual contributions to this book notwithstanding, we conceive of it as a collaborative endeavor tackling the powerful but often surreptitious experience of living in an increasingly connected and mediated world. As Appadurai (1996) famously put it, our era is characterized by disjunctures between and across ethnoscapes, ideoscapes, mediascapes and others. These interlocking scapes have intensified cross-cultural contact and spawned a dual process of cultural fusion and fragmentation that scholars increasingly capture with the vocabulary of hybridity, pioneered by Nestor García-Canclini (1989) and Homi Bhabha (1994) among others. That the local–global encounter is always already hybrid is relatively clear. Less evident are the epistemological, ontological and political implications of hybridity. If ethnography is to take a leading role in illuminating the articulation of globalization and localization, it is imperative that ethnographers make a commitment to exploring and understanding the forces that shape different forms of hybridity.

This commitment is important for the development of global media studies. Unqualified theoretically and empirically, the argument that hybridity and borderlessness embody resistance rather than accommodation appears hopeful at best in an age of globalization contingent upon human economies enmeshed in the institutions that provide the ideological base for consumer culture. In postcolonial studies, the concept of hybridity itself is at the center of a heated debate concerning the cooptation of concepts of cultural specificity by global capitalism (Kraidy, 2002). To ferret out this connection between ideology and experience, or in more ethnographic terms, between history and biography, it is crucial to understand how cultural *influence* has been understood in international communication theory and research, and how the idea of hybridity itself has been used to theorize influence in global culture.

Mass media influence on society and culture is a contested issue in the field of international communication. In the 1940s, exponents of early theories of media influence, commonly referred to as "magic bullet" or "hypodermic needle" theories, believed that the media, especially television, had powerful effects on audiences. Since then, the debate about the socio-cultural influence of the mass media has not met with agreement among scholars as to the level, scope and implications of media influence. After the dominance of international communication research and theorizing focused on nation-building and national development during the 1940s and 1950s, media/cultural imperialism emerged in the 1960s as a critical alternative to the instrumental rationality of the modernization paradigm in which development communication was grounded. During the 1960s and 1970s, numerous studies demonstrated how greatly unbalanced media flows were between the haves and the have-nots, with the West, especially the United States, the leading exporter of media and popular culture, and smaller developing nations net importers of American and other Western cultural commodities.

However, while a constellation of cultural imperialism studies (Galtung, 1971; Mattelart, 1972, 1977, 1983; Schiller 1969, 1976; and many others) interrogated how the economic inequities between the Western countries and the rest of the world were reflected in international media and information flows, these same researchers stopped short of engaging the "feudal" inequities and cultural practices that media users faced in their everyday lives. One of the critique of cultural imperialism's shortcomings was its assumption of effects in the realm of the "everyday" without actually studying how people made meanings out of media messages. This translated into a weak theorization of the issue of "culture" in cultural imperialism research (Fejes, 1981). It has also been argued that the cultural imperialism thesis does not apply in some national contexts such as China (Lee, 1984) and Brazil (Straubhaar, 1984). Others criticized cultural imperialism on an ideological level (Rogers and Schement, 1984), exposing their own ideological biases in the process. In the last decade, international communication has moved into a fragmented eclecticism in which there is a movement away from "cultural imperialism" and towards "cultural globalization." While some have welcomed this development (see Tomlinson, 1991 and 1999), others have warned of its pitfalls (Curran and Park, 2000; Nordenstreng, 2001).

In this environment, an ethnographic approach to the local–global nexus is useful to the extent that it contextualizes different hybridities and thus moves away from grand theories such as "cultural imperialism" and "cultural globalization" towards a more contextualized and comparative approach to the operation of power in culture. As the local becomes increasingly enmeshed in the global and vice versa, international communication has also expanded its boundaries to include approaches based on the interpretive social sciences such as cultural sociology and anthropology, and on the humanities such as literary criticism. It is these developments that lead us to the designation "global media studies" which indicates the inclusion of a broader spectrum of approaches to media and culture than traditional international mass communication research. The resulting challenge is that as ethnography has been included, and thus appropriated, for the study of global media, our understanding of what constitutes ethnographic research changes as well.

Ethnography and its theoretical and epistemological tensions

This changing understanding of what constitutes "ethnography" in the context of global media studies brings us back to the challenge formulated in the first chapter of this book, and again summarized in the introduction to this chapter: how can ethnography as an essentially local endeavor contribute to the growth of media studies increasingly concerned with globalization? This issue can only be resolved through a detour through the theoretical and epistemological tensions inherent in the ethnographic turn in media studies, which can be traced back to the formative years of active audience research in Great Britain.

Two texts have been foundational to the active audience formation in British cultural studies. Stuart Hall's seminal essay on encoding/decoding (1997) and David Morley's *The Nationwide Audience* (1980) launched a decade of interpretive audience research which included Ang (1985), Buckingham (1987), and Hobson (1982). This research tradition attracted a large number of adherents, interested in its theoretical sophistication and interdisciplinary orientation. Against cultural imperialism's monolithic conceptual structure and pessimistic views on domination, they suggested more variegated theoretical options and upheld the possibility of alternative "readings" of mass mediated texts. Also, the active audience formation emerged as a visible strand in the interdisciplinary project of cultural studies, and gained widespread interdisciplinary exposure as a result of the burgeoning interest in and increased institutionalization of that project. Despite its success, however, the active audience tradition has elicited criticism, discussed in this book in Chapters 1 (Murphy and Kraidy), 2 (Algan) and 3 (Couldry).

Most importantly, the qualification of the qualitative audience studies in the active audience formation as "ethnographic" is controversial. Nightingale (1996) has argued that most studies conducted under the active audience rubric were more "documentarian" than "ethnographic." In media studies, the ethnographic designation was more a rhetorical strategy to disassociate cultural-studies-based audience research from functionalist perspectives on the audience such as "uses and gratifications." Another explanation lies in the rocky relationship between cultural studies and much of the social sciences. When cultural studies incorporated audience research, according to Nightingale (1996), "the cultural studies audience experiment was suddenly open to methodological demands and criticism from social scientists" (p. 108). Ethnography was thus invoked as method, while in practice qualitative audience research differed from ethnography because of the lack of sustained engagement in the field and the focus on letters of interview transcripts at the expense of the numerous details, events and observations that anthropologists are trained to record and interpret in ethnographic fieldwork. This prompted some anthropologists to remark about audience studies that "despite their considerable theoretical sophistication they are ethnographically thin" (Abu-Lughod, 1999). In this book, we (Chapter 1) and Couldry (Chapter 3) contextualize that criticism, while chapters by Darling-Wolf (Chapter 7), La Pastina (Chapter 8), Akindes (Chapter 9), de Almeida (Chapter 10), Podber (Chapter 11) and others, clearly demonstrate that media scholars can produce excellent ethnographies based on prolonged fieldwork, thick description, and deep translation.

The lack of long-term, embodied fieldwork is perhaps what is behind the weakness of *cultural translation* in those qualitative audience studies. Advocating a naturalistic line of inquiry, qualitative audience research in cultural studies depended heavily on "the authenticating quality" (Nightingale, 1996, p. 111) of relatively raw data in its analysis. To be fair, this tendency is undoubtedly grounded in the critical imperative to unmask power differences in social science research. From that standpoint, including as much as possible the "voice" of the researched balances the power of representation vested in the researcher. This commitment to multivocality, however laudable, can lead to ethnographic thinness if taken too literally. This is especially true of cross-cultural contexts. Despite their feminist and critical grounding, many studies conducted in the 1980s under the active audience rubric in cultural studies were not in fact cross-cultural, but largely consisted of researchers working in their own cultural milieu. As such, the weakness of cultural translation was not a fatal flaw.

In the context of *global* media studies, however, a lack of cultural translation is in effect a deadly blow to qualitative audience research. This is because the culturally specific meanings that have long been ethnography's bread and butter cannot be adequately rendered without a complex and multifaceted process of cultural translation. Our contributors have also underscored the importance of cultural translation. Juluri's title "Ask the West, will dinosaurs come back?" connotes the translative dimension of ethnographic work (Chapter 12). Similarly, Couldry's treatment of the ethnographic problematic of "being there" to "reveal" what he calls "the systematic order of a wider culture" (Chapter 3) and Darling-Wolf's grappling with "multiple selves" (Chapter 7) address what is mainly a tension associated with cultural translation. The cross-cultural rendering of experience in terms intelligible to an audience mostly located outside of the space of fieldwork is at heart a process of translation laced with considerations of class (Podber, Chapter 11), race and ethnicity (Akindes, Chapter 9; Murphy, Chapter 14; Kraidy, Chapter 15), and gender (Darling-Wolf, Chapter 7; de Almeida, Chapter 10; La Pastina, Chapter 8). From this internationalist and cross-cultural perspective, Nightingale's assertion that "translation is crucial and inescapable in cultural research" (1996, p. 111) is foremost in importance.

Towards a translocal ethnography in global media studies

The theoretical and epistemological tensions inherent in ethnography's move into media and cultural studies (Murphy, 1999) emerged at the precise moment when media studies is grappling with the phenomenon of globalization. The dilemma of whether to sacrifice the breadth that is essential for an understanding of globalization to gain in ethnographic depth necessitates new deployments of ethnography, one that is locally based but globally engaged. At this conjecture, we believe that Marcus's idea of "multi-sited ethnography" (1998) is a productive epistemological choice for studying complex, multilayered and geographically diverse dynamics. Coupled with translocal ethnography, a critical theory of hybridity helps focus on the diffuse workings of power and counter-power. As Marcus (1998) put it, ethnography should help in disentangling "accommodation" and "resistance" in cultural dynamics, in order to understand "the uncompromising sense of paradox in the intertwining of diversity and homogeneity that will not allow an easy parsing of these two terms" (p. 61). For García-Canclini (1989), understanding the paradox of cultural mixture does not entail a final theory of hybridity with a stable ontology and a clearly preferred epistemology. Rather, as Rosaldo writes in the preface of the English translation of *Culturas híbridas*, "the term hybridity, as used by García-Canclini, never resolves the tension between its conceptual polarities" (1995, p. xv). Because of this theoretical instability, empirical examinations of hybrid cultural contexts must be flexible and comparative. After all, theories of hybridity help us understand the local not merely as a locale, but as a crossroads of transcultural influences. We thus believe that a translocal ethnography is a productive methodology to study the hybrid cultural processes at the heart of globalization.

Appending the prefix "trans-" to local as a qualifier of the kind of ethnography we are advocating expresses our belief that ethnography's importance lies more in its capacity to comprehend the articulation of the global with the local, than in its supposed ability to understand the local in isolation of large-scale structures and processes. A translocal ethnography builds on that to focus on connections between several local social spaces, exploring hitherto neglected *local-to-local articulations*. In terms of transnational cultural influence, translocal ethnography reformulates Galtung's "wheel model" (1971) of cultural imperialism by shifting the focus of research on connections between several points on the periphery of the wheel, without pre-determining that such connections must necessarily go through the core. Ethnography then is a productive methodological and theoretical choice that is well suited to unearth the socio-cultural practices that are generated and in turn preserve the working and agenda of globalization. It is important to note that the ethnography we are discussing here is not only the traditional ethnography of anthropology, which focused on tradition, nor the ethnography of sociology, with its focus on modernity, but an ethnography that is, out of epistemological and political necessity, fundamentally multisited and interdisciplinary.

Furthermore, the idea of a *translocal* ethnography is born out of the paradox that in times of globalization, a rigorous ethnography *must be local and at the same time cannot be only local*. In other words, ethnography's commitment to cultural specificity and *in situ* empirical work must be upheld at a time when the "ethnography" moniker is used to indicate allegiance to a certain discourse in cultural studies (Nightingale, 1996), rather than an empirical commitment to understand how lives are lived locally. While we do recognize the importance of *critical* ethnography as an epistemological *discourse*, we firmly believe that a methodological commitment to empirical field ethnographies enhances the quality of research and furthers a progressive political agenda.

Marcus's (1998, p. 71) own differentiation between realist ethnography, or the method of traditional ethnography, and a modernist ethnography more concerned with large-scale international processes, further helps us in accentuating the distinction between *local* and *translocal* ethnography. As we see it, translocal ethnography is necessary to render globalization intelligible through the lenses of various locals. Our notion of translocal ethnography then comes close to Marcus's ideal of "multi-sited ethnography." Marcus (1998) writes that

> in multi-sited ethnography, comparison emerges from putting questions to an emergent object of study whose contours, sites and relationships are not known before hand, but are themselves a contribution of making an account that has different, complexly connected real-world sites of investigation.
>
> (p. 86)

It is in this context that we believe this book to be a multisited ethnography. Taken together, the geographically and epistemologically diverse contributions to this book can be said to constitute a scenario for multisited ethnographic work encompassing diverse "local" settings in Brazil, Denmark, India, Lebanon, Mexico, rural Appalachia, and elsewhere. They represent a dialogical process and polyvocal account between ethnographers and through ethnographic texts of what and where fieldwork is and how it should relate to the formation of global media studies.

Conclusion

As the implications of global media are being debated, translocal ethnography can play an important role in developing the field of global media studies. In addition to the necessity of sophisticated cultural translation and the reorientation of ethnography to a translocal focus, we would like to conclude with two broader issues that frame ethnographic research, and follow up with two related agendas. The two issues are (1) the communal character of audience experience, and (2) the material conditions that ground and shape audience interaction with the mass media. A commitment to a social understanding of audiences refocuses ethnographic attention from individual negotiation to sociocultural mediation, while an engagement with the material and structural forces that shape translocal processes means a recuperation of a qualified political economy perspective on media audiences.

Collectively, the chapters in this book heed Willis's (2000) assertion that there is a need to move away from the "dominant individualistic view" of cultural negotiation, and re-engage the notion that cultural creativity is usually collective and socially originated. This entails an understanding of meaning-making activities as intrinsically framed, enabled, and constrained by powerful external structural determinants. When taken together, they show that for media researchers, such a return to structural concerns must involve a combined commitment to macro and micro questions of power and identity that move beyond singular text- or place-focused resistance and accommodation studies and towards a translocal understanding of globalization.

That the cultures of globalization are hybrid is becoming conventional wisdom. However, what is missing is a systematic examination of the shades of cultural hybridity and the social, cultural, political and economic agendas and forces that contribute to their formation. Hence the two related agendas that should be initiated to remedy this gaping hole. First, global media scholarship must make *a commitment to empirical research* to complement its theoretical arguments. This should not be misconstrued as a dismissal of the discursive in favor of methodological fetishism. Rather, our point is grounded in the belief that dialogue between theory and research is crucial for intellectual activity that has meaningful implications for the everyday. Second, we advocate that global media studies *embraces real interdisciplinarity*, because the complexity of globalization and its multifaceted processes require diverse expertise. Namely, we call for research and theory that cuts through the categories of the political, economic and cultural. Transnational capitalism has successfully blurred the boundaries between these spheres, and extended this mixed reality to all aspects of our lives. If our scholarship is to have any relevance, it is imperative that we catch up. The best place to begin is everyday life, where the political, economic and cultural are articulated through the mediated. Herein lies the promise of translocal ethnography.

References

Abu-Lughod, L. (1999). The interpretation of culture(s) after television. In S. Ortner (ed.), *The fate of "culture": Geertz and beyond*. Berkeley: University of California Press.

Ang, I. (1985). *Watching Dallas*. London: Routledge.

Appadurai, A. (1991). Global ethnoscapes: Notes and queries for a transnational anthropology. In M. Fox (ed.), *Recapturing anthropology: Working in the present* (pp. 191–210). Santa Fe, NM: School for American Research Press.

Appadurai, A. (1996). *Modernity at large: Cultural dimensions of globalization*. Minneapolis: University of Minnesota Press.

Bhabha, H. (1994). *The location of culture*. London: Routledge.

Buckingham, D. (1987). *Public secrets: EastEnders and its audience*. London: BFI.

Curran, J. and Park, M. J. (2000). *De-Westernizing media studies*. London: Routledge.

Fejes, F. (1981). Media imperialism: An assessment. *Media, Culture and Society* 3(3) 281–289.

Fox, M. (ed.) (1991). *Recapturing anthropology: Working in the present*. Santa Fe, NM: School for American Research Press.

Galtung, J. (1971). A structural theory of imperialism, *Journal of Peace Research* 8(2), 81–117.

García-Canclini, N. (1989). *Culturas híbridas: Estrategias para entrar y salir de la modernidad*. Mexico City: Grijalbo. Translated as *Hybrid cultures: Strategies for*

306

Entering and Leaving Modernity (1995). (trans. S. López and E. Schiappari). Minneapolis: University of Minnesota Press.

Hall, S. (1997). Encoding/decoding. Reprinted in A. Gray and J. McGuigan (eds), *Studying culture: An introductory reader* (pp. 90–103). London: Arnold.

Hobson, D. (1982). *Crossroads: The drama of a soap opera.* London: Methuen.

Kraidy, M. (2002). Hybridity in cultural globalization. *Communication Theory* 12(3), 316–339.

Lee, C. C. (1984). *Media imperialism reconsidered.* Beverly Hills, CA: Sage.

Marcus, G. E. (1998). *Ethnography through thick and thin.* Princeton, NJ: Princeton University Press.

Mattelart, A. (1972). *Agresion desde el espacio: Cultural y napalm en la era de los satelites.* Chile: Ediciones Universitarias de Valparaiso.

Matterlart, A. (1977). *Multinacionales y sistemas de comunicacion: Los aparatos ideologicos del imperialismo.* Mexico: Siglo XXI.

Mattelart, A. (1983). *Transnationals and the Third World.* South Hadley, MA: Bergin and Garvey Publishers, Inc.

Morley, D. (1980). *The Nationwide audience.* London: BFI.

Murphy, P. (1999). Media cultural studies' uncomfortable embrace of ethnography. *Journal of Communication Inquiry* 23(3), 205–221.

Nightingale, V. (1996). *Studying audiences: The shock of the real.* London: Routledge.

Nordenstreng (2001). Epilogue. In N. Morris and S. Waisbord (eds), *Media and globalization: Why the state matters* (pp. 155–160). Lanham, MD: Rowman and Littlefield.

Rogers, E. and Schement, J. R. (1984). Introduction to "Media flows in Latin America." Special Issue of *Communication Research* 11(2), 159–162.

Rosaldo, R. (1995). Foreword. In N. García-Canclini, *Hybrid cultures: Strategies for Entering and Leaving Modernity* (trans. S. López and E. Schiappari) (pp. xi–xviii). Minneapolis: University of Minnesota Press.

Schiller, H. (1969). *Mass communications and American empire.* New York: Augustus M. Kelley.

Schiller, H. (1976). *Communication and cultural domination.* White Plains, NY: International Arts and Sciences Press.

Smith, A. D. (1990). Towards a global culture? *Theory, Culture and Society* 7(2–3), 171–192.

Straubhaar, J. (1984). Brazilian television: The decline of American influence. *Communication Research* 11(2), 221–240.

Tomlinson, J. (1991). *Cultural imperialism.* Baltimore: Johns Hopkins University Press.

Tomlinson, J. (1999). *Globalization and culture.* Chicago: University of Chicago Press.

Willis, P. (2000). *The ethnographic imagination.* Cambridge: Polity Press.

INDEX